Why are we badly governed? Why has a system of government—the envy of the world as recently as the 1970s—developed so many defects? Why is there such a gulf between political classes, who seem to believe the position satisfactory or inevitable, and the general public, increasingly disaffected by politics and government?

Personalities matter in politics, but too much current discussion fastens on them. With that focus one may easily conclude nothing has changed. We have had presidential Prime Ministers before. We have had relations between Prime Minister and another leading minister as tense as those said to exist between Blair and Brown. But if one looks beneath the surface we find great changes in how government and the political system function. They can reasonably be called revolutionary and are in many respects disturbing. That is the argument of this book.

The book argues that the defects are not attributable to one political party. Some factors are outside politicians' control: the globalisation of economic activity; the changes in international politics after the end of Soviet Russia; the adverse consequences of more dominating and competitive media. Some other factors are widely recognised: the decline of the Cabinet and the marginalising of Parliament; the influence of spin on our political culture; the increased role of political and special advisers. But others are not as well understood. Among them are the decline in the authority of many ministers, the undermining of the constitutional position and consequent effectiveness of the civil service, the fragmentation of government and the public sector into a mass of bodies with complex but ill-defined relations between them, and the ramifying of a system of government which, despite its protestations, is less interested in delivering results than managing news.

The book traces these developments, especially over the last 25 years, but most intensively since 1997. It looks to a major change in the ways of government. It doubts whether a change of Prime Minister or party would remove current defects. It considers other possible alternatives, particularly a constitutional change to a 'presidential' system of government, or the introduction of a legal constitution. It concludes by arguing that, although venturing in new and untried directions might seem attractive, improvement—radical improvement—of the system we have is more likely to achieve better government and restore public confidence.

British Government in Crisis

or

The Third English Revolution

SIR CHRISTOPHER FOSTER

·HART·
PUBLISHING

OXFORD AND PORTLAND, OREGON
2005

Hart Publishing
Oxford and Portland, Oregon

Published in North America (US and Canada) by
Hart Publishing c/o
International Specialized Book Services
5804 NE Hassalo Street
Portland, Oregon
97213-3644
USA

Hart Publishing is a specialist legal publisher based in Oxford, England.
To order further copies of this book or to request a list of other
publications please write to:

Hart Publishing, Salter's Boatyard, Folly Bridge,
Abingdon Road, Oxford OX1 4LB
Telephone: +44 (0)1865 245533 or Fax: +44 (0)1865 794882
e-mail: mail@hartpub.co.uk
WEBSITE: http://www.hartpub.co.uk

British Library Cataloguing in Publication Data
Data Available
ISBN 1–84113–549–6 (hardback)

Typeset by Hope Services (Abingdon) Ltd.
Printed and bound in Great Britain by
MPG Books, Bodmin, Cornwall

To our grandchildren—Emily, Arthur, Miles and Max—

Whose generation's task it will be to clear up the mess
ours has made

Contents

Introduction

WHAT HAS GONE WRONG?

W E ARE BADLY governed. Some reasons for this are now widely acknowledged: Cabinet being replaced by prime ministerial government; the dominance of a political culture of spin; the rise of unelected special advisers and political cronies to positions of great power; the marginalising of Parliament and the substitution of the media as a 24 hour a day forum for political debate; but most important our inability to restrain a perilous and deeply flawed foreign policy in Iraq or to bring about a lasting improvement in our public services despite more billions spent on them. We have a government which seems to think leadership consists in issuing never ending, but frequently changing, streams of instructions and then is surprised the public sector does not immediately jump to it and implement the latest.

But there is much more—and more fundamental—than that which I will argue has been a revolution in how we are governed, with an outcome as yet too unstable to last. We seldom any longer produce good new laws. No surprise that almost as soon as one law is passed another initiative leads to another law on the same topic. Our white and green papers are so spun as to be normally uninformative and often unintelligible. The civil service is in danger of being politicised and demoralised. The structure of government and the public sector has become too fragmented to be manageable. The PM is too grossly overloaded to achieve what is expected of him. He has no time, if he had the inclination, for much beyond spin and over-hasty decision-making. The job has been refashioned to suit only people with similar attributes to his.

However, though the Blair administration has made government worse, the debilitating revolution started well before his. This book is my attempt to understand what has happened and what can be done about it. In different capacities, I have spent more than 40 years advising or commenting inside and outside government. I started to feel something was seriously wrong when after several years I again found myself near the centre of power as an adviser on rail privatisation. I had been involved in another major policy failure, the poll-tax, but had believed that fiasco was due to one person's wilfulness, namely Margaret Thatcher, and could have been averted but for her. The origins of rail privatisation convinced me something was systemically wrong. We no longer had—as I remembered us having in the 1960s and 1970s—the time or the capability to be thorough enough to explain to ourselves, to Parliament and the public just what we were attempting, and therefore to make reasonably sure what was practical and would work.

Like many others—all the more so because I was a long-term Labour sympathiser—I had hoped Blair would rescue and improve government. From my vantage-points as a non-executive board member of Railtrack, vice-chairman of the RAC and then chairman of the RAC Foundation, I have seen attempt after attempt fail to get a decent, workable, environmentally-friendly transport policy. A flawed rail privatisation, which could have been put right, has been turned into a disaster from which the railways may never recover. Meanwhile road congestion grows and we have no sensible policies to tackle it, only unending spin. I looked to see if similar factors have held back improving education, the NHS, and crime and disorder. I believe they have.

This book is an attempt to explain what has gone wrong and an apology for my failures, especially over the poll-tax and rail privatisation. If one believes, as I do, that British government in the past, though full of imperfections, was better, then one is under an obligation to say how and why. In this book's first chapters I have attempted an honest assessment—much helped by others who knew it—of the strengths and weaknesses of what I call the Old Regime, that is, before the Revolution; also of why it fell; and whether, if improved, it might have developed into something more satisfactory than that which we now have. I believe it could have done.

I then describe the changes in how we are governed which took place under Thatcher. I also review the failure of the poll-tax. Then I consider the counter-revolution John Major attempted and, after it failed, the further decline in the quality of government which his administration brought about. To explain where we are now I discuss Cabinet, news management, the altered standing of ministers and the undermining of the civil service under Blair. I discuss the plight of the railways as a concentrated example of most of the failings of modern British government combining to make a difficult situation worse. I summarise the Revolution before considering what is likely to happen next and what I believe most needs to be done.

I am grateful to those with whom I have discussed these matters over many years and in particular for the generosity of their recollections and comments to many friends and acquaintances who have commented on draft chapters of this book. It would be invidious to single them out, but some have given me unbelievable help throughout this project, several more have commented on every chapter, others on all those of which they had direct experience:

Andrew Adonis, Christopher Brearley, Sir Patrick Brown, Lord Butler of Brockwell, Chris Castles, Sir John Chilcot, Sir Geoffrey Chipperfield, Vic Cocker, Lord Croham, Tam Dalyell, MP, John Edmonds, Professor Andrew Evans, Lord Freeman, Sir John Garlick, Professor Stephen Glaister, Sir Terence Heiser, Professor Eric Hobsbawm, Lord Hoffmann, David Holmes, Professor Christopher Hood, Sir Robert Horton, Lord Howe of Aberavon, Lord Hunt of

Tamworth, Professor George Jones, Edmund King, Sir Timothy Lankester, Professor Martin Loughlin, Lord MacGregor of Pulham Market, Anthony Mayer, Professor Iain McLean, Sir Nicholas Monck, Lord Morris of Aberavon, Sir Patrick Nairne, Nigel Ogilvie, Sir Edward Osmotherly, Francis Plowden, David Rayner, Lord Richard, Sir Michael Scholar, Andrew Smith, John Smith, John Swift, Lord Waldegrave, John Welsby, Lord Wilson, Christian Wolmar and Philip Wood, but also serving civil servants in many departments and other public servants who by convention are not named. None is responsible for my use of those recollections and comments.

At my old friend, Tam Dalyell's, suggestion, I had useful conversations with a number of current MPs: Kevin Barron, Andrew Bennett, Jon Cruddas, Louise Ellmann, David Hamilton, Tom Harris, Gerald Kaufman, Andrew Lanslie, Helen McEchan, Anne Mackintosh, Theresa May, Clare Short, Chris Smith, Graham Stringer and David Wright. I interviewed some because they were ex-ministers, but most because as recent arrivals in the Commons I was interested in their appraisal of their roles as MPs. Again, though I could not have written my chapter on Parliament to-day without what they told me, none is responsible for the use I have made of what they said.

My greatest thanks goes to my wife for her patience, to Jo Abbott, who was my secretary at the RAC Foundation, for her indefatigability in collating and circulating chapter drafts, and in arranging meetings, and to Sebastian Foster for editing my typescript.

Christopher Foster
London
December 2004

PART 1

THE OLD REGIME

1

Parliament

Of Parliament:

. . . its various members ought to represent the various special interests, special opinions, special prejudices to be found in that community. There ought to be an advocate for every particular sect and a vast neutral body of no sect—homogeneous and judicial like the nation itself.

Bagehot (1867)[1]

Of Accountability:

Democracy is government by explanation.

A.J. Balfour[2]

THE PRINCIPAL FUNCTION of Parliament, and particularly the House of Commons, has not been to be part of government or a legislature, which in any true sense it is not, but to hold ministers to account. To do that effectively, it has been important that members between them should have a wide range of experience and be in contact with as many opinions as possible at home and abroad. So constituted, it has also been able to provide enough ministers of quality and some in each generation who were outstanding. Governments showed their strength and cohesion, or their weakness, through their performance in the House of Commons. The accountability of the Executive to Parliament, though not without shortcomings, remained effective until near the end of the 20th century.

PARLIAMENT AND THE EXECUTIVE

The British constitution, because forged in 17th century battles between Crown and Parliament, is bi-partite, not tri-partite: the position of the judiciary (and the civil service) being derived from the powers of the Crown and not separately entrenched in law.[3] In Britain sovereignty is said to belong to Parliament, or more strictly the Crown in Parliament. However, the monarch's veto on legislation has long been theoretical and the House of Lords' veto limited

---

[1] Bagehot (1997) 16.
[2] Quoted in Howe (1994) 77.
[3] Tomkins (2003) chs 2 and 3.

by Parliament acts and conventions, leaving the Commons intact so that in practice, because of direct election, it possesses the sovereign power of Parliament. However, its sovereignty is legal fact, not political reality. Rather, as the public lawyer John Griffith has said, practical sovereignty belongs to the Executive, which has the Crown's governing powers, provided it has the support of the Commons, a fact modified but not replaced by entry into Europe.[4] Every generation needs to ask how effective, without being disabling, are the checks on that sovereignty, which Parliament and other elements in the constitution provide. That question precipitated the Civil War and the Glorious Revolution. In the 1920s, a lord chief justice wrote a book about *The New Despotism*.[5] In 1978 Lord Hailsham claimed sensationally that we have an 'elective dictatorship', a phrase so catchy that it is still used, despite great changes in the checks and balances on the Executive since then.[6]

THE SEPARATION OF POWERS

What Bagehot called the fusion of ministers and Parliament—the fact that the first are drawn from the second—has been the strongest argument against what has been mis-called the separation of powers between Legislature and Executive (mis-called because what would have been involved was the separation of people into different institutions.[7] The powers are already separate.)[8] Eulogising the British constitution in the 18th century, Montesquieu had thought the separation of powers between its Executive, Legislature and Judiciary its best protection against the tyranny he observed in France.[9] He assumed each would have a distinct motivation: to govern, make laws and enforce them, but Jeremy Bentham pointed out that such separation in Britain was largely a fiction. Cabinets then contained several judges as well as peers and MPs. Judges sat in Parliament and Cabinet. MPs were regularly elevated to the bench. Bentham argued that they did not have distinct motivations according to their function, but were equally motivated by financial self-interest.[10] He was right to believe that the art of constitution-making was to find expedients—usually laws, rules and conventions—which would have the effect of constraining people's private interests and aligning them with whatever was held to be the public interest governing the performance of their public functions.[11] It was a

---

[4] Griffith (1963) 401–2; also Smith (1999) 11.

[5] Hewart of Bury (1929).

[6] Hailsham (1978); Daintith and Page (1999) 17.

[7] I am indebted for this point to Professor George Jones.

[8] Also Tomkins (2003) ch 2.

[9] Montesquieu [1748] Book XI, ch VI.

[10] Bentham [1776] (1948), mainly ch 3. Even into the second half of the 20th century MPs were often made judges.

[11] Most extensively explored in relation to the government regulation of industry, Laffont and Tirole (1993).

point, too, of which the authors of the American constitution were well aware, though too few contemporary reformers are.[12]

But such expedients do not need such separation. It has been the opposite of British practice in Parliament, Cabinet and political decision-making which has valued bringing together people of different background and motivation.[13] Because ministers sit in Parliament, they become better known and their characters better understood, which enhances their practical accountability. The effectiveness of that accountability was most considerable when a wide range of experience and knowledge found expression in the Commons, as happened both in its corrupt period until the mid-19th century and during its period without substantial allegations of corruption until near the end of the 20th century. The effectiveness dwindled thereafter when charges of sleaze and corruption led to severe limits being set on MPs' ability to gain and use outside experience. They powerfully reinforced other reasons why it not only became dominated by professional politicians, but discouraged them once elected from broadening their experience and understanding.[14] How that happened and its consequences for government will be important later. Sadly the crude doctrine—that it implies separate institutions, not just separate powers—has returned inappropriately to influence ideas on constitutional reform.[15]

THE REFORM OF PARLIAMENT

Parliamentary corruption was significant while its members were actively making laws and many were government placemen; when Whitehall and Westminster worked through trading favours, while courtiers on the make unashamedly surrounded kings. In the 18th century the crown deliberately overcame the political instability of the 17th century—between court and country, region and religion—by systematic corruption mainly to secure a majority in Parliament. Many seats were for sale for money or favours. Once in Parliament MPs could, and many did, make money by promoting, supporting or sometimes opposing private bills to serve a multitude of private and local interests.

Because central government had little to do with the economy; because there was parliamentary resistance to any form of centralised, crown-directed protectionism; because there were enough places in which industry could develop unaffected by local restrictive practices and perhaps because of the

[12] Madison, Hamilton and Jay (1992) 263–7, 'Ambition must be made to counteract ambition'.

[13] Lord Hoffmann in conversation, and in his excellent Hoffmann (2001) has drawn my attention to the importance of getting past the arid formalism of dogmatic interpretations of the doctrine of the separation of powers to what really matters; to its applicability in British circumstances; and to the good sense of James Madison in *The Federalist* in recognising that separation need not and cannot be absolute, Madison, Hamilton and Jay (1992) 246–47.

[14] Riddell (1993) 19–23. The idea of parliament as the prime focus and disseminator of public opinion is in Crick (1964) 273.

[15] Bingham (2003); Oliver (2003) 345–47.

influence of Adam Smith, this corruption did not check the industrial revolution and therefore the take-off of economic growth. However, it did withstand efforts to reform Parliament and administration, not only by radicals and revolutionaries, but even by the Younger Pitt as Prime Minister.[16]

This 'market-place' Parliament survived the 1832 Reform Act. It was at its height in the 1840s and 1850s when the statutes needed to build the railways were passed with extensive corruption.[17] A multitude of rail and other statutes, serving private interests, dominated the legislative programme.[18] As in the US Congress 150 years later, it was difficult to pass legislation which did not benefit powerful monied interests (but not impossible, as the anti-slavery movement, repeal of the corn laws, the factory acts and parliamentary reform showed)[19].

By the 1860s, parliamentary corruption appeared so scandalous as to prompt reformation: a tremendous clearing up of its processes and procedures that has lasted into our day. Gladstone was probably most responsible.[20] The impetus was preparation for the 1867 Reform Act. It raised the prospect of an equally corrupt Parliament composed more of representatives of the middle and lower middle classes. It therefore posed the classic dilemma of how to make democracy safe for the ruling classes. Educated on Plato, Aristotle and Livy, and so well aware of democracy's instability, they knew the ancient democracies had transferred wealth from rich to poor and had fallen partly as a consequence. To restrain headlong democracy—Carlyle called it 'Shooting Niagara'—they replaced corruption with political, judicial and administrative integrity.[21] At the same time, the development of better processes of parliamentary accountability exposed old ways of trading favours within government. Exposed, they were largely eliminated.[22]

THE REAL SAFEGUARDS

In *The Federalist* James Madison stressed how safeguards against excessive power tending to corruption are best built in when a constitution was con-

---

[16] Ehrman (1969) 223–36, 282–326.

[17] Lewin (1936); Alderman (1973); Foster (1992) ch 1.

[18] Rail and many other private laws were effective because of the self-interest of those who composed bill committees, though unsurprisingly better at safeguarding promoters' and landed interests than rail-users' long-term interests, Foster (1992). Members of congress may accept contributions to their election funds from promoters. Hence the strong impact vested interests have on much US legislation.

[19] McLean (2001) 46, shows that votes for such measures were usually smaller and across parties.

[20] Morley (1906) ii, 239, also 363 said that while Gladstone believed parliamentary procedures were of the first importance to the efficiency of government, he left no papers about it and therefore Morley would not elaborate on it. Subsequent biographers have followed his example. But see Ostrogorski (1902).

[21] Carlyle [1867] 1899, 1–48.

[22] I am indebted to Professor Dawn Oliver of University College London for this point. I discuss corruption more fully in Foster (2001).

structed, difficult thereafter.[23] But Gladstone's generation managed it. The standing orders established in the anti-corruption drive of the 1860s built on ancient custom that only the Crown, not Parliament, could originate taxation or expenditure. Only government, and no individual MP, could propose or modify any tax proposal or expenditure item and only one such proposal could be discussed at a time.[24] Moreover, Gladstone kept absolutely separate the discussion of raising revenue—in the budget—from discussions of expenditure, later collected in the annual expenditure statement.[25] Under his influence, the Commons adopted standing orders to prevent a member chairing a private bill committee in his own financial interest, or packing it with fellow MPs with the same or a similar interest: for the first time chairmen of bill committees became, and have remained, neutral. These changes to standing orders, when adopted elsewhere in the Commonwealth, became known as the 'Westminster rules'.[26]

A further protection was that ministers came to introduce almost all legislation for the government (in contrast to the United States, where bills are introduced by senators and members of congress who are not part of the executive).[27] This practice, together with party discipline, further prevented MPs from using their power to block and amend legislation as a lever to get ministerial decisions on other matters in their favour (known as 'log-rolling'), except when the government has a small majority. Moreover, when bills are going through committee, British ministers normally successfully resisted amendments, other than their own, until the 1990s.[28] These rules were reinforced by the growth of party discipline allowing an elected government to have a substantial chance of carrying their legislative programme while they retained a comfortable majority. Almost all MPs were whipped so that their votes could not be for sale. An outcome was a strong protection against backbenchers achieving or materially influencing legislation at the behest of vested interests or their own inclinations.[29] With over 600 MPs, no vested interest was likely to have enough members in its pocket to pass or defeat legislation improperly. It remains the only respectable, but powerful, argument, for more than 600 MPs (though the enormous workload English MPs now have as constituency social workers (see below chapter 10) may now be another).[30]

By such arrangements Gladstone's generation deliberately destroyed most of the opportunities for jobbery and log-rolling which had been such a prominent

[23] Madison, Hamilton and Jay (1992) 260–67.

[24] That only the Crown, that is government, could make expenditure proposals was an ancient convention, Daintith and Page (1999) 107–9.

[25] Reid (1962).

[26] Reid (1962) 11.

[27] cf. Amery (1953) 12.

[28] Both John Stuart Mill (1910) 231 and Walter Bagehot (1997) 60, 89, pointed out that laws are not well made in committee, an opinion Hobbes, Blackstone, Bentham, Rousseau and Madison also held and a truth that many contemporary parliamentary reformers are in danger of forgetting. For the other citations, Waldron (2001) 43, 51–53.

[29] Also Oliver in Heywood (1997).

[30] I am indebted to Rt Hon John MacGregor for this point.

feature of the 18th-century and earlier 19th-century Parliament.[31] Together they prevented Parliament, and Commonwealth Parliaments based on the Westminster model, from developing like the US congress. Its committees normally consider individual expenditure proposals and related tax proposals together, which allows their members to practise 'pork-barrel' (a term used when the money flows into election or party funds rather than into politicians' pockets) and log-rolling politics. By contrast, members of Parliament, apart from ministers, had and still have no direct decision-making powers over public policy. Except when the government has a small or no majority, parliamentary rules have successfully ensured that MPs do not have improper, or corrupt, influence over public legislation. But they were still free to challenge ministers with all the opinions—their own and other people's—they believed relevant to an issue.

These and other late Victorian changes altered the functions of Parliament under the constitution. No longer the legislature in a strict sense, it *ratifies* laws (which whipping in general makes a formality); but does not for the most part originate them or decide their content. Besides being a nursery for ministers, the importance of MPs lay then and until recently, (1) in the pressure of their opinions on ministers, the value and variety of which depended on the breadth of their experience, and (2) broadened by that experience, in the shrewdness and understanding they developed in penetrating ministers' evasions and disclaimers to hold them truly accountable, as well as (3) to some extent in their effectiveness in mobilising their opinions through the Parliamentary Labour Party, the conservative members' 1922 committee and other backbench committees. Their effectiveness was enhanced because they became MPs after a career or occupation which also gave them knowledge as well as an understanding of people. In that way they were influential, embarrassing ministers to do better, altering ministerial decisions, preventing or forcing changes in legislation. These late Victorian changes altered what the corruption of MPs—as distinct from ministers—could achieve. And there it stayed, until the sleaze allegations of the 1980s and 1990s, not because of superior moral virtue—it is wiser to assume human nature remains the same—but because of safeguards built into the system.

ACCOUNTABILITY AND MINISTERIAL RESPONSIBILITY

The origins of ministerial responsibility were in the 17th century constitutional invention by Parliament that the king's ministers were accountable to it, not to

---

[31] John Dunn in Dunn (2000) 63–69, argues how difficult it is to design procedures to avoid corruption. However, the late 19th century adoption of the appropriate Parliamentary rules, and of a civil service chosen by merit and with tenure, as well as the greater influence of whipping in Parliament, have been responsible for providing such safeguards for MPs, ministers and officials.

the Crown which had been the Tudor position.[32] Even before there was a Cabinet in the modern sense, two conventions developed regarding the collective and the individual responsibility of ministers. Ministers were not held personally responsible for policy, because that by convention was a collective responsibility, though they usually answered for government policies as they affected their department. But they were held responsible for everything else to do with their departments. In the middle to late 19th century that classic theory found expression first in prime ministerial statements;[33] and then in constitutional textbooks.[34] Again as early as the 17th century, the judges came to regard Parliament as a more sensible check on the Executive's misdeeds than the courts.[35] The appropriate punishment might be the resignation of the minister or even the ministry. Such punishment demonstrated the sovereign political power of the Commons over the Executive.

The historically-minded think first of the greatest occasions. Of Chamberlain brought down in the two-day debate over the fiasco of the Norway campaign, knocked out by speeches by Attlee, Admiral of the Fleet Sir Roger Keyes, L S Amery and Lloyd George of which best remembered is Amery's heavy punch from Cromwell: 'You have sat too long here for any good you have been doing. Depart, I say, and let us have done with you. In the name of God, go.'[36] Or of how, less well known, in another debate after the fiasco of the Charge of the Light Brigade in the worst days of the Crimean War, a speech by Lord John Russell brought the Aberdeen government down, as a speech by Sir Geoffrey Howe, also on resigning from the government, was to bring down Margaret Thatcher.[37] Conversely, an anthology could be made of the speeches by which great orators have extricated themselves from tight corners, as did Lloyd George over the Marconi and Maurice affairs; another of failures to deliver a knock-out blow, as Neil Kinnock failed to finish Margaret Thatcher in the Westland debate in 1986 or Michael Howard, Blair, in 2004 over Iraq; and a third of when lesser ministers failed to extricate themselves, as John Nott over the sinking of the Belgrano or when Leon Brittan as Home Secretary pleased nobody by his equivocations over capital punishment.[38]

But to limit accountability to presumed offences is misleading. Whatever ministers do in Parliament, like announcing a decision or explaining a bill, is rendering an *account* to Parliament which only becomes an offence if Parliament judges it one. Not only what ministers say to Parliament, but also the

---

[32] Tanner (1928) 50; Marshall (ed) (1989) 2.

[33] E.g. Earl Grey in 1858, quoted by Woodhouse (1994) 5, 6; Lord Salisbury in 1878 and Gladstone in 1883, quoted by Madgwick in Herman and Alt (1975) 77–78.

[34] Bagehot (1997) ch 5; Dicey [1885] (1959) 329, 364, 374–75, 382–83; Anson (1908) 387–401; Jennings (1959) 112–14; Woodhouse (1994) ch 1, 2.

[35] Woodhouse (1994) 4

[36] Jenkins (2001) 576–82.

[37] Ridley (1970) 431–33; Molesworth (1886) iii, 34–38.

[38] Nott, *Hansard*, 3/4/82; Dalyell (1987) 14–15. I am indebted to Ruth Winstone of the House of Commons Library Parliament and Constitution Centre for these references.

white papers and other public documents they lay before it, give an account of their policies. Edmund Burke's great speeches may have been meant more for reading than hearing.[39] Was he not called the Dinner Bell of the House of Commons? But there have been great occasions like Sir Robert Peel holding a packed Commons silent for four hours as he explained his reasons for changing his mind on Catholic Emancipation and persuaded enough to follow him into the division lobbies to secure the measure.[40] Or Gladstone's great budget speeches ordered like a white paper, full of statistics and closely reasoned, when he too held the House in rapt attention for hours on end. Effective instances can be found throughout parliamentary history until not long ago. For example in 1974, in my own recollection, Tony Crosland, bound by an undertaking made during the election campaign, had to defend his decision to let the Clay Cross Councillors off the surcharges which the law had placed on them for defying the previous government over council housing rents. Even so experienced a parliamentarian and debater was daunted by the ordeal of preparation and by the knowledge that many of the best debaters as well as the best informed opinion in the House, even in his own party, believed the retrospective law needed to let them off was wrong.[41]

However the daily bread of accountability was not grave offences and stupendous explanations, but the mass of lesser matters—from failure to recognise or deal with a problem, or wasting money to incompetence—for which peers and Commons expected an account from ministers.[42] Accountability from major to minor matters has always been the staple fare of Parliament and has influenced the development of many procedures used to handle parliamentary business: debates, committee work and parliamentary questions. So the Commons has been able to extract information from the Government, frequently against its will, and therefore on occasion to embarrass ministers.[43] The consequent embarrassment was also in the media. From earliest times until the 1980s, Parliament was reported in the media where such embarrassments, even over minor matters, could be prominent.[44]

More prosaically, ministers may be challenged to show that they know what they are talking about; that their policies are coherent and that they can answer questions raised by the opposition and their own side of the House. Committees could be a more penetrating, because sustained, mechanism than questioning on

[39] Though his effectiveness as a parliamentary orator is stressed both by Ayling (1988) e.g. 26–28, and O'Brien (1992) 139–44.

[40] *Hansard*, 5/3/1829, 728–80. I am grateful to Ruth Winstone for drawing my attention to this stupendous speech.

[41] My own personal experience as one of his advisers at the time.

[42] Woodhouse (1994) 28–38.

[43] Complaints about Parliament's declining ability to call the Executive to account, because of declining reputation, increased interest in personalities rather than issues and less full reporting in the media, were heard in the 1990s, Woodhouse (1994) 17. But the scrutiny of the Executive still seemed often intimidating enough to us in the 1960s and 1970s.

[44] MPs' letters go straight to ministers; other complaints go lower down and may never reach them.

the floor of the House. Parliamentary questions were once more effective than now because it was easier to get through a minister's defences by asking supplementary questions. The recent practice of announcing new policies to the media rather than to Parliament was not only a matter of ministers' wishing greater publicity. It moved accountability, as we shall see, to a forum with different objectives, priorities and standards of truth and fairness in debate.

Parliamentary accountability worked best when legally and practically an activity was under the minister's control. The main reason why the mid-19th century attempt to devolve powers to independent boards and other agencies was reversed, was because they were found not effectively accountable to Parliament unless ministers controlled them.[45] Parliamentary accountability was more suited to an age before nationalised industries and other large non-departmental public sector bodies. The line usually adopted, that ministers were responsible for policy and the boards for day-to-day operations, was an awkward fudge, both because in practice the distinction between policy and operations was fuzzy and moveable, but because ministers could not in any direct sense control board policy.[46] Parliamentary accountability worked better with the large people-factories, which most home departments once contained, issuing licences, inspecting activities, distributing benefits and so forth. There the hierarchies were in control and therefore the minister on top, in the limited sense that, if even the most junior official transgressed, the problem could be soon investigated and brought to the attention of a minister who often had no previous awareness of the activity in question, but then had to defend it. Parliamentary procedures almost always meant there were a few days to establish facts, which was one reason—the sheer variety of questions asked was another—why departments did not develop the kind of instant data banks, which they were to be so criticised for not having in 1997, when information technology was available.

Parliamentary accountability presumed that through a statement, contributions to debate, answers to parliamentary questions and letters, or through a process of discovering documents or taking evidence in a parliamentary committee, enough evidence could be found to convict ministers of an offence or show them innocent. That offence was rarely a breach of the law, more often maladministration, but most frequently that the truth had not been told about a developing policy or executive action. Parliamentary scrutiny has been thought most relevant when the offence was ill-defined in law or concerned ministers' and officials' use of their discretion within the law. In those circumstances judgment on the issue depended on the opinion of a minister's peers in the Commons or Lords. Its longstanding success depended, literally and historically, on a forensic age, when Parliament as a high court believed that, even with offences imprecisely defined, it was sufficiently small, cohesive and

---

[45] Lubenow (1971); Bagehot (1997)102–5; Baldwin (1995)110–11.
[46] They had more, but even then, limited power, when the industries were in deficit. Otherwise they were trusts with substantial discretion. See Foster (1971).

non-partisan, and that its members knew each other well enough, both within and across parties, to act as a jury with a substantial chance of seeing through to the truths behind ministers' words.[47] Those acts of judgement were easier, because, until the 1980s, poor accommodation crowded MPs together in the smoking and tea-rooms and in the corridors. Now they can spend most of their time in their offices with their researchers and need not know each other well. Yet still many MPs believe that face-to-face, they can detect a lying minister.

TRUTH AND OBJECTIVITY

Important was ministers' obligation to tell the truth or, more accurately, not to tell untruths which, as we had once learned, was why John Profumo fell.[48] I remember Harold Wilson in Oxford, returning as an honorary fellow and dominating the Jesus College senior common room, a few days before the crucial debate—I believe he rehearsed his speech to us—as he told us that it had nothing at all to do with sexual morality or a breach of security, only with being found out in lying to the Commons, as years later one was to be told that Clinton's tribulations, though empowered by his sexual foibles, were because of his alleged perjuries. When I became a civil servant—despite what we all knew about *raison d'état* and the occasional cases, beloved of old ethics textbooks, when it would be more honourable or in the public interest not to tell the truth—we knew such lying was fraught with difficulty, best kept to a minimum. On the rare inescapable occasions, it was best left to old hands who had the wisdom, experience and reputation to get away with it. This attitude was reinforced in those days of long departmental hierarchies by the fact that the more senior officials did not want to be lied to by their juniors. That it was wrong to lie and that one had better be ready to face the consequences if one did, was an important part of most education. Public service tended to attract those who thought in such terms. But most practical people accepted it was better and safer not to lie, if for no other reason than the high cost of being found out and the effect on one's career and family, if one were. Whatever other morality was rejected, few rejected this aspect, if only on utilitarian grounds. After all it was an age when the City worked on the principle that someone's word was his bond.

I recall many occasions among officials or with ministers, when the most convenient answer to a parliamentary question was noticed not to be true. In Robert Armstrong's version of Burke, being economical with the truth was all right.[49] Its acceptability rested first on the logical demonstration, which many had been through, that it was strictly impossible to tell the whole truth about anything, since there was always an infinite amount one could say about every-

[47] On the connection between the forms and history of parliamentary accountability and its origins as a high court, see Maitland (1908); also Marshall and Moodie (1964) 178–80.

[48] There were also security reasons for his fall.

[49] Burke said 'but, as in the exercise of all the virtues, there is an economy of the truth'.

thing. There was also the common sense point that one need not volunteer an answer to a question which one had not actually been asked, especially given the scope MPs then had to ask supplementary questions. But the frisson of fear which could attack ministers was salutary, as they realised that they were on dangerous ground when penetrating supplementaries were asked by chance or by guile. The more the answers were tried out with their officials in advance, the clearer it became how vulnerable ministers would be if they strayed from the truth. One saw the folder in which officials dealing with the issue exhaustively set out far more supplementaries than would ever be asked as well as the truthful answers to them. It gave officials an opportunity, as well as an obligation, to set out what facts they knew—statistical, scientific, economic or other—which they believed relevant to an issue, given the short time they had to compile it. Ministers were bound by a need not to be factually misleading, but also that their answers should reflect government policy truthfully. Nevertheless when MPs were only fishing to find out what ministers were up to while developing a policy, a minister could usually fall back on the convention that nothing was government policy until approved by Cabinet, though he was still expected not to tell an untruth about it; but if it were maladministration or anything else for which he were ministerially responsible, there was no similar bolthole.

There were matters about which ministers and officials could not tell the truth to Parliament.[50] Some were commercial in confidence, but they were rarely matters of high policy. Some were secrets which could not be disclosed because of their value to an enemy of the state; but there was a convention for dealing with them: they might be disclosed to the leader of the opposition or other member of the shadow Cabinet under the confidentiality of the privy council oath to which they too belonged. They might be trusted with the secret because they could become Prime Minister or Cabinet minister entrusted with the same or similar secrets. If they could not be trusted because the secret could not command bi-partisan support, then it probably should not be a state 'secret.'

There were rogues among ministers, who at times and from certain aspects included giants like Disraeli, Salisbury, Lloyd George and Churchill, whose great ambitions could override the conventions and make them mislead their colleagues and Parliament. Ministers, great and small, would not have been human if at times they had not hoped they could get away with a convenient untruth.[51] Hence the importance of trust between ministers and their officials— often exemplified in my experience—when ministers would try out lines of defence, and then being told sadly they would not do, until a safe one were found. There were occasions, as with Salisbury in foreign policy and most Prime Ministers since Churchill and Attlee over nuclear policy, when *raison d'état* had a similar, more defensible consequence of lying to Parliament. But the general

---

[50] There were also stock answers, readily recognised, by which ministers fend off questions before they were ready for them like ' I have no plans for X' or 'That is a speculative question.'
[51] Dale (1941) 110–16.

presumption was that ministers would always not want to tell an untruth to their colleagues or to Parliament. The consequence of Eden's lying to the Commons in December 1956, when he denied he had any foreknowledge of the Israeli attack on Egypt, was not a happy precedent.[52]

As late as the mid to late 1980s, one could find many permanent secretaries who would say they had never, or perhaps only once, had any difficulty with the minister over truth-telling over such a matter in a ministerial statement or answer to a question. One civil servant told me of his shock when a Cabinet minister in the early 1990s, having been told that as a matter of fact that X could not be a valid reason justifying a huge expenditure on Y, simply replied that he would take the risk of being found out telling a lie to Parliament. Yet ministers still avoid telling an untruth to Parliament when pointed out to them, especially if they believe the civil servant might be ready to go through the complex and insidious process of making a formal complaint against them. The possibility of their being a minute—as the Butler inquiry should have found in 2004 (see below chapter 17)—showing what the civil service believed to be the truth, remains a discouraging one if an inquiry or tribunal were to call for the relevant papers.

Nevertheless one must not exaggerate the penetration the Commons normally used when interrogating the Executive. Supplementary questioning, whether on the floor of the House or in committees, even then, was a poor substitute for the relentless cross-examination possible in a law court or in the US Congress.[53] Committees rarely had the knowledge, the staff or the discipline to be so formidable. The traditional approach was often inadequate for assessing departmental performance or the performance of any particular on-going activities, which became more important as the constraints on public expenditure growth grew severe from the 1970s and efficiency in its use therefore mattered more. As over the years the private sector has shown, greater efficiency requires a basically different approach and more regular fit-for-purpose and systematic information (see below chapter 10). Another problem was the growth of rules and regulations which practically were outside parliamentary scrutiny; secondary legislation which received little attention; and tertiary legislation which was outside it altogether.[54] But, despite such shortcomings, the House often did expose ministers for what they were, good and bad.

PARLIAMENT AS A NURSERY OF MINISTERS

As significant, that political education they gained in Parliament trained many to become good, and some very good, ministers. There were obscure 18th century PMs, but there were also Walpole and the two Pitts. Wellington may have called the Derby Cabinet in 1851 the 'Who? Who?' Cabinet. Among its

---

[52] Hennessy (1989) 167.
[53] From my own personal experience of both parliamentary and congressional committees.
[54] Baldwin (1995) 80–121.

unknowns was Disraeli. Salisbury's first Cabinet may have had no one else of quality except Lord Randolph Churchill. But what was remarkable over the centuries, until the end of the 20th century, was what high average quality people with broad experience were attracted to Parliament and became ministers, and how in every generation several were outstanding.

CONCLUSION

Besides its vital functions in maintaining a government in power, especially when it has a slender or no majority, and as a nursery of ministers, commentators from Bagehot to Bernard Crick and Peter Riddell have rightly maintained that its prime function has been to call ministers to *account* on whatever they and their departments do: to challenge ministers over their past and proposed actions; to influence ministers by expressing their opinions on them and ultimately to approve or disapprove their policies and actions, whenever ministers, willingly or unwillingly, give an *account* of the actions and policies for which they are *responsible*. This function—first shaped in its bi-partite battles with Tudor and Stuart monarchs—and its elected status until recently gave the Commons its great authority.

However, the Northcote Trevelyan reforms of the civil service—replacing patronage by merit and political impartiality—were to introduce a third element into what had previously been a bi-partite constitution, not the judiciary as a check upon the integrity of ministerial power as in the United States, but by setting up a countervailing, but supportive, force closer to ministers.

2

The Constitution Acquires a Third Element: The Civil Service

Cabinet ministers have . . . a great deal too much to do and much more to do than ministers in other countries.

Lord Hailsham (1978)[1]

It is extraordinary that in our system of government we both have more ministers than others and in my experience more . . . put-upon ministers than others.

Chris Patten (1986)[2]

I wondered once again at the unique quality of the British civil service: the capacity of its top people to develop a genuine loyalty to a minister who wasn't here yesterday and will be gone tomorrow.

Barbara Castle (1974)[3]

THE DOCTRINE OF ministerial responsibility for everything meant British ministers had more legal responsibilities than their democratic counterparts elsewhere: among them handling complaints, making appointments, preparing laws, policymaking, decision-making, bargaining with Treasury, negotiating with many others, managing news, even for managing their departments. To perform and be accountable for so many functions, while seeming on top of all their departments, ministers relied on a special close partnership with their civil servants, unique to Britain and other nations with a Westminster-style constitution. Unless this chapter seem but a rhapsody for a bygone age—which is not intended—the system of government described had many shortcomings, as will be later apparent. But, while it lasted, it let ministers discharge so many functions and enabled them to cope with an ever increasing workload.[4] By convention, though not in law, the civil service became the third element in the British constitution.

---

[1] Hailsham (1978) 208–9.
[2] Interviewed by Hennessy (1989) 323.
[3] Castle (1980) 130.
[4] Morrison (l959) ch 14 remains an excellent account.

GROWTH OF THE RELATIONSHIP

After the 1945 election had been fought in the middle of the Potsdam conference, only Attlee and Bevin changed in the British delegation, replacing Churchill and Eden. Everyone else, down to Attlee's valet—such were the days—carried on, as did the policies, to the astonishment of the other world leaders.[5] Permanence, continuity and seamless transition have long been characteristics associated with the British civil service. Its excellence in these and other ways depended on traditional relationships with ministers. In the 18th and early 19th centuries, the relevant relationships altered from those between monarch and ministers to ones between ministers and their advisers. Much of the control of Parliament by Crown and ministers depended on their packing public offices with 'placemen', often relatives or protégés. Such relations were often mired in corruption and patronage, faults vividly described by Dickens and Trollope. Following the 1854 Northcote-Trevelyan Report that system was gradually cleansed, not only because of the rise of the middle classes and of professionalism, but more because new sustained party allegiances in Parliament made it politically embarrassing, even dangerous, for an incoming administration to rely on the protégés of past administrations, likely to be disobliging if not disloyal.

The 1918 Haldane Report extended that partnership to meet the more complicated requirements of busier government when large executive ministries emerged from the First World War, though still about one-tenth the size of their modern counterparts.[6] The Report's impact came through two closely-linked ideas. First, government required investigation and thought in all departments to do its job well: 'continuous acquisition of knowledge and the prosecution of research' were needed 'to furnish a proper basis for policy'. Government bills and decisions could no longer safely rely on the expertise of ministers, MPs and outside opinion. Second, ministers could not provide an investigative and thoughtful government on their own. Neither could civil servants, but a partnership between both could. It must be extended, however, from the cluster of officials round a minister, typical of 19th century government, to embrace whole departments as the repositories of relevant knowledge and opinion.

Haldane did not say how to develop such investigation and thought, except that they should be grounded on a distribution of responsibilities between ministries which has mostly continued to this day. Haldane did not describe partnership because he saw it as normal practice. A way of defining his position is to contrast it with Woodrow Wilson's, who, as a professor of politics at Yale,

---

[5] K Harris (1982) 266.
[6] Haldane (1918); Haldane—who was later to be Ramsay Macdonald's first Lord Chancellor—had been a colleague of Lloyd George's in the Asquith government when he had modernised the War Office. The Prime Minister gave him the job of considering what the organisation of government should be post-war.

and later as US president, had lasting effect on Americans' very different view of politician-civil service relationships. One recalls an obscure nineteenth-century German political philosopher only because of his influence on Wilson. He, Blunstchli, observed that since laws could never be detailed enough to prescribe what should be done in every case, there must be administrative discretion in decision-making.[7] How could it be disciplined so as to be a legitimate inter-pretation of the law?[8] Wilson's answer was also Germanic, indeed Weberian.[9] Once the laws were made, politicians should tie the bureaucracy down to the greatest extent possible by rules to constrain their administrative and executive actions, and they should be published, as they still are in the USA, running annually into thousands of pages.[10] Such a rule-based administration had been established between his 1887 article and his becoming president in 1912.[11] Though congress may challenge these rules, political accountability in America has been as incoherent and ineffective as it is now becoming in Britain.[12] Instead, effective accountability for these rules is to the US courts, while in con-tinental Europe it is usually to institutions of administrative law.[13] Court-based accountability remains important because in its various American and conti-nental European forms, it is the other main way of limiting the unbridled power of the executive, should the British partnership alternative appear irretrievably broken down.

Given these bureaucratic rules, the Wilson approach required the greatest possible separation of powers between politicians and officials, the latter taking the decisions on specific cases to reduce political interests and corruption influencing administrative decisions. Its practical effect is still observable, though somewhat eroded by the politicisation of the top levels of the US execu-tive.[14] Through the US spoils system presidents exercise some power over administrators through political appointments, needed in the US model to control the officials below and avoid rule by bureaucrats. However, appointees to senior positions have many different backgrounds, motivations and interests. Once appointed, they can be hard to get rid of, therefore to influence, so that the

[7] Bluntschli (1898) 521–23. In 1690 John Locke had similar, but fuller and more exact, thoughts on the practical necessity of administrative discretion in interpreting the law, Locke, [1690] (1924) 199–203.

[8] Dicey was among those keenest to limit ministerial and official discretion, but was only able to make it plausible because of the extreme *laissez-faire* position he took up, Jowell in Jowell and Oliver (1989) 3–8.

[9] W Wilson (1887) 213–14.

[10] Breyer (1982).

[11] In practice, unlike Britain, each part of the federal bureaucracy came to make the rules for itself because American politicians never had time to devise them. How the US courts exercised this func-tion was not codified until the Administrative Practices Act, 1946, see Breyer (1982); Oliver (2003) 323–24.

[12] Campbell & Wilson (1995) 251. I am indebted for this interpretation of Haldane to Thomas (1978). Later I found a similar idea, though not the metaphor, in Dale (1941) 121–30.

[13] On the difficulties of rule-based administration, see Jowell in Jowell and Oliver (1989).

[14] Wilson was an admirer of Northcote-Trevelyan and had hoped to administer government through a wholly merit-based civil service, but the US spoils system was too strong.

White House is often unable to overrule their decisions or co-ordinate their behaviour.

Haldane's solution to this problem of administrative discretion was equally, but differently, Germanic, indeed Hegelian. Instead of *separation* of powers, or functions, between temporary politicians responsible for policy-making and permanent administrators responsible for implementation, he advocated *fusion*—his word—that is, partnership.[15] His ideal was an ever-present, indissoluble symbiosis between minister and civil servants so that they were almost one person, a less mystical forerunner remaining the closeness once expected between a wise monarch and his trusted counsellors.[16] In 1988 a permanent secretary, Sir Brian Cubbon, described his role, mathematically rather than mystically, as 'the reciprocal' of the minister.[17] The product of any number and its reciprocal equals One.[18]

The constitutional implications of Haldane were plain. Civil servants had a duty to provide advice—intelligence and thought—or, in more modern words, recommendations between options, based on information and analysis. But the decision on what to do remained the minister's or Cabinet's, depending on its importance. To enhance that advice, civil servants must be independent of political party.

Occasionally ministers under political pressure might be tempted to cut corners. Their officials' lesser temptation to do so was reinforced by their having a different motivation from ministers; by their appointment through competitive examination to tenured pensionable careers and by ministers having almost no power over their posting and promotion, so achieving the independence from ministerial influence over appointments which *The Federalist* had believed vital as between different elements in the constitution. In the 1920s Sir William Beveridge, once a permanent secretary, could say that the relationship between minister and permanent secretary was like that between man and wife, except that the minister did not choose the permanent secretary and could not divorce him.[19] As late as the 1960s, the civil service still put every obstacle in the way of moving those who no longer had the minister's trust. Castle in my time could not get rid of her permanent secretary.[20] Though he

---

[15] An early discussion of the idea is Shaffer (1973); also 'Mackenzie and Grove (1957).

[16] Interestingly, Bagehot used the same word 'fusion', to refer to the ideal relation between executive and legislature that is the antithesis of the separation of powers, Bagehot (1997) 8. An important difference is between the use of fusion to describe the relations between individuals in parliament and Cabinet where the people are the same but the powers different and here where the people are different but the powers the same.

[17] Sir Brian Cubbon, quoted by Hennessy (1989) 508. Sisson (1959) 3, speaks of high-level administrators as 'nearer being a bit of the minister's mind'. I am indebted to Neville Johnson of Nuffield College, Oxford and Professor George Jones for this reference.

[18] Sir John Garlick suggested this rationalisation.

[19] Thomas (1978) 43–45.

[20] In practice it worked to her and my advantage, though neither of us expected that. Padmore stopped being an effective policymaker, and for 2 years the lead in policy-making, *faut de mieux*, fell to Castle and me, much as in the Treasury when after 1997 it was to fall to Gordon Brown and Ed Balls.

tried, Wilson could not get rid of the Head of the Civil Service. As we shall see, the growing influence of politicians in the appointment and promotions of civil servants, especially after 1997, undermined civil service independence and the influence of the values they were meant to uphold.

Legally this relationship was named the Carltona principle.[21] Examining the legitimacy of civil servants taking decisions for ministers in 1943, the court upheld it.[22] Ministers could not in law delegate their responsibilities, but the same thought underlay Haldane's notion and Cubbon's expression of it more than sixty years later: ministers and their civil servants were, if not one legal person, then an organic unity for decision-making purposes. The presumption was that civil servants were so close to ministers and knew their minds so well that they would take the same decisions ministers would take, given the law and the substance of government policy on the matter.[23] Reciprocally, ministers would not take a decision without their officials' advice and therefore without heeding constraints imposed by the law, government policy and the principles of administrative law (see below chapter 3).

EXPERIENCE OF THE RELATIONSHIP

There were many signs of close partnership in the 1960s. Appointed special adviser and chief economist with deputy secretary status in 1966,[24] I was told that my minister was surrounded by a close palisade of senior civil servants, usually under-secretaries; each watching over her interests on a given policy front; noting daily occurrences and media reports; monitoring all interest groups and their views; watching the opposition, updating the comprehensive files; and advising the minister whenever called to do so.[25] The ring round Barbara Castle was hermetic. As a temporary, I could not be part of that ring because I could not be responsible for anything except my own advice and for the advice of those working for me. Though a few under-secretaries were eccentric and one or two not industrious, they were impressive: men, and the occasional woman, of weight and intelligence—which some were at pains to veil—rapid and agile with the written word, not easily moved to enthusiasm, mostly methodical, some, but far from all, not as quantitative—or as responsive to economics and the other social sciences—as a young economist would have wished, shrewd at spotting dangers for their ministers and themselves, above all able to deal on equal terms with senior representatives of the interest groups, with whom relations were a principal part of their job. Many were novelists *manqué* in that

---

[21] See Daintith and Page (1999) 40–41; also Wade and Forsyth (1994) 358–59; Freedland (1994) and (1995); Oliver (2003) 207–8.

[22] Several judicial decisions reinforced fusion, Daintith and Page (1999) 40–41.

[23] Dale (1941) 120–25; Munro (1952); Brown and Steel (1979) 129.

[24] Though because of my youth with the pay of an under-secretary.

[25] By Sir John Moore, then Principal Establishment Officer at the Ministry of Transport, later second secretary in the Civil Service Department.

they pondered with fascination the characters of those with whom they had to deal, analysing their professional strengths and weaknesses, usually in carefully guarded language to which one had to learn the code. Judgement was the most admired quality. It meant a strong appreciation of the realities of a situation: what could be done and what not. Among those realities were the people who had to be persuaded in nationalised industries, local government or elsewhere— the Establishment indeed—to do what a minister wanted. Between them they had massive experience, not only of everyday occurrences, but some would have been involved in rarer events: how to deal with a major rail accident, a strike, the need to get rid of the chairman of a public body who could not be sacked. There were also folk memories of how bye-gone ministers and officials had handled unexpected events, capable of substantiation in the files. Between them they possessed what a Cabinet secretary, Burke Trend—himself a master of the written word, able to write a complete White Paper at a sitting without alteration—was to refer to as 'the departmental store of wisdom.'

Civil servants were almost always present when ministers met to do business and when ministers met outsiders officially. They listened into ministerial telephone calls and accompanied ministers to take a note at outside meetings, afterwards debriefing those who needed to know. A practical reason for these practices was that in a long, busy day, it is not always easy to remember who said what to whom and what ministers wanted done. (As the Ecclestone and second Mandelson resignation episodes, and the Hutton and Butler Inquiries, later showed, there are always people ready to put an unattractive gloss on a conversation which needs a note written at the time to refute it robustly.) The private office controlled a minister's diary and expected—with discretion—to know where a minister was and how contactable at any time. (Robin Cook's falling out with Ann Bullen showed what can happen when a minister feels unable to be frank with his diary secretary about private engagements.[26])

I remember a bizarre instance. Knowing that, if he called Barbara Castle directly, her private office would overhear him, Tommy Balogh, then Wilson's policy adviser, called me, saying that he wanted to meet her and the other transport ministers urgently on a matter he could not discuss over the phone. I arranged it with some difficulty, not wanting to be overheard. So Barbara Castle, Stephen Swingler, John Morris and I met him in a borrowed room in the House, realising the department would know if we met in one of their rooms. The phone rang. It was her private office, ostensibly to tell her of a diary change, but really, we knew, to let us know we could not escape their vigilance. Barbara then turned to Tommy, who had not only forgotten what he wanted to say, but thought she had wanted the meeting, not he.

Inevitably approached by all sorts of people in their political and social lives, ministers obeyed the precept that whenever an approach became serious, they would ask for a letter to be sent to them at their department, so the request could

---

[26] N Jones (1999) 197–8.

be processed within the official machine. Ministers met outsiders in the House of Commons, their constituencies and their social life to discuss issues, even reaching conclusions, which, however, had to be translated by officials onto paper with supporting argument to get through the Cabinet system, or to be a basis for departmental action. Ministers could not reach a decision in private, with each other or someone else. Neither could an official.

Ministers' private secretaries were judged by the quality of the relationship between the minister and the department. They used their discretion over ministers' private lives, but were expected to inform the permanent secretary of everything important they were up to in their official life, not unreasonable given the need to brief and debrief them for any contact. A private secretary to a junior minister, Stephen Swingler, who did not inform his permanent secretary about some negotiations his minister had with another minister—which the minister had expressly asked him to keep quiet about—was carpeted.[27]

The civil service would go over all written and other media communications, including speeches—except party political ones and even then officials might check facts—to avoid mistakes of fact and law or departures from government policy. They would generally prepare first drafts of all papers and letters. Churchill's civil servants in No 10 acquired the skill of writing Churchillian prose, an example followed by others close to ministers—Roy Jenkins and Dennis Healey required their private secretary on occasion to imitate their prose styles—if they could write well and the minister had a recognisable style.[28]

Underpinning their knowledge of their job was an exhaustive, but marvellous, filing system. Everything was written down. Almost every meeting discussed a paper, which was revised as it rose through the hierarchy towards the minister or was sent down again by her. (There was no problem of identifying who suggested, and who authorised, every significant change to a paper, as there was to the 2002 Iraq dossier.) Every meeting, every lunch, was minuted. When appointed, I was given a full-time filing clerk to set up and maintain all the economists' and mathematicians' files, which Bert Green did very well.[29] The importance of files meant a determination to get them into order before someone left their post. The highest praise the best under-secretary in the department received from his successor was that the files he left behind when promoted, reinforced by a few retrospective notes for the record, made clear not only how every issue had been handled, but also the strengths and weaknesses of the courses of action for other issues likely to arise.[30] The best files inherited were contingency planning, if not meant as such. Moreover, their existence facilitated the rotation of officials from one post to another, usually every three

---

[27] Personal knowledge.

[28] Colville (1987) i, 190–91; information from Sir John Chilcot when Jenkins' secretary and Sir Nicholas Monck who had been Healey's.

[29] His job was to avoid duplication and filing unimportant drafting changes.

[30] C P Scott-Malden as recalled in private conversation by his successor, Sir Peter Lazarus, as railways under secretary, later permanent secretary.

years or so, which was to get fresh minds in post every so often. It also served to discourage the possibility of too close or even improper relations building up with outside interests.

No nonsense about competing for posts. Promotions were aimed at getting the right person in post and ensuring that senior officers obtained the right mix of experience to prepare and test them for top positions.[31] A huge amount of time in departments and at the centre of the civil service was spent deciding who should go where in their career development.[32] Departmental high-fliers were systematically tested by their being posted to the Treasury, No 10 or Cabinet Office as well as into the depths of a large executive activity.

The process of deliberation, especially in the home policy departments, was often not as quantitative, economic or otherwise analytical as it could have been. Nevertheless it far exceeded the minimum evidence judicial review required. Its model form was rather that of a much more mature, though more worked-up and thorough, essay that an undergraduate classicist or historian might write, setting out the pros and cons of a thesis before drawing conclusions for his tutor. Challenged and tested at every stage as it moved up the hierarchy, this process of serial tutorials up the hierarchy was appropriate for many purposes, e.g., for much casework, but not for all. Often slow and cumbersome, it sometimes seemed to slow down a proposed change deliberately; or delay it to ensure there was enough pressure for it. Civil servants could use their contacts in other departments to brief other ministers against policies they did not like as well as policies other ministers genuinely did not want. Even so, in most cases it enabled ministers to reach an informed decision on the basis of the evidence provided. Moreover, ministers seldom wanted an intellectual solution to political problems, rather one which took into account public opinion and pressure group interests and which they could defend politically. If they pressed for an intellectual approach, as with local authority grants, they got it.[33]

POWER WITHIN THE EXECUTIVE

But one must not be starry-eyed about the relationship. As Burke Trend had expressed it in the early 1970s, it remained broadly true that 'the machine wins every time'.[34] Too great civil service power had led to departments securing an unhealthy monopoly of advice to ministers. The 'office view' on a matter could be difficult to challenge. Until the mid-1960s the permanent secretary often had the departmental hierarchy under his control. Attlee referred to the 'autocracy'

---

[31] Though a special adviser, my deputy secretary status meant I sat on the departmental management board where I had plenty of opportunity to see this going on.

[32] Information from Lord Croham who was Head of the Civil Service.

[33] In this case it was to protect ministers from the charge of being political in the allocation of funds between local authorities.

[34] Hennessy (1989) 537.

at the Post Office when he was postmaster-general.[35] Macmillan's permanent secretary told him it was unconstitutional for him to consult anyone else in the department, as Roy Jenkins was also told at the Home Office, wondering at the contradiction between a permanent secretary who was personally liberal, but regarded it as wrong for any opinion to reach the minister which he had not approved.[36] Crossman spoke of the 'secret discussions' among civil servants before submissions came to him which might have been more accurately described as meetings to prepare submissions for him.[37] He found his permanent secretary insistent that she comment on what went to ministers.[38] Submissions to him, with which she disagreed, went forward, but with such pungent comments that subordinates were wary of crossing her views, especially given that she was generally right.[39] Like many other departments, the 1960s saw Transport show greater tolerance: different ideas could be put to ministers by civil servants, if first circulated on paper. If suggestions took account of criticisms, and the views of relevant interests, they would reach ministers. By the end of the 1960s, Douglas Allen, as Treasury permanent secretary, allowed papers to go straight to ministers, provided they were always copied to him so that he could intervene.

Despite more voices reaching ministers in the 1960s and 1970s, the balance of power stayed with the machine. But ministers and officials were seldom at loggerheads. Working relations were usually good, though, even at its best, the decision-making process could seem opaque to ministers sitting on top of it. A Jenkins, Castle, or Healey, Heseltine, Ridley or Lawson could almost always get their way. But many others often stood up to their officials. I recall the London Motorway Box in 1969. By then Dick Marsh was minister and my own position was weaker, not helped by his return to a more traditional view that he did not want a choice put to him, rather a single recommendation, which he would decide if he could handle politically. Departmental stubbornness in favour of the Box was grounded, from officials' standpoint not unreasonably, in the fact that a long and expensive inquiry process—a court-like rather than economic process—favoured it. Yet it seemed plain to us economists that the economic and many traffic-engineering arguments were against it. The arguments supported Marsh's own view.[40] The box was dropped.

To overcome the office view, even the strongest ministers benefited from:

- a team of junior ministers who—far from common given the haphazard nature of many ministerial appointments—worked constructively together.

[35] K Harris (1982) 90, 590.
[36] R Jenkins (1991) 181–84. Jenkins' view of Home Office elaborated in Headey (1974) 210–20
[37] Crossman (1975) 26–31.
[38] Crossman (1975) 51–55, 65–66.
[39] Information from Sir Geoffrey Chipperfield, then at MHLG.
[40] It is relevant that as a London MP Dick Marsh was dead against it before he received our arguments; but still the strength of opinion within the department that the conclusion of an independent inquiry should not be overturned was such that it was the next government that finally killed the proposal off.

Our team at Transport did. Barbara's subsequent team—for her disastrous Industrial Relations bill—did not;

- special advisers. In those days when they were mostly technical advisers, their main strengths were that they could track down and challenge the evidence, on which advice to her was based, as well as improving both access to outside analysis and advice and that done internally. Special advisers improved these processes provided they actively engaged with civil servants in developing practical policies, or alternatively confined themselves to speech-writing and constituency relations.

ADAPTABILITY OF THE RELATIONSHIP

But for virtually all ministers the advantages of partnership far out-weighed the disadvantages. Its flexibility allowed the machine to adapt to ministers' different styles and appetites for business. They could deal with the idiosyncrasies of Ernest Marples, whose working day lasted from 4am to lunch-time, after which he slept before going down to the Commons. He hardly entered his department, insisting meetings took place at his home—the small compensation being a glass of Chateau Marples—and of Duncan Sandys, who would not leave a phrase unturned when discussing documents, and worked so thoroughly that he needed a double-shift system in private office to get through no more work than other ministers did.

They learnt to know how extensive the advice a minister wanted and how best to present it. There were always voracious readers like Barbara Castle and Margaret Thatcher and those who, like Ernest Bevin and later Michael Heseltine, depended almost wholly on talk with their officials. Some, like Castle demanded they were always given a choice of decisions, though one were recommended. Others wanted a single recommendation to accept or reject, before being given another option. Some still have a lawyer's ability to master a brief. Others take longer. Some want copious information: Tony Crosland—to whom I was also a special adviser—required a vanload of papers sent to his home for his 1975 Transport Review, as much as if writing a book. Others want summaries on one or two sheets of paper. Some are efficient and well organised, some not industrious. Some have a zest for arbitrary decision-making without close attention to the evidence. A few avoid a decision if they can. They vary in what interests them within their departments and in their willingness to delegate to junior ministers.

Partnership allowed the civil service to adjust to these differences in ministerial styles, priorities and workload. (The most important post an ambitious young civil servant had was as head of the minister's private office.) It did not try to negate differences in personality but, individually and institutionally, it provided structure, processes and constant sources of advice, which made ministers more effective, more than in other government systems, which also provided structures, but where the advice was not as bespoke to meet every minister's needs. Writing about politics, in terms of personalities and without regard to structure or process, distorts, but to allow no influence of personality differences on power is mistaken. Much of the dialogue the nation was later to laugh at in *Yes, Minister* came from the need for usually successful tact in steering ministers around pitfalls.[41]

Ministers did not realise how much thought went into making them more effective.[42] They would never see the detailed notes that accompanied ministers moving department, setting out their preferred ways of doing business, attention span, strengths, foibles, how they could be pleased and how annoyed, preferred times of working and methods of relaxation, family and personal friends to be allowed special access, and so on. (I remember the long note her private secretary, John Gunn, wrote when Barbara Castle left for her new job at Employment and Productivity.) It was the silk on the upholstery of the Rolls Royce service the civil service offered and it appealed to civil servants to be as closely interested in their ministers as much as it did to understand characters in a good novel.

STRENGTHS OF THE RELATIONSHIP

Civil servants developed a first-rate capability for protecting ministers' short-term interests, especially when confronted, as always happens, with unexpected events. Particularly, but not only, in Private Office, they could give ministers crucial psychological support at times of stress, because they were trusted, leak-proof and always on the ministers' side, more than their party supporters in the Commons who might fancy their chances as rivals or be envious. Moreover, there were the discouraging examples of ministers who had rejected their embrace: Neville Chamberlain (and Sir Horace Wilson) in pursuit of appeasement; Eden over Suez; Tony Benn (and his special advisers) at the Department of Industry; and all too many after 1997.

Furthermore, partnership helped ministers, who generally had to learn on the job. That is far from saying that ministers should always do what their civil servants tell them and not listen to other people. John Stuart Mill in his day stressed the importance of local government as a nursery for ministerial talent, still true.[43] However, the 'companionable embrace' of the civil service was an additional and more important training ground, arguably the most significant contribution of the relationship to democracy.[44] The theory and usually the practice were that understandably most ministers had little experience in their

---

[41] See a discussion on how to handle ministers with Lord Bancroft, dismissed as Head of the Civil Service by Margaret Thatcher, Hennessy (1989) 509.

[42] Based on the note I saw written when Barbara Castle went from Transport to DEP.

[43] Mill (1910) ch 15.

[44] Castle (1984) 35, talked of the 'administrators' companionable embrace'.

backgrounds—even if clever or experienced in other ways—to head large government organisations with a wide and unpredictable spread of difficult decisions and without a common measure like profit to help them. Moreover, as Bagehot noted, ministers seldom go where they have most experience or expertise. Neither in Britain do they stay in any one post for long. To make democracy work, the axiom was that through some experience in their background—as businessman, magistrate, trade union official, schoolmaster or whatever—they could be helped to realise their potential in government. Rather that than government by experts of any kind. Whatever their background, officials preferred strong ministers—able to stand up to their colleagues and to Parliament—rather than weak ones.

And it generally worked. At worst, if they stuck to their admirable, probably unadventurous, written brief, they would rarely be humiliated. They could be an actor, even a parrot. More frequently, they would marry their own judgement and experience to what the civil service had to offer and produce something better than either could separately. At best, even the greatest and most self-reliant benefited from their help. As a consequence, the civil service came to respect and admire not only the best but also good ministers. Ministers came to trust and rely on these civil servants, especially those close to them, though they would never forget, if they were wise, that the minister's interest and that of the departmental machine must often diverge. As a consequence of these strengths, but particularly the last, ministers were able to perform far more functions—except those concerned with politics, party and constituency—indeed do more things at once, and to appear wiser, more knowledgeable than they could have done on their own. Furthermore the processes underlying the decisions they took, meant the evidence on which they were based, the consultative processes gone through, the reasons for the actual decisions taken, could be revealed voluntarily or if Parliament demanded it. Despite the fact that over time ministers' responsibilities grew, yet with few exceptions, and even though notoriously many ministerial careers end in tears, their performance was enhanced by the partnership. A rewarding contrast is between Roy Jenkins among the best as Home Secretary and Chancellor, where reasoned but politically astute decision-making was required, and his comparative failure as president of the European Commission where face-to-face horse-trading was *de rigueur*.

CONCLUSION

The efficient secret of Haldane partnership enabled ministers to do more work and appear more on top of their job than in other government systems, though nowhere else were they so dependent on their officials.[45] The gradual, and then

---

[45] Campbell and Wilson (1995) 19–20.

more precipitate decay of this relationship after 1979, meant ministers' and officials' ability to get through as much business with thoroughness and effectiveness was much reduced. After 1997 it was not unreasonable to say that in practice, if not in law, special advisers had replaced civil servants as ministers' *alter egos*.[46] As we shall see, it had painful consequences for both the efficiency of government but also for the values by which it operated.

[46] Oliver (2003) 238.

3

Decision-Making: The Exercise of Ministerial Power

> ... several things should be left to the discretion of him that hath executive power. For the legislators not being able to foresee and provide by laws for all that may be useful to the community, the executor of the laws, having the power in his hands ... has ... a right to make use of it for the good of the society.
>
> *John Locke* (1684)[1]

MOST OF WHAT ministers, or civil servants on their behalf, do, is taking decisions within the law and bounds set by government policy. The kinds of decision made varied between departments, but most secretaries of state themselves: make executive decisions generated by departmental activities; allocate and authorise expenditure; decide how to respond to serious criticisms in Parliament, as by setting up an inquiry or other expedient; decide how to handle business with colleagues, Parliament and the press or unexpected emergencies like dealing with a strike; and make public appointments.

Decision-making was and remains the most evident expression of ministerial power, far more than lawmaking, something often forgotten by those who have recently argued for the replacement of our political by a legal constitution.[2] Some decisions were urgent, some needed a rapid response, while some, involving wide and slow consultation might proceed through green and white papers: not only major legislation, but a Defence proposal to buy equipment from abroad or DHSS needing to deal with the suddenly perceived dangers of lead in petrol (see below chapter 4).

THE PRACTICE OF DECISION-MAKING

Ministers were involved in most decisions until the First World War, when comparatively few were made; but, especially during the two world wars, their

---

[1] Locke [1690] (1924) 199. Locke attributed that right to 'the Common Law of Nature'.
[2] Oliver (2003).

number increased and civil servants progressively came to take more.[3] Ministers' interest in taking decisions grew in the 1960s; but the number to be made grew faster, so that civil servants made increasing numbers of the less important decisions for them. Civil servants maintained that formal and informal signals from ministers, indicating policy changes, were usually easily picked up by civil servants without much discussion and reflected in their decision-making.[4] Even so, the law, the convention of ministerial responsibility and, more recently, media pressures gave ministers many more decisions to take than other nations' ministers or a private sector CEO.

Reasoned decision-making drew on many ministers' common experience. Many were lawyers, but more able to rise higher in their profession and remain MPs than now.[5] Many had been magistrates.[6] Many MPs—Labour as well as Conservative—came through local government as mayors and aldermen in days when they were automatically magistrates. Some had similar experience in the colonies. Indeed, sitting in judgement was part of the professional activity of many occupations from colonial administrator or military officer, to trade union official, schoolmaster and even school prefect. Weighing evidence, oral and written, was a familiar activity. Indeed the standard form of the traditional civil service minute identified the issue, set out the relevant evidence and law, put the main options, and then the main advantages and disadvantages of each before making a recommendation. As long ago as 1940 Oliver Lyttelton, a rare businessman who was also a successful minister, remarked on civil servants' tendency to assume ministers knew nothing about a subject; but their defence would have remained that, as in a court of law, ministers needed to review relevant evidence before making up their minds.[7]

Some decisions were based on recommendations made by officials with quasi-judicial authority, like inspectors and regulatory authorities, or by public inquiries or the Monopolies Commission which operated under court-like procedures. As with the Motorway Box (see above chapter 2) a minister found it harder to overturn their recommendations: he would have to give reasoned arguments in public why he should do so.

Though the load varied between departments, ministers might find ten or more significant decisions a day in their evening and weekend boxes, or to be discussed at meetings sandwiched between other activities. How carefully ministers scrutinised the requests for decisions which filled their evening and week-

---

[3] For the growth in the decisions ministers had to make in the First World War, see J Harris (1997) 198. Oliver Lyttelton, businessman and politician, could say at the end of the Second World War that the occupation of a minister had turned from that of a policymaker to an administrator in his lifetime, Chandos, (1962) 146.

[4] Private information.

[5] This point came home to Sir Henry Brooke, as head of the Law Commission, when he read the Commons Reports on the 1965 Law Commission debates when many of the contributions of the lawyers who took part were excellent.

[6] Foster and Plowden (1996) 201–7. In 1895 20%; in 1992 only 4% of ministers had been JPs.

[7] Chandos (1962) 202.

end boxes might be hard to tell. A tick and their initials were often all that was needed. Officials took dozens more in the secretary of state's name, but he or she was accountable for all to Parliament. Making decisions was occasionally agonising, often enjoyable, usually interesting, but, even when routine, proof of the power which had attracted most into politics. Some could be as important as legislation. Many might interest Parliament or the press but, even if not, were practice for greater decisions. Many clustered round the institutions and public bodies a minister had to handle habitually. They were ways of getting to know, and learning how to persuade, people in nationalised industries and elsewhere who frequently had different backgrounds, aspirations and motivations from their own. If good working relationships were to be maintained, the handling of decisions was as important as the decision itself. A spin-doctor can often gloss as a triumph a decision which has soured personal relations, even irreparably.

CONSISTENCY WITH THE LAW

Announcing a decision, ministers and civil servants had once written formal letters to chairmen of public bodies, MPs, members of the general public or anyone else, tending to start, 'I am directed by the Minister under . . .', followed by a reference to the statutory power. Towards the end of the 1950s they were usually replaced by informal, less bureaucratic letters which no longer referred to a statute or a regulation.[8] However, if there were doubts whether the minister had the necessary powers, departmental lawyers were consulted. That ministers must operate only within the law, remained well understood.[9] After a fire at a steel plant, Tony Benn telephoned the British Steel Corporation from his car, ordering it to be closed down for two days, only for officials to remind him that for him to do so was beyond his legal powers. If the issue seemed important enough, such powers might be sought in new regulations or a bill.[10] As a member of a public body in the 1990s, it was a shock to receive a letter from a departmental minister demanding that many millions of our budget should be spent on a large project with a negative return, but of high interest to his constituency. Had civil service advice that this request exceeded his powers, as it did, been ignored? Or was the advice no longer there? Then and later ministers were more often to insist on such actions and get away with them, though they had not the legal powers.

---

[8] I was told under the influence of Ernest Gowers' campaign for plain English.
[9] Craig (1994) 4–7; Jowell in Jowell and Oliver (1989) 3–23.
[10] Until the 1933 Donoughmore Committee there were doubts if secondary legislation was consistent with the Rule of Law, Jowell in Jowell and Oliver (1989) 6.

CONVENTIONS: CONSISTENCY WITH DEPARTMENTAL POLICY

Standard practice was that, before a minister took a decision, he would receive a file with the case particulars, the relevant law, regulations, government policy and similar decisions previously made. Benn complained he was expected to accept 'recommendations' for decisions put to him. I doubt it, but if he disagreed with a recommendation based on precedent, he should have gone through the evidence and arguments put to him, on which the recommended decision was based, showing why he disagreed and on the basis of what evidence and arguments, then giving reasons for his preferred decision. Moreover, for fairness and consistency, such a change in departmental policy sets a precedent for subsequent decisions, whether taken by ministers or officials. In that sense ministers could overturn a 'recommendation' by spelling out a new policy in such terms, but could not do it by being in any other sense 'political' or arbitrary.[11] As late as the 1970s a junior minister at the Home Office, who habitually took arbitrary and inconsistent decisions, was moved when officials pointed this out to the secretary of state.[12] The exception proves the rule. When Jenkins was Home Secretary, Jersey still had capital punishment. A recommendation for the death penalty—consistent with the law there and with every Jersey precedent in its use—came for his approval. Believing it would affront British public opinion, he turned it down.[13]

CONVENTIONS: CONSISTENCY WITH GOVERNMENT POLICY

However, where a departmental policy had been agreed by Cabinet, even by one of a different party, and became government policy, or touched other departments' interests, ministers had to be ready to argue for their proposed policy changes before a Cabinet committee or even at Cabinet. One can see Benn's permanent secretary, Sir Anthony Part, endlessly trying to persuade him to take an issue to Cabinet and abide by its decision, whatever the manifesto or Labour's National Executive Committee said.[14]

Or in Parliament. A decision justified in Parliament had authority as much as in a court of law, an especially valuable validation when the law did not provide a precise answer, as over a difficult issue of war or peace, or in reviewing the sentence of or pardoning a criminal, or of justifying a controversial planning decision. To give an extreme example, before incorporation of the European

---

[11]   Benn (1990) 187, 210–12.
[12]   Private information.
[13]   Remembered by Sir John Chilcot. It was the last such recommendation from Jersey.
[14]   As Crossman had attempted strenuously but not as successfully, not seeing why Cabinet's judgement should always be preferred to his own, Wilson dealt with him more rapidly, Howard (1990) 265–66.

Convention on Human Rights whether a Myra Hindley should be kept in prison was considered better decided not by an official under rules or a judge, but by a Cabinet minister responding to public opinion and able to defend his decision in the Commons. His was a more authoritative expression than the courts of how public opinion wanted administrative discretion used.[15] A good performance on such an occasion ranked high in all quarters of the House, helping prove the quality of a good minister. It was a way of earning promotion.[16] Since the department's reputation was raised, it had a positive effect on the morale of the civil service and the respect in which it held a minister.

NATURAL JUSTICE

Though I do not recall hearing the British lawyers' phrase, *natural justice*, used, I am assured that it was well known to civil servants who regarded it as a guide to proper administrative action by them and by ministers, not only a set of rules for the courts.[17] It implied being systematically fair.[18] It generally required that the views of interested parties were considered, and that any other relevant evidence was sought and weighed, before any decision.[19] How these principles were interpreted depended on the significance of the decision, work pressures and the ability to secure ministerial time. It underpinned the convention that if one party to an issue could see a minister, fairness required that any other party of substance should see the minister as well. If the minister were too busy to see all, then an official should see all.[20]

As a decision travelled up the hierarchy towards the permanent secretary and the minister, an official might stop it, noting either there was ample precedent for it or that it was sufficiently like a decision the minister had already taken not to burden her with it, since her or his consistency made plain what the answer would be. Economising on busy ministers' time was an important considera-

---

[15] Subsequently the courts, using the European Convention on Human Rights, have ruled against ministers.

[16] Kavanagh (1990) and Riddell (1993) 272.

[17] By two permanent secretaries, Sir John Garlick and Sir Peter Baldwin. Ingrained in the system was that ministers' and officials' decisions must be *consistent*, both with each other and government policy, otherwise described as not being 'arbitrary', 'irrational' or 'unreasonable'; e.g., Wade and Forsyth (1994) 399–402 (*legal*, that is not *ultra vires*, and *fair*); Craig (1994) 281–334; Wade and Forsyth (1994) 463–70 (the equivalent to what the USA knows as due process); Breyer (1982) 346–50. The Sainsbury criteria in 1992, and the *Better Regulation* unit criteria in 1998, for good regulation were similar, Daintith and Page (1999) 277–78. Administrative law regards *legality, rationality* and *propriety*, otherwise *fairness,* as required of ministerial and official decision-making. They are different words for the same qualities. For this I am indebted to Professor Loughlin.

[18] An account of 'fairness' as it appeared to a Cabinet secretary, can be found in Hunt (1993) 120–21.

[19] However just whose views should be considered in making a decision could be a difficulty, just as rights of representation are often difficult for lawyers. Baldwin (1995) 36.

[20] Cf Lord Diplock, 'Exposition of the Process of the Principles of Judicial Review', in *Council of Civil Service Unions v Minister for the Civil Service* [1985] AC 374 at 408, quoted in Wade and Forsyth (1994) 1012–14.

tion, that was never given sufficient weight when their decisions were reviewed in the courts. The courts always assumed that ministers had all the time in the world for their decisions. But except in a few cases, there was nothing like the time for the length and elaborateness of the simplest court procedures. Besides, much of the relevant evidence was on file.

THE PUBLIC INTEREST

Another important convention was that any ministerial decision must be in the *public interest*, an apparently slippery concept often found in statutes and administrative law, and frequently believed to be so ambiguous as to be meaningless.[21] To the best of my knowledge, it was not defined in statute or rules, but if so, like *natural justice*, it was kept in the bottom drawer, not on display. Yet ministers and civil servants gave it a meaning.[22] As best I can judge, it had three elements:

• Ministers could not give electoral or party political—let alone their own political or financial—advantage as a reason for a decision, certainly not in Cabinet or before Parliament, but also not in private with their officials. At the same time officials were perfectly aware ministers must face electoral and other political consequences of different courses of action. The convention was frequently observed by a minister asking for officials to recommend the decision they believed right or in the public interest, and let him see if he or she could live with it politically. If so, they had provided a public interest recommendation he or she could accept;
• In parallel it was usual to consider the 'right' decision and afterwards separately, but before it was firmed up, the question of how to put it over publicly, rather than attempt both simultaneously or address the second question first as became standard at the end of the 20th century;
• Attempts might be made to modify a decision or proposal if that might gain a wider consensus for it without undermining its original objectives.

As recently as 2002 on retiring as Head of the Civil Service, Sir Richard Wilson repeated the view that government should be driven by public interest considerations:

> It is however fundamental to the working of our constitution that governments should use the resources entrusted to them, including the Civil Service, for the benefit of the country as a whole and not for the benefit of their political party; and that opposition parties should feel confident that this position is being respected.[23]

[21] The notion that public offices are to be used in the public interest and not in the interest of the office-holder comes from common law, Oliver (2003) 97, though interestingly she uses the concept but does not further define it.

[22] The very existence of an impartial civil service pre-supposed a public interest as distinct from private interests. Not officials but ministers were meant to define it, Marquand (2004) 107.

[23] R Wilson (2002).

FORMAL CRITERIA

Though it did not persist long enough to become a convention, another 1960s development made it easier to separate out the political element in ministers' decisions, until gradually jettisoned from the 1980s, precipitately after 1997: the publication of formal, usually economic, criteria was introduced, both to get better, because more logical and better-evidenced, decisions, and to help ensure consistency between them. When we introduced systematic cost-benefit analysis into the appraisal of road schemes shortly after the Humber Bridge,[24] the main opposition from civil servants was from fear it was a Trojan horse to enable politicians to get inside the process and select individual schemes on purely political grounds. Preferable for them in that era would have been a signal of a policy change from ministers, for example, that greater weight should be given to regional or safety or environmental considerations in developing and selecting road schemes, the exact choice being left to them.[25] Logically they were wrong since formal investment criteria could be as much a protection against the corrupt or purely political decision making they feared. But historically they were to be proved right. [26]

THE PLACE OF POLITICS

These conventions were a vital means of avoiding politicisation of the civil service, since officials did not have to advocate political advantage when discussing an issue with ministers. What was in it for ministers? Most probably accepted it as right. Many ministers took decisions they believed right despite their difficult politics. Marples pressed on with parking meters despite their great unpopularity. One was thrown through his front window. Crosland negotiated an Icelandic fish agreement believing it to be generally right though against the interest of his constituency, Grimsby. All believed it was for ministers to supply the politics. But they had better be able to defend their decisions in those terms in Parliament or to the media (let alone, as scarcely happened, if challenged in the courts). Otherwise the opposition and informed opinion would be howling for their blood. Moreover, there were usually enough MPs on

[24] Also for rail and other public transport schemes. There had been rudimentary CBA for roads.
[25] The era of cost-benefit analysis—from the late 1960s and 1980s—was a protection against ministers being able to influence the choice of road schemes and alignments on political grounds. In recent years the most obvious exercise of resurgent political power has been the removal of politically contentious road schemes from the programme, whatever their public benefits.
[26] A still more sophisticated technique to deter political decision-making and keep it in the public interest was the use of regression analysis as developed in the 1970s to allocate funds between local authorities. One observed, then and since, ministers using the limited freedom they had to choose between equations.

their own side, disliking a blatant, though admiring a concealed, political manoeuvre, to discomfort a minister, if too overtly political. The game, if it were a game, was for a minister to take a decision which was a political winner, while being able to justify it as in the public interest.

Ministers in many circumstances could be adroit enough to find a genuinely defensible reason against what they did not want to do for political reasons. The confusions that can arise over ministers taking 'political' or policy decisions unilaterally are amply illustrated in Benn's diaries, particularly those for 1974–6, where here, as in other aspects of his political style, though not content, he was a forerunner of the Thatcher era. One strand is shown by his determination not to cancel Concorde, although most of Whitehall, and—instinctively or rationally—many ministers, wanted to cancel it because of its rapidly increasing costs.[27] Benn's political reason was patently that it would be a local political disaster for him in Bristol where it was made and he was an MP; but he could use neither national nor local electoral advantage as an overt reason for not cancelling it and could have been subject to parliamentary obloquy or judicial review if he had. His task was to find a reason in the public interest against cancellation which Cabinet would agree was defensible. But earlier ministers had tied up contractual arrangements between governments and manufacturers to make cancellation impossible, except at incredible cost.[28] Thus he found, as ministers before him had frequently done, a reasoned argument which could stand up in Parliament.

There were rare exceptions—perhaps portents for the future—where no other reason than electoral advantage could be given. The decision to build the Humber Bridge was tantamount to a manifesto commitment, made before the 1966 election—a category of promises which once did not have the legitimacy it later acquired—despite its non-existent economic return. It over-rode the normal decision-making processes within the Ministry of Transport. Not entirely without precedent—old hands blenched at the memory of the premature approval of the Hunstanton-Godmanstow by-pass to help a bye-election—it was still a rarity causing uproar in Whitehall, going all the way to Cabinet, and becoming highly visible outside it. It became a precedent for some years not to be lightly repeated by ministers, particularly as the empty bridge long remained a white elephant.[29]

There were ministers adroit enough to hoodwink Parliament, but the fear of not doing so successfully was a powerful discipline on the boldest and least principled. However, sometimes politics needs what the law can never provide: an

[27] Benn (1990) 116, 125, 159–60.
[28] Roy Jenkins had found it unbreakable in 1964 and Heath again in 1970. Julian Amery as minister of Aviation had so tied the contract deliberately to stop the French breaking the contract, Howe (1994) 56.
[29] Embarrassing to us because I was asked to join in objecting to what Barbara Castle had done over the Humber Bridge, as logically I should have done, given our crusade to extend the use of cost-benefit analysis.

opaque decision because there is not enough political consensus to support a clear-cut one. Such endeavours require the wiliest of politicians if they are to be constructive. Outstanding was Lloyd George. His masterpiece was the Anglo-Irish Treaty of 1921 by which he ended for 50 years endless disruptive argument over Ireland's future.[30] He did it by a series of subterfuges, ambiguities and working on the prejudices and fears of his fellow negotiators from Ireland and Ulster so that they were cajoled into a form of words that did the trick without the possibility of re-opening. But, given parliamentary and civil service vigilance, such tricks require a master-hand.

ARM-TWISTING

But could not ministers just instruct someone to do something? In principle they could within their departments, but having to give a reason for doing so, defensible before Parliament if required, was a powerful protection against sheer political interference. As will appear in chapters 4 and 11, the autonomy of many public bodies made even reasoned instruction virtually impossible until the 1980s. With nationalised industries and bodies in receipt of public expenditure, ministers could sometimes use arm-twisting to get the actions they wanted and for which they did not have the formal powers. Arm-twisting might either be silent, as it generally was, or blatant.

I recall a silent example as a member of the Post Office board in the late 1970s. We presented the board's corporate plan to the secretary of state, Eric Varley. It requested funds to invest in infrastructure needed to meet the beginning of a boom in demand for telephony. The minister commented on it, then switched into a discussion of threatened closures of sub-post offices and poor local service in his constituency, allegedly because of understaffing. The Post Office got the funds it then believed it required, though less than were needed to meet the actual growth in demand, later to be a prime motive for privatisation. But Varley's own concerns were met without anything as crude as a bargain. One had seen such arm twisting going on in a minor way all the time with the nationalised industries and other public bodies: that which cost them little relative to their budgets (even in deficit) could be helpful to ministers as such or as constituency MPs.[31]

Cruder arm-twisting took place on the rare occasions when ministers met such people as nationalised industries' chairmen without others present. In such ways ministers could extend their influence beyond their statutory powers, but not much. The independence and robustness of boards and board chairmen—and the jealousy of Cabinet colleagues—limited the effectiveness of arm-twisting and kept it cheap. It was reinforced by still detailed Treasury control

[30] McLean (2001) ch 7.
[31] Foster (1971) 99–118.

over expenditure in days when ministers had almost no freedom to go outside the detailed allocations they had negotiated with Treasury, but had to go to it to authorise virtually anything different, another Gladstonian legacy. Authorisation required a publicly defensible, that is a *public interest,* reason.

In other cases where it has been felt that ministers were especially likely to be tempted to make political decisions—like rail branch closures, planning permissions and grants to local authorities—more or less elaborate procedures grew up to prevent it. Though, as indeed with rail closures, cumbersome procedures could be a political manoeuvre to deter some decisions.

ABSENCE OF SERIOUS CORRUPTION IN THE BRITISH EXECUTIVE

Partnership with their officials—much better than the courts or departmental ethics officers[32]—protected both against the infiltration of corrupt decision-making, if protection were needed. British ministers have long not been corrupt and remain so. But from the 17th to the early 19th centuries corruption was as commonplace as in many nations one now judges corrupt. Lord Chancellor Westbury in 1865 was the last minister to resign because of the corrupt use of ministerial power: in his case, nepotism.[33] While a few corrupt appointments may seem no more than petty corruption, a system will be corrupt which substantially allows ministers to make the appointments they please, an issue which began again to cast a shadow over some appointments around the end of the 20th century. Westbury marked a turning point because what he had done for a few relations was no more than had been standard among ministers some years earlier. It would not have led to his resignation then, had it not been for the hypocrisy that he had also been a great judicial reformer purging the corruption of the courts, and he was also unpopular because of his habitual sarcastic invective.

In 1892 Gladstone told his Cabinet to drop their public company directorships. Mundella still had to resign as President of the Board of Trade in 1893 when his department investigated a firm in which he had been a non-executive board member until 1892, though no one suggested he had behaved improperly, only carelessly.[34] Even so, Salisbury relaxed the policy in 1900, so that half his Cabinet had company directorships.[35] It was reintroduced and maintained after 1906, when the incoming Liberal Prime Minister, Campbell-Bannerman, asked his new Cabinet to reveal all their directorships, and in most cases give them up, because he did not want his front bench to be known as a 'sty for guinea-pigs'.[36] Some such conflicts of interest remained. Lord Beaverbrook was a Cabinet minister in both world wars while personally dominating the contents

---

[32] Thompson (1995).
[33] Molesworth (1886) iii, 258–61; Vincent (1978) 208.
[34] Armytage (1951) 300–05.
[35] Searle (1987) 44; also Roberts (2000) 540.
[36] J Wilson (1973) 496; Searle (1987) 3.

of his newspapers (the *Daily Express, Sunday Express* and the *Evening Standard*), though not uncriticised.[37] Farmers and landowners were much longer exempt from any requirement that they should not continue to run these businesses when in ministerial office.[38]

It helped that, before the rise of the Labour Party, most Conservative and Liberal MPs had sufficient private income; but occasionally a prominent one, even a minister, might emerge whose means were slender, or who was so extravagant as to put him at risk. Disraeli came close, but the worst was Lord Randolph Churchill: a brilliant orator, dazzling minister, but a financially insecure younger son. As Chancellor of the Exchequer he put information in the way of Lord Rothschild. Much of it was tips about the intentions of the British and foreign governments to borrow money or award contracts which enabled Rothschild to be first on the scene. It was worth Rothschild's while to lend Lord Randolph substantial sums, to the extent that when he died he was about £2 million (in modern money) in debt to Rothschild's bank.[39] On a smaller scale, Jimmy Thomas, an old Labour colleague of Ramsay MacDonald's, who stayed on as a minister in the National Government, passed information to shady, but close, business friends, who had also lent or given him money without obvious reason—in one case nearly half a million pounds in modern money—but he had to resign, not for financial corruption, but because he had passed them budget secrets.[40] An extraordinary case, not found out during his lifetime, was that of Sir Samuel Hoare. When foreign secretary in 1938 and 1939, he received in modern money £60,000 a year from Beaverbrook, a substantial supplement to his (in modern money) £150,000 ministerial income.[41] Beaverbrook's daughter called him 'father's spy in the Cabinet'.[42] The morality of the time, as for centuries past, regarded such behaviour as unwise. It risked making a minister financially dependent as much as had Robert Walpole's, Edmund Burke's, Benjamin Disraeli's, Winston Churchill's and Peter Mandelson's large borrowings from patrons to buy a house to fit their conceptions of their social positions.[43] Yet in these cases, including Mandelson's, one doubts whether receiving home loans from friends amounted to corruption in the sense that they altered decisions ministers made to their own or someone else's corrupt advantage.

[37] Chisholm and Davie (1992) 165–67, 412–13, 437–38, 440.

[38] But there came to be safeguards. Sir John Kerr in conversation recalled when, as a private secretary, Margaret Thatcher suddenly had to leave a meeting on farming and none could replace her in the chair because all had farms. The meeting could not be reconvened until a minister could be found to chair it who had no such interest.

[39] R Foster (1981) 331, 395.

[40] Marquand (1977) 784–86.

[41] Chisholm and Davie (1992) 352–53. Hoare had been a member of the Royal Commission chosen to investigate the 1922 Lloyd George honours scandal, Searle (1987) 372–73. Beaverbrook had also financed Edwin Montague when secretary of state for India, but that instance was complicated by the close relationship he had with Montagu's wife, Chisholm and Davie (1992) 164–65.

[42] Kidd (1987) 163.

[43] Ayling (1988) 34–8; Blake (1966) 251–53, 420–44, also 754.

Such lapses rightly did not affect the reputation or the reality of British ministers as not being corrupt. Most lapses at worst involved passing political insider information, which cannot be so easily policed, not the corruption of a decision the minister had the power to make. It remains a remarkable record in that, possibly except for the far from proven allegations against Neil Hamilton, there is no known modern example of a minister found to have used his or her wide-ranging powers corruptly on behalf of an outside interest. After 1997 the Ecclestone case was to resurrect this possibility as was a reported deal in 2004 between the Labour party and the unions (chapter 12).[44]

It is not accidental that allegations of serious ministerial corruption ended with the rise of the modern civil service. The best protection of the lawfulness and probity of ministers' decisions—and therefore against significant government corruption—was that they have taken decisions with their civil servants, giving their reasons for any departures from previous departmental policies. So it became difficult for ministers to misuse their power for electoral advantage or their own financial advantage.

Less easily policed has always been ministers leaking information which in some circumstances may have been of financial use to the recipient, as it was to Rothschild. In relation to MPs, the use of insider information was considered not reprehensible until about the 1960s. It was and remains hard to monitor. While a minister would not take a decision without officials present or on the basis of a submission put to him, he can talk to friends in his club or at the dinner table, he can give them a tip they can use to their financial advantage or, if he is ready to take the risk, to his own. In part the culpability of ministers in the Marconi Affair turned on whether they had used insider information to their financial advantage and, if so, whether it was blameworthy.[45] Similarly with Jimmy Thomas and Samuel Hoare. Were they paid from friendship or because the insider financial or political information they provided was useful to their paymasters? In any case was it reprehensible by the standards of the day? But, however personally reprehensible, such leaking cannot even then have affected their decisions as ministers since government decision-making was already well protected systemically from corrupt influences. If—as again became common at the end of the 20th century—decisions were once more to be made without civil service safeguards, they could more easily become arbitrary, political or corrupt.

[44] *Times*, 26 July 2004. If true, in return for contributing to party funds for the general election, the unions were promised legislation on corporate manslaughter, extending European directive rights to temporary and agency workers, and a debate on re-nationalising the railways at the 2004 party conference.

[45] Press and opposition asserted the ministers made the money from abuse of government contracts which would have been illegal. The Commons concluded their gains were lawful because made through insider information, Jenkins (1988) 250–55; Donaldson (1962).

ABSENCE OF OFFICIAL CORRUPTION

Since the last quarter of the 19th century, we have had and still have an incorruptible civil service. Civil servants, more than ministers, are worth the attention of corrupt influences because they advise ministers and take most decisions in government, including those on contracts, so that the bending of the rules, which international experience suggests are of the greatest financial interest to business, are mostly under their control.[46] Examples of corrupt official behaviour have been few.[47] But there are, and long have been, many corrupt civil services in the world.

As well as traditions of integrity and probity handed down, the principal protections against civil service corruption have come from appropriate and enforceable laws and regulations; from the same, albeit by private sector standards complicated, procedures that protect them as well as ministers; by their rotation between posts; from high enough salaries, pensions and, above all, sufficient protection of tenure, to deter civil servants from succumbing to corruption. Suddenly at the end of the 20th century these too were under attack.

CONCLUSION

A decision-making system developed which depended on trust between ministers and officials and the sanction of effective parliamentary accountability. It lasted as long as they did. It was also in general much quicker and less rule-bound than the more bureaucratic or judicial procedures common in other countries. That meant administrative decisions could be far more responsive than they, directly or indirectly, to political judgement and, through that, to public opinion. But its acceptability, legitimacy and protection depended on procedures, which while modified to suit the importance or sensitivity of the decision, gave reasonable assurance that the decision had not been arbitrary and had been fair.

---

[46] Rose-Ackerman (1999) ch 3.
[47] An account of protection against fraud and the rare cases of it—Sir Christopher Bullock, Air Vice-Marshal Howard, George Pottinger and a few in the civil service—is in Neild (2002) 90–94 and 217–21; Hennessy (1989) 374–79.

4

Laws That Work

If Princes consider laws as things imposed on them, they have the appearance of fetters of iron but to such as would make them their choice as well as their practice, they are chains of gold.

Marquess of Halifax (1688)[1]

Shortly before he died, I invited Clement Attlee to Chequers where he had spent the happiest days of his life (having ensured that Chequers without his wife would not be too upsetting). Following his stroke, he found questions difficult so I put questions to him. "If you were in this chair" I asked him, "what subject would you put higher in the system of priorities . . ." Immediately he answered, "Transport". I moved Barbara Castle there . . . within a very short period.

Harold Wilson (1976)[2]

MANY MINISTERS NEVER led on major legislation. Several departments seldom, if ever, had a major bill. But for ministers, introducing a significant bill was among their most prized, if intense, activities. As, if not more, important than drafting the law itself was clarifying and evaluating the policy on which it was based after consultation with the interests concerned. However, implementation of a new statute, or a major policy change, depending on circumstances, could be almost automatic.

MINISTERS' POWER TO CHANGE THE LAW

A straightforward implication of Cabinet Government, and the legal sovereignty of the Crown in Parliament, was that ministers could change the law, if they could obtain Cabinet agreement and carry a bill through Parliament. The process of bill preparation was intended to produce both a bill, and a reasoned explanation of why it was needed, and why judged capable of implementation. Occasionally legislation was rapid to meet a sudden emergency or horrific case, but usually ministers were expected to take time to set out their intentions and, after these had first gained Cabinet approval in principle, explain them in a statement to Parliament or a preliminary white paper. They would then consult

[1] Halifax [1688] (1704) 102.
[2] H Wilson (1976) 31.

interested parties so as to be able to persuade Cabinet colleagues their proposals had enough support. After that, ministers and civil servants spent much time developing and discussing the details of the policies that finally emerged, if it were major legislation, in an authoritative White Paper explaining the policy and how it would work, and then as a bill, all needing Cabinet approval.

BILL PREPARATION

The division of preparatory work on bills between ministers and their civil servants varied over time and between departments. Ministers' input was dominant until the late 19th century. What strangely came to be known as Gladstone's 1844 Railway Nationalisation Act, he drafted.[3] It anticipated, indeed bettered, 1980s' privatisation statutes in the simple ingenuity with which it motivated the railways to be efficient.[4] But Gladstone was a genius and his bill was neutered in committee, possible as Parliament was still a legislature. Gladstone discussed important bills in Cabinet, as a deliberate tactic to work up a sense of solidarity among its members.[5] A few ministers continued to write bills into the 20th century; though, unless lawyers, they ordinarily used a draftsman to draft in legal language.[6] Cabinets still went over the detail of important bills.

Around the turn of the century, civil servant input into bill preparation increased.[7] The Liberal administrations after 1906 introduced several bills on old age pensions, unemployment, national and medical insurance, requiring an unprecedented amount of analysis and expert support, so increasing civil servants' input. Some involved Lloyd George in massive detailed preparatory work as Chancellor of the Exchequer and principal instigator.[8] But by the inter-war period and into the 1950s, the civil service contribution was normally

---

[3] Foster (1992).

[4] McLean and Foster (1992); Foster (1992) ch 2; Matthew (1986) 67, 119–20.

[5] Matthew (1995) 107–8, 119.

[6] Gladstone framed most of the clauses of the Irish Church Bill, Mackintosh (1962) 251. Morley said of him that since Pitt he was the only statesman capable of framing such a statute and of expounding it with lofty and commanding power, Morley (1905) i, 898. Gladstone's 1844 bill on railway regulation, which he himself drafted, was a classic of its kind: see Foster (1992). Gladstone was still involved in drafting in 1889: Shannon (2000) 418–20, as was Haldane after 1906. Before he became Solicitor-General, Geoffrey Howe drafted an Industrial Relations Bill deliberately in plain English, but in vain, as it was rejected by the parliamentary draftsman, a decision Heath upheld as Prime Minister, Howe (1994) 46–49, 58–60; also Howe (1992).

[7] E.g. J Harris (1997) 173–75. By contrast the preparation for the Old Age Pensions Act of 1908 was amateurish, without expert analysis or even the relevant actuarial calculations, Bunbury (1957) 71. So was Lloyd George's bill on site value rating, which was why it was dropped, McLean (2001) 163.

[8] Bunbury (1957). Drawn from the memoirs of W J Braithwaite, the civil servant most responsible for the National Insurance Act of 1911, it gives an excellent picture of ministers and civil servants interacting while preparing a major bill.

dominant.[9] An exception was that ideological baggage, and Labour party controversy over forms of public ownership, meant ministers led by Herbert Morrison gave great attention to the detail of nationalisation statutes: an unfortunate example in its consequences.[10] In this long period bills, and sections of bills, were often initiated by the civil service, or after 1965 by the Law Commission to rectify inadequacies in past legislation.[11] Or by ministers.

But the division of labour varied: for example, preparation of the 1944 Butler Education Act had to overcome two obstacles. The secular authorities and educational pressure groups must be persuaded the bill protected their interests. Then there were the special concerns of the churches, particularly difficult to meet in the past. R A Butler agreed that the civil servants led by Neville Heaton had found acceptable solutions to persuade the first set of interests to implement it; but satisfying the second was more difficult.[12] To solve that problem he took on consultations himself.[13] But the detail was mainly Heaton's and his team of officials.[14] The Butler Education Act was among the most successful statutes ever, remaining the foundation of education policy for 44 years, adaptable even to comprehensive education.[15] A disadvantage of that adaptability was that a drains-up analysis of the kind which a new bill would have needed, could have unearthed and solved important problems.[16] While the 1944 Act was a great success, going comprehensive did not work as well, at least in the terms hoped for by those behind it.

Similarly, in founding the National Health Service, the detail could be left to officials, but Bevan had to take on the most difficult problems, among them squaring the doctors. He could not persuade them to become civil servants. He had to settle for their self-employed status. The more a minister allowed the detail of a bill to reflect compromises between the various interests, the more work could be left to officials. But if a bill were controversial, while civil servants could prepare the ground and clarify the issues, the interests opposed, as Aneurin Bevan put it, expected to see the minister, the organ-grinder, not the monkey. However, once the interests had been talked round and politically

---

[9] Information from Sir Henry Brooke. An exception was Henry Brooke who, when Minister of Housing and Local Government from 1957, was already immersed in the detail of the policies behind the bills he piloted through Parliament. Such prior expert knowledge was rare.

[10] Chester (1975). My own thoughts on these statutes' failings are in Foster (1971) and (1992) ch 3.

[11] A standard ingredient of a file handed over by civil servants to their successors was their thoughts on where statutory powers might well be improved when an opportunity arose. Such thoughts were often the source of civil service contributions to a bill or sometimes were the basis of a complete bill. Generally they were useful, tidying up, rather than radical changes.

[12] As a deputy secretary, he was my colleague at Transport, a reticent, shy, highly intelligent, academic-seeming man; he was spoken about with awe as the architect of the Butler Education Act.

[13] Butler in Herman and Alt (1975) 197; also Howard (1987) 134–38.

[14] I came to know Heaton well after he had been several years at the Ministry of Transport.

[15] Loughlin (1996) 383.

[16] The comprehensive problem was another example of the problem called NOSSO in this chapter. Crosland was told he could not draft legislation to force local authorities to go comprehensive. Other non-statutory means had to be found to persuade them.

acceptable compromises made, then as with the Butler Education Act or the Act founding the NHS—with one reservation to be discussed—there was no serious problem with their implementation when passed. Those involved just went ahead and did it.

THE 1964 LABOUR GOVERNMENT: MANIFESTO CHALLENGE

The 1964 Labour victory meant many new bills.[17] Officials would have combed the manifestos during the election to have what were called *full submissions* ready immediately afterwards. They were intended to test the meaning and good sense of what might be hastily cobbled words, the product of rushed political expediency—with scant attention to practicality—when the manifesto was written; then to relate them to existing policies; and in what was meant to be, but was not always, a constructive spirit, suggest that they, or something like them, could be carried forward into new policy or law. (The declining receptivity of governments from the 1980s to this form of challenge, and its banning from 1997, helps explain why so many ill-considered and redundant bills started to clog the legislative process.) Behind this expected challenge, then the constitutional duty of civil servants, was sound British empiricism. What was the real problem, if any, underlying what—as always with manifestos—may not have been carefully chosen political words?

So the 1964 manifesto committed the government to a new 'integrated' transport policy. The rail and road unions—papering over the cracks between them—had inserted this slogan into the manifesto, mainly because the railway unions hoped to protect railway jobs. The real issue, as the new minister of transport, Tom Fraser's, officials persuaded him, was how did one meet the problem, despite the recent Beeching cuts, of an ever increasing railway deficit about which the ministry was being continually bludgeoned by the Treasury? The plain fact, they thought, was either that one closed down more of the railway system, or found a justifiable reason to persuade Parliament and the Treasury to provide permanent subsidy.

Fraser's acceptance of that common sense led, first, to the ignominy of a special ministerial Cabinet committee set above the ministry and then to Barbara Castle replacing Fraser. The department, shamed and humiliated, quickly stirred itself to meet Barbara Castle's requirements. Within a few weeks, she rushed us into a draft White Paper which was turned down by that ministerial transport committee on advice from all round Whitehall. The smiling permanent secretary, responsible for the full submission to Fraser, took me, as Barbara's special adviser, before its corresponding official committee. Everyone

---

[17] The 1964 bills introducing corporation tax and capital gains tax were particularly demanding. There had been a similar increase in legislation in 1945. While these two Labour administrations had initiated substantially increased legislation, there was not much of a let up in 1970 and not a marked increase in 1974.

has career memories which make him or her shudder. Under Sir Eric Roll of DEA's chairmanship, first, Sir Richard Powell of the Board of Trade, then Douglas Allen of the Treasury, were followed by others who tore our proposals to shreds. I particularly remember George Pottinger of the Scottish Office, later disgraced in the Poulson Affair, who introduced himself, not ingratiatingly, as 'the Smiler with the Knife'. All these high-sounding new bodies to integrate transport, what were they for? What would they actually do? Had we persuaded anyone in the transport industry they were necessary, or would work? It was humiliating (though 30 years later many final, let alone preliminary, white papers, were to be as shallow and insubstantial, especially after 1997). But they were right. We were sent off to 'Do Better'. For me it meant losing the next weekend. Struggling with all I had been told about the new science of logistics, I wrote a 50 page blue-print for what became the National Freight Corporation, which, by and large, and worked up after rapid consultation, was judged able to meet the political demand for freight integration, while not being stupid.[18] The creation of Passenger Transport Authorities—still with us—met the political demand for passenger integration.[19] We produced a second preliminary White Paper, setting out our broad intentions. It was accepted by that committee and by Cabinet.[20]

PREPARATION FOR THE 1968 TRANSPORT ACT

More than a year passed before the bill was ready. Meanwhile most discussion, in which I (or my staff) took part, as a special adviser and an economist, was between officials.[21] After preliminary discussions with ministers of what was to be in the bill—in which I also took part—officials constructed a work programme whose main purpose was to decide how its subject-matter needed to be apportioned between the policy areas of the different under- and assistant secretaries; what issues needed to be discussed between them and which with other departments, as well as when the Treasury must be brought in.[22] Because reforming the railways raised business and organisational issues judged outside the competence of ministers and administrators, a special committee was set up under John Morris as parliamentary secretary: a main board member from

[18] Also Castle (1984) 98, 109–10, 114.
[19] The political demand for integration in 1997 led to the creation of a Council for Transport Integration, which may have done many other things but not much new to address this hoary problem.
[20] Ministry of Transport (1966).
[21] The exact process may have varied between departments, for they had their own traditions, but not, I think, the overall form.
[22] In retrospect what seems incredible now was how tightly scheduled those meetings were and how seldom were their timings changed. Ministers' private offices were briefed to discourage altering their meeting timings, because of all the re-scheduling and wasted time that caused below.

Shell, a Lazard's director, a specialist in capital appraisal techniques, a Treasury under-secretary and two rail board members.[23]

Thereafter for months the diary was a mosaic of hundreds of meetings, most between officials. For virtually each one a paper or papers were written or revised. Ministers were assured some clauses were technical. They were barely discussed. They mainly dealt with interaction with other legislation and regulations. Some largely followed model forms used in the past and were also not much discussed as a consequence, less than was sensible with hindsight: for example, setting up the National Freight Corporation and the National Bus Corporation as new nationalised industries. Many issues were discussed with the Treasury because of their financial implications, and others with the Ministry of Housing and Local Government because of their consequences for the local planning system.

The purpose of this work was to assure ministers and civil servants that our proposals were coherent and would work; but, as important, that all within the industry understood them too; that their concerns raised in consultation had been addressed; and solutions capable of implementation had been found. Questions about the White Paper sections and later the bill clauses would be put to Barbara Castle—generally with Stephen Swingler or John Morris present—often in several meetings to ensure their sense was what ministers intended; or if that proved difficult—because of difficulties with Cabinet colleagues or powerful vested interests or because difficult to reconcile with other statutes—to find an acceptable compromise.[24] Evidence from any relevant party, advanced in the consultation process, was reviewed and the minister approved the weight given it.[25] Some objected to the policy itself. Some, even from unions and trade associations, was ideological or political. But much, which was helpful, was about the practicalities of implementation. If the outcome were unlikely to please a party, she would decide if she, another minister or an official would try to overcome the opposition face-to-face.

As special advisers our main role was to ensure that ministers' concerns about what was politically desirable, and the interests of the broad electorate as distinct from the pressure groups, were given due weight in the official consensus-seeking. As economists, mathematical modellers and analysts, another role was to help ensure that relevant research from round the world was not neglected, but also through analysis to attach weights to the interests of the pressure groups involved.[26] This modelling and analysis could be politically important

[23] The outsiders were distinguished: John Berkin, John (later Lord) Cuckney, John Hunt (later Lord Hunt of Tamworth) and Professor AJ Merrett.
[24] In the 1970s Sir Patrick Nairne, then Permanent Secretary at Health and Social Security, found Barbara Castle also ready to devote many hours over instructions for a complex bill.
[25] A few ministers—here, John Morris, to be Attorney-General 30 years later—had been trained as lawyers, but it did not make their legal knowledge the more relevant: the disciplines of the legal mind were no more useful than political experience, wisdom about people and common sense.
[26] The tool was cost-benefit analysis which involved putting a money value as far as possible on a proposal's consequences for each interest insofar as they were significant. There would also be unquantifiables which ministers could take into account.

since it might help ministers strike acceptable compromises. These calculations need not be elaborately researched: rough calculations could often give sufficient indication of relative importance. But some were.[27]

Some—especially the nationalised industries—were endlessly—many, like the trade associations and unions, the second a Labour innovation, frequently—consulted. Consumer and single-issue interests, then far less organised, scarcely got a look in.[28] Ministers saw themselves, through their backbenchers and their constituency and other contacts, representing consumer interests. When Christopher Hall, an ex-newspaperman and I, both special advisers, suggested opinion surveys to test public support—as over seat belts, the breathalyser and other policy issues—Barbara Castle slept on it and rejected the idea as undermining ministers' and backbenchers' contributions to policymaking. However, canvassing backbenchers was not her strong-point. When not in the chamber or voting, she used her time in the House to go through her many red boxes at which she was tireless. But in Stephen Swingler, one of the parliamentary secretaries, she had the perfect conduit, as she did not in her later ministerial career. He regularly discussed the Bill with Labour backbenchers in Annie's Bar in the Commons, an important part of the process. As Barbara Castle, without a Swingler, was to find in her next department, a backbench revolt can bring a minister down.[29] If our ideas were acceptable to Labour backbenchers, our bill would have an easier passage through the House and was more likely to be acceptable to swathes of public opinion. A lesser motive was to help find friendly backbenchers to endure the rigours of the bill committee.[30] I was occasionally present, because backbenchers, who had been got at by their constituents or for other reasons took a close personal interest, would have questions which one had better be able to answer. Some had been railwaymen, professional truck or bus drivers or union officials. There was a strong chance they knew what they were talking about. If 'the boys' had a good point, it would be brought up with Barbara Castle and officials.

Putting a bill together was made easier because of newspaper discussion of large parts of the bill in advance, when the views of the principal interests concerned would be reported as a matter of course. Barbara Castle encouraged me to lunch with the broadsheet correspondents. Michael Bailey of the *Times* and Adam Raphael of the *Guardian* were worth talking to because deeply know-

---

[27] One such was on Track Costs. Another was Alan Wilson's mathematical demonstration published as a White Paper that any good to Bristol from building Portbury docks would be more than offset by the damage it would do to trade in the South Wales ports and Southampton so that the overall economic return would be negative with more losers than gainers. Later he became Sir Alan Wilson, Vice-Chancellor of Leeds University, and, by 2003 the government's special adviser on higher education.

[28] Middlemass (1979) 371–85, Olson (1971).

[29] One can only speculate over how Swingler would have helped her avoid the debacle over *In Place of Strife*.

[30] I listened to several ministerial conversations on this point.

ledgeable about both people and issues. If told something in confidence, they kept it. A programme of speeches and statements in the House—some initiated by us, some by the opposition—also canvassed opinion.

The output was first a set of five white papers explaining the policy in detail—a related one on London Transport—and then a bill. Towards the end, officials worked up its clauses in the non-legal form, that is plain English, appropriate to *Instructions to Counsel*, and then discussed them, my staff or I again being present.[31] The civil servants would cap the process at the end by issuing volumes of comment on the bill—*Notes on Clauses* and later *Notes on Amendments*—magnificent elucidations and explanations of what was in the bill, gilding the lily, it then almost seemed; but reading them, one felt at last that something coherent and defensible had been realised. These notes were of great help to ministers in the House.

In sum, while many bills involved ministers in shorter but similar work, a large bill involved ministers in several meetings a day with their civil servants over a long period, as well as occasional meetings with colleagues and consultations with lobbies. It also took up a substantial amount of civil servants' time across much of the department and in other departments with an interest, for about a year before the Bill was introduced into Parliament. Throughout, successful legislation depended crucially on what has since decayed: an iterative process between ministers, officials and knowledgeable people elsewhere to make sure the bill reflected the policy of ministers and was workable.

It was essentially no different in 1974 when I helped John Silkin put together the Community Land Bill, though it was patently a political bill where winning over the opposition was scarcely tried.[32] Personally he was heavily involved in many meetings as, to an influential extent, was Harold Lever who took a deep interest in it as Chancellor of the Duchy of Lancaster and an old property hand. Whether bills started as a manifesto commitment, a minister's idea, from within the civil service or indeed whatever their origin, those which entered Parliament and came out as statutes were very much the minister's. In substance, but not in legal form, they had their stamp all over them.

Indeed it is tempting to look back—not on a Golden Age because there were many obstacles to good and effective government—and believe that, whereas the difficulty since the 1970s has been that good, or at least plausible, policy ideas are often reflected in bad legislation—usually because a department has attempted too many bills at once and at a furious pace—then good legislation sometimes embodied poor, over-ambitious or infeasible policies, though that

---

[31] Later in the 1970s special advisers were less often present when officials met on their own, in my judgement an unhelpful delimiting of boundaries.

[32] The act did not survive the next Tory government. Its misfortune was that it was kept separate from the reform of local government finance, while they should have been tackled together, a political commitment taken before the election.

was not true of the 1968 Transport Act which, in several respects, remained the basis for transport policy for twenty years and more[33].

There were incentives to induce ministers to spend time on important Bills. Some were personal: to be remembered for a well-regarded Bill that might even be a footnote in history books or justify a chapter in their memoirs. Some were parliamentary: not to be disgraced by being left speechless in the House of Commons. Or even to be applauded, there or in the media. But perhaps the most significant incentive to be thorough was provided by the Cabinet system through which, first in informal, bilateral meetings and then more formally in Cabinet committees and perhaps even in Cabinet, colleagues, briefed by their own civil servants, would scrutinise the advancing measure. To avoid being scorned by a Butler, a Crosland, a Callaghan or a Healey was a powerful incentive to take pains. If there were a drawback, it was that reforming legislation was not passed in all the areas that arguably needed it, since the time could not always be found to persevere with such an intensive process even then.[34] Or, if it were done without effective enough consultation—like Barbara Castle's later union legislation or going comprehensive—the first became a political disaster and the second slowly emerged as a very limited success. Indeed Tony King said that transport was perhaps the only area in which it was clear the first Wilson administration had discharged its manifesto commitment.[35] But the administration was responsible for other statutes, which made a difference and historically were more memorable, like Roy Jenkins' civil liberties reforms at the Home Office.

Because of this approach, practically complete, already well-scrutinised, Bills entered Parliament. Neither House would accept an incomplete bill in those days.[36] A major change in a bill thereafter was because of a change in policy, as for example when Jack Jones, the formidable General Secretary of the TGWU, started by being keen on the tachograph in the Barbara Castle bill—the so-called spy in the cab—which would have reduced accidents by limiting drivers' hours, only to find much later that he could not carry his members with him. They wanted unlimited overtime and not to be snooped on.

Because of the consultation and preparation undertaken, ministers by the end knew a bill inside out. Although a junior minister would carry it through committee, the departmental minister was expected to deal with second reading, turn up in committee from time to time and to be knowledgeable about the bill on these occasions. Some did more, but other preoccupations usually prevented them. Another consequence of thorough preparation was that amendments

[33] My own view is that if we had been aware of, and had tackled, the NOSSO problem, its effect could have been as lasting as the Butler Education Act. Passenger Transport Executives still survive.
[34] Particularly true of the 1970s in my experience, where the preparatory work was done, for example, on local government finance and housing, without proceeding to legislation.
[35] King (1975) 286–87.
[36] But it had to after 1906, the period before the 1980s when legislative ambitions also outran the resources available, Bunbury (1957) 163.

could almost always be resisted. Virtually all reached the bill committee from the vested interests. Their substance was already known because of thorough consultation. In the *Notes on Amendments* civil servants would point out that they reflected some familiar point of view already rejected, or were based on a misunderstanding, or were there to cause political mischief. They were usually right. Perhaps too seldom was an omission or an improvement in drafting acknowledged. Therefore, being an MP on a bill committee could appear a superfluous labour, but nothing like to the extent it had become by the end of the century (chapter 10). At least the bill, and the oral and written explanations given of it, remained intelligible.

SHORTCOMINGS OF CORPORATISM

This approach to legislation has been criticised as corporatist, giving too much weight to vested interests, especially producer ones.[37] That was true if ministers did not know or stand up for the wider public interest. Given all the pressures upon them, in my judgement, technically trained, but politically sympathetic, specialist advisers helped them do so. (Ministers need special advisors. As will be argued, it is how they are used that matters.) But insufficient weight given to wider public opinion was not an argument against consulting minority opinion, which was often more strongly felt and more knowledgeable about the issues in hand than general public opinion. Broadly there are two kinds of occasion when minority opinions should be given special weight.[38] One is where consumer minorities feel strongly about a matter: in our case the users of lightly-used, mostly rural rail branch lines, but a better example might to-day be those who enjoy, as distinct from those who merely disapprove of, some country sports. Another is insofar as producer and worker interests, though inevitably minorities, have more understanding of practical problems of implementation than can any politician or official. A successful political system is not one that just counts heads. Strength of opinion and hands-on knowledge also matter for successful, workable policy. In my own experience, explaining what we were doing over a year to successive middle management courses at the British Transport Staff College, Woking, and then being closely questioned into the small hours after dinner, was invaluable.

IMPLEMENTATION

Before the bill entered Parliament, substantial progress would have been made with the rules and regulations needed to establish the framework within which

[37] Oliver (2003) 11. Corporatism was pervasive in its influence on government, Middlemass (1979).

[38] Of course ministers may also decide to give special weight to minority views because of religious belief or matters of conscience.

the new policy or activity would operate. Iterative consultation, drawing ministers into the detail where it proved intractable, provided all were committed, meant implementation of new policy through legislation was hardly a problem. The spadework had been done and all were cognisant of their new roles.

Sometimes the implementation of an act or important policy change affecting an on-going public service or major executive activity could be as straightforward. So well did the ministry know local authorities and the construction industry—so much did all want a better system—that setting up regional Road Construction Units for national highways went well. But in many cases persuading the executive branches down the line to alter their behaviour radically could be laborious. It took a committee headed by a minister to persuade the Highways side of the ministry to adopt cost-benefit analysis for highway investment appraisal.[39] We then had to out-post the Highways Economics Unit under Geoffrey Searle. He was first-class at overcoming technical and other opposition from engineers, but it took until after a change of government to become established.[40]

It sometimes took extreme energy to get something moving, but, if it were important, some official could usually be found who had the drive and tenacity for it: MHLG officials for upping the building of council houses to 300,000 a year under Macmillan; Ronnie McIntosh for quickly setting up a structure of regional economic planning agencies under George Brown; or Otto Clarke or David Serpell for major reforms of the control of public expenditure. Otherwise they could be re-organised, have new duties given them, but they, almost as much as, even more than nationalised industries and other statutory public bodies, expected to be left to interpret how they did their job.

NO STATEMENT OF STATUTORY OBJECTIVES

While much of the 1968 Act lasted—some to this day—one wrinkle of the British constitution (NOSSO) deadened its impact on the railways.[41] The nearest Barbara and the rest of us had come to being introduced to its existence was during a class act by the department's distinguished chief lawyer, Richard Hankey, a son of Lord Hankey, the first Cabinet secretary. At a late stage, Hankey performed brilliantly before ministers, doing his excellent best to twist the words in the draft instructions, showing how apparently precise words could be hopelessly vague, so telling us that we needed lawyers to turn it all into

---

[39] Chaired by Neil Carmichael who had become a parliamentary secretary. I sat on it.
[40] Less lucky was the endeavour led by Alan Wilson and David Quarmby, later joint managing director of Sainsbury's, to get mathematical modelling incorporating congestion and economic evaluation standard in urban transport planning. The campaign for it went well but the computers used were too slow and expensive to run. That arch-enemy of the use of economic techniques, Colin Buchanan's dissenting judgement on the Roskill Commission, did not help either.
[41] Years later Professor Martin Loughlin of LSE made me realise its full significance.

safe legal language. In passing I remember him explaining why 'maximisation', as in the maximisation of profits or efficiency or of consumer benefits, could not be written into a bill as the statutory duty of a public body. Puzzled, I asked why, and was told it was because of the impossibility of proving in a court of law whether it had been achieved, an important difficulty since technically we would have preferred the railways', and some other nationalised industries' objectives, to be required to reflect quantitatively in their decision-making—through cost-benefit analysis—the impact of their activities on some social costs, particularly their impact on road congestion.[42] Innocent of the full significance of his remarks, we lost an important trick, not realising that part of our policy depended on them interpreting their powers and duties as we wanted them to.

David Marquand is right in saying that in some respects *laissez-faire* remained British government practice long after the death of 19th century economic liberalism. Ministers could not instruct statutory bodies.[43] They always had the discretion to exercise their powers and duties as if a public trust.[44] Sometimes their prime duty was defined as to exercise their powers and duties in the public interest. Ministers could not sack their chairman, though they could not re-appoint them and hope they would resign if the minister showed no confidence in them. But once ministers had appointed a successor, they could not instruct him either, if he chose to use his discretion within the law. It is not accidental that it was over such bodies ministers had most to resort to arm-twisting (above, chapter 3), but that was not easy if they were profitable or had ample funds. How to get either kind of public body to do what ministers wanted on a contractual or quasi-contractual basis, while protecting them from excessive ministerial interference and motivating them to be efficient, was an unsolved problem into the 21st century, as we shall see.[45]

The root problem was lost in the mists surrounding the origins of doctrine of ministerial responsibility: either ministers were fully responsible for an activity or that activity had to have discretion—the model was often that of a public trust—to interpret the duties laid on it by statute.[46] English law found no satisfactory *quasi-contractual* way in which a public body could be motivated to pursue a duty laid down by ministers to achieve certain outcomes with discretion being only over how they achieved those outcomes, that is over inputs

---

[42] It was in my mind because of the cost-benefit analysis I had done on rail and other schemes. In the 1970s there was a brief but sensible attempt to run London Transport with the duty of maximising passenger miles carried per £ of subsidy. On the analytical and practical problems see Foster (1971) pt 1, and (1992).

[43] There were technical reasons why ministers scarcely ever issued general directions to nationalised industries as they were empowered to by statute, but also the important and interesting reason that, if they did, they might be presumed to have taken over full responsibility for the nationalised industry.

[44] On the influence of public trusts in shaping public corporations, see Foster (1992) esp ch 3.

[45] See Richard Pryke and John Dodgson's successive books on how the nationalised industries disappointed expectations of improved productivity.

[46] Discussed in Foster (1971) 27–28.

(subject to a profitability or maximum subsidy constraint). It was a serious problem with all the nationalised industries. Similarly, as Martin Loughlin has shown, we never developed the law needed to regularise satisfactory relations between central departments and local authorities, delimiting what each could do.[47] (It was because local authorities were considered to have similar discretion whether to adopt comprehensive education, that Crosland did not try to force them to do so through a statute.) NOSSO was the Achilles' heel, responsible for endeavours after 1979 to centralise, but actually weaken, government as ministers struggled to impose their will (below, chapter 11).

After Barbara Castle moved on, the interpretation of much of the policy we had worked on was at the discretion of British Rail. Crucial to getting more freight from road to rail, was that British Rail should work closely with the new National Freight Corporation to that end. It refused. If it did not move freight to and from railheads in its own trucks, it would rather not have it. A rail board member was also dispatched to state they would not work out the marginal cost of different traffics and routes, though a key policy developed by the Rail Inquiry to which they were a party.[48] Consequently there was no adequate financial reporting on loss-making services. Inexorably the railway deficit started to rise again. A few years later the railways were—not for the first or last time—again effectively bankrupt.

Yet despite occasional intransigence—which in my experience normally involved resentment over what was seen as undue interference in how public bodies ran their affairs—the norm was different. If ministers could persuade officials that what was being attempted was in the public interest or had over-whelming political support from the Cabinet, they could get enough consen-sus—aided by officials who were expert in manoeuvring the interests they knew so well—among those who had the power to deliver, there was normally no further problem in implementing a policy which had been well-designed as part of a lengthy consultative process. But to be successful ministers had to accept the realities of power and the law.

One reason for so limiting ministers' ability to give instructions was their impermanence, here to-day, gone to-morrow. To have permanent effect the changes they made had to be acceptable to those implementing them, but also to the opposition. One day I was telephoned: would I lunch with Michael Heseltine, then junior opposition transport spokesman? Barbara encouraged me to do so. Over lunch in the Guards' Club he and his boss, Peter Walker, grilled me over some of the proposed controls over the nationalised industries in our bill: were they meant to improve public policy and efficiency, or were they Trojan horses for mischief making? Persuaded they were intended to help make

---

[47] Loughlin (1996).
[48] The importance of getting 'sound costings' from BR merited mention in Barbara Castle's diary, Castle (1984) 141.

them more efficient, they said they would not press their opposition to them, but consider the relevant provisions constructively.[49]

The problem was the obverse of the incredulity that Crossman and Tam Dalyell, as his PPS, felt when they saw policy carrying on as if nothing had changed after the 1964 election.[50] Parliamentary democracy required that a previous minister's policy was not so entrenched in new ways of working that it could not be altered, even reversed by a new minister, especially after a change of government. In days when it was rare for new laws to follow rapidly in the same policy area, the need to change the law might be some protection against too much change, but not much. Such flexibility was a source of ministerial power, but could impede sustained administrative improvement to increase efficiency, an issue which however became of greater importance following the public expenditure crises of the 1960s.

CONCLUSION

Ministers have always had constraints on their power. They included Parliament (which effectively killed the Chamberlain government, Eden's Suez policy and devolution in the 1970s); pressure groups (like the British Medical Association, which killed Bevan's wish to make doctors into civil servants, and the TGWU who temporarily killed the tachograph); and limits on expenditure (which prevented the NHS getting rid of waiting lists and other public services like housing and prisons getting rid of their queues and overcrowding). Motivating those involved in implementation could be a problem—as it still is—unless they had not only been consulted, but persuaded what their role should be, especially insofar as implementation depended on the co-operation of public bodies with deeply held views of their own and enjoying considerable legal and administrative autonomy. However, the difference between then and now was that in that past, ministers had enough time to go through extensive consultation processes while turning policy into legislation. They also needed to persuade their Cabinet colleagues that the measure was something they could defend in Parliament.

---

[49] As I recall the main issue on which they were persuaded was over the intention to establish marginal costs for each unprofitable rail service on a sound basis and then determine which was worth subsidising after cost-benefit analysis of the options.

[50] Dalyell (1989) 120–22.

5

Cabinet Tries to Cope

Cabinet is a democracy, not an autocracy; each member of it, including the Prime Minister, seeks to convince his colleagues as to the course to follow. The Cabinet bears his stamp, it is true, on each and every policy issue, but it is the Cabinet not the Prime Minister who decides. The growth of the Cabinet committee system is one factor which would restrain the overweening desire of a would-be dictator. More and more decisions have to be taken there, or prepared there for Cabinet. Where there is general agreement on the committee, he would have to be a brave or rash Prime Minister who sought to overrule such a decision. He would not last long.

Harold Wilson (1976)[1]

HOBBES, TROUBLED BY the anarchy of the English civil war, and the failure to construct a sustainable constitution during the Commonwealth, thought that only the single-minded rule of one person—the Sovereign—could avoid chaos and restore order.[2] Britain has not had a monarch since William III who could fit Hobbes' requirement. Instead the development of Cabinet and Cabinet Government has been the means by which the British political system—until the 1980s—tried to develop enough unanimity—Cabinet solidarity—to have the strengths of government as if by a single purposive mind while avoiding the pitfalls of absolute power.[3] For about two and a half centuries Cabinet had the ultimate power within the Executive.[4]

Many Prime Ministers—Lloyd George, Attlee, Macmillan, Wilson and Heath—and their Cabinet secretaries, improved its methods of working as government business increased.[5] Opinions vary when it was most efficient. Douglas Allen, head of the civil service under Wilson and Callaghan, believes it was in the 10 years after 1945 when papers were circulated sufficiently long

---

[1] H Wilson (1976) 8–9.

[2] Hobbes [1651] (1996) 130–34.

[3] About the only disagreement I have with Jeremy Waldron's superb book is his over-reliance on voting in Parliament as the means for resolving political disagreement: Waldron (2001) 33–45, but more generally chapters 2 and 3. More important was Cabinet whose job it was to put together policies and bills likely to command a majority in parliament.

[4] This chapter, and discussions of Cabinet and the Cabinet system in later chapters, are based on Foster (2004).

[5] An interesting account of Hankey's setting up of the Cabinet system with proper agenda and minutes is Amery (1953) 74–80.

before meetings for members to be adequately briefed.[6] But it long remained an efficient mechanism, though struggling to cope with an ever-growing workload.

THE EFFICIENT SECRET OF THE CONSTITUTION

In the late 17th century, the Privy Council was superseded as the central organ of government by what later came to be known as Cabinet. The council had not only been a source of policy advice to the Crown, but an executive, an active organisation of administration in undivided charge of a national bureaucracy.[7] Not only was accountability to shift from the Crown to Parliament, but executive authority for the most part went from the council to the great officers of state individually without providing for any one of them to have over-riding (chief executive) powers to co-ordinate or over-rule the others.[8] Nevertheless Cabinet in place of council was to develop a collective responsibility for policy and administration, but also a role in co-ordinating the activities of the departments of state in relation to both.[9]

Bagehot's description of Cabinet as the hyphen or buckle between Legislature and Executive—a committee from the first which headed the second—was a key element in his own demolition of the idea, drawn from Montesquieu and Blackstone (but, as we have seen, already refuted by Bentham (above chapter 1)), that the separation of powers between Executive, Legislature and Judiciary was the fundamental reason for the success of the British Constitution.[10] The truth was that its success or, as Bagehot put it, its efficient secret, lay where people from the first two overlapped at that hyphen or buckle: in the *separation* of legal powers between legislature and executive, but their junction or *fusion* as people.[11] Like Parliament, Cabinet's deliberations and authority gained from the breadth of experience around the Cabinet table which included vital legal experience: at a minimum that of the Lord Chancellor, but many other kinds of experience. Political memoirs and diaries frequently recall proposals being challenged by colleagues' knowledge from outside politics.[12] Bagehot could have added that the Cabinet is an example of fusion in another sense: the separation of powers between ministerial heads of departments. They have their separate

---

[6] Personal communication; also J Harris (1997) 401–5.

[7] Elton (1959) 420–21.

[8] In practice as individuals, though most powers were vested in the Secretary of State without further designation, so that technically powers could be exercised by any secretary of state. I am indebted to Lord Hunt of Tamworth, who has been Cabinet secretary, for the point that none was given CEO powers.

[9] Some quasi-judicial ministerial decisions by law are not subject to collective Cabinet control or consideration: e.g. determining planning appeals.

[10] Bagehot (1997) 10.

[11] Jeremy Bentham had practised a similar demolition in Bentham [1776] (1948) esp ch 3.

[12] My own memory is of Harold Lever, who had been a property developer, taking an intense interest in the Development Land Bill, as Chancellor of the Duchy of Lancaster.

powers; but their fusion as people round the Cabinet table in collective responsibility for government was also complete.[13]

COLLECTIVE RESPONSIBILITY

The 18th century established the convention of Cabinet collective responsibility.[14] Its main requirement was that government policy was that of the whole Cabinet, so that the government resigned if successfully censured in the Commons.[15] For about a hundred years governments resigned when they lost the Commons' support over a major policy issue. During this period, the constitutional requirement of collective responsibility was well aligned with the political requirement that the government needed to command a majority in the House of Commons. It corresponded to an early stage in the development of political parties when members were readier to vote against their parties on particular issues or even cross the floor. The emergence of cohesive national parties meant governments resigned thereafter because they lost their majority, felt they had too small a majority to continue, or dissolved Parliament to fight an election. Still collective responsibility survived. The odd exception like the resignation of Sir Samuel Hoare as Foreign Secretary in 1935 proved the rule. The Cabinet had approved the Hoare-Laval pact but, when published, it proved so unpopular, the Cabinet withdrew its support for it. Hoare resigned because his new found disagreement with the rest of the Cabinet was exposed.[16]

A second part of the convention was that no minister should publicly disagree with government policy. Any who did should resign. Earlier, Cabinet colleagues had often disagreed publicly.[17] The case which established collective responsibility in this regard was that of Lord Thurlow whom, as Lord Chancellor, George III following custom had personally chosen.[18] William Pitt as Prime Minister persuaded George III to sack him in 1791 because in the House of Lords he had opposed the establishment of a sinking fund, though the proposal was government policy the Cabinet had agreed. Many ministers have since resigned

[13] Attlee excluded several departmental heads to keep the Cabinet small. It worked while what they did was of little interest to Cabinet, but they felt second-class ministers, though on Cabinet committees.

[14] Jennings (1959) 134–35. However note Sir John Anderson's 1946 view 'Theoretically, the responsibility of each individual policy pursued in his own department rests upon [its minister] alone. No other minister—not even the Prime Minister—has any legal power to override him', quoted by Daintith and Page (1999) 30.

[15] Campbell and Wilson (1995) 10–13 mislead, when they suggest collective Cabinet decision-making was the essence of collective responsibility; rather it was approval or disapproval of proposals or decisions put to it, sometimes, but far from always, discussed.

[16] Mackintosh (1962) 443; R James (1970) 62–64; Nicolson (1966) 230–34.

[17] J H Plumb traces back to Walpole the realisation that a Cabinet minister should resign if he disagreed with his colleagues, quoted by Hennessy (2000) 39.

[18] H Wilson (1976) 72–76. Thurlow was one of the best parliamentarians of his day, Bagehot (1997) 53.

over policy differences.[19] Among them have been Joseph Chamberlain over protection in 1903; John Burns and John Morley over entry to the First World War; under Ramsay MacDonald, Oswald Mosley over economic policy and Trevelyan over the failure of his education policy as well as, eventually, the Cabinet's surviving free traders;[20] Eden and Cranborne over Munich;[21] Bevan, Wilson and Freeman in 1949 over prescription charges;[22] Boyle over Suez; Thorneycroft, Powell and Birch over public expenditure in 1957;[23] under Wilson, Mayhew over the navy programme and Cousins over incomes policy.[24] There were to be Heseltine, Lawson and Howe under Margaret Thatcher, Clare Short and Robin Cook under Blair.[25]

However the Hoare-Laval pact was not the only case when the pure constitutional convention—that ministers had publicly to agree the Cabinet line or resign—was watered down.[26] Disraeli could not dismiss Salisbury in 1877 when they disagreed over the Eastern Question. Joseph Chamberlain did not disguise his disagreement over protection in Cabinets in which he sat, but was too strong to be ousted. Rosebery as Prime Minister, and Harcourt as leader of the Commons, disagreed over almost everything.[27] Churchill sat as a free trader under Baldwin. In 1928 Lord Birkenhead as Lord Chancellor was openly against a bill on women's suffrage he was introducing in the Lords. John Elliott and Oliver Stanley did not resign over Munich. Jim Callaghan in 1969 egged on opposition to *In Place of Strife,* Harold Wilson's and Barbara Castle's attempt to discipline the Unions. Moreover there have been several agreements to differ in public. Women's suffrage was an open question under Asquith. Initially the free traders in Ramsay MacDonald's government in 1931–2 were allowed to dissent from the protectionists as were the pro and anti common marketeers from each other in Wilson's second administration. All these examples paved the way for the Major administration—and later on in the Blair administration—when ministers hardly hid their disagreement over many issues.

Nevertheless the *Ministerial Code* still states that ministers must uphold the convention. Over the years that convention has been applied increasingly widely to include members outside the Cabinet, junior ministers and finally parliamentary private secretaries. In recent times that included about a hundred 'ministers' and therefore a sizeable proportion of government-side MPs.[28] In parallel, changes in the Cabinet system provoked, for example, Herbert Morrison's contention that, despite the development of Cabinet committees on which some

[19] Madgwick in Herman and Alt (1975) 80–87.
[20] Marquand (1977) 540–41, 592, 725–30.
[21] Nicolson (1966) 322–27.
[22] K Harris (1982) 473–80; Pimlott (1992) 157–72; Ziegler (1995) 82–88.
[23] Horne (1989) 70–78; Thorneycroft in Herman and Alt (1975) 110–17.
[24] Pimlott (1992) 388, 409–10; Ziegler (1995) 252.
[25] Howe (1994) 637–68; Lawson (1992) 958–65. Heseltine's can also be seen as a protest at the Prime Minister overriding what he saw as the proper processes of Cabinet Government.
[26] Madgwick in Herman and Alt (1975).
[27] R James (1963) chapters 10 and 11; Gardiner (undated) ii, 258–422.
[28] Woodhouse (1994) 170–71.

members of the Cabinet do not sit, all ministers are still bound by the decisions of such committees as if of the whole Cabinet.[29] Although binding on all government by convention, Cabinet decisions have no legal authority.[30] Neither are there rules on the decisions Cabinet must take. This fact was to make it possible to diminish the functions of Cabinet at the end of the 20th century without altering the law, when the convention of collective responsibility altered from an agreement not to disagree publicly after there had been Cabinet discussion, or the opportunity for one, into a binding discipline to accept the Prime Minister's decisions, even when there had been no opportunity for serious discussion.[31]

THE DEVELOPMENT OF CABINET

Cabinet solidarity is a quality intrinsic to an effective executive.[32] It does not require collective decision-making, if by that is meant one that emerges from discussion around a table, an almost fatal endeavour, but it implies reasoned approval of definite proposals put to it.[33] Even that may not be easy as Gaitskell, and later Dell found, horrified by Cabinet meetings where ministers talked rubbish after reading economic briefs they did not understand.[34] Many Cabinets became so argumentative that it was surprising more Cabinets did not break up for this reason, especially on important issues over which they disagreed strongly. They did not because they did not want to hand government to the opposition; because as individual ministers they did not want to leave office and, as Nigel Lawson was to say, once ministers are in Cabinet they became pre-occupied by their departmental business.[35]

PRIME MINISTERS AND CABINETS

While many differences in relations between Prime Ministers and Cabinet reflected differences in personality and reputation, the increase in the volume and complexity of business, the growing importance of interdepartmental issues and central handling of major policies, as well as the greater intrusiveness of the media, made Prime Ministers' chairing Cabinet and its leading committees more

[29] Morrison (1959) 25. The Home Affairs Committee in WW2 became parallel and equal to Cabinet: Mackintosh (1962) 425.

[30] Jennings (1959) 276. Because the Cabinet is a creature of convention, it cannot make law, unlike the Privy Council which can pass orders-in-council. I am indebted to Professor Martin Loughlin for this clarification.

[31] Daintith and Page (1999) 52.

[32] Mount (1992) 116.

[33] In their otherwise excellent book Campbell and Wilson (1995) 11–12, seem to think collective responsibility requires collective decision-making.

[34] Hennessy (2000) 163.

[35] Lawson (1992) 127–29.

demanding and time-consuming, difficult and often conspicuous. Churchill said of his second administration that two or three problems were discussed at Cabinet meetings, each of which would have occupied a full Cabinet meeting before the First World War.[36] Despite Churchill's rambling, if entertaining, diffuseness prolonging Cabinet meetings in the 1950s, somehow the business got done; but Wilson's tendency to allow everyone to talk too much slowed down what Cabinet could achieve, though part of his great tactical skill in handling opposition. So, to Crossman's concern, did Wilson's too frequent re-shuffling of ministers for them to grip their departments.[37] Endlessly observed in the Crossman, Castle and Benn diaries, but not unprecedented, were the chairing strategies and tactical manoeuvring needed to achieve enough consensus to reach any conclusion, rather than one Wilson particularly wanted; but again one should not confuse such greater prime ministerial activity within Cabinet with increasing power.

Although the necessity for practising the arts of chairmanship has grown with complexity, they have always been essential to Cabinet Government.[38] Charismatic Prime Ministers—Gladstone, Churchill, Macmillan, Wilson, Blair—have often been the worst chairmen; the least charismatic—Attlee and Douglas Home—the best. But all Prime Ministers found it easier to run a Cabinet whose members are in broad agreement, and feel involved and committed to its policies.[39] However, there is no necessary correlation between skilled chairmanship to keep Cabinet together and a Prime Minister using that skill to get his own way. Moreover, not all Prime Ministers had personal political objectives and, on most issues, did not have them most of the time, as Macmillan and Wilson explicitly stated.[40]

The younger Pitt, Palmerston, Lloyd George, and Churchill had at times dominated their Cabinets, especially in wartime, as Margaret Thatcher and Blair were to do, though most faced rebellion in the end. Crossman, an early proponent of the view that the Prime Minister had acquired presidential power, tried to blunt the significance of a Cabinet being able to end the career of a Prime Minister by arguing it would need to be veiled in such a cloak of conspiracy that a Prime Minister could maintain effective control of its business until the last catastrophic moment.[41] But several Prime Ministers lost the support of their Cabinets and went in varying circumstances: Palmerston, Asquith, Lloyd George, Churchill, Eden and later Thatcher. Only one can plausibly be said to have dismissed his Cabinet—MacDonald—and the price was his becoming a prisoner of the Conservative party. Macmillan was mistaken in dismissing a

---

[36] Hennessy (2000) 206.
[37] Crossman (1975) 78. Campbell and Wilson (1995) 48.
[38] Pimlott (1992) 520–21; King in King (1985) 114–18; but see Morley (1906) ii, 23.
[39] Many Prime Ministers and Cabinet ministers have said this and some have seen it as contradicting the presidential thesis: H Wilson (1976) 2–5.
[40] King in Skidelsky (1988) 54–55; also King in King (1985) 51, 115.
[41] Crossman in his introduction to the 1963 edition of Bagehot.

third of his Cabinet in July, 1962 and Thatcher's purges to secure colleagues to her taste would ultimately fail to secure their lasting loyalty.[42]

DEVELOPMENT OF THE CABINET SYSTEM

If Cabinet consensus means such close partnership that every contentious issue is hammered out by Cabinet together—what one may call the first classic model of Cabinet—one must go back to the era of genuinely small government before the 1867 Reform Act, but even then the conduct of the Crimean war over-stretched that mechanism with almost disastrous military consequences.[43] Provoking the establishment of a War Committee to rescue the war, it helped breed the Cabinet committee as a smaller, more effective instrument.[44] Committees became more frequent.[45] By the 1870s a committee of the Cabinet was formed to keep the foreign secretary to the government line on foreign policy.[46] In 1882 Gladstone's practice of often bypassing Cabinet ostensibly to avoid leaking led to a Cabinet committee on 'leakage'.[47] For a while such *ad-hoc* committees lost their importance in the systematisation of Cabinet committees which was begun in defence in 1906 and became comprehensive in the First World War, when the first Cabinet secretary, Hankey, initiated procedures still recognisable.

It took on the form under Attlee that continued in reality until after 1980, and in appearance until today. In this second classic phase as the committee system developed after 1916—but more especially at its height between the 1940s and the end of the 1970s—there was no less discussion between ministers than previously, though pressure of work made brevity more appreciated. However, on almost all issues, except the most important or contentious, it took place before Cabinet in bi-laterals between the Cabinet ministers whose departments were most concerned or face-to-face at Cabinet committees.[48] Typically, proposals by departmental ministers would be considered at Cabinet committees chaired by a senior minister and including ministers with little or no departmental interest in the subject. This process usually ensured that proposals were looked at in the perspective of overall government policy and plain common sense, and was thus a safeguard against ministers becoming captive to their officials, their prejudices or their friends. When all has been said about disputes over the Cabinet

---

[42] H Young (1989) 331–36. Thatcher thought that by replacing wets and difficult dries by professional politicians, they would be readier to toe the line: King in Skidelsky (1988) 51–64; but see Lawson (1992) 479.

[43] Walker (1970) 40; Mackintosh (1962) 138.

[44] H Wilson (1976) 62.

[45] Cabinet committees can be traced back to 1716: Hennessy (2000) 46.

[46] Lord Derby: Mackintosh (1962) 305.

[47] Matthew (1995) 115.

[48] Herman and Alt (1975) xvii, are surely right to criticise those who regarded the move from what I have called the first to the second classic phases as marking the disintegration of Cabinet Government.

table, most matters have always got through expeditiously and uncontroversially, many improved by colleagues' comments in Cabinet committee.

There is a long tradition of some issues not coming to full Cabinet for discussion and decision, particularly the budget, but also aspects of defence, foreign and nuclear policy.[49] Whatever excluded ministers may have felt, this practice did not always increase prime ministerial power. Often the reverse, particularly, but not solely, because Prime Ministers have always discussed budgets with chancellors of the exchequer, and in such bi-laterals have occasionally felt unable on their own to resist measures, which they did not like, against strongminded chancellors like Peter Thorneycroft, Nigel Lawson or Gordon Brown.[50]

As its processes changed and developed, one can see the same conflicting forces shaping the Cabinet system as made prime ministerial power fluctuate: the almost relentless growth in government business; the Prime Minister's wish to control the Cabinet better either for policy reasons or to expedite business; the desire of Cabinet ministers to be involved in and agree many aspects of that business; and the Prime Minister's continual need to placate many of them. Despite its committees becoming practically more important than Cabinet, the rationale of the system remained the need for ministers' proposals to pass the personal scrutiny of their colleagues, particularly those in other departments with an interest in the policy. They would be briefed by their officials to support a proposal, or to be effective, and, it was hoped, constructive critics of it, if they had the personality and temperament.[51] Extensive discussion in Cabinet itself was a last resort for still contentious business.

Several Prime Ministers altered the Cabinet system to increase its capacity as the pressure of work increased, principally by further expansion of the structure of Cabinet committees; but without lasting success, since the problems increased more than enough to fill the new capacity. Churchill's government was successful in fighting the war, but, especially towards the end, he left most domestic matters to others. Even so Churchill's in-tray was often congested.[52] Attlee looked back on Ramsay MacDonald's government, in which he was postmaster-general, as too overloaded with departmental business to concentrate on dealing with the slump of the 1930s.[53] To remedy that he tried making Cabinet smaller by excluding several ministers who were heads of departments, but in doing so created as many problems as he solved. Churchill tried 'over-lord' ministers to supervise more junior Cabinet ministers, but that failed. Acutely aware on becoming Prime Minister of the difficulty of working the Cabinet system in

---

[49] R A Butler in Herman and Alt (1975) 193–99; H Wilson (1976) 59; Hennessy (1995) 85–90; Mackintosh (1962) 135; Mount (1992) 121–28; Morgan (1997) 605–6. The atom bomb was never discussed in Cabinet or defence committee until after Nagasaki, only between Churchill and Anderson: Hennessy (2000) 51. Under Attlee, decisions on nuclear matters were made by a small Cabinet committee, of which Gordon Walker had been a member, not by the PM alone: Walker (1970) 89.

[50] In Herman and Alt (1975) 207; also Lawson (1992) 649, 664–65; Dell (1997) 223–41, 490–540.

[51] On the development of the Cabinet system see Walker (1970).

[52] Colville (1987) ii, 249.

[53] K Harris (1982) 85–89 and Appendix 3.

the early 1950s, Macmillan asked Attlee, then opposition leader, how to lessen *The Burden on Ministers*, as the report Attlee made was called. His main recommendation was greater use of Cabinet committees. Yet it was without much benefit, to judge by complaints about overload towards the end of Macmillan's regime.[54] Wilson brought innovations into the Cabinet system to which he gave considerable thought both before and between his administrations.[55] Heath tried a different method from Attlee's to reduce Cabinet size. He combined several departments into mega-departments, but that created its own problems (below chapter 6).

Because of the growing need to reduce business coming to Cabinet, the papers, decisions and minutes of Cabinet committees, unless challenged and so forced onto the Cabinet agenda, were held to have the same status and binding effect as Cabinet papers, decisions and minutes. By the first Wilson administration, government business had become so heavy, he required even ministers questioning a Cabinet committee's treatment of their own business to get the committee chairman's agreement before bringing it to Cabinet.[56] Only the Treasury retained an automatic right of appeal to Cabinet. Even so, as late as that administration, achieving collective responsibility still required full Cabinet to approve white papers, page by page.[57] To the ministers involved, Cabinet discussion could occasionally seem unsatisfactory.[58] Among the Cabinet papers in 1968 I had a hand in, the whole Cabinet went through a White Paper on *Road Track Costs*, full of calculations and analysis, which was held to need such Cabinet approval as a main plank of transport policy.[59] So one sees Crossman struggling with issues, like many ministers before and since, which he had neither the time nor expertise to understand.[60] In almost every aspect, the solutions which the Prime Ministers suggested were administrative reforms of the Cabinet system alleviating the problem, but not ending it.

CABINET SECRETARIAT

If the use of committees was one means of enabling Cabinet to get through more business, development of the Cabinet secretariat was a second. Hankey established it in 1916.[61] Before then, the conclusions drawn at a Cabinet meeting

---

[54] Hennessy (1995) 166–67.

[55] H Wilson (1976) 42–76.

[56] H Wilson (1976) 65–66; S James (1992).

[57] H Wilson (1976) 52–53. He said the practice ended in the mid-1970s, because Cabinet Office clearance of papers with departments had improved so as to make it unnecessary. An issue is that, even if they improved then, was the improvement maintained? How has the quality of government papers been maintained since Cabinet, or the Cabinet secretariat on its behalf, stopped clearing them?

[58] E.g. Crossman (1975) 34–36.

[59] Crossman (1976) 541. Tony Harrison, another economic special adviser, and I were allowed virtually to write that white paper, so specialised were its contents.

[60] Also the nationalised industries' white paper: Crossman (1976) 524.

[61] Mackintosh (1962) 353.

depended on how the Prime Minister summarised them in a letter to the Crown.[62] After 1916 Cabinet minutes recorded them and gave them authority. The Cabinet secretariat became one of the most efficient government mechanisms, handling the increasing masses of paper with never flagging facility even in the 1970s.

But from the start its acceptability to other ministers depended on it being neutral between ministers. That tradition continued until almost the end of the 20th century. The briefs it provided for the Prime Minister for every Cabinet and the chairman of every committee meeting brought out the issues to be discussed, especially those where there was still disagreement between departments. A chairman who followed such a brief could be sure he would miss nothing important and might be helped to find compromises. But it was not part of their job to help the Prime Minister or other minister impose their will on Cabinet. Therefore it was against the ethos of the secretariat to be constructive in the sense of brokering new solutions to unsolved problems. Theirs was a genuinely collective Cabinet resource.

Until the 1970s neither Prime Minister nor Cabinet had other resources to help them find solutions to intractable problems. Wilson's first policy unit under Tommy Balogh might have attempted it, but he had 'ferocious tantrums' and was hostile to most civil servants.[63] I quickly learnt in 1966 that the last way to sort out a problem with civil servants was to involve Tommy in it. Besides, his cast of mind was critical, not constructive. By contrast the Cabinet Policy Review Staff created by Heath was intended to contribute to collective decision-making by Cabinet and its committees. Later, one was to find the Prime Minister's policy unit under Wilson, Thatcher and Major acting as best they could as the PM's eyes and ears, but seldom intervening effectively in policy-making, while under Blair, as we shall see, they did their best to take it over from Ministers.

CABINET PAPERS

The third means of securing effective collective responsibility was through the drafting of Cabinet papers. One can hardly over-state the extent to which government activities were dominated by ministers, helped by civil servants, making policy recommendations in papers which would then be turned by often iterative steps into Cabinet papers. Among these steps would be interdepartmental discussions between officials and, if necessary, official committees,[64] to clarify issues as much as possible, before ministers met to negotiate agreement on those papers; then waiting to see if the relevant Cabinet committee agreed and, if it did not, setting the interdepartmental machinery going again to find a

[62] Walker (1970) 50. Frequently referred to in Prime Ministers' biographies.
[63] Ziegler (1995) 180–81.
[64] Official committees date from 1930s: Walker (1970) 68.

compromise; until finally getting the imprimatur of Cabinet.[65] All these steps could recur several times. In substance such Cabinet papers sought colleagues' approval at various stages of policymaking and preparation of legislation. Often as important, they would state an intention to alter a policy which did not require a change in the law. Knowing when Cabinet approval was needed became an art form; but experienced civil servants had learnt when such a policy change could safely be left to a departmental minister's discretion and when seeking colleagues' approval was wise. If a minister could not persuade his or her Cabinet colleagues of the merits of a policy, neither party nor Parliament was likely to be persuaded.

INTERDEPARTMENTAL ISSUES

Most policy initiatives and proposals reached the centre of government from Cabinet ministers and their departments. There were constitutional as well as practical reasons why, since the powers and duties conferred by statutes on government ministers were, and remain with few exceptions, exercised by departments. However, an increasing number—not only the most important—required interdepartmental consideration and co-operation. One reason for this—going back into the 1960s—was a more concentrated interest in particular groups of citizens: the poor, the long-term unemployed, those made unemployed after major closure in a particular industry, those on bad estates. Yet Cabinet committees—the traditional instrument for interdepartmental co-ordination—tended to work better with routine or relatively non-contentious policy issues. They were more re-active than pro-active, better able to handle government business submitted to them by departments. They had not the resources to put policy proposals to departments. They were better at following up action agreed by Cabinet, resolving conflicts, agreeing policy than at developing it. Until the CPRS was created, there seemed no better alternative to ministers patiently and sometimes exhaustingly talking the issues out across the table of a Cabinet committee.

THE FUNCTIONS OF CABINET

At best, the system in its second, as indeed in its first, classic form, given the reduced volume and more often exclusively departmental focus of the work Cabinet then had to do, satisfied important criteria. It provided *leadership*, especially when there were foreign and domestic crises or other unexpected events, and projected the government's public image with varying success. In working

---

[65] An account of this is to be found from the inside in Kaufman (1980) chapter 7. It is largely repeated in his 1997 edition as if it remained true, which it did not.

up what became the final and approved Cabinet paper and associated entry in the Cabinet minutes, it provided a process for *legitimating* policy proposals and decisions. It reflected the fact of individual ministerial responsibility for each of them, but ensured *collective responsibility* and therefore commitment of the whole Cabinet as well. If it reflected most shades of opinion within the party, as was common, its decisions would more likely be supported in Parliament, though such variety of opinion might make it harder for a decision to be reached. It was a way of ensuring that the Treasury's interest in a policy, and any other *interdepartmental* aspects, had been covered.[66] All departments and therefore ministerial interests could have their input into any issue so that no aspect of government responsibility need be overlooked. As they went through often numerous drafts, such papers were vital negotiating documents, altered to reflect agreements reached with Cabinet colleagues, individually and collectively over that policy, becoming proof that the Cabinet's collective responsibility for policy had been discharged. At worst, a Cabinet might become fractious, obsessed and inward looking. At its best, it provided for the rigorous and systematic discussion and development of proposals and important decisions to ensure their *thoroughness and practicality*, qualities expressed in well-drafted public papers, internal blue-prints for implementation and legislation as relevant. It brought to bear other senior ministers' perspectives on issues, often able to take more detached and objective positions than could a minister immersed in a topic. Its conclusions were a basis for government's *accountability* to Parliament. It confirmed the Prime Minister as *primus inter pares*, reinforcing his strength if he were strong, while compensating for his weaknesses, if weak, like Ramsey Macdonald or Eden. At the end of an administration, when often some of the best ministers had tired, it could accelerate its disintegration through the interplay of conflicting personalities as under Asquith, Attlee or Wilson. In no circumstances did it allow the PM, or expect to allow him, to have the domination of a president over the executive—not even Lloyd George or Churchill in war—though he might seem to be dominant through personality. It could also allow him to appear not much more than the chairman of the Cabinet, like Campbell-Bannerman, Baldwin, Douglas-Home or Attlee, if that were the impression he wanted to give or suited his temperament.

CONCLUSION

Cabinet was an ingenious, and perhaps for more than two centuries, an effective way of co-ordinating government, while restraining any absolutist tendencies a Prime Minister might develop. Extended by the use of committees into the Cabinet system, it remained effective in developing and implementing policy

---

[66] Whenever a paper involved public expenditure or tax, the Treasury had to have been consulted.

with thoroughness and effectiveness, for controlling the executive and managing its relations with Parliament until the 1970s. Moreover as long as Cabinet ministers collectively felt able to disagree with the Prime Minister when an issue seemed important enough, we retained a Cabinet system. Whatever the complexity of the committee structure, whatever the matters which did not come to full Cabinet, it still required ministers, including the Prime Minister, to run the gauntlet of scrutiny in an iterative process from some of their colleagues—usually a substantial number if the matter were important—before their notions became government policy. Except sometimes in war and over Suez—as was no longer true after 1997—it succeeded in preventing a Prime Minister, or any other minister, from taking a major decision without recourse to one or more Cabinet colleagues. That was the essence of the old Cabinet system.

But by the end of the 1960s its effectiveness was fighting a losing battle with overload. After the Heath reforms, it was hard to see what further improvements in its machinery would help Cabinet cope with a still increasing and more contentious workload without sacrificing tenable collective responsibility. The 1970s tested it to destruction.

6

Overload and Gridlock: The Old Regime's Decline

> Julius Caesar was able to write, dictate and read at the same time, simultaneously dictating to his secretaries four letters on the most important subjects, or, if he had nothing else to do, as many as seven.
>
> *Suetonius*[1]

> Joe, the trouble is that when old problems recur, I reach for the old solutions. I've nothing to offer any more.
>
> *Harold Wilson to Joe Haines* (1974)[2]

During the 1970s one heard more often that British government was overloaded.[3] But that was the symptom. Rather successive governments showed an inability to solve apparently intractable problems. More than a decade was needed to discover feasible, because by then politically acceptable, solutions.

WHAT IS OVERLOAD?

Since the 1930s, few ministers have made a virtue of seeming to have all the time in the world and also being competent and effective.[4] Neither have officials. Young civil servants with nothing to do, playing cricket in the corridors of the Admiralty belong in the distant past.[5] While one has met senior civil servants who have the knack, apparently effortlessly, of regularly arriving late and leaving early, while doing more than was expected of them and never putting a foot wrong, such paragons have been rare among them and among senior ministers.[6]

---

[1] A questionable attribution, though quoted by Grabsky (1997) 43; Plutarch (undated) 189, refers to him practising dictating letters on horseback and keeping two scribes busy 'or, as Oppius [a lost life] says, even more.' I am indebted to David Holmes for this gloss.

[2] Haines (2003) 110.

[3] A key article in creating this realisation was King (1975).

[4] Any slackening under Churchill is debatable by the test of how many papers came to the PM: Hennessy (2000) 93–94.

[5] A pre-war memory of Sir James Jones, later permanent secretary, DOE, 1972–5. One can get a sense of the amplitude of civil service life in the 1930s in Dale (1941) and still immediately postwar in Munro (1952).

[6] One was John Locke, of legendary economy in the competent use of his time, as I remember him in the 1960s. He became head of the Health and Safety Executive.

Some ministers may not have managed their working lives well. One reason why Crossman—not the best minister in the memory of his best known permanent secretary—was so overloaded that he did not have much permanent impact on departmental policy, was that he wanted too long to see every letter sent out in his name and attempted to personalise them rather than giving general instructions to his civil servants on what he wanted, trusting them to make the actual decisions (unless they presented new problems) and write the actual letters.[7] A few had extravagant private lives.

Even in the 1970s Sir Douglas Wass, Head of the Treasury under Healey and Howe, believed the ministers he knew had the time they needed to make rational, considered decisions, as some did, if they had organised their lives well.[8] Others appearing busy may have been examples of what was later dubbed Laughrin's Law: 'Ministerial diaries abhor a vacuum. So ministerial business automatically expands to fill every waking minute of a minister's day unless this is countered by a reverse irresistible force.'[9] But most senior ministers were busy, however one judges the importance of what they do. A senior minister, who did not attempt fundamental reform as was common in the past, could always find plenty to do in Cabinet, in departmental decision-making and office routine. Most needed, and indeed wanted, to spend the day in Whitehall and the evening in Westminster to get their work done. They had to find substantial time for both, no longer true by the end of the century.

One must not exaggerate the burdens of office or underestimate its joys. Most ministers coped remarkably well most of the time, given the pressures. Peter Shore spoke of the adrenalin rush from the interest and excitement of office, which enabled most to do much more than they had ever thought possible. Some ministers have always had enough energy, capability and decisiveness to take considered decisions on every matter put to them, as well as to resist too much encroachment on their time by the media, speech-making and deputations. However, the difference between a minister working at full stretch and being overloaded can be a fine one: Attlee, perhaps the most effective Prime Minister—heading an administration with more solid achievement than any other—found his workload heavy but not insupportable.[10] Despite frequent exhaustion, Pitt, Palmerston, Gladstone, Lloyd George, Neville Chamberlain (in domestic affairs) Churchill (before his second administration), Butler, Macmillan (until he was ill), Wilson, Barbara Castle, Jenkins, Heath, Carrington, Healey, and later Margaret Thatcher, Geoffrey Howe, Nigel Lawson and no doubt many others seem to have coped with attention enough to whatever was put to them. Roy Jenkins—wrongly, I believe—wrote of

---

[7] Howard (1990) 266–67; Tam Dalyell remembers being given the job of reading through many of these letters as parliamentary private secretary.

[8] Private communication from Sir Douglas Wass. Sir Nicholas Monck, who was Healey's private secretary during the IMF crisis, saw him as outstanding in his intellect, resilience and use of time even in that disaster.

[9] Laughrin (March, 1996).

[10] Hennessy (2000) 161.

Barbara Castle as having made 'exhaustion into a political virility symbol and [being] foolishly critical of those who did not believe that decisions were best taken in a state of prostration.' But the difference between them was one of style: she gloried in seeming rushed, almost overloaded. He preferred appearing relaxed.[11] In short, MPs foresaw the pressures they would be under in office, but most still sought and enjoyed it. Most dreaded becoming opposition spokesmen again, or as Healey put it, 'returning to the world of shadows.'[12]

INTRACTABLE PROBLEMS

However, even before the 1970s, administrations with a high proportion of competent ministers and no obvious passengers in important positions— Attlee's in his early years, Macmillan's, the first Wilson administration— seemed overloaded: their members knew they were not solving some problems they had set out to solve.

But frequently that was because of their nature. Since the Second World War, British governments have been criticised as facing, but failing to solve, the economic and political problems of a nation in relative decline. But, attempting to increase, even stabilise, Britain's rate of economic growth to equal those of other advanced economics by Keynesian demand management and interventionist industrial policies, while maintaining full employment, a leading role in international affairs and a strong overseas defence presence, was impossible, even if ministers had had all the time in the world to devote to nothing else. Demanding, and in the end unsuccessful, attempts to avoid devaluation, rein back pay and prices, and find industrial strategies that might persuade firms to invest more, took up endless Cabinet time even before the 1970s. Trying to provide effective public services, given their defective management, while keeping public expenditure under control; or to make the so-called basic industries more productive, was hopeless, given the practical autonomy nationalised industries had, but also caused conflict within Cabinet. The retreat from empire was demanding of ministerial and Cabinet time as ministers argued over bases and weapons, trying to strike a balance between economies in defence expenditure and retaining a place for Britain in world affairs.

THE 1970S

Even so, the 1970s were a period of exceptional turmoil in the memories of those in government.[13] Ministers were persistently overstretched. Lord Croham, when head of the civil service, suggested that in his experience many were over-

---

[11] He admitted both his relaxed style and hard work: R Jenkins (1991) 225–26.
[12] In the memory of Sir Nicholas Monck.
[13] Campbell and Wilson (1995) 72.

loaded, without appearing so publicly or knowing they were.[14] By the end of the Heath government, Lord Hunt, then Cabinet secretary, said ministers were so tired they no longer took decisions in a sensible way.[15] By the mid-1970s Cabinet overload seemed so serious that Barbara Castle said of Harold Wilson he was 'working under such intense pressure on every front that I suppose he is at his wit's end to fit everything in;'[16] while Crosland said, 'all that we can do is to press every button we have got.'[17]

When head of the Central Policy Review Staff in the early 1970s, Lord Rothschild was shaken, observing ministers taking too many decisions. They could not spend the time on them which in his judgment a reasonable person would expect to spend, like, say, the senior executives of a large firm like Shell, where he had been director of research.[18] As a distinguished scientist, he gave a questionnaire to those ministers he could persuade: to test their decision-making ability when tired at the end of the day, usually with unflattering results unpopular with them.

Indeed, a common reaction to overload is to reduce not the number of decisions taken, but the care with which the relevant arguments are absorbed, weighed or challenged. Its more ordinary symptoms in a malfunctioning government are decisions taken without enough preparation and care. Poor legislation and rushed decisions can be as much a symptom of ministerial overload as were the repeated sequences of sudden and difficult Cabinet meetings called for by the economic and other crises of the 1960s and 1970s. At worst, the ultimate shortcoming of an autocrat is the willingness to take crucial decisions, like Blair invading Iraq—or, to give an extreme example, Hitler invading Russia—without effective preparation or challenge. It is the final corruption of absolute power. Instead ministers are likely to be at their most effective when, as Lloyd George and Churchill did tirelessly in war-time, they challenge the advice they are given and each other's proposals and decisions, not when they allow others to take important decisions for them unquestioned or when, insufficiently challenged, they indulge their impulses.[19]

THE HEATH GOVERNMENT: 1970–74

The reasons for slowness in recognising the need for new policies differed between the Conservative government, which broadly showed too much unanimity, and Labour governments, which showed too little. The Heath government's greatest success was entry into Europe, a policy on which Cabinet was

[14] Lord Croham, quoted in Hennessy (1989) 486.
[15] Campbell (1994) 577; also Stuart (1998) 78.
[16] Castle (1980) 473, also 12–13.
[17] Hennessy (1995) 163.
[18] Hennessy (1989) 248–49.
[19] Grigg (2002) ch 9, 10, passim; Churchill was always demanding answers and responding to those around him challenging his abundant, but sometimes zany, ideas: Annan (1995) 46–47.

agreed.[20] But it was overwhelmed almost at once by recurrent severe economic crises—and politically contentious measures to deal with them—as well as by Northern Ireland where for a time it seemed turmoil might develop into uncontrollable chaos.

Before the 1970 election Heath was deliberately friendly to the unions, entertaining and even playing The Red Flag on the piano to Vic Feather, Jack Jones, Sid Greene and other union leaders in his flat at the Albany.[21] But his government believed it had prepared more carefully for office than any previous one.[22] Among its preparations had been a more drastic and confrontational industrial relations bill than Castle's.[23] An example before its time, of what the 1980s would call 'conviction politics', ministers did not consult the TUC over it.[24] In Jim Prior's view—first as minister of agriculture and then leader of the Commons—both its severity and the failure to consult with the unions were bad mistakes from which he thought he had learnt when preparing his own industrial relations bill under Thatcher. (She was to stigmatise it as wet and replace it with more radical legislation than Heath's.) Prior believed it would have been shrewder to have copied *In Place of Strife* almost to the letter, so disarming the angry, prolonged opposition to their bill in Parliament.[25] Moreover, it was a wasted effort because a technical defect let the unions sidestep it.[26]

Like Wilson, Heath wanted voluntary agreements with the unions. However, as voluntary policies failed and unemployment reached a million in 1972, he made his U-turn, floating the pound, but resorting to statutory prices and incomes policies which still failed to achieve wage restraint.[27] Industrial unrest increased. The Heath Cabinet—in Jim Prior's opinion—was more united in its views than any recent Conservative government before or since.[28] (One sign of amity was that unlike virtually all later Cabinets, it almost never leaked.[29]) But its unanimity was part of the problem. The neo-liberal economic policy and policy towards the unions, which Margaret Thatcher was to adopt, was not represented in the Heath Cabinet, not even by Thatcher. Enoch Powell—excluded by his racist Rivers of Blood speech—held such views outside the government, as did junior ministers like Nicholas Ridley and Sir John Eden who resigned.[30] John MacGregor, who headed Heath's private office from 1965 to 1968, was to recall years later how proto-Thatcherite the speeches and policy documents

[20] Hennessy (2000) 346; also Nott (2002) 137; private information.
[21] Hennessy (2000) 332.
[22] Prior (1986) 71; Stuart (1998) 81. Campbell (1994) 312–13, quotes Hurd as saying the programme was neither precise nor practical enough.
[23] Howe (1994) 58–65.
[24] Campbell (1994) 364–65.
[25] Prior (1986) 72.
[26] Campbell (1994) 463, but see Howe (1994) 62.
[27] Prior (1986) 74–76 also saw this move as a mistake.
[28] Prior (1986) 66.
[29] Howe (1994) 72–73.
[30] Campbell (1994) 448–49; Nott (2002) 133, who was Economic Secretary from 1972, is good on this.

were in substance and tone, which he had helped prepare then. So were those on the party manifesto at the shadow Cabinet conference at Selsdon Park, shortly before the 1970 election.

But Heath's 1930s experience made him—like most of his generation on Right and Left—implacably opposed in practice to any policy that might lead to substantial unemployment. The last time the ruling classes had stood up to the unions was over the 1926 National Strike. While an immediate victory, it had divided those classes sharply, a division the guilt-inducing unemployment of the 1930s had reinforced.[31] One did not have had to see the Jarrow marchers to be affected. As a young child I can recall the poignant, unsettling and momentarily devastating effect on a right-wing middle class household in a quiet central London street—and on me—of hearing the first Welsh miner singing loudly and well for alms at a time when the police kept all beggars, drunks and vagrants off such streets. That sense of shared guilt meant that Heath, when the crisis came, would not adopt monetarist or quasi-monetarist economic policies.[32] His apparent conversion to proto-Thatcherite economic policies was superficial and did not last. When statutory prices and incomes policy failed, he had nothing to fall back on. Strikes mounted, intensified by the inflationary effects of the 1973 oil price rise. A 'siege mentality' developed in Cabinet.[33] Public Services broke down. Britain seemed ungovernable. The coal strike made Heath call an election which he lost.

THE WILSON AND CALLAGHAN ADMINISTRATIONS: 1974–9

Wilson at once abandoned the statutory incomes policy, but had to return to a voluntary policy in 1975. He struggled to avoid making it statutory against a background of mounting inflation. After he resigned in 1976, a deteriorating pound and a shortage of reserves brought in the IMF.[34] Both statutory prices and income policies and savage, recurrent and divisive public expenditure cuts, were needed to meet its conditions. Because of union pressure to protect jobs, those cuts were concentrated on capital expenditure with ultimately serious consequences for the quality of much public sector infrastructure. Protests mounted—not only in Britain—against increasing public expenditure feeding through into higher taxation. Electorates started rebelling against local tax increases. Before the end of the 1970s, Cabinet itself could be found arguing over the detailed figures in individual prices and wages agreements.

Unlike Heath's, the Wilson and Callaghan administrations were not like-minded. Ministers had such diverse views that they disagreed, not only over

---

[31]   Not just on the left. One only had to read Harold Macmillan's *The Middle Way* (Macmillan, 1938).

[32]   Prior (1986) 73–74; Nott (2002) 146.

[33]   Prior (1986) 90.

[34]   Ziegler (1995) 443–49.

economic policy but much else. Re-negotiation of entry into Europe exacerbated differences in Cabinet which never healed.[35] In 1975 Roy Jenkins wondered why perhaps the most intelligent and experienced Cabinet in recent British history chose that autumn of roaring inflation and sterling collapse to bring forward divisive legislation for the nationalisation of shipbuilding and the aerospace industry.[36] Later, Healey recalled discussions of devolution and of forcing worker representatives onto PLC boards as occupying endless Cabinet time while the country moved relentlessly towards the Winter of Discontent.[37] Part of the problem was that the Left, disappointed by what it had not achieved in the first Wilson administration, and helped by small or non-existent parliamentary majorities, insisted on Left initiatives. No Labour minister seemed to take seriously enough the malign economic disincentive effects of low and heavily taxed profits, and high marginal income tax rates. Instead left-wingers, made restless by what they saw as the modest progress of the first Wilson administration, urged more active industrial and redistributive policies for which there was not political consensus. Furthermore, at a time of generally declining industrial profitability, they advocated more public ownership and more interventionist industrial strategies.

Despite Wilson and Callaghan's skilful chairmanship, ministers became increasingly argumentative and fractious, preparing the scene for the splits which led to the formation of the Social Democratic Party and the acute division of Labour into Left and Right after 1979 that helped keep the party out of power for 18 years. Wilson did not help by remorselessly not sending his best people where they were best fitted. Healey did not get the Foreign Office. Crosland, with disabling bitterness, did not get the Exchequer. Callaghan would not take Industrial Relations.[38] Giles Radice, a friend and disciple of Crosland, Jenkins and Healey, has described how intense rivalry between those three, who all had similar political beliefs on the right of the Party and used to be friends, promoted and prolonged Cabinet conflict. In particular Crosland as Foreign Secretary, losing the intellectual economic argument, yet going on and on using his intellectual prestige to divide the Cabinet against Healey during the IMF crisis, in retrospect seems unforgivable.[39]

Neither did it ever come right. The Heath, Wilson and Callaghan administrations did not develop the single-minded will to develop the sustained strategy needed to outwit and defeat entrenched opposition from the unions; or to overcome their own reluctance to drop too simple Keynesian policies, or risk unemployment. Cabinet did not learn from its IMF experience.[40] By 1978 the Public

---

[35] Hennessy (2000) 364–69.
[36] Jenkins (1991) 427.
[37] Healey (1989) 450–61.
[38] Radice (2002) 220.
[39] Radice (2002) 250–66. More favourable to Crosland's interventions is Jeffreys (1999) 207–16.
[40] Burk and Cairncross (1992) 225–28.

Sector Borrowing Requirement was again £9 billion.[41] A decade of conflict ended with corpses unburied and rubbish accumulating in the streets, and the slow dying fall of the Callaghan government. Evidence of how slow the Labour Party was to learn the lessons of the IMF crisis was in the left-wing and statist Labour Party manifesto for the 1983 election. Healey described it as 'the longest suicide note in history.'

DEPARTMENTAL OVERLOAD

Gridlock had other consequences. When in the 1970s, the going got rough, many ministers spent less time in their departments. Many became so busy that they had to delegate too much on trust to officials and frequently resented it. Often the delegation was more than officials wanted who had been used to closer working relationships to help them know what ministers wished. Senior civil servants made repeated journeys to private office in the hope that their bit of business, marked for action, would have returned in the red box. Covering notes to ministers could become shorter and more exclamatory in the hope brevity would catch the eye. Papers in their boxes, which in calmer times ministers would have found time to challenge in a meeting, would instead prompt a scrawled question. Especially, as tiredness built up before the holidays, papers, which might once have been read thoroughly, would be initialled as a mark of tacit, if sometimes reluctant, approval. All led to ministers complaining, not always reasonably, that they were presented with *faits accomplis*, too late for them to do anything about it. Heath's creation of mega-departments made it worse—a deliberate tactic to reduce Cabinet overload.[42] But without enough thought on how the ministers heading them could reduce their own now increased load.

It was my own experience with Tony Crosland, who was intellectually cleverer than Barbara Castle and in many respects had greater potential. But because of the brigading of three departments into one under Heath, his mega-department at Environment, which at that time included Transport, had more daily business than Transport had had in the 1960s. Three other major policy areas were ripe for pungent analysis and fundamental reform. Each could usefully have resulted in major legislation, rather than the patchwork of fudge which was all there was time for. But the department's sheer size and scope would have defeated the most energetic and determined minister. He let John Silkin, another Cabinet minister in DOE, get on with one, land taxation, which was a manifesto commitment, but in doing so in my judgement missed a perfect opportunity to deal with it as part of the reform of local government taxation

---

[41] Though a lower % of GDP than in 1976. However inflation and unemployment were both rising.

[42] Campbell (1994) 314–15; Hennessy (2000) 336–40.

through basing rateable values on actual values before and after development.[43] He dispatched a second issue, local government finance—where he had an excellent team to advise him on what needed doing to save local government while making it fiscally responsible—to the Layfield Committee whose good report languished.[44] He allowed the third important issue, housing, to be worked on within the department, also by a first-rate team of insiders and outsiders who produced more than enough evidence and analysis on which to base a housing policy.[45] But because of the pressure of Cabinet and urgent departmental business—and also his preferred methods of working—he would not spare enough time for progress meetings to steer it to avoid it getting bogged down in official conservatism. Nothing happened before he moved on to the Foreign Office, though he saw off an initiative, a portent of the future in that it emanated from the No 10 Policy Unit and was top-down, politically-driven rather than emerging from an analysis of the problem in consultation with those who knew and understood it. It recommended the sale of council houses. Welcomed by Wilson, it was negatived by Crosland as no doubt good short-term politics, but bad long-term since it would starve the cities, especially London, of housing for public sector and other low paid workers, as eventually it has.[46]

Instead he concentrated on transport, then among DOE's responsibilities, but not the hardest problem then.[47] On this he worked as he preferred, waiting for a mass of papers to be prepared for him on which he then worked intensively at home.[48] Not an easy strategy for a busy minister.[49] Moreover an increasing part of his time, as the economic crisis worsened, was spent preparing for Cabinet on macro-economic policy where he was an expert.

Thus for all these reasons, an outstanding, but severely overloaded, minister contributed no lasting reforms at DOE at a time when several were badly needed. Ironically, a solution to the problem of how to ensure effective financial accountability in local government could have allowed substantial devolution to it so as to reduce central government overload. Regional devolution as worked through in the more careful, well-defined way it was in 1978, as it was

[43] Foster, Jackman and Perlman (1980) esp. 458–82.

[44] The report was interesting, but there was no way there was time or inclination for it to be acted on by Crosland or his successor, Peter Shore.

[45] Department of the Environment (1977a), (1977b).

[46] It was because of his successor, Peter Shore's enthusiasm for it that I felt unable to continue as his adviser. It needed more time to work up as a policy to be applied in areas where there was ample housing or more generally to the most dilapidated public housing. Otherwise it would prove, as it did, a regressive measure.

[47] The problem was that the railways had done almost nothing to improve their efficiency, were in mounting deficit and there was no political will to cut back on services, as our policy in the 1960s had entailed, when they were not cost-effective in achieving measurable social ends.

[48] Another reason for the prominence he gave to the transport review was that Fred Mulley jealously kept Crosland out of most day-to-day transport business which, as a very experienced minister, he could do. A review was Crosland's only way into this policy area. I am indebted to David Holmes for this.

[49] The Foreign Office also found this working method and his unwillingness to accept more than one red box a night, very difficult: Radice (2002) 247.

not in 1997, might have had similar effect. In many departments ministers did not have the time or energy to engage in the process of extensive consultation and consensus-seeking—which was a strength of the British administrative system—to achieve the thorough fundamental reforms that many policy areas needed and might have been expected from a left-leaning administrations.[50]

CONSEQUENCES OF THE 1970S

Four seem especially worth mentioning:

(1) In 1977 Margaret Thatcher sets up the Stepping Stones project through which John Hoskyns—to be the first head of her Policy Unit—developed an economic policy for a Conservative government in collaboration with Keith Joseph, Geoffrey Howe, John Biffen and a handful of right wingers.[51] They agree macro-economic policy should move further from Keynes towards monetarism than Healey had gone.

(2) That project also decided on a tougher and more calculating approach to the unions, accepting substantial unemployment might have to be accepted as the necessary price for breaking union power.[52] Healey, starting his account of his chancellorship, ruefully quoted the Austrian-American economist, Joseph Schumpeter in 1946:

> . . . the real problem is labour . . . Unless socialization is to spell economic breakdown, a socializing government cannot possibly tolerate present trade union practice . . . As things actually are, labour is of all things the most difficult to socialize. Not that the problem is insoluble. In England, the chances for successful solution by the political method of democracy are greater than they are anywhere else. But the road to solution may be tortuous and long.[53]

By 1978 Callaghan, now Prime Minister, who had led the successful opposition to Barbara Castle's attempt at trade union legislation and had supported dismantling Heath's Industrial Relations Act, told Healey he was so disenchanted with the unions he wanted legislation to control them. Healey reminded him of his role in defeating *In Place of Strife*.[54]

The Stepping Stones project went further. Curbing 'trade union power was the starting point for everything . . . It would be necessary to change the unions' power and role by law. This in turn would require a long programme of one to two years to build public support.'[55]

---

[50] Not even in education despite Callaghan's great concern about it, Morgan (1997) 140, 141.

[51] Hoskyns (2000) 39–65.

[52] Hoskyns (2000) 124–25. They hoped union legislation might avoid it, but that was hardly a sanguine hope.

[53] Quoted in Healey (1989) 378.

[54] Healey (1989) 398.

[55] Hoskyns (2000) 42–43.

(3) The Heath, Wilson and Callaghan Cabinets' economic failures undermined the reputation of collegiate Cabinet Government.[56] Cabinet disarray in the 1970s made Margaret Thatcher, watching from the back-benches, determine to run government differently.[57] It was the forbidding experience Blair also drew on when he re-designed government.

The dilemma was well illustrated in the 9 Cabinet and 15 other ministerial meetings needed over the IMF crisis. John Morris—then fighting cuts in Welsh expenditure—remembers them as crowded into a short time, even two very long meetings in one day.[58] Under Callaghan's masterly chairmanship ministers argued themselves into accepting the harsh IMF conditions and distributing the cuts between them. They were also a defining moment for Cabinet and the Cabinet system.[59] How, can be seen in a later exchange between Edmund Dell, a Cabinet minister as Healey's No 2, who called them a 'farce and a dangerous farce at that,' and John Hunt present as Cabinet secretary.[60] Dell said:

> Nine meetings while the market was impatiently waiting for a decision. In a sensible system of government Callaghan would, after discussing with Healey and Foot [as Employment Secretary] and possibly, as a matter of *amour propre*, with Tony Crosland, have told the Cabinet, 'It is my responsibility. We have to cut public expenditure. Do not be so stupid as to resign, which I actually know you are not going to do anyhow and bring the government down and let Thatcher in. The party would never forgive you'

He was echoing Thatcher and Blair's reaction to these agonies of Cabinet Government of which the IMF saga was perhaps the worst, but not the only, example. Hunt reacted:

> I don't think collective responsibility is a myth. I think it is a reality. It is cumbersome . . . It has all sorts of disadvantages and it is possible it may need to change . . . probably under any of these systems it is going to be a bit of a shambles. But I do think it has got to be, so far as possible, a democratic and accountable shambles.[61]

The Dell view that such contentious issues required prime ministerial, rather than Cabinet, government won in the 1980s.

(4) Most ministers still seemed appreciative of the support they had from their civil servants: among them Heath, Whitelaw, Wilson, Callaghan, Jenkins and Healey.[62] However, in both parties some started to claim they needed more

---

[56] King (1975).

[57] Hoskyns (2000).

[58] Personal information from Lord Morris of Aberavon.

[59] On Callaghan as a masterly chairman, see Morgan (1997) 531–32; Healey (1989) 431; Hennessey (2000) 388.

[60] Hennessey (2000) 388–89; Morgan (1997) 551, says Dell was the only major critic in the Cabinet thinking these Cabinets a shambles, but that does not make him less far-sighted.

[61] Dell and Hunt quoted in Hennessy (2000) 388–89.

[62] Politicians generally remained satisfied with the service they got from civil servants until the 1980s, and this is borne out by interviews: Campbell and Wilson (1995) 31; also Pimlott (1992) 623;

political support in government. Douglas Hurd, when Heath's political secretary in Downing Street, saw Heath become too dependent on his officials, distancing himself from the better political advice he needed.[63] Noting that ministers immersed in paperwork were finding it hard 'to think politically about their daily problems', he called for more political advisers, an understandable reaction when the Prime Minister was a permanent secretary *manqué*, found officials more congenial than politicians and when Cabinet itself was overtired and short of talent.[64] Under Wilson and Callaghan such views were endorsed, particularly on the left. Barbara Castle remarked:

> I thanked God for the allies I have got in the ministerial team and for the special advisers. Without them a minister is almost certainly swamped by the sheer pressure of the top officials surrounding him—or her.[65]

and on officials:

> how I welcomed their frankness when they disagreed with me and only asked that their views should be balanced by the attendance round my discussion of dedicated socialists who were in deep agreement with my policy.[66]

Left-wingers like Benn, aiming at a centralised economic planning system and more left-wing policies, and neo-liberals like Keith Joseph, wanting to overcome union and other corporatist opposition to releasing market forces, drew a similar constitutional message from government failure.[67] To overcome opposition to their policies, politicians must resume power from civil servants. In the 1980s this line of thinking was to lead to conviction politics rather than more political advisers, at the end of the 1990s to both. It was an incomplete, even the wrong, message to have drawn from the experience of the 1970s. So was the opinion Thatcher, and later Blair, formed that successful politics now required prime-ministerial, or quasi-presidential, government, replacing Cabinet Government.

CONCLUSION

The 1970s tested the old ways of governing Britain. Despite its quality, the British political system could not cope with a Tory government without the courage to abandon the Keynesian consensus or Labour ones unable to agree on

---

Whitelaw (1989) 328–29. Though Healey could be critical, e.g. (1989) 402, 427 ff, he often indicates his appreciation of his officials; on Heath's exceptional reliance on officials see Campbell (1994) 490–92; on Callaghan see Morgan (1997) 510, 526, though it took him time to become comfortable at the Home Office: 293–96 and Foreign Office, 409–11.

[63] Campbell (1994) 326, 492. Heath's problem was a tendency to get drawn into labyrinthine detail, rather than concentrate strategically on the top political issues.

[64] Hurd (1998) 76–77.

[65] Castle (1980) 209; but see 331, 733.

[66] Castle (1980) 225.

[67] House of Commons Expenditure Committee (1997). For left-wing views see Morgan (1984) 88, 516; Sedgemore (1980).

fundamental issues. Rather than overload, it was the difficult and divisive nature of many of the problems overload masked, even more the prolonged unwillingness of successive governments to drop failed economic policies and adopt ones that might work. Apparently endless wrangling in Cabinet over the best way forward was all too publicly visible. Gridlock, and because of it overload, persisted because unsolved problems endlessly recurred on the Cabinet agenda. In too many government departments serious problems, which needed systematic investigation leading to carefully worked-out and implementable reforms, were not adequately addressed. Trust in the political system, once high among the public, declined significantly.[68]

Several more far-sighted reforms might have increased the effectiveness and efficiency of government and eased the load on ministers:

• Well thought out devolution which actually reduced the load at the centre;
• Finding a solution to the NOSSO problem (above chapter 4) which could have made relations with the nationalised industries and other public bodies less time-consuming and wearing;
• Developing civil service management skills and techniques, perhaps even dividing it in two: a smaller part around ministers performing their traditional policy advisory and constitutional functions and a larger concentrated on efficient management of the public sector;
• Setting up well-funded, politically impartial institutes—British Brookings— available to government and sizeable opposition parties—to prepare the longer-term reforms for which ministers no longer had the time.[69]

But there was not the time to effect such innovations either. Similar problems attacked other nations, many like Canada, Australia and New Zealand with democratic, Westminster-style constitutions.[70] There, too, these difficulties prompted argument about the adequacy of traditional forms of government and how they could be altered to fit the modern world: at first on the virtually unquestioned presumption that we should keep the processes of Cabinet Government and parliamentary democracy. So a concatenation of adverse circumstances tested to incipient destruction a system of government which had evolved to meet changing circumstances for almost two hundred years, a process completed by Margaret Thatcher's imperious will to humble the unions and to regain power from officials.

[68] Kavanagh in Almond and Verba (eds) (1980).
[69] The embryo of one such, founded with Ford foundation money, was the Centre for Environmental Studies, of which I was director from 1976 to 1978. With the 1979 election approaching I asked Michael Heseltine—the shadow secretary of state for the environment—if he would continue us. He said he would if we would design a housing policy which a Conservative government might adopt. But the partisanship of the time was such that none of CES' able housing experts would consider it. So CES was closed down when the Conservatives came to power.
[70] Campbell and Wilson (1995) 72–97.

PART 2

FIRST STAGES OF REVOLUTION

7

Margaret Thatcher

We must have been the most divided Conservative Cabinet ever.

Jim Prior (1986)[1]

... What about the deliberate use of fear as a political weapon, albeit within her own party and administration? Fear is not a morally attractive weapon; even Machiavelli acknowledges that. But is it sometimes a necessary weapon? Given the sheer scale of everything that Mrs. Thatcher has wanted to achieve, could she have achieved it with only love and rational arguments as her weapons? Could the inevitable and massive resistance have been overcome without the use of fear? I wonder; I am inclined to doubt it. But it is at least a good question.

Anthony King (1988)[2]

UNDER MARGARET THATCHER the institutions of Cabinet and the Cabinet system survived but their operation was altered, driven by the experiences of 1970s and by her personality. Government came to depend so much on her force of character and indefatigability, that its weaknesses were apparent before she fell, exemplified in the poll-tax fiasco in which I was personally involved.

HERESTHETIC

In democracies, where political opinions usually lie from right to left along one dimension, party leaders try to place themselves in the middle to gain or retain a majority.[3] Strong movements to left or right from within their party may stop them doing so, as with Labour in the 1980s and the Conservatives after 1997. Or politics may become multi-dimensional making an election-winning strategy less predictable, as after 1974. But, unless parties occupy the middle ground, they cannot win power. That is the median-voter hypothesis.[4] Once there what

---

[1] Prior (1986) 134.

[2] King in Skidelsky (1988) 64.

[3] 1906 and 1945 may seem exceptions to this generalisation, However the Liberals came in with a large majority partly because the Conservatives were so divided over tariff reform, while in 1945 the middle ground had temporarily shifted to the left because of the war and the suppression of normal economic concerns.

[4] Downs (1957).

loses them power is normally perceived incompetence, in modern times usually economic.[5]

Occasionally a political leader has a purpose for which he does not have majority support—in Cabinet, Parliament, the electorate or some combination of the three. In his brilliant work on the topic, Iain McLean calls this phenomenon heresthetic or the art of political manipulation.[6] He instances three outstandingly successful examples before Thatcher's, all with lessons for understanding the Thatcher era and since.[7]

The first was Sir Robert Peel repealing the Corn Laws in 1846 against the convictions and economic interests of the majority in his Cabinet, the parliamentary Conservative party he led and the electorate, still small, all dominated by landowners. Repealing the Corn Laws would increase imports, bringing down wheat prices to the poor's benefit, but reducing agricultural rents, the landowners' main source of income. Peel hid that he was a Ricardian, economic liberal. The Corn Laws must go both because he believed—whatever landowners thought—that free trade was necessary for economic prosperity and because the suffering and famine they provoked among the poor were intolerable, especially in Ireland.[8] He gradually gained a Commons majority through persuading the opposition parties and about one third only of the Conservatives to vote for repeal. However, the majority of his own Conservatives still voted against him, a prospect no other Prime Minister had even to consider until Blair in the second Gulf war.[9] He persuaded the Leader of the Lords, Wellington—as a landowner, like most peers, strongly opposing repeal—that the Queen's peace and the country's governability, especially in Ireland, were at stake unless these Laws went. Convinced by this argument, Wellington used his great influence to persuade enough peers to vote for repeal. But Peel's success smashed the Conservative party until Derby and Disraeli put it together again.

The second example was when Disraeli and Derby, leading a resurrected Conservative party, passed a Reform Act in 1867 more extreme than Gladstone had proposed for the Liberals and carried it against the initial instincts of the majority in Cabinet and Parliament.[10] To do it Disraeli confused everyone— even it is suggested himself—by his brinkmanship, dazzling rhetoric and the

---

[5] Hibbs (1987).

[6] McLean (2001)10, *passim*.

[7] The other outstandingly successful heresthetic before Thatcher has least to offer towards an understanding of British politics after 1979. When there was a majority against every solution to the Irish problem Lloyd George used sheer cleverness and guile to find one in 1922, which lasted until 1968. In small things it was fairly common, because un- or only briefly noticed, for ministers to do what they thought right, even if not supported by majority opinion. The major issues provided the test.

[8] Wellington sussed him out from the start: Longford (1972) 357–68.

[9] McLean's statistical analyses show fairly conclusively that the 55, like Peel, for the most part voted against their electoral and economic interest: McLean (2001) 45–56.

[10] McLean (2001) 57–86 to which again I am greatly indebted; but also Blake (1966) 450–77 and Roberts (2000) 86–98.

complexities of various systems of electoral reform.[11] His motive seems to have been his belief—found in his romantic novel, *Sybil,* but against the evidence and presumptions of class politics—that the Tories could win elections with an expanded franchise. Salisbury, his successor as Conservative leader, turned that dream into a remarkable third heresthetic reality by taking steps to create the Tory workingman, inspired by loyalty to the Crown and imperialism to vote against his class interest and return conservative governments, more often than not, until the end of the 20th century.[12]

Like Peel, Thatcher in her first administration was in a minority in Cabinet and probably in the party. Her opposition to majority opinion in her Cabinet was also grounded on economic doctrine, but Friedman rather than Ricardo, though John Nott, an economic liberal, thought her own instincts protection-ist.[13] Like Peel, she broadened her support through another important and emo-tional issue: in his case famine and disorder because of the Corn Laws, in hers ungovernability and disorder because of the unions. Like Disraeli, she used rhetoric to get her way, but with a wider audience, first party conference and then the public with whom she was remarkably successful.

But there was another different heresthetic feat important for the future of the Conservative party, which, unlike Disraeli and Salisbury, she did not realise, despite her instinct for what would be popular. By the 1970s the number of nat-ural Tory voters, which they had established, was in rapid decline. She thought she had re-established her party as that of business entrepreneurship, lower taxes and smaller government, the equivalent of the US Republicans. But she had not. The middle classes went on deserting it. Like Lloyd George, she missed her chance to rebuild her party for the future: in his case to merge Labour with the Liberal party as the dominant party of the left, in hers to build the images of Essex man and the hard-nosed blue-collar worker—hard-headed, anti-union, anti-government, low tax and Thatcherite—into a party able to command a continuing majority.[14] Neither she nor her immediate successors had Salisbury's constructive gift.

MARGARET THATCHER AS PRIME MINISTER

While her approach achieved the practical effect of a strong and for many years successful government, it was tailored to the style and capacities of one person. No previous Prime Minister had been as persistently disdainful of her colleagues or as often openly contemptuous of their opinions: neither the most authoritarian,

---

[11] Bagehot (1997) 164–65 in the introduction to his 1872 edition, contrasts Disraeli's obfuscation of the issues when presenting parliamentary reform with the normal clarity with which issues were discussed in Parliament.

[12] McLean (2001) 87–112; Roberts (2000).

[13] Nott (2002) 183.

[14] Grigg (2002) 108, 200–2.

Wellington, who started by expecting to give his ministers orders, but learnt that lesson; nor Gladstone, who, as he grew very old, lacked patience in dealing with his ministers; nor Lloyd George using his prestige from winning a war to impose his will on his coalition partners, but with abundant charm and patience in day-to-day dealings with ministers. Even one of the cleverest ministers close to her, Nicholas Ridley, admitted what he called her 'bossiness'.[15] Though one or two would recall as fun her imperiousness, and even the lashes of her tongue at them, they were the exception. Geoffrey Howe described it as, 'the undivided sovereignty of her own opinion, dressed up as the nation's sovereignty'.[16] David Howell said that,

> If by conviction government, it is meant that certain slogans were going to be elevated and written in tablets of stone and used as the put-down at the end of every argument, then, of course, that is, indeed what happened . . .. Of course there is a deterring effect if one knows that one's going to go not into a discussion where various points of view will be weighed, but into a huge argument where tremendous battle-lines will be drawn up and everyone who doesn't fall into line will be hit on the head.[17]

Heseltine once returned from Cabinet saying he had lost the battle over an issue, 17 to 1, 17 for him, her against.[18] Few could persuade her to change her mind. One had to choose the right moment.[19] Like others among her close civil service aides, Charles Powell sometimes could. 'But she would not admit it. She always had to be right and you just went along with it.'[20] She was among the worst chairmen because she started with her own opinion on a topic and then often did all she could to stop contrary opinions being expressed, sometimes being appallingly rude to her colleagues, even mocking them or raising her eyebrows heavenwards as they spoke.[21] Why did she do it? One of her official secretaries, after a particularly vigorous put-down of a Cabinet minister, remembers suggesting she telephoned him to apologise. She did not resent the suggestion, but seemed surprised he thought it necessary, so blindingly obvious the truth seemed to her. He doubts if she bothered to make the call.[22] Though many colleagues asserted they liked her personally, her approach would have been less divisive if had she been less ready to put down or even humiliate colleagues in Cabinet or before their officials, or worse, to get Bernard Ingham to leak derisory comments about them to the media.[23] One private secretary remembers Whitelaw and Carrington repeatedly dropping in on each other to consider how they could defuse rows.[24] While many past ministers had leaked

---

[15] Ridley (1991) 35; also 26, 266.
[16] Hennessy (2000) 434.
[17] Hennessy (2000) 401.
[18] Private information.
[19] Private information from several sources.
[20] Kavanagh and Seldon (1999) 182.
[21] Nott (2002) 201–2.
[22] Private information.
[23] Nott (2002) 184–85, 240–41, 314; private information.
[24] Sir John Chilcot.

their disagreement with the Prime Minister to the press—notoriously Callaghan and others over *In Place of Strife*—Prime Ministers had seldom leaked against colleagues, as her colleagues persistently believed she did.[25]

How did such an abrasive person become Prime Minister? Under the old Tory methods of leader selection, which depended mainly on how Conservative leaders judged each other, she probably would not. But when the party was moving to replace Heath, and Whitelaw was too loyal to stand in the first round, she suddenly gained a formidable reputation as shadow chancellor for mauling Healey during the 1974 Finance Bill, especially over the Capital Transfer Tax.[26] The opportunity played to her rhetorical gifts and her determination, willingness and ability, developed as a tax lawyer, to soak up massive briefing fast, a capability she retained almost to the end.[27] She was often pleasant socially, and as leader of the opposition she had not the power base to be authoritarian; but Heseltine believed that already part of her character, recalling his dismaying experience as her junior transport spokesman from 1968 when he heard her lecturing representatives of the transport sector rather than listening to what they had to say.[28]

She was a new phenomenon in British politics, more like Reagan and other recent American presidents, in that—alongside her determination—her greatest quality was rhetoric, an actor but with more than an actor's ability to establish an inner ideological coherence and tone in everything she said and did. As a consequence her ability to handle the media, especially the right-wing press was exceptional.[29] Her relentless scrutiny of papers put to her fastened on sentences, phrases, even words she would worry at until sure they amounted to a statement or speech fitting her conception of her Thatcherite persona.[30]

Important for her impact on government was that hers was the antithesis of the reasoning and reasoned approach previously central to British government. Not for her the process of identifying the problem, amassing the evidence, weighing the options. Her legendary work capacity was not devoted to such uses of reason as debate among colleagues and in Parliament. Before the 1979 election she told Sir Anthony Parsons, then ambassador in Teheran, 'Do you know there are still people in my party who believe in consensus politics . . . I regard them as Quislings, as traitors.'[31] Instead she went for *conviction politics* with a tenacity that stood her and her close associates in good stead in her battles with the unions and over the Falklands, but a habit caught by others in her Cabinet, making many of them readier to stir up and confront opposition than

[25] H Young (1989) 193, 196. Ingham (2003) ch 14, denied doing so except in two cases.
[26] Heseltine (2000) 160–61; Lawson (1992) 13; Prior (1986) 99–100.
[27] Howe argues that by the time of the Madrid summit her readiness to be briefed intensively had declined: Howe (1994) 578–79.
[28] Heseltine (2000) 117.
[29] Prior (1986) 134–35.
[30] Hoskyns (2000) has several accounts of what hard work it was when she challenged almost every word they wrote for her.
[31] H Young (1989) 223.

was sometimes necessary or wise. The increasingly bad relations with local government, which were to exacerbate tensions over the poll-tax, were one disastrous example. Bad for Cabinet solidarity was that Cabinet ministers began to hold, and not always resolve, differing convictions, as over Europe.

That her own thought processes were hostile to deliberation is a not insignificant explanation of what happened to government. To a large extent she re-designed the Cabinet system to suit her cast of mind—which could be flexible—rather than just to outmanoeuvre the Cabinet majority against her economic and union policy. She could perform U-turns, as over the Channel Tunnel, Maastricht and, retrospectively, sanctions against Iran. She could distance herself, if need be, from policies that did not work without seeming to do so. But mostly she wanted to get her way. Nigel Lawson defended himself and other ministers against the charge that they should have made a firmer stand against her over important issues:

> Most Cabinet ministers, particularly after a longish period in government, tend to be pre-occupied with fighting their own battles . . . and lose interest in the wider picture . . . It was noticeable that towards the end those colleagues, who most bemoaned the lack of collective discussion of issues outside their departmental field, were busy making private bi-lateral deals with Margaret over issues within their own departmental responsibility.[32]

But it was more than the normal diffidence of not wanting to seem a busybody. She did not want ministers commenting on each other's business, though that had been the essence of Cabinet Government.[33] To speak out of turn was to risk acute, crushing personal attack. And banishment from Cabinet, almost invariably after a brief lapse of time.

HER HISTORIC MISSION

When she became Prime Minister, she used the dedication and personal devotion of her No 10 staff—for she was kind and considerate to them and their families—to build a commanding position, so that she could perform what with hindsight seems her historic mission. She used her outstanding rhetorical skills and force of personality to put over her monetarist economic policy, to defend the severe unemployment that followed and, crucially, to break the power of the unions which had defeated governments in the 1970s.[34] After the 1979 election

---

[32] Lawson (1992) 129; also 122, 583.

[33] Campbell and Wilson (1995) 198.

[34] Preparations for this strategy for Thatcher had been made in opposition by John Hoskyns, who became the first head of her No 10 Policy Unit, under the aegis of Keith Joseph and with the increasingly warm co-operation of Geoffrey Howe who was to describe its output, the *Stepping Stones* report, as 'apocalyptic . . . more subtle and likely to be more effective than anything we had produced thus far.' Hoskyns (2000) 39–65; Howe (1994) 104–8. Hoskyns had been a soldier turned successful businessman, building his own IT firm, before joining Thatcher in opposition.

Howe pressed ahead with planning the new economic policy with, as he describes it, the warm support of his Treasury officials, though achieving the control of the money supply required was not easy.[35] Principally because of Jim Prior's determined opposition, planning the destruction of trade union power was harder. Norman Tebbitt had to replace Prior for a drastic enough Industrial Relations Act to reach the statute-book. Meanwhile severe control of the money supply defeated attempts by private sector trade unions to achieve inflationary wage increases. But there were false starts before coal stocks at the power stations could be built up, the NUM trounced and the public sector unions defeated. John Hoskyns' achievement as the first head of her Policy Unit was to have done the planning necessary to defeat the miners and to have persuaded Margaret Thatcher—against her instincts because she was not a strategist or games-player—to delay battle until they were sure she could win.[36] Luck played its part. She would not have succeeded, but for a split Labour opposition and the great political and military success of the Falklands War. Otherwise the Wets in Cabinet would probably have watered her policies down. Nevertheless the greatest credit for these economic achievements, which had eluded governments throughout the 1970s, is hers.

MARGARET THATCHER AND CABINET

After 1979 ministers entered Cabinet expecting it to be as collegiate as Heath's had been. She preserved the formalities of Cabinet Government to the end. All collective decisions were legitimated in Cabinet or Cabinet committee minutes. She started by using her Cabinet conventionally for most purposes.[37] But to get her own way she took trouble to select the order in which ministers spoke and to prime those she hoped would say what she wanted to hear on matters she cared about.[38] Even so, she could not have carried her neo-liberal economic policies and her campaign against the unions after extensive discussion in Cabinet committee and full Cabinet, any more than Gladstone could carry Irish Home Rule or Wilson, the reform of trade union legislation.[39] Therefore, Thatcher by-passed Cabinet over economic policy from the start, holding

---

[35] Howe (1994) 125–32.

[36] Hoskyns (2000) *passim* from 97ff. He has copious illustrations of how difficult it was to get past her instinctive belief she knew the right thing to do and persuade her to do something different. Also how hard Ronnie Millar and others had to battle against her equally instinctive choice of the wrong arguments and less vivid words even in the speeches which were to make her famous. Also Howe (1994) 147.

[37] Prior (1986)133.

[38] Private information.

[39] An account of how it happened is in Foster and Plowden (1996) esp. the Introduction. A longer account is King in King (ed) (1985) which however does not discuss the machinery of government questions central here.

breakfast meetings before Cabinet with those who thought like her: among them Geoffrey Howe, Keith Joseph, John Nott and John Biffen.[40]

The paramount importance of those issues may reasonably justify the means she took. While disliking parliamentary debate, she was assiduous in touring the corridors and tearooms to discover what backbenchers thought.[41] If she could carry them and the party, she was less concerned about Cabinet.[42] Gilmour reported no Cabinet discussion of economic policy in the vital first year.[43] Prior did not know VAT was to go up by 15% until it was announced.[44] The first Peter Walker, as minister of agriculture, heard of the abolition of exchange controls was on radio. Howe later protested he simply had not realised how deep the Wets' misgivings had been over economic policy since she did not give them the chance to express them to their colleagues.[45] Not able to make himself heard, one Wet, Ian Gilmour, made critical public speeches, while still a Cabinet minister.[46] By mobilising support in Cabinet and Cabinet committee, Prior achieved more emollient union legislation than she wanted, but such manoeuvres became harder later.[47] When she had a Cabinet majority against her resisting public expenditure cuts in 1981, she did not give in, but showed her strength by starting to reshuffle the Cabinet.[48]

After the Falklands war she insisted more on *conviction politics*. On great and small issues the habit of evading Cabinet discussion was catching. She found she often succeeded without attempting Cabinet consensus: indeed without persuading the pressure groups affected by a policy; or capturing public opinion; or appeasing sections of her party. Since opposition was frequently based on doubts about her policies' feasibility rather than their desirability, she was often proved politically right afterwards by belated public support as well as within her own party.[49] But not always. She banned the unions at GCHQ without bringing it to Cabinet. Cabinet did not hear of her agreement with Reagan to ban using British-based bombers to bomb Libya until the night of bombing.[50] She was not interested in Cabinet's views, which would have been hostile.[51] Margaret Thatcher's by-passing or steam-rolling of Cabinet colleagues opposed

[40] Howe (1994) 147–49; Ian Gow, David Wolfson and Denis Thatcher were frequent attenders. Prior (1986) 133.

[41] Helped in this most by her first PPS, Ian Gow.

[42] Dunleavy and Jones in Rhodes and Dunleavy (1995) 295–96.

[43] Gilmour (1992).

[44] H Young (1989) 149–50.

[45] Howe (1994) 148–49.

[46] Howe (1994) 168.

[47] H Young (1989) 193–98.

[48] Lawson (1992) 107–8.

[49] However, as judged by monthly Gallup polls, she was the second least popular Tory leader since the war: 'Her peaks of popularity did not approach Callaghan's in the 1970s, Wilson's in the 1960s, Eden's and Macmillan's in the 1950s or Attlee's after the war. Her troughs, however, sank lower than those of any other Prime Minister' Crewe in Seldon (ed) (1996) pp 401–3.

[50] H Young (1989) 475–79.

[51] Mount (1992) 122–23.

to her suited a situation where she and those close to her had a clear, well-defined agenda and when she paid relentless attention to detail to ensure she got what she wanted. Given her approach, it is hardly surprising that full Cabinet discussion of policy became rare.

By the mid-1980s Cabinet itself had become little other than a formal or ritual occasion.[52] Nigel Lawson regarded Cabinet meetings as the most restful and relaxing event of the week.[53] She started with many in Cabinet she did not agree with. When she could, she replaced Wets with Drys. Increasingly important though was her belief those replacements would not challenge her, but she was not a good picker of people in her own interest, sometimes preferring impressiveness to solid worth.[54] Though there were throughout many able people in her Cabinets, by the end those who thought like her and had worked most closely with her to achieve her objectives had gone, some forced out by her. Instead she ended surrounded by colleagues who in her terms, whether she knew it or not, were mostly Wets.

HER USE OF THE CABINET SYSTEM

Though the committee structure covering all aspects of government survived, she had fewer, and used them less, than Callaghan had. Instead there was the *ad hoc* committee. But choosing such a committee of those best qualified to progress a matter, as had happened in the past, was not the same as picking one to get the outcome she wanted, as she did, even against the wishes of the Cabinet majority, not for all measures, but for those she particularly cared about.[55] This practice biased scrutiny since it ensured it was done by those favourable to a measure. Most official committees had disappeared which had once gone over difficult material before it reached ministers. The time-pressure on ministers had become so great, and the need to be away from London—for example on European business—so insistent, that regular meetings were hard to schedule.[56] So, as time passed what Lawson called 'creeping bi-lateralism', that is, meetings between herself and the departmental minister, became her preferred and usual vehicle for scrutiny. The guarantee of the reasonable thoroughness and practicality of new measures was no longer through the constructive criticism of other Cabinet colleagues, but through her own inexhaustible appetite for papers and minute attention to detail. Collective responsibility was replaced by her relentless interrogation of her ministers about the effects of their policy proposals. Less effectively checked and balanced by her Cabinet colleagues, whether a measure got through came to depend more on her personality and judgement.

[52] Private information.
[53] Lawson (1992) 125.
[54] Ridley (1991) 35.
[55] Lawson (1992) 127; Baker (1993) 255–56; King in King (1985).
[56] Butler (1999).

Her use of bi-laterals sometimes made the handling of interdepartmental issues more difficult, except insofar as ministers took the initiative to settle issues among themselves.

COLLECTIVE RESPONSIBILITY

That prime constitutional safeguard, Cabinet collective responsibility for government policy and executive action, was undermined. Ridley, among her strongest supporters, tried to re-define the convention as one of her singular responsibility. He argued:

> Ministers in Britain, like their counterparts in America, are 'hired and fired' by the person in whom the power of the Executive is vested. They do not have positions in their own right . . . they are there to help the Prime Minister and at the Prime Minister's pleasure.[57]

A novel interpretation, but it did not work. Though indefatigable—sleeping four or five hours a night—she found all power could not be concentrated in the Prime Minister. To take a routine example, she was at her best as in bus policy, where she had a minister ideologically and personally congenial, and a policy proposal not her own. Nicholas Ridley's own conviction politics made him wish to privatise and deregulate busses, but she required extensive research and analysis—with substantial academic and practitioner input—to convince her and Whitehall of its practicality.[58] Most consequences were correctly predicted (but not all, not the rapid resurgence of the wish to create local monopolies and the inability of the competition authorities to move quickly enough to prevent them). There were other examples of the benefits of her attention to detail. But even in the best circumstances, her scrutiny was no substitute for detailed collective discussion between departments and with all interested external parties before publication to discover what was capable of effective implementation.

When the chemistry between her and the minister was bad, the process could be tempestuous and less effective. No wonder some ministers kept the working up of a pet proposal to themselves as long as possible—unchallenged and unscrutinised—and then slipped it through, not easy, by choosing a time when she might be too busy to notice. But there were havens where even junior ministers could do something they believed worthwhile: John MacGregor as a minister in DTI remembered the freedom and encouragement Keith Joseph and she gave him to work up measures to free small businesses from red tape, while she scarcely concerned herself with what the Home Office was doing under Whitelaw.

---

[57] Ridley (1991) 26–30.
[58] Private information.

DECLINE IN CABINET SOLIDARITY

Cabinet solidarity—another plank of the constitution—withered. Evading discussion in Cabinet, Cabinet committee or bi-laterals, some colleagues pursued policies of which she did not approve.[59] Lawson refused to adopt progressive fiscal measures to offset the regressive effects of the poll tax and make it more palatable. In 1987 Lawson decided to shadow the mark off his own bat. Furious when she found out, there was nothing she could do about it.[60] He had all the levers. Towards the end she did not always get her way in Cabinet, as over the Hillsborough agreement.[61] Or over the future of Hong Kong.[62] Earlier it was rumoured that Carrington and Gilmour had to threaten resignation to stop her pressing further the terms she had renegotiated on Britain's contribution to the EC budget.[63] Howe and Lawson had to threaten resignation to get agreement over the Madrid summit.[64] All these divisions were to be grist to Blair's mill when he prepared for government.

She became increasingly isolated.[65] In 1988 Willie Whitelaw—her lightning conductor with the rest of the Cabinet—retired. Publicity misfortunes made her closest supporters, Parkinson and Ridley, resign. She clashed with Tebbitt. She provoked the resignations of Heseltine, Biffen, Lawson and Howe, and so brought about her own downfall, proving, as some said, that Cabinet Government still worked. But not until that astonishing end. A Cabinet which works only to engineer a Prime Minister's downfall is hardly a promising example of collective responsibility and Cabinet solidarity.

The point is not to diminish Margaret Thatcher's greatness or many of her colleagues' ability. She was not just a remarkable, but a great, Prime Minister and one can argue how necessary were her greatest achievements and also her ruthlessness and single-mindedness in attaining them. Neither did her greatness end with the Falklands War. Her leadership and determination forced through and extended the privatisation programme. Her astonishing *rapport* with Reagan and Gorbachev let her play an important role in helping ease Russia's end as a superpower. But to Blair and his associates reflecting on her experience, more seemed necessary to ensure lasting prime ministerial power.

---

[59] See King (1985) 116–89.
[60] Thatcher (1993) 703 wondered whether she should have sacked Lawson; also Kavanagh and Seldon (1999) 199.
[61] Austin Rover to General Motors: Kavanagh and Seldon (1999) 201–3; Thatcher (1993) 437–38.
[62] H Young (1989) 431.
[63] Nott (2002) 186.
[64] Howe (1994) 578–79; Lawson (1992) 927–36; Ridley (1991) 209–10.
[65] H Young (1989) 452–7.

CONCLUSION

Palmerston, Lloyd George and Churchill had long periods of almost personal rule in wartime. In peacetime, Lloyd George, buoyed up by his war-winning prestige, but leader of a coalition dominated by Conservatives and of a divided Liberal party, was in no position to do so for long. The 1980s saw the longest period so far in which a Prime Minister tried to dominate her colleagues when Margaret Thatcher increasingly by-passed the procedures of the old Cabinet system to get her way which she often, but not always, succeeded in doing. It was the first peacetime attempt at presidency and it failed.

Having accomplished her historic achievement of solving the problems that successive administrations had failed to solve in the 1970s, she or another—a Salisbury to her Disraeli—almost certainly had it within their power to forge first a Cabinet and then a party machine able to redesign a Conservative Party to win a majority in the 21st century, based on self-interest, low taxes, a smaller government and strong business support. But her temperament, her arrogance towards her colleagues and her insistence she was right in small matters as well as great, did not let her do so, in the end overwhelming her great gifts. The inference was not widely drawn that the British constitution is not at its best under an executive leader opinionated on every topic, but under those who, while necessarily engaged in foreign and economic policy, do not neglect their roles as chairmen and mediators between colleagues, showing their leadership qualities principally in reacting to unexpected events. To find national leaders as ready to alienate their friends and antagonise their possible supporters, while unwilling to compromise even over insignificant issues, one has to reach back before Prime Ministers to James II and even Charles I.

But no single example better illustrates the dangers of her kind of government than the poll-tax.

8

The Poll-Tax[1]

The great man stopped in his tracks and glared. His shoulders heaved, went into *rigor*; his face became empurpled and sweat poured down his forehead, cheeks and end of his nose. He wrestled with some deep impediment of speech; finally burst, spluttering out the single word—'TROUBLE.' Then he turned on his heel.

Alan Clark on Whitelaw on the poll-tax[2]

T
HE POLL-TAX FIASCO merits discussion both as an extreme example of Margaret Thatcher's methods and of (mistaken) political judgement overriding institutional scepticism. Her longstanding hostility to the rates—at least since 1974—and persistent championship of the poll-tax from 1985 to the bitter end were to help bring her down. Almost alone among her Cabinet colleagues, Nigel Lawson opposed her.[3] He wanted rates kept, but reformed.[4] He disbelieved the political good sense of the poll tax. What remains extraordinary is how ineffective his opposition was, despite being Chancellor, even on this major issue of taxation policy. Moreover his refusal to co-operate in raising grant to local authorities and to take other measures to offset its political consequences would contribute to its failure. Like many others he seldom stood up to her in person.[5] However, in his memoirs he had been as trenchant as any about her 'delusion of self–sufficiency', her 'distrust of any colleague who was not a yes-man', her authoritarian conduct of meetings and her abuse of them 'as a means of getting her own way irrespective of the merits or political costs'.[6] Perhaps that is why neither he nor officials could overcome her intransigence.

Yet he claimed that over the poll-tax, she observed the proprieties of Cabinet Government because in 1985 she chaired innumerable meetings of the E(LF) Cabinet sub-committee; since many departments had local responsibilities, two

---

[1] I have been helped in this account by several concerned, among them Christopher Brearley, Sir Terence Heiser, Anthony Mayer (head of the Local Government Finance Studies team from October 1984 to March 1985), several still serving civil servants, and William Waldegrave. As always, how I have used their comments is my own responsibility.

[2] Clark (1993) 195.

[3] He would have threatened resignation over it if he believed that would have stopped her and if he had not saved that threat for what he judged a still more significant policy issue: the exchange rate and Alan Walters' role over it: Lawson (1992) 122, 583, 960–66.

[4] Lawson (1992) 573–75.

[5] Private information.

[6] Lawson (1992) 123, 128 and private information.

thirds of the Cabinet were on it, as was the chief whip; there were departmental studies, as well as a Green Paper leading to public consultation and two and a half years of intensive ministerial discussion.[7] But what failed its trial over the poll-tax was Cabinet Government as Margaret Thatcher had re-created it, not its more robust previous forms. Not that there was ever a golden age of Cabinet Government but, that said, it was a travesty of Cabinet Government, made so by her characteristics as chairman already mentioned. One cannot prove that the poll-tax fiasco would not have happened in the 1960s or 1970s—*In Place of Strife* went far before being stopped by Cabinet discussion—but some factors suggest why it might not have done.

As recently as 1981 a working party chaired by Terry Heiser, later permanent secretary of DOE, had concluded that:

1. Despite its difficulties rates were the least worst local tax;
2. Alternatives to it, like the poll and other taxes, could probably only supplement it;
3. The poll-tax might seem unfair and would be difficult to collect.

Despite Margaret Thatcher's opposition, the then secretary of state, Heseltine, accepted rates should be retained. A Green Paper expressing those findings went to Cabinet who discussed and endorsed it after further examination by Whitelaw.[8] Hers was a reluctant acquiescence. Heath had promised the abolition of rates as long ago as 1974. She had campaigned against them then and disliked breaking a promise.

So Thatcher remained implacably opposed to rates.[9] Meanwhile various expedients had checked local expenditure growth, but more sustainable measures were needed if increasingly acrimonious annual battles with local authorities were to be avoided (below, chapter 11).[10] To find them DOE proposed a review to cover local government structure as well as finance, but in October, 1984, she instructed Patrick Jenkin, who had replaced Heseltine, to concentrate on finding an alternative to rates.[11] Indeed she insisted from the start that the review might recommend anything but the rates. It was entrusted to a task force, not to an interdepartmental Cabinet committee, because she believed that Whitehall through its traditional mechanisms would never be radical. Sir Terry Heiser, now permanent secretary, picked a small high-quality team for William Waldegrave as parliamentary secretary. To give the greatest scope to radical ideas and as part of a highly confidential exercise Waldegrave was to report directly to her, not through Patrick Jenkin, the secretary of state, or senior officials, though Kenneth Baker, the minister of state, involved himself closely

---

[7] Lawson (1992) 561–62.

[8] Department of the Environment (1981); Heseltine (2000) 207–8; Butler et al (1994) 29–34.

[9] Thatcher (1993) 644–47. Ridley (1991) 32, 119. Another reason for her hostility was that she saw it as a tax on home improvement: Ridley (1991) 128.

[10] Loughlin (1996) 92–95.

[11] Thatcher (1993) 642–44.

in the team's work and Waldegrave briefed Jenkin. Even so it was a then unprecedented overturning of the convention of ministerial responsibility.

Waldegrave's Local Government Finance (LGF) team was not short of relevant expertise. Its DOE members had ample experience of working in local government finance. The Treasury provided one member, but she, given its confidentiality, was not to report back to the Treasury on the development of the policy, as would have been normal and wiser.[12] The team under Waldegrave was not to consult all departments with an interest in local government, but only with experts with advice on how the tax might work. The Institute of Fiscal Studies and experts from LSE helped calculate its effects on households. Lord Rothschild led four more advisers, so-called Wise Men, of whom I was one.[13] The team's remit was to report to a Cabinet meeting at Chequers six months later. Until then, Mrs Thatcher had no contact with its deliberations though all involved knew her hostility to the rates.

This approach—of allowing a departmental team to investigate an issue of serious interest to other departments—departed radically from normal procedure which was to set up a Cabinet committee of officials under neutral Cabinet secretariat chairmanship. So there was no equivalent to the one which had successfully scotched our early half-baked ideas on transport policy in 1966 and encouraged us to do better. For most purposes such official committees were dead. The traditional mechanisms of collective responsibility were eroded by her further requirement that the team should not discuss the policy proposals it was developing with officials in other departments, including the Treasury, until after the principal decisions had been taken. There was no counterpart to the structure of interdepartmental meetings I had known in the 1960s and 1970s allowing issues concerning other departments to be threshed out so that their ministers could be well briefed for subsequent Cabinet committee and Cabinet discussion; though—more relevant for local government finance than for most issues—the interests of many other departments were directly concerned: Education, the Home Office, Employment, Health, the Scottish and Welsh Offices as well as housing and transport within DOE. Neither was discussion allowed with local government. Since 1979 the onslaught of legislation attempting to curb the growth of local expenditure had created such hostility between central and local government that easy, open discussion between them would have been impossible.

Cabinet discussion of the team's conclusions took place on an Away Day at Chequers on the basis of a slide-show: no papers circulated, only one member of the LGF team present. Nearly half the Cabinet was there.[14] Though Nigel

---

[12] The team had two DSS officials to help reconcile the poll-tax and the social benefit system. It also consulted with the Home Office, but only over the problem of identifying those liable to pay the tax.

[13] We worked as individuals, not as a team.

[14] Butler et al (1994) 70.

Lawson was at an inescapable engagement abroad, Peter Rees, Chief Secretary to the Treasury, replaced him. Because of her refusal to allow the team to discuss their proposals with other departments, ministers reached Chequers unbriefed. No one—certainly not the absent Lawson—expected a decision then to proceed with the poll-tax.[15] However her opening statement fixed on it: 'I am convinced by the argumentation of William and Kenneth. What do you think?'

All present were on the back foot from the start. The team's presentation had covered many other matters: the case for annual elections, elected mayors, unitary authorities, nationalising non-domestic rates and profound changes to the grant system among them. Moreover, the team well understood there were difficult issues to be overcome because of the regressiveness of the new tax compared with rates and the need to establish its collectability. Yet these difficulties were not properly discussed. Ministers were reeling from the adverse political consequences of rates revaluation in Scotland and growing threat of budget revolts by the most left wing local authorities. Attention fastened almost entirely on the politics of the poll-tax. To Lawson's subsequent horror, the meeting decided on the poll-tax with no dissentient ministerial voices: not provisionally or in principle, subject to overcoming the problems of its regressiveness and its collectability, but formally as the basis for further work.

The subsequent E(LF) Cabinet committee discussions were therefore based on a *fait accompli,* but in addition various checks and balances within the machine did not work as they would have done in the 1970s or earlier. At its first meeting Lawson tabled a paper recommending rates reform rather than the poll-tax. She ruled it out of order since the decision to proceed with the poll-tax had been taken. After that, the Chief Secretary rather than he attended EL(F). So the poll-tax after Chequers was discussed in a Cabinet committee dominated by the Prime Minister, who was helped by the fact most others on the committee were against the rates, against which they had been strongly briefed through party sources and had not been sufficiently briefed through any source on the even greater political and practical drawbacks to the poll-tax which needed to be overcome. Its members were quickly discouraged from intervening by the Prime Minister.[16] One inescapable reason why other departments did not bother to brief their ministers, as they once would have done, was because the Prime Minister's impatience with argument made most ministers reluctant to face unwinnable rows with her and therefore dislike briefing which implied they should engage in such rows. The proposals were published in the Green Paper, *Paying for Local Government,* in January, 1986. The Cabinet meeting, which formally approved it, was that at which Heseltine had already just resigned

[15] 31 March 1985. I was not invited, though involved in briefing for it. My dismay was twofold. The strong caveats and necessary conditions required, which had been stressed even by those who saw possibilities in the scheme, were not given enough weight in the discussion. Then a decision was taken not in principle to explore the proposal further and in doing so to assess its advantages and disadvantages, but to adopt it *tout court.*

[16] Private information.

because frustrated by her from bringing to it his misgivings over Westland.[17] Lawson had reluctantly agreed because she had been persuaded to retain rates alongside the poll-tax in what was called dual running.[18] However, Nicholas Ridley dumped dual running at the 1987 party conference. The poll-tax on its own became a manifesto commitment at the 1987 election.

In the years before its introduction, instead of taking steps to offset its regressiveness and solve the practical problems, if that were possible, ministers cut grants to local government which raised the prospective average annual poll-tax from a modest £50 a head initially to about £350. Together they turned a difficult policy into an impossible one. William Waldegrave recalls what he calls the 'dumb insolence' of non-cooperation in the Treasury, which ensured its failure. Years later the fifth secretary of state involved, Chris Patten, whose fate it was to implement it, remembered telling Margaret Thatcher:

> We needed a lot more money to provide a safety net for people to prevent the poll-tax doing what it did do, which was to act as a heat-seeking missile against floating voters in marginal constituencies . . . Margaret, who was usually spectacularly good at identifying the impact of tax changes on what she would call 'our people', was distracted by the debate about shadowing the German mark.[19]

An otherwise excellent book, *Failure in British Government: the Politics of the Poll Tax,* followed Lawson's lead in seeing the poll-tax as an example of Cabinet Government working which it was not.[20] Unrealistically, given Mrs Thatcher's attitude towards dissenting chancellors, let alone officials, the book argued civil servants should share the blame because they did not blow the whistle against the poll-tax.

One of its authors, Andrew Adonis, conveyed these two lessons to Tony Blair when he joined his staff in 1996:

- The fiasco was a failure of Cabinet Government and reinforced the case for prime ministerial government;[21]
- To protect the Prime Minister against the repeat of such a fiasco, he needed to be surrounded by more political and politically aware advisers who should take over much of the civil service's policymaking role.[22]

---

[17] A Cabinet meeting I, as part of a consortium to build a Channel crossing approved at the same meeting, was eagerly awaiting. At the time I had no inkling that there would be no discussion in Cabinet and that our particular scheme had already been lost. Neither would it have made any difference if Heseltine had stayed for the approval of dual running. Despite his responsibility for the 1981 Green Paper at no stage had he been involved in discussions over the poll tax.

[18] Kenneth Baker gives an account of the main meeting of E(LF), 20/5/85. Most ministers approved. Brittan, Lawson and Rees did not: Baker (1993) 122; on Lawson's approval of the Green Paper, see Baker (1993) 126.

[19] *Sunday Telegraph*, 23 March 2003.

[20] Butler et al (1994).

[21] Butler et al (1994) ch 8, 14.

[22] Butler et al (1994) ch 9, 14; also private information.

Was the disaster caused by insufficient political advice?[23] Not plausibly. It was politics, or rather the political will of the Prime Minister, which most prevented searching discussion of the issues and swamped civil service advice on the difficulties to be overcome. Many ministers were around to give political advice, eight in DOE alone. The discussion at Chequers in March, 1981, and in E(LF) subsequently was almost entirely political. After she had decided on the poll-tax, neither its fairness nor collectability could be got sufficiently on the agenda for solutions to be reached, though there were enough warning signs. Dual running, which would have kept the level of poll-tax down, was not finally abandoned until November, 1987, at a Cabinet committee where Lawson argued vigorously for keeping it. The Scottish poll-tax was already creating uproar as the English poll-tax was still passing through Parliament. Perhaps Adonis' point was that ministers were not good enough at politics.

Rather Margaret Thatcher's ways of working round Cabinet could make it difficult for ministers and officials alike to press impartial, objective advice. Her own final comment that no sooner had they established the poll-tax in a workable form—though untrue—than it was abolished, was a sad comment on the lack of attention—despite official advice—given to fairness, thoroughness and practicality years before when it should have been.[24] In short the fiasco showed not the shortcomings of the Cabinet system, but of the system it had become under a Prime Minister who actively discouraged frank, open argument; whose conviction politics excluded discussion of feasible measures from the start; and who had learnt how to work round the Cabinet system to get her way.

After the 1997 election Adonis joined the No 10 Policy Unit of which he became head in 2001. Rarely has one book, which misinterpreted an event, had such an impact on the workings of government, though it was not the only influence propelling Blair in the direction he took in reforming the centre of government.

The fiasco was all so unnecessary.[25] Better communication, as in the old Whitehall, would have quickly shown how unnecessary replacing rates by the poll-tax was; what serious difficulties needed to be overcome and how—just— they might have been, if it had to be a poll-tax. A more objective approach would have started with a thorough review of rates. Why then replace them? Four main reasons were given:[26]

---

[23] Thatcher (1993) 642, though it became a rallying point for those who opposed, both in her party and on the left.

[24] Thatcher (1993) 642.

[25] My own position was that I was invited back with Lennie Hoffman and Tom Wilson as one of four advisers under Lord Rothschild's leadership, until after the Chequers meeting when we were told we were no longer needed. I had been one of the team—before and after the Layfield Report— waiting to help Crosland reform local government finance. I had co-authored a book on the topic, which came out in 1980, intended as a contribution in the Brookings style (chapter 9). It advocated reforms in the grant system, many of which this review endorsed, and the reform of rates into a property tax, which it did not, but which was close to what Lawson wanted.

[26] E.g. Baker (1993) 115–16.

1. One, strongly influential with the Prime Minister, was the plight of the elderly widow or widower paying unabated rates on the family home though the children had departed. But the poll tax threw up its own anomalies. There was to be the family of four—grandparents and parents—but with one income, paying four poll taxes instead of one rates.[27] Besides, if this anomaly were thought particularly deserving, a special rebate could have been devised, with rather less difficulty in identifying deserving cases, than the poll-tax was to throw up.

2. There was the heated political fall-out from the Scottish rating revaluation in 1984, conveyed to the PM by George Younger and other Scottish Conservative MPs, shaken by the effect on their popularity of the resulting increase in domestic rates. But its main cause in Scotland was a shift of burden from non-domestic rates onto the domestic ratepayer which could have been solved by decoupling non-domestic rates from domestic rates, which incidentally is what was done. A bolder solution to the revaluation problem, favoured by Lawson, would have been to replace periodic revaluations by continuous indexing of rateable values, replacing them by actual sale prices whenever a property was sold.[28]

3. In a time when, as so often, public expenditure was under pressure, it was galling to the Treasury, and infuriating to other spending ministers whose budgets had been cut back, that increases in local expenditure were harder to control. Richard Jackman, Morris Perlman and I had considered this problem in our book and suggested how the grant system might be improved to reduce local authorities' tendency to spend more. These and other changes in the grant system—including the nationalising of the non-domestic rate to make it a close-ended grant with increases in it linked to inflation—were adopted to remove the perversity that local authorities could increase their grant from central government by spending more. If local authorities were not cutting back on expenditure as much as the Treasury would have liked, a robust reaction would have been to point out that the macroeconomic concern that it would be reflationary was fallacious[29]. From that standpoint it did not matter if a ratepayer spent the money or if it were taken from him and spent by local government. So the issue was presentational, except that it seemed unfair that public expenditure by central departments should be cut back more than local expenditure. Still there were further measures which could have been taken within the rating system: for example, though not without practical difficulty, requiring local authorities to publish their budgets before an annual local election or annual referendum. As it was,

---

[27] Howe (1994) 603.

[28] Lawson (1992) 574. A scheme for it had been devised in Foster, Jackman and Perlman (1980) 397–412. By excluding increases in value from home improvements until the property was sold another of Thatcher's objections to rates could have been met, Thatcher (1993) 644–45.

[29] Foster, Jackman and Perlman (1980) 369–89.

rate-capping was introduced, which achieved the task in most local authorities, but with increased acrimony.

4. A further problem affected a few authorities where the number of 100%
rate rebates was high. Since they did not pay rates, their interest was to
increase rates and enjoy benefits from the additional expenditure. Besides
rate-capping, which initially had worked in almost all authorities, and nationalising non-domestic rates, there were other ways in which this problem could
have been tackled. Among them was applying the same mechanism to rates—
that is, reducing the rebate to less than 100%, but compensating for it by a
matching increase in social security benefits—as was to be applied to the poll
tax, so that at the margin 100% of any increase in local expenditure would
have been met by the ratepayer[30]. No doubt there would have been strong
objections, but it would still have been part of a more familiar system and a
less regressive tax than the poll-tax. Another perceived injustice would have
remained in that some earners in a household had votes, but were not the
ratepayer. Later research done for DOE showed, however, that in practice
most non-ratepaying members of households contributed to the rate-bill.
However, such remedial measures were overwhelmed by a general perception
of an extreme left campaign against the government as much by local authorities as by the unions.[31] It came to be believed that stronger measures were
needed to ensure local accountability; but whatever they were they could have
been more easily grafted on to the rating system. They did not need a new tax.

These issues were well known to most involved from the start. But without
anyone being given the chance to explore them with Mrs Thatcher, with
officials in other departments or with the Cabinet committee, from the start the
message from the Prime Minister was that retention of the rating system was not
acceptable. If rates were out, what was in? A local income tax was ruled out.
Only a third of adults paid PAYE and the Inland Revenue could not code Pay-
as-You-Earn returns to place of residence.[32] The EC would not permit a local
VAT. It could have led to huge price differences between neighbouring authorities.[33] The presentation at Chequers explored the option of a tax which was
60% rates, 40% poll-tax, but that was turned down. That left the poll-tax as the
only feasible option.[34] The Local Government Finance Team and its advisors

---

[30] Baker (1993) 127.

[31] At one point there was a draft bill, never published, to make it possible to put some local
authorities into bankruptcy. As partners in Coopers and Lybrand, Sir Kenneth Cork and I were canvassed about becoming the joint insolvency commissioners for Liverpool. There was even discussion of how we would enter City Hall: would it be by helicopter?

[32] Baker (1993) 117–18; Ridley (1991) 126–27; there were concerns that a local income tax would
have been misused by some Labour local authorities. A more intractable problem was the
Treasury's refusal, as always, to hypothecate or share its principal tax.

[33] It was also argued it would have encouraged cross-border shopping: Baker (1993) 117.

[34] Butler, Adonis and Travers (1994) credit me as the author of the poll-tax. This is only true in the
sense that if rates, income and sales taxes were ruled out, the only possibility left was the poll-tax
which might be made to work if its redistributive impacts and practical difficulties could be overcome.

were fully aware of the regressiveness and collectibility problems to be over-come and warned ministers about them:

1. One set was practical. How did one authenticate the number of residents in a household? What about the problems posed by students, gypsies, lodging houses and establishing identities? As early as Chequers ministers had been warned of these difficulties. As had been discussed with the Home Office, the only satisfactory way of identifying who in a household was liable to pay poll-tax was through a national identity card system. In any sensible policy-making no decisions would have been taken until after full discussion with local authorities to test practicality in these and many other dimensions. The blowing up of the space shuttle on the same day drove discussion of the Green Paper from the media, but when the full impracticality of the poll-tax became known during the ensuing consultation period, the political momen-tum behind the tax was too great for it to be aborted; or the necessary modifications to be made until too late. Franker discussion than was possible with Thatcher should have prevented that happening.

2. Another was that replacing rates by the poll-tax would be regressive. Professor Tom Wilson, another of we four wise men, made the point espe-cially strongly. The rider I made was that it would be unacceptable unless means could be found to offset that regressiveness. To demand of any single tax that it should be progressive was absurd. The effects on income distribu-tion of the whole system were what mattered. Several were possible. Some, which were canvassed, depended on banding the poll tax so it had features of a property-tax.[35] I spent an hour with Nigel Lawson—the only meeting I had with him—to persuade him to offset this regressive effect by announcing that he would not lower higher income tax rates as much as otherwise intended, but he would not do that.[36] It is unwise to pursue a fiscal policy a chancellor is against, certainly if he refuses to co-operate so as to mitigate its adverse effects.

3. There are always losers from any tax change who complain more than the gainers praise it. For a while the extent of these effects was hidden among the averages, but it became clear later. Since, as has been argued, the case for introducing poll-tax *per se* was non-existent and offsetting all these gains and losses difficult, it should have prompted second thoughts about the policy. But again it was too late.

4. Protests—as with the introduction of the separate water-rate when there was no serious problem—would have been much fewer if the tax had stayed at £50 a head as first calculated or even the £140 re-calculated when approved

[35] Richard Jackman and I worked out what we called the Dublin airport alternative which depended on hypothecating central government grant as if paid for by receipts from the standard rate of income tax and allowing local adjustments to that.

[36] Lawson (1992); he recalls my pressing him on the poll tax. My memory is that I urged him to mitigate its redistributive effects by continuing dual running and various offsetting tax measures.

at the Chequers meeting.[37] Thereafter a series of ministerial decisions from 1987 cumulatively led to the average annual poll-tax bill being some seven times higher than first predicted. Treasury ministers, who significantly and knowingly reduced central government grant rates to local authorities, did the greatest damage. Because of the high gearing—non-domestic rates having become not variable and in effect part of the grant system—a reduction in grant led to a big percentage increase in poll-tax. If grant rates in 1988 had been at 1984 levels, it is just possible there would have been no uproar. However, Cabinet colleagues did not work well together to help each other mitigate these adverse effects. In particular Lawson would not help by increasing grant to lessen the level of poll tax required.[38]

---

[37] Baker (1993) 118–19, 123.

[38] Baker (1993) 138–39. Among them was getting rid of the original idea that rates and the poll tax should run together for several years: Ridley (1991) 124–25.

9

Major: The Counter-Revolution That Failed

It was much more what Cabinet Government is supposed to be like. It was much more rational . . . the problem was that when people began to be disloyal later on, they were not very frightened of him.

William Waldegrave[1]

ON SUCCEEDING MARGARET Thatcher, Major intended to restore a more collegiate government, but divisions within the Cabinet, and after 1992 a small and dwindling majority, made it impossible. Instead the Cabinet, the Cabinet system and the cohesion of government deteriorated. A government with many talented and experienced ministers became less effective than Margaret Thatcher's had been. External factors also made government more difficult: the ever greater intensity, intrusiveness and destructiveness of media interest; the greater speed of change which seemed to be required; and the growing impact of global developments, and sudden overseas events, on domestic affairs.

THE CABINET AND CABINET SYSTEM UNDER JOHN MAJOR

1990 was an opportunity to revert to a more collegiate—yet rigorous and thorough—government and to revive meaningful collective responsibility and cohesive Cabinet solidarity. Another Prime Minister—Howe and Lawson still in the Commons, Heseltine and Hurd still in Major's Cabinet, perhaps others—might have done it. With a united Cabinet and party, Major himself might have done so. But Margaret Thatcher wanted John Major because she thought him 'One of Us' and that she could control him from beyond her political grave. Others wanted him because he was her antithesis. But he was neither an executive leader in her mould nor as good a chairman and mediator between colleagues as Wilson, Callaghan or Alec Douglas-Home had been.

---

[1] Quoted in Hennessy (2000).

Nevertheless he wanted to, and for about two years did, restore a more collegiate style of government.[2] At his first Cabinet he asked Douglas Hurd to report on Jordan.[3] Heseltine, returning to Cabinet from exile since Westland, asked a question, almost unthinkable under Thatcher. The atmosphere relaxed. Others asked questions too. For a while a collegiate atmosphere reigned. Robin Butler commented that Major's early Cabinets were like the Prisoners' Chorus from Beethoven's *Fidelio* where the prisoners, released from their chains, start celebrating diffidently and gradually gain confidence until they are heard revelling in their newly found freedom.[4] Hurd was often heard trying to help bring order by summarising points at issue, setting out the pros and cons.[5] Major was a great setter-up and user of Cabinet committees for policymaking. The more collegiate spirit survived, despite ups and downs, and growing difficulties, until after the 1992 election, when it started to fade.

A more politically acceptable replacement was quickly found for the poll-tax. Major inherited the 1991 Gulf War, but gained popularity as a war leader, his lack of bombast and ordinariness impressing the troops there, as later in Bosnia, when he visited them.[6] He had considerable negotiating skills, which he used to good effect at home and abroad, usually gaining much more than he gave away. The negotiations preceding Maastricht were a personal triumph for him, though they stirred up antipathy between pro and anti-Europeans in the Conservative party which was later to cause so much trouble.[7] But he did better in these negotiations than Margaret Thatcher would have done. Entry into the ERM at first seemed like another success in the war he was determined to fight against inflation.[8] It did not turn into a disaster until after the 1992 election. His unexpected victory in that election was another triumph for him. His greatest achievement was the Citizen's Charter in 1991, a new consumer-focused philosophy of administration and of participatory democracy which was to provide new and lasting objectives for the public services.[9] Rarely for him, he believed in it strongly.

A strong Prime Minister would have found it difficult to re-build collective responsibility and Cabinet solidarity; maintain the Cabinet's role in legitimising decisions; encourage objectivity in policy preparation; and take over Margaret Thatcher's role in scrutinising policy proposals. But Cabinet discussion all too soon became rancorous. Major's position was weakened by the need to include Thatcherites in his Cabinet.[10] Appealing to both sides on Europe, John Major

---

[2] Kavanagh and Seldon (1999) chapter 8; Hennessy (2000) chapter 17; Kavanagh in Kavanagh and Seldon (1994).

[3] Private information.

[4] Kavanagh and Seldon (1999) 224.

[5] Private information.

[6] Freedman in Kavanagh and Seldon (1994).

[7] Wallace in Kavanagh and Seldon (1994).

[8] Jay in Kavanagh and Seldon (1994).

[9] Cabinet Office (1991); Willman in Kavanagh and Seldon (1994) 64–65.

[10] Campbell and Wilson (1995) 103.

united his party and Cabinet immediately, but divided it more in the long run.[11] Disagreements over Europe encouraged some to be fractious over other matters. But, as important, many ministers had long been in office and were tired. Many thought themselves at least John Major's equal and as likely to be right. Neither did Major find his Whitelaw to help smooth over Cabinet's widening divisions. Heseltine, who became his deputy Prime Minister, had outstanding talents, might have made a fine Prime Minister, but was no Whitelaw. Yet within his Cabinet, he had John Wakeham who chaired half his Cabinet committees and would probably have been as good as Whitelaw at soothing ruffled feelings, conciliating divisions of opinion and achieving Cabinet solidarity.[12] But almost as soon as the 1992 election was over, the Conservative standing in the polls plunged and never recovered.[13] The Labour opposition at last revived and showed an ability to attack.[14]

Margaret Thatcher had followed many earlier Prime Ministers in avoiding reading the newspapers. She relied on Bernard Ingham, her press chief, to tell her what she really needed to know, so keeping her mind, and more of her time, free for government. She got on well with most newspaper proprietors because they saw her as a hero, but John Major and his ministers were not so seen.[15] Thatcher's seemingly endless honeymoon with most media ended. The lobby hung around Downing Street to observe if Cabinet stayed late. If it did, it sensed disagreement and rang its Cabinet contacts in the afternoon for a story. Therefore to appear unanimous, Cabinet started ending promptly, however unfinished its business, but in vain. The media had their claws into ministers in its endeavour to make them part of their entertainment industry. Ministers, including the Prime Minister, started to announce policies to the media before bringing them to Parliament or sometimes to their colleagues or their officials. Under media spotlights, conviction politics often turned into spur-of-the-moment politics. Some ministers were better copy than others. Several had to resign because of scandals nothing to do with their job. Ministers' principal accountability under Thatcher had not been to Parliament but to her. Now it shifted to the *Today* programme. The price paid for this shift in accountability to the media was that eventually they, more than the opposition, destroyed government by exploiting divisions between ministers. By the end of Major's administration a 'Cabinet of chums' was said to have become a 'Cabinet of vipers'.[16]

Under a weak and inexperienced leader and with little discipline, Cabinet itself became 'like a rather disorderly board of directors, where many speak and

---

[11] Riddell in Kavanagh and Seldon (1994) 51–55; Hennessy (2000) 456–57.

[12] Wakeham chaired a Liaison Committee at the end under Thatcher to pull together planning and timetabling for the weeks ahead: Kavanagh and Seldon (1999) 231–32.

[13] Seldon in Kavanagh and Seldon (1994) 39–43.

[14] Riddell in Kavanagh and Seldon (1994) 55–56.

[15] Hennessy (2000) 471.

[16] Kavanagh and Seldon (1999) 226.

few listen', as Bagehot described it, but with vastly more business.[17] Major was not a man to impart a sense of vision—when asked to provide vision, he famously disclaimed it—even direction, let alone strategy, to his Cabinet.

Moreover the old disciplines were lost. The fall in the number of Cabinet papers—that is, policy documents circulated to the whole Cabinet—from 340 a year under Attlee and 140 under Heath to 20 a year under Major had been almost linear.[18] Among the reasons given for that decline since 1979 were that:

- The huge increase in legislation characterising the Thatcher years made it impossible for ministers to read their papers and master their briefs;
- Events were now moving so fast that a Cabinet paper written one week might be out-of-date by next week's Cabinet meeting. Yet while foreign policy, and occasionally defence and major industrial disputes, can move so fast that reports to Cabinet must be oral—as has always been recognised—most issues, certainly policy issues, coming to it can be more considered. Besides, civil servants had honed the skills of writing and altering Cabinet papers at speed, even as crises developed;
- It would reduce leaking.[19] But most Cabinets have leaked and this one continued to leak.[20] The lack of Cabinet papers did not reduce the frequency of leaks, but their accuracy, because ministers came away with various impressions of the oral summaries they had been given at Cabinet, often revealing the truth after the first few years: a picture of frequent disagreement, confusion and lack of reasoned argument and objectivity in policy formulation;
- Under Thatcher fewer papers written for Cabinet were more than offset by similar and as thorough papers written for Cabinet committees and for bilaterals with her.

However, what characterised the Major administrations was not so much the further drop in papers written for the whole Cabinet, but the decline in the number and shortening of most written for Cabinet committees or meetings with the Prime Minister. So sensible discussion between ministers on the basis of clear statements of the issues became difficult.[21] Instead, ministers reported orally to Cabinet and Cabinet committees on the progress of their business, which could include reporting progress or lack of it on a policy or issue, seeking approval of a white or green paper or bill or their reactions to press comment. Therefore the only account many Cabinet ministers had of other departments' policies or

---

[17] Bagehot (1997) 10.
[18] Butler (1999).
[19] Ridley (1991) 37–38; Prior (1986) 134.
[20] Matthew (1995) 115, but also see Mackintosh (1962) 257, for other early examples; Crossman (1975) 580.
[21] A good description of her handling of Cabinet and Cabinet committee is in Baker (1993) 255–60.

policy proposals was oral, given by the minister in Cabinet, or, if they were absent from it, as recorded tersely in the Cabinet minutes.[22]

When Thatcher's voracious appetite for paper and rigorous determination to get to the bottom of issues and drive through what she wanted were withdrawn, Cabinet colleagues continued deeply divided, not only on Europe, which would have happened anyway, but on many other topics. The Cabinet often became indecisive, a tangle of shifting alliances and without papers, therefore with diminished ability to master complex issues. Hence the Cabinet system did not return to its old ability to process government business. It did not resume enough Cabinet solidarity to be effective. Having to write a paper, or papers, on a topic was no longer the way departments were motivated to think matters through clearly when initiating or implementing a policy proposal. Attempts were made to arrange Cabinet committee meetings to develop fellow feeling and agenda-based discussions among ministers, but with many ministers disinclined, and many often away in Europe, formal meetings became harder to arrange and worse attended.[23] Furthermore, while in the past an occasional minister may have tried to override the normal civil service practice of free discussion with officials in other departments relevant to an issue, including the Treasury, civil servants now found ministers often trying to block such discussion, simply because of many deep policy disagreements around the Cabinet table.

So leaking killed collective responsibility, Cabinet solidarity and the use of the Cabinet system to achieve thoroughness or demonstrate practicality. Kenneth Clarke said, because of Cabinet becoming as leaky as a sieve, ministers would not bring their business there. Though Major had started seeking consensus in Cabinet, increasingly he, too, would bring less to Cabinet after 1992 for fear of leaks.[24] Cabinet did not discuss *Back to Basics*, which had a short-run success (though by 2002 it had made Major seem hypocritical).[25] Robin Butler recalled that the inability to bring pit closures or the complex issues surrounding Britain's membership of the Exchange Rate Mechanism before Cabinet or Cabinet committee showed how fear of leaks—driven by disagreement—stopped proper discussion.[26] When initiating proposals departmental ministers found they had a choice: they might ask the Prime Minister to put it on the Cabinet agenda, or for him or the deputy Prime Minister to set up a group to consider it. Or he or she might believe it sanction enough if they persuaded the Prime Minister on a matter with minimal or no consultation with other

---

[22] Harold Wilson (1976) said the habit of starting a Cabinet minute with a précis of the relevant Cabinet paper, even if it were not delivered, goes back to the 1920s, but what is there to précis with no Cabinet paper?

[23] Private information.

[24] Hennessy (2000) 444.

[25] Currie (2002).

[26] Hennessy (2000) 459; Stephens (1996) 262–63. Major had been much identified with entering the ERM. His prestige and effective power dropped on exit.

ministers affected. Decisions began to be taken in what was called the political Cabinet or in more informal meetings, usually without officials present to take minutes and record decisions. The decision to abolish the National Economic Development Council was taken by a few ministers coming together by chance behind the Speaker's chair just before the 1992 election, furious because of the ribbing about that election they had just had from its union members at the Council meeting.[27] A growing habit of taking decisions without officials present led to a weakening of partnership between ministers and officials. Such informal decision-making was a recipe for subsequent misunderstanding of what had been decided. The legitimation of government decisions could become almost a game. It was no longer possible to say who had executive supremacy: neither the Prime Minister nor Cabinet nor any particular collection of ministers.

Policy direction changed frequently as bright ideas were taken up, even during the passage of a bill. Quick changes in policy direction had been evident, as we have seen, in bills on local government from the early 1980s. Later into the 1990s it afflicted housing, education, industrial relations, criminal justice and social security. This over-rapid succession of policies, especially in the 1990s, was itself caused partly by too rapid a rotation of ministers, each seeing legislation as a lasting memorial. Other causes of excessive new and unclear legislation, more marked under Major, were the fertility of political think tanks, pressure groups and lobbyists. As important was that an almost sure way of attracting media attention was for ministers to announce their thoughts on changing the law, however provisional or ill thought-through. The source of policy change might be little more than off-the-cuff remarks, perhaps made as an instant response to a challenge on radio or TV.

As a consequence—after a lull in the growth of legislation in 1990–2—not only was legislation in spate but also its preliminaries, proposals for legislation: the police were assailed within two years by five major sets of proposals on police reform and four on criminal justice.[28] National initiatives—especially in education and training—were rolled out without waiting for an evaluation of the pilot projects which sensibly preceded them. Hence many, often conflicting, quickly and poorly-conceived policy initiatives—as on health, education and criminal justice—were not worked up in detail. So they did not command assent, particularly from those whose everyday lives would be affected by them, but also often from fellow ministers before or after their legislation. Later in the decade, new ideas on GP fund-holders and cross-district referrals did not work because not enough attention had been given to making them practical.[29] The quality of much new legislation had so declined that judges for the first time felt they needed to take into account white papers and what ministers said in

---

[27] As chairman of a NEDO working party, I happened to be at that meeting. Also private information.

[28] J C Hoddinott, president of ACPO, Chief Constable of Hampshire, on policy reform at Coopers & Lybrand (1994). Lord Chief Justice Taylor made a similar remark.

[29] Glennerster in Kavanagh and Seldon (1994).

Parliament to help them make sense of opaque bills, ironically at a time when the full explanatory documents, which might have been helpful, were less likely to have been written.[30] The depths of that era of ill-considered legislation came in statutes restraining dangerous dogs and establishing the Child Support Agency.[31]

Most ministers, forced to rely on their own judgement, did the best they could in the circumstances. The quality of government in a department came to depend most on the quality of its minister, his or her fixity of purpose and length of tenure, for in many departments the rotation of ministers was rapid. Little changed in the Foreign Office, Defence or the Northern Ireland Office. Relations between ministers and officials remained as close, trusting and productive as ever. Peter Brooke and Patrick Mayhew—ministers in the old style—are to be credited with easing the transition to more constructive politics in Northern Ireland. Many others did their best, but, without a controlling intelligence and under intense media pressure, there was little continuity of policy in many departments. As a consequence the notion of a minister needing to pursue a policy consistent with government policy as approved by Cabinet virtually disappeared. Without Cabinet or other legitimation of the change in policy, Redwood and Hague in succession pursued different policies in Wales. An Education Secretary, who was Catholic, and a junior minister, who was not, seemed to put tussling over religion at the centre of education policy. Douglas Hurd was considered the last home secretary to do a proper job going through the papers before making up his mind.[32] Under pressure Baker, Clarke and Howard left very different and sometimes conflicting imprints on law and order legislation. Howard and Anne Widdecombe openly wrangled over Home Office policy. As would not have happened under Margaret Thatcher, privatisation or rather mutualisation of the Milk Marketing Board took place with ample consideration for the needs of farmers, but without serious attention to establishing competition or consideration of the needs of the consumer.[33] Transport policy did a U-turn. The turnover of transport ministers was rapid. After 1994, the Roads Programme was repeatedly cut back. Though there was a promising green paper, successive ministers ducked any attempt to introduce road pricing to check traffic growth.[34] Succeeding ministers, even before 1997, did not build on John MacGregor's foundations to ensure rail privatisation worked as best it could.

Major was not much help in preventing or sorting out such difficulties, sometimes because he had his own views; but also ministers and officials could find him not on top of the issues.[35] Rather than the Cabinet secretariat trying to

[30] The key case was *Pepper v Hart* [1992] 3 WLR 1032: Loughlin (1996) 256. It was standard practice on the continent.
[31] Hansard Society (1992) 388–98.
[32] Private information.
[33] Personal experience.
[34] Foster in Seldon (2001); RAC Foundation (2002) chapter 1.
[35] Campbell and Wilson (1995) 216.

resolve interdepartmental differences in its traditional neutral and objective fashion, ministers found his Policy Unit sometimes trying to broker solutions ideologically and frequently adding to rather than resolving disagreement by doing so.[36] Moreover a pall was cast over his administrations by the expectation he would lose in 1992, the virtual certainty he would do so in 1997 and the severe difficulty of contending with a small majority between those two elections.

THE EXAMPLE OF RAIL PRIVATISATION

It is not my present purpose to try to persuade the reader that still nationalised railways could have coped with the more than a third increase in passenger traffic that followed privatisation, though I doubt it.[37] Moreover BR's management would have been overstretched if it also had to take on the planning, preparation and execution of large-scale, network-wide project management on an intensively used railway, even if the Treasury had funded it, which it would not have done. The Treasury's dead hand was the prime practical reason for the privatisation of this, as of other, nationalised industries, though there was the expectation based on other privatised industries' experience that rail cost efficiency and customer service quality would be improved.

Neither will I argue—then the focus of most public discussion—whether it was wise to separate train from track ownership, though in practice this separation has led to comparatively few problems.[38] The Labour government retained the vertical separation of train from track among its few givens when reviewing the railways in 2004. It has also become central to rail regulation and the interoperability of rail systems throughout Europe.[39] Nor will I

[36] Campbell and Wilson (1995) 246.

[37] Many argued for nationalisation—and still do—despite all the evidence against nationalisation as a means of securing consumer responsiveness and productive efficiency. My own analysis is mainly in Foster (1992). I believe that without privatisation, the railways could not have been modernised. Copious evidence shows that British Rail had been inefficient in managing demand, costs and investment: Foster (1963); Joy (1973); Serpell (1983); Wolmar (2001) chapters 2 & 3. However, from 1982, under the first Bob Reid and John Welsby, BR had its best top management ever. Sir Robert Reid—only the second lifelong railwayman to do so—became chairman in 1983, being succeeded by his namesake, Sir Bob Reid in 1990. John Welsby became Chief Executive. Though successive governments, since Beeching in the early 1960s, had refused to allow it to rationalise its network, it became Europe's most efficient railway in its use of resources, through judicious cost-management and market pricing: UIC Comparisons in *Rail Gazette International,* March, 2003. Even so, at privatisation the government provided £15 subsidy for every £1 paid in fares on some regional services: private information. The East Coast Main Line and the first part of the Channel Tunnel rail link were modernised with reasonable efficiency and without undue cost escalation.

[38] That trains were built which created difficulties for the track for which they were supposedly designed and that allegedly some train companies took less trouble to stop their wheels going square has been blamed on vertical disintegration, but both causes and remedies are more complicated than that suggests. Under-appreciated during privatisation was the need to devise mechanisms to ensure integrity at the wheel-rail interface.

[39] Borne in on me at a Rail Forum conference on European Railway Policy, 15th April 2003, where almost all speakers were players in the industry.

argue whether rail privatisation created too many bodies. Though some relations between them proved difficult—mostly between government bodies; and between them and the industry—yet innumerable large private firms have continuing contractual relations with as many as 100 other firms.

Rather my focus is on shortcomings of the privatisation process. It would have been as flawed whatever the outcome, whatever the structure chosen. Though I will contend (below chapter 16) that actions from 2000 caused the real disasters, and—contrary to what was widely maintained—rail privatisation was a modest success until then—those shortcomings were not atypical of government failings of the Major era—different from those of the Thatcher government—which elsewhere also undermined its ability to design and secure fundamental reforms.

- 1990 and 1991 were wasted while an interdepartmental committee of junior ministers argued ferociously at a high level of abstraction about the structure to be chosen. The PM, rather than mediating between them, characteristically had his own views, wanting a return to a regionally-based system. An early White Paper setting out the problems privatisation was intended to address and the options to be examined would have shown—if the industry had been properly consulted—that some options lengthily considered before the 1992 election were too abstract and impracticable for serious consideration, so releasing time for more detailed investigation of options which had stood up to initial scrutiny.[40]
- Such a White Paper was not published after the 1992 election, during which rail privatisation became a manifesto commitment Instead a preliminary White Paper was rushed out, which the new transport secretary, John MacGregor, had inherited. The option chosen surprised the BR board. The White Paper contained little detail, papered over the cracks of past differences at Cabinet level and bore slender resemblance to what was to come.
- Rail privatisation was the most complicated of privatisations.[41] Exceptionally able officials were involved, but by then cuts in senior policymaking—and even more analytical—manpower had taken its toll. No longer—as had been true in 1966—could resources with relevant experience be quickly drafted from elsewhere in the department to develop a deep analysis, prepare options

---

[40] It might be objected that the non-production of White Papers was a symptom, not a cause, of an insufficiently detailed privatisation, but attempting a comprehensive White Paper tests how coherent and practical the policy is. It also invites meaningful comments from those in the field best qualified to judge its sense and practicality.

[41] As MacGregor's non-political special adviser from a month or two after the 1992 general election until I joined the Railtrack board in 1994, I was persuaded that vertical separation was possible and that on-rail competition was not. From my previous experience with the privatisation of BAA, BT and electricity, I believed there would be improvements in efficiency and productivity, as for 6 years there were. But I failed to get a better split of regulatory responsibilities, which had already been decided with the Treasury, or a comprehensive, well-argued white paper. I had moved to Railtrack before the Department of Transport became involved in the maintenance contracts.

and engage in thorough worthwhile consultation. Neither did Cabinet have the discipline or coherence to agree on an option and, having done so, stand by it. John MacGregor knew the full 5 years before the next election were needed to handle the complex issues it raised and that therefore speed was essential.

- One way the 1992 White Paper was misleading was in over-stating the extent of competition already judged possible. Extensive competition was introduced to the railway through franchising and outsourcing, but on-rail competition between different train companies competing on the same route was practically impossible, except in a few areas.[42] However, differences of opinion within Cabinet, and ideological prejudice, made it impossible to be open about this, a further source of confusion, since almost the only competition in this area was between participants in the policy process vying to delay admitting there could be no such competition.

- MacGregor wanted later to produce a real—second stage—white paper to explain his vision and overall strategy in addition to the many consultation documents produced on detail. It was badly needed to explain how everything was meant to work and attract comments on practicality. But continuing disagreements between some ministers in other departments were judged to make that not practical for fear of re-opening those disagreements.[43] Later, for such a massive change, separate—third stage—white papers on each of the main players in the re-organised industry—train companies, track authority, maintenance and renewal companies, rolling stock companies and the regulators—would have given clear guidance to those drafting the bill; and to those drawing up, and later implementing, the contracts and other relationships between the 100 bodies created. Public, Parliament and industry would have known in detail what was intended and whether those involved thought it workable.[44] Many problems, which were to haunt the industry, would have been exposed, solved, or the regeneration of the railways through privatisation abandoned, or taken more slowly. The ultimate justification of well-written, substantial white papers is that drafting them may expose aspects and implications of a policy which has not been sufficiently thought through. (As I have argued (chapter 4), there were indeed serious shortcomings in government in the 1960s and some in the 1968 Act. However, a preliminary and later several explanatory white papers were written on the main topics and thus what was done then was done with extreme thoroughness and the closest

[42] More than one company operated on some routes, but genuine competition between different companies operating in different time-slots and providing different services is limited.

[43] I published a much-shortened version of what its contents might have been as Foster (1996b) largely unnoticed, certainly not as a blueprint for the industry with the authority its publication as a detailed White Paper would have given it.

[44] A far from unimportant issue, like what was to be done with BR's research facilities, could not have been buried: what happened was that they were allowed to vanish. But BR research was not allowed to vanish entirely. It was sold to the Atomic Energy Authority, which continues to thrive as a consultancy on the purchased intellectual capital.

collaboration over detail with those in the relevant nationalised industries, and with Barbara Castle when any difficult issue came up.)

- Substantive discussion and determination of the issues were further delayed by the tactic of drafting an enabling bill flexible enough to allow virtually any form of rail privatisation to be adopted. Though ingenious, it was a downward departure in legislative drafting, necessary because government had not yet decided the form privatisation was to take. Even so, the bill was yet another to reach Parliament incomplete and needing copious amendment. Indeed the statute that came out of Parliament was hardly recognisable as the bill that went in. So Parliament, public opinion and the railway industry had no chance of discussing the actual model chosen.

- Content and timing were altered after the bill went through Parliament, all to get the whole thing over before the election. The train operating and the track maintenance companies were to have been franchised completely before Railtrack was sold. That would have been sensible since both would have been in existence before the more difficult details of Railtrack's privatisation were finalised. City and political pressures before the election reversed the order.

- Moreover from 1992 to 1997, there were three secretaries of state for transport, five including Malcolm Rifkind at the beginning and John Prescott/ Gavin Strang in 1997. No wonder subsequent Conservative transport secretaries of state developed their own interpretations of what was intended, even more Labour ministers afterwards.

- After 1992, it soon became clear the Government would lose the next election. Under such circumstances it is never wise to engage in radical reform, which experience shows inevitably takes a number of years to bed down, when at best the next government is indifferent or at worst—as in this case—hostile to what one is doing. (There was no equivalent to the behind-the-scenes lunch Barbara Castle encouraged me to have with Peter Walker and Michael Heseltine to reassure them that the long-term financial reforms to subsidy we were proposing were managerially sensible and worth their support. Or the behind-the-scenes conversations with the opposition for reassurance British Airways' privatisation would not be undone.[45] Rather the objective was to make it practically irreversible. Neither were there the equivalent to the conversations Stephen Swingler—and sometimes I—had with ex-railwaymen (and truck driver) MPs in the House. Nor the sessions I had with each successive intake at the then British Transport Staff College at Woking where before and after dinner we talked about all the issues as they arose, all valuable input into our constructive work.)

Yet rail privatisation was a success until 2000 by all objective tests other than yielding a well co-ordinated investment strategy (below, chapter 16). Its failings

---

[45] I am indebted to David Holmes for this information.

were principally political: not that any particular politician was to blame, but the whole process of devising new policy initiatives, and turning them into legislation, under Major had become so hasty, overcrowded and under-consulted—as it has continued under Blair—as to make many new policies—for example, in education, health and crime and disorder—flawed and ineffective, though ultimately, rarely with such substantial consequences. Among the mistakes made:

- The roles of the two regulators were muddled, a failure that produced endless friction later. Though deliberately done, I attribute this failure to fix regulatory responsibilities sensibly again to the absence of an adequate description of them in a White Paper or other explanatory memorandum, both initially and when the arrangements were changed after 1997. If properly explained, the very idea of one, an agent of government, setting train service outputs and subsidy and a second, an independent economic regulator, controlling operating and infrastructure spending—moreover doing so at different times—would surely have been seen to be politically unworkable, as indeed it was, though only altered ten years later.
- The first, the *Office of Passenger Rail Franchising* was intended to be an agent of the department of transport—though independent enough to award franchises without political second-guessing—and, as such, provider and guardian of public money: to negotiate the franchises; determine the subsidy each train company received, and therefore indirectly every other part of the system; what minimum service they were to provide for that subsidy; and to monitor their performance. With more time—as should have been taken—to improve financial and operational records—not only the performance but the proceeds would have been better, because bidders would have had more certain information to go on. Labour's opposition threats of re-nationalisation also blighted the bidding process.[46] But in the circumstances OPRAF did as well as could be expected.
- The department initially wanted OPRAF to be the economic regulator as well. But that would have provided the rest of the industry with no safeguards against OPRAF's decisions on the extent and quality of service required for the money given to the train companies. However, the work of the second regulator, the *Office of the Rail Regulator,* was originally and sensibly expected to focus on approving and resolving disputes over the multitude of inter-company agreements, while ensuring that franchising and other outsourcing was as competitive and fairly conducted as possible. Because the Treasury was the source of the money needed to balance the industry's profit and loss accounts, and originally Railtrack was presented as staying government-owned when the legislation and licences were drafted, profit (RPI-X)

---

[46]   D Helm 'A Critique of Rail Regulation', Beesley Lectures, 17 October 2003, 3.

regulation of Railtrack seemed inappropriate.[47] However, the statute defined ORR's duties similarly to those of regulators of privatised industries making monopoly profits, another recipe for confusion. Moreover, the Conservative government later decided to privatise Railtrack. To reassure investors, cost regulation was needed, not as usual to protect consumers against unreasonable profits, but to determine what was a reasonable level of Railtrack costs for the government to finance and to provide an incentive for it to cut that level of costs over time.[48] The initial 1994 cost review wrongly concluded that Railtrack had overestimated its operating costs by about 25%, particularly its maintenance and renewals requirements.[49]

- Another mistake, late in the 1992 Parliament, was the government's decision to freeze most fares. Overall passenger demand had been flat for about 50 years, though with cyclical fluctuations, while rail freight had fallen. When demand rose cyclically, management's sensible reaction, backed by government, had been to curb it by raising fares so as to avoid excessive overcrowding, the need for substantial new investment and to improve financial performance.[50] To increase track capacity on busy routes to accommodate higher demand would have needed yet greater subsidy, as it still does. However, better marketing after privatisation achieved large increases in off-peak traffic BR had not achieved though without an increase in net revenue.

- An important misjudgement was over the privatisation of BR's maintenance and renewal facilities. From the mid-eighties there had been significant improvements in BR productivity, less so in infrastructure maintenance and renewal—British Railways Infrastructure Services (BRIS)—which nevertheless achieved a productivity improvement of about 10% in 1987–8[51]. The consensus among BRIS engineers planning its privatisation—most destined to be transferred to go to one or other of the 13 maintenance contractors—was, first, that a one third reduction in BRIS staff costs was possible—it was achieved in the three years up to privatisation in 1996—and, second, that a further reduction in total M & R costs could be achieved over the three years after privatisation through new capital equipment and the ending of old Spanish customs and other inefficiencies. One of the mysteries is that once these new companies were bid for and acquired by construction and engineering firms, the second round of promised productivity improvements were

---

[47] However a preliminary Railtrack review of track access charges was conducted in 1994 before privatisation.

[48] Its form was the usual one of costs being allowed to rise by total allowable costs, increased to allow for inflation but reduced by a pre-determined percentage each year: RPI-X. See Foster (1992).

[49] A balance-sheet restructuring was therefore undertaken to allow Railtrack to float, borrow the extra funds it needed for maintenance and renewal, and start on the West Coast mainline and Thameslink 2000.

[50] Of the 35% increase in passenger demand after privatisation, nearly half of that increase was due to cyclical factors.

[51] I am indebted to Jim Cornell for this estimate. He was head of BRIS at the time.

not realised.[52] The contractors had three years before their contracts came up for re-negotiation in which to pocket all additional profits so made, but they would, or could, not realise them. Rather they then demanded more money. Insufficient competition had developed to prevent them doing this. Nevertheless to suggest, as some have, that such outsourcing of contracts was bound to fail is wrong.[53] Maintenance is satisfactorily contracted out in many industries, many of them safety-critical. The relations between airlines, aircraft manufacturers, airports and air traffic control regimes are at least as complex as the post-1994 relations in the British railway industry. Yet air travel is sufficiently, but not absolutely, safe.

All other privatisation had such defects which in general were remedied subsequently by co-operation between government, regulator and the private interests involved. In this case these flaws, even the last, were similarly redeemable. But it was not to be. Privatisation was completed just before the 1997 election. As we shall see, the new government was not interested in such co-operation.

CONCLUSION

The 1980s and 1990s saw changes in Cabinet Government as Margaret Thatcher increasingly by-passed and John Major failed to restore it. He was neither the person to build a more robust prime ministerial power base, nor to return to a more robust and painstaking form of Cabinet Government. To find a comparison one needs to go back to monarchy: more active than Richard Cromwell, possibly the closest comparison is with Richard II following the greatness of Edward III. By the end of the Major government a Justinian or Napoleon was needed to codify and otherwise pull everything together. Leo Abse believes John Smith would have attempted it, but that has to be pure speculation.[54]

---

[52] Or insofar as they were, the decline in unit costs from higher productivity were not reflected in the second (1999) contract renegotiations.

[53] Wolmar (2001) 231–38.

[54] Abse (2003) 1–12.

PART 3

BACKGROUND TO THE REVOLUTION

10

The House of Commons: Less Representative, Less Effective

There has been a change this century, and particularly over the last generation, in the attitudes of the majority of politicians. Instead of life in the Commons being the off-shoot of social and economic positions outside, it is now the centre of their lives and ambitions.

Peter Riddell (1993)[1]

Being an MP is a part-time job. There is not enough work to make it full-time. Some try to make it full-time by engaging in futile activities which make it worse.

An ex-minister and old parliamentary hand (2003)[2]

I WILL NOT ATTEMPT a full account of changes in Parliament from the 1980s but only summarise the more important, especially those in the Commons which have reduced its ability to hold the Executive to account.[3]

CHANGING COMPOSITION OF THE HOUSE

Some changes affect MPs directly. The experience and knowledge which helped MPs hold ministers to account had two main sources: their careers and contacts before they became MPs; and the contacts and jobs, many paid, they built up as MPs. Their previous occupations—as businessmen, manual workers, trade union officials, lawyers, other professionals and a host more—and their part-time activities subsequent to election, meant almost always some had direct experience of issues raised in the House. Or could readily consult a friend or acquaintance who had. That breadth of experience, and knowledge of people in and out of Parliament, gave them their power: as RA Butler said, 'a Prime Minister couldn't really wield dictatorial power if it were against the wishes and will of the back-benchers.'[4]

---

[1] Riddell (1993) x.
[2] In an interview with the author.
[3] Riddell (1993) (1998) and (2000). Chapter 1 above argued that most of its other functions can be subsumed under accountability or are secondary.
[4] Butler said Eden had backbench support over Suez: in Herman and Alt (1975) 203.

The breadth of that experience declined from the 1980s. Fewer had substantial previous careers.[5] They became MPs younger. Since leaving university most had short spells in political or related employment while making the contacts to get a seat. The proportion of MPs who had had proper jobs outside politics before entering the Commons fell from 80% in 1951 to 40% in 1992.[6] Even Sir Patrick Mayhew and Michael Howard, who only became MPs in their forties, had tried several times before. Paddy Ashdown at 42 was almost unique among leaders of his generation in being truly a late entrant to politics. In 1981 Anthony King defined a career politician as someone who 'is committed to politics. He regards politics as his vocation, he seeks fulfilment in politics, he would be deeply upset if circumstances required him to retire from politics. In short, he is hooked'.[7] An inducement to becoming a career politician and entering the Commons early was that the sooner one did, the more likely and sooner one might become a minister.[8] Greater career specialisation outside politics also made it harder—even for lawyers and journalists—to combine a successful outside, and a parliamentary, career as had once been common.[9]

Not so much the number, but the quality, of outside part-time jobs available to MPs declined. As an indicator, towards the end of the 19th century 36% of the 460 largest companies had chairmen who were or had been MPs. Still about 20% between the wars, it fell to 4% in the 1970s.[10] In their generation a few, like Jim Prior and Lord Carrington, still obtained top chairmanships and directorships after office. Many acquired board directorships, though usually of smaller companies.[11] But, by the end of the 1980s, the outside world's willingness to pay even ex-ministers had declined sharply. At the same time the salaries of those they saw as their equals outside Parliament shot up. Many MPs felt under more pressure to supplement their incomes.

As we have seen (above, chapter 1) the safeguards the Gladstone era had introduced effectively stopped MPs having an improper influence on the content of legislation or on ministers' decisions. Speaker Weatherill, at the end of the Thatcher period, said examples of sleaze were few in his day and always dealt with by the House.[12] However, the tiny Major majority after 1992 meant defection of even a few could have brought the government down.[13] The behaviour of a very few, ready to threaten this—not always for money—was grist for

---

[5] John Morris remembers Attlee's advice, which he ignored, to establish himself in his profession before going to the Commons.

[6] Sampling *Dod's Companion* suggests most had worked in jobs unrelated to politics, but only for a few years.

[7] King (1981).

[8] Riddell (1993) 263, 269–70.

[9] Riddell (1993). John MacGregor has pointed out that many MPs leaving in 1997 were in financial difficulties, see Trustees (1998).

[10] Riddell (1993) 23.

[11] Cook (1995) 131–33.

[12] Sutherland (ed) (2000) 167.

[13] Oliver in Heywood (1997) 123–42.

the media, who played it up for all it was worth, and brought the Commons into public disrepute.[14] Large majorities after 1997 and 2003 ended that short period.

The remedy for this short-term problem was worse than the cause, Through using the notion of 'conflict of interest', a new Committee on Standards in Public Life greatly diminished the possibility of MPs taking on outside activities—paid or not—which would broaden their experience in ways relevant to the business of the House.[15] By 2000, witnesses to that committee agreed the problem was much diminished by the procedures its first chairman, Lord Nolan, had recommended and by the return of the Blair government in 1997 with a huge majority.[16] But at immense cost. In a few short years Nolan was to show himself more an enemy to the Commons than anyone since Cromwell, when he emasculated it by sending Colonel Pride to purge it of more than half its membership, so creating the Rump Parliament.[17]

So by the beginning of the 21st century, MPs had been transformed from a body with a wealth of experience—in a broad, yet real, sense representative of the nation—into career politicians, most with little past or present experience outside politics. They could spend their lives among their own kind and others in the political classes, instead of week in, week out—in board, trade union, charitable organisation or wherever else in the real world their part-time occupations took them—having to explain just what they thought the government or their own political party were up to.

By the century's end increasing their incomes mostly depended on their becoming and staying ministers, though greater competition meant few stayed ministers long. Keeping their incomes meant not losing their seats. If they did—or otherwise retired from Parliament—their likeliest source of future income would be a peerage or other political job in the gift of the PM. Political parties tried to gain more control over those whom constituencies selected for Parliament. The Labour Party did so successfully as part of the campaign against Militant. By 1997 Blair, as head of the party, exercised great, though not complete, control over who was selected for seats and who might be de-selected once there.

ALTERED CONDITIONS OF WORK: MINISTERS AND BACKBENCHERS

Significant changes in how Parliament worked also made it harder to hold ministers to account. Poor accommodation had crowded MPs together in the smoking and tearooms and in the corridors.[18] They could now spend much of

---

[14] Neill (2000) paras 2.2–2.3; Leigh and Vulliamy (1997). A prominent case was that of Sir John Gorst who tried to trade his vote, asking in return that a hospital in his constituency should not be closed by the government.

[15] Nolan (1995).

[16] Neill (2000).

[17] Clarendon [1645 73], 1826 edn, vi, 215–17; Tanner (1928) 152–53.

[18] I am grateful to Tam Dalyell and Andrew Bennett in particular for these observations of change.

their time in their new offices with their staff and need not know each other well. So MPs began to lose that ability they once had in penetrating ministers' defences which depended on their getting to know each other intimately. Moreover they could as easily watch or listen to speeches on TV in their offices as in the chamber. An emptier chamber made what they said there less challenging to ministers.

Cabinet ministers had spent many evenings in Parliament going through their boxes, but also talking to Cabinet and backbench colleagues. No longer. After 1997—and even more from 2003 when most evening sittings ended[19]—ministers and backbenchers saw each other less, except at arranged meetings.[20] The informal, but often significant, accountability that comes from a chance meeting in the corridor or a chat over tea became rare. Neither, except when they spoke, did many senior ministers commonly turn up to debates about their department's business, or stay to listen once they themselves had spoken. Many—particularly the older ones like Margaret Beckett and Michael Meacher, but also Patricia Hewitt and Hilary Benn among newer members—had enough sensitivity to backbenchers to take trouble over what they said and give fine performances, but others regularly made Labour backbenchers cringe as they sat behind them; and yet in some cases they were even promoted.[21] Others spoke as if in media sound-bites, a few as if no more than playing a record. Ministerial speeches and statements now rarely conveyed new information or indeed well argued old information. Many MPs concluded that ministers had sometimes not troubled to brief themselves on the matter in hand, and that a few, even without shame, sometimes did not know what they were talking about. A glance into the chamber might reveal no more than a junior minister and maybe a whip attending. Their own speeches, however pertinent, could be as if flung into a void.

Parliamentary questions had been a penetrating means of inquiring into ministerial or departmental fault. But MPs now had staff generating massively more questions. More got written answers. Furthermore ministers became cynical in planting questions among their supporters to curtail the opposition's opportunities. Every government-side MP might be handed a wad of 'soft' questions ministers wanted asking. Many questions could be answered easily, but many were political, many obscure. Many required factual answers with tenuous relationship to ministerial accountability. Oral questions could once be more effective because of the greater possibility of penetrating a minister's defences by asking supplementary questions. But the pressure of MPs to have their questions asked, soft and hard, meant supplementaries were often crowded out. The activity of

[19] By 2004 more than a third of MPs wanted their nightshift back, G Hurst, *The Times*, 5th January 2004; also M Chittenden, *Sunday Times*, 4th April 2004.

[20] Already, when I was interviewing MPs mainly in mid-2003, several who had voted for ending sessions regretted it. By 2004, 241 signed a motion to reverse that decision. Amazingly in opposing the reversal, *The Times*, 5th January 2004, did not mention the plight into which it put ministers who for many years (chapters 3, 15) had been expected to work during the day in Whitehall and in the evening in Westminster.

[21] Private information.

a persistent questioner like Tam Dalyell over the sinking of the Belgrano, by which he could return, question-time after question-time, further briefed to ask more penetrating questions, became impossible.[22] Margaret Thatcher and John Major attended substantial parts of important debates. Blair was rarely in the Commons—dropping in for only 5% of votes—except for Prime Minister's Questions and the few other times he spoke.[23] Even in the Iraq debates he did not stay to listen.[24] The contrast with Macmillan, Wilson, even Gladstone in his 80s—patient through hours of debate—could not have been greater.

THE MEDIA TRUMPS PARLIAMENT

Other important changes were in the power and attitude of the media. After 1990 the media undermined parliamentary accountability by depriving MPs of publicity. Simon Jenkins, as editor of *The Times*, scrapped its dedicated parliamentary page, because he asserted it was only read by MPs. It was a symptom of both rapid decline in media attention to Parliament and of media takeover of the Commons' function of accountability.[25] That catastrophic decline, precipitous since 1992, in the attention the media gives Parliament—so that nothing spoken after 4.30 pm is reported and most important matters are in the media before they reach Parliament—has been as much cause as consequence of the fall in the quality of proceedings on the floor of the House.[26]

Prime Minister's Questions now regularly gained most media attention. Once Prime Ministers—up to the first Wilson administration—would not have answered a question belonging to a departmental minister, but increasingly the Prime Minister replied to questions for which he was not statutorily responsible. By the end of the 1990s, it had become a weekly bullfight in which Prime Minister and leader of the opposition gored each other—nothing to do with accountability—and repeatedly exhibiting the raucous activity which the polls showed the public disliked. But many of their followers, at least, were curiously enlivened or depressed by their success or failure.[27] Oddly at the start of the Blair government, William Hague had repeatedly trounced Blair, but it had not seemed to matter to Blair's followers because of his great superiority on television and radio. By 2003 Labour MPs were reassured that Blair habitually defeated Iain Duncan Smith. His replacement by Michael Howard brought back

[22] Dalyell (1987) 14–15.

[23] Cook (2003) 472.

[24] *The Times*, 2nd January 2004, reported his voting record improved to 9%, perhaps because of a greater need to influence backbenchers. On Gladstone, see Jenkins (1995) 301, 445–7, 601.

[25] On changes in the reporting of Parliament see Riddell (2000) chapter 160; before he died Jenkins, almost 80, was the last survivor of more than 400 years of parliamentary rhetoric, perhaps the only member of either House Peter Riddell told me he would go out of his way to listen to as an orator.

[26] Marr (1995) 105–61, esp. 107; Jenkins (1991) 565.

[27] Riddell (1998) 31; private information.

into that arena an opponent more effective than William Hague at cut-and-thrust, though frequently out-shone by the PM. But was that a quality by which a future PM should be chosen?

COMMITTEES

The post-1979 House of Commons committee structure—with a committee shadowing each government department—ought to have made ministers more easily accountable. To some extent it did, but growing partisanship made many committees—with their in-built government majorities—reluctant to criticise ministers. A committee chairman remarked how much easier, because of partisanship, it was for a committee to be critical on comparatively minor issues than on ones of the first political importance.[28] Some had no inclination to be penetrating and exhaustive—so it seemed to Whitehall—rather only to browbeat a civil servant to disclose anything to embarrass a minister.[29] To lessen pressures on ministers' time they interviewed officials as had previously only happened before the Public Accounts Committee and one or two specialised committees.[30] At times they found it difficult to interview ministers and civil servants they wanted.[31] In defending their ministers' policies rather than accounting for their actions, officials found it harder not to appear *political*.

Most committees preferred concentrating on policy, though ministers with their own policy ambitions rarely heeded their ideas.[32] Since 1997 many committees' principal aim has been to maximise media attention which they have found easier with many short reports than with lengthy substantial investigations.[33] One MP recalled the dismay felt after 9 months' work on what they thought was an important subject: it was by then so out of touch with what was commanding public attention that they could not even get a Westminster Hall debate on it.[34]

When committees turned to issues of accountability, relying largely on part-time academic help, they had not the resources for thorough audit and review of individual issues or of departmental performance.[35] Therefore seldom has there been rigorous investigation. Since 1997 the readiness of committees to criticise the government has increasingly depended on whether it had a chairman—like

[28] Private information.
[29] Private information.
[30] E.g. the old Select Committee on Nationalised Industries which was, however, mostly concerned with their accountability, not policy.
[31] Drewry in Jowell and Oliver (1989) 156–58; Woodhouse (1994) 242–43.
[32] Drewry in Jowell and Oliver (1989) 141–64; Woodhouse (1994) 177–217; Riddell (2000) 92–95.
[33] When motivated more by a wish to get a story into the media than to achieve a penetrating and rigorous examination of an issue, expert witnesses could find their questioning unimpressive.
[34] Private sources; also generally my own, admittedly limited, experience.
[35] Even if they had, there would be persistent difficulty in their securing all the papers from departments on individual issues and departmental performance since their rights to demand papers are limited, unlike those of the House of Commons as a whole. Woodhouse (1994) 178–80, 192.

the redoubtable Gwyneth Dunwoody of the Transport Committee—who had a flair for leading and inspiring a committee, and some among its Labour majority, who had lost hope of ministerial office, and were readier to be critical of the government. The decline in the number of Conservative MPs made it sometimes hard for them to spare time for select committees, again reducing their impetus to be critical. As time passed and there were more 'have-been ministers' and 'never-will-be ministers', more committees became stringent in their inquiries and trenchant in their reports. But without routine information or resources of the right kind, with limited ability to press for answers from ministers and civil servants, and without a tradition of pressing their inquiries home, they are usually less effective instruments of accountability than they could become.[36]

Select committees gained from the collapse in the PM's authority in 2003, attracting more media attention. However, the real limits to their effectiveness are how slow ministers generally are to respond to reports as tradition dictates they must; how unsatisfactory government participation in debates on them normally is; and how seldom even the best reports have noticeable effect on what government does. Civil servants point out that, unlike bill committees and the Public Accounts Committee (PAC), but like many debates and other meetings, select committees have no definite functions in the administrative process, and therefore little leverage, to force departments to take them seriously.[37]

An exception, the PAC, has almost the reverse strengths and weaknesses. Legally it may hold officials to account because Parliament gives permanent secretaries as accounting officers a personal responsibility for safeguarding propriety, regularity and value for public expenditure, distinct from any ministerial responsibility. It has a large and dedicated staff—which it had been able to expand while Whitehall staff was cut—able to secure the papers it needs under confidentiality arrangements which are not disabling. Though the topics it investigates are thinly spread over departments and agencies, they cover all aspects of accountability—bar that for policy—including financial and administrative questions, but also now extending to performance review. Its reputation remained high and its activities can be feared.[38] In the National Audit Office it has a more powerful resource than any other parliamentary activity. If genuine accountability, rather than attracting media attention is the objective, it could be the model for the future.

---

[36] Financial if not performance review in the modern sense was closer to the brief of the old Estimates Committees set up in 1912, and in 1971.

[37] Private sources.

[38] Drewry in Jowell and Oliver (1989) 156–58. Even so, it has never explicitly sought a resignation of an official. In general the mechanisms—with the PAC at their apex—which control public money, remain sound in traditional terms. A useful account of them and how they developed is Daintith and Page (1999) 104–206.

LEGISLATION

Not to legislate—that is settle the content of bills—but to ensure new bills are fit for purpose, well integrated into existing law and wholly explicable, has always been a prime focus for parliamentary scrutiny and therefore ministerial accountability. But since the early Thatcher days, the virtual doubling and poor quality of much legislation have overwhelmed bill committees. Discussion throughout Parliament, but particularly in bill committees, was made less meaningful by the fall in the quality of government papers, most evident since 1997. Either the green papers and white papers on which intelligent debate could be based were not there, or they were jazzed up with irrelevances—for example, lists of what were claimed as the government's previous achievements—interspersed with matter in boxes often without obvious relationship to the main argument; and with that argument incomprehensible and incomplete (chapter 14). PR documents in fancy covers and written in sound-bites by spin-doctors are seldom informative in the long tradition of blue-books and white papers of the past. MPs often found them in any serious sense unintelligible.

Too often bill committees demonstrated the random, lack of concentrated thought ministers frequently now gave bills before introducing them. Civil servants commented how difficult it had often become to interest junior, let alone senior, ministers in the content of bills, presumably because it had little effect on their advancement or retention.[39] Not infrequently it was all too obvious when more than one department was involved in drafting a bill, now more common in the interest of more joined-up government. Frequently their different points-of-view were not reconciled before the bill entered Parliament.

Many bills were unintelligible, despite explanatory memoranda. Too many poorly drafted and incomplete bills, their sense altered by amendments arriving at all stages, made impossible any intelligent, constructive scrutiny of legislation by Parliament. One MP remarked that as a solicitor he could not imagine sending a barrister into fight with such poor documents and weak briefing as ministers customarily had in bill committees. The House of Commons Library did its best to replace this function of explanation—which government and the broadsheets no longer performed—by producing short papers trying to explain many matters before the House, but they had not the authority comprehensive and comprehensible government explanations would have had.

Backbenchers admired the agility and knowledge of some ministers—it may be invidious to single out Michael Meacher or Nick Raynsford for, no doubt, there were many more—showed in guiding a bill through committee, but others' lack of understanding of their own bills was all too apparent.[40] They could

[39] Private information.
[40] To a large extent re-drafting was taken over by the Lords, which, composed of people most of whom had had much broader experience, had a larger knowledge base from which constructive comment might emerge.

hardly speak without reference to officials in their box.[41] MPs on both sides might admire the skill with which those leading for the opposition performed their thankless task, but seldom did the government accept an opposition point.

Some government and opposition MPs drew satisfaction from brokering amendments, which might patch patent inadequacies. But with discussion severed by increased deployment of the guillotine, a plethora of government amendments as late as report stage, and other amendments from all quarters, those in the Lords waiting for these bills observed some emerging from the Commons with no greater or even less coherence than when they went in. As a consequence of much effort in the Lords, they almost invariably became coherent and reconciled with previous law. By that time they seldom required interpretation by the judges because of legislative incompetence.[42] But by then their connection with the original policy initiative could be slender. Often all that government seemed to care about were initial favourable notices in the media, not what happened afterwards.

An exception that became more important from 2003, but which no more than proved the rule, was when draft bills were presented for preliminary discussion or there was other pre-legislative scrutiny. Then it was just possible that, if enough Labour MPs got together, they might persuade the government, usually through the Parliamentary Labour Party, to drop the bill or some part of it or at least have a serious re-think. But the motive again was usually to try to alter the policy rather than improve its thoroughness or its practicality, though there was often improvement at this stage, especially with highly technical bills, through the intervention of interested parties[43]. The Lords had become the real lawmaker in that it tended to question and repair the imperfect bills. The absurdity was that the talent and industry of hundreds of people in both Houses were being used first to complicate, and then rectify, the drafting of bills. That whole endeavour would have been unnecessary, if ministers had continued to go through the processes necessary to produce a decent bill described in chapter 4.[44] Through them they had first developed and tested their policies for good sense, public acceptability and practicality before drafting bills which were complete before entering Parliament and already judged to be capable of implementation. In that sense, though in the circumstances vital, so much Commons and Lords' intensive labour could be called a waste of time.

---

[41] Some have told me that this was said of a few ministers even in the 1970s.

[42] Information from Lord Hoffmann. The judges still needed to interpret but seldom because of their technical incompetence, most often because of difficulties in reconciling them with other law. A good account of how the Lords scrutinises legislation is in Oliver (2003) 191–93.

[43] In the past much of this improvement would have been secured at consultation stage before bills entered parliament, but with highly technical bills, this extra stage was an improvement.

[44] The UK has no equivalent to the French *conseil d'état* and *conseil constitutionnel* which scrutinise bills before they enter the legislature: Oliver (2003) 15.

CONSTITUENCY BUSINESS

Old hands and ex-MPs were astonished by the attention newer MPs gave constituency business. But it was without exception true of the backbenchers I spoke to and, from what they said, true of their acquaintances among MPs. Many found it where they were most able to exercise freedom of judgement and achieve outcomes they felt unequivocally worthwhile.[45]

It takes up overwhelmingly the greatest part of their time in their constituencies—where most English MPs feel the need to spend an increasing proportion of their time—but also in Westminster. It—and party seminar-like meetings in which policy is discussed—have replaced MPs' paid and unpaid outside interests as the main source of the knowledge they use for their job. As recently as the early 1990s MPs spent on average 20 hours a week on constituency matters.[46] In 2003 some questioned reported they spent a third or more, and some more than half their time on it.[47] A workload of 1000 cases a month did not seem excessive. Almost without exception, and across parties, they said it was their most worthwhile and enjoyable activity, despite, or perhaps because of their being deluged by constituents' visits, letters and E-mails.[48] A new MP found he spent his first 18 months replacing his predecessor's inefficient 'surgeries' by sophisticated computer systems to provide instantly the information, and the often stock form answers, he needed, rather than go through the protracted process of asking government for that information, or relying on government help-lines. Older MPs thought they needed such back up to keep happy and busy the secretaries and other staff they could now afford to employ.

As local authorities turned more into central-government agencies and lost local profile, constituents with worries became readier to go to their MP than to their local councillor. Some MPs saw themselves rather as a frequently used court of appeal when a constituent could not get redress from the council or other local agency. Some said local councillors could not compete with the resources MPs had. Several said that their best moments were when constituents wrote them a particularly appreciative letter or E-mail. In this way they felt they had influence and gained respect.

---

[45] Elsewhere constituency business could be still more demanding. A Philippine congressman told me he spent 70% of his time on constituents, almost all about local matters and had 46 staff to help him. It made it much harder to get into the national policy questions which were his main interest.

[46] Power (1998).

[47] I spent some time with a number of MPs to discover how they spent their time, how worthwhile they found their various activities and how the functions they performed might be improved. They are listed in my *Acknowledgements*. They are not responsible for my use of what they told me. I am indebted for this inspiration to Tam Dalyell.

[48] True of the sample of MPs I spoke to. Scottish and Welsh MPs could hand much of their constituency work to their regional counterparts. Even so it was surprising how many of them maintained a strong constituency presence; but perhaps not so because of the importance of their grass-roots for re-election.

Moreover it was how to get known locally. Many incidents interested the local press. Particularly if they could sort out an important local problem, they could increase their chances of re-election and ward off the possibility of de-selection. Their constituency business was overwhelmingly local in that both issues and most answers were found there. So they built up networks of those in positions locally to help them deal with the difficult cases. Some told me they estimated that perhaps only 5% to 10% of the matters they dealt with involved any contact—through letter, meeting or PQ—with any minister or otherwise with a Whitehall department or public body at national level. Only a few saw their inquiries as a means of becoming better known to ministers to help advance their own careers.

Hence the high proportion of newer MPs previously employed, or otherwise engaged, in local policy networks (below chapter 11). About 60% of Labour MPs—more of those first elected since 1997—have been local councillors.[49] Others have been local government officers or have worked elsewhere in the public sector. Rapidly declining numbers have been manual workers, in the armed services, in business or have practised as lawyers. Even the once high number of teachers among Labour MPs is declining as they age and are not replaced. The fall in the number of lawyers with substantial court experience—once there always were many outstanding ones—has meant the Attorney-General must be appointed in the Lords. Harriet Harman, when appointed Solicitor-General, was neither a barrister nor a solicitor with a certificate to practise in the High Court.[50]

TALENT, BUT NO LONGER NURSERY?

The other active function of the Commons has been as the nursery for most ministers. There have long been complaints that the pool of talent from which ministers are drawn is small.[51] Just before he died Roy Jenkins opined that the quality and standing of MPs had never been lower. Many have spoken similarly. But that is an injustice. Were the majority who lurk in Chips Channon or Harold Nicolson's diaries, or in memoirs of both sides of the House, remarkable? What of those knights of the shire and silent trade unionists unquestioningly supporting their governments?

It would be wrong to suppose MPs less intrinsically able than their predecessors. It is casual empiricism, but the ministers and ex-ministers I have met seem as intrinsically able as many ministers I have known in the past. So do MPs. There may not seem as many giants, but survival of the fittest depends on processes that encourage it. If fewer have the chance to become giants, that depends on nurture more than nature.

---

[49] Based on a 10% sample of *Dod's Companion*.
[50] Howe, 7 October, 2002.
[51] Riddell (1993) and (1998) 27.

The unintelligibility and waste of much Commons' work makes the prospect of ministerial office more enticing. But the impression has grown that promotion to ministerial office is a lottery and has little to do with merit. Who become ministers depends most on how well known they are known to Blair or Brown or those close to them. While Prime Ministers have always shown a tendency to prefer their friends, Blair and Brown's absence from the House made their circle of acquaintances smaller. Another factor is how well they are thought to perform to the media. Yet another is that they remain 100% loyal to Blair (or Brown). A Mowlam or a Short may be allowed a few outbursts, but one must not be tiresome.

If, as has been argued, so much of what MPs do is unintelligible, or not noticed by senior ministers, or drudgery to rectify the omissions of the Executive, how can they be expected to shine, except, if they are lucky, in ways the media appreciate? Thus the chances an MP has of demonstrating his or her real ability to be a good minister—as opposed to a good media blocker—are fewer than previously. Even more serious, the lower status they have, and diminished status they can acquire by comparison with the past, do not give them the chances they once had to acquire a public reputation. Subsequent chapters will indicate why ministers currently find it harder to be as successful as their predecessors. Again the context in which they work shapes how they appear and how they develop, not their ability, which is probably not less than their predecessors'. Moreover their frequent greater distancing from their civil servants does not allow officials to give the close aid which was once so important in helping them make the best use of their abilities (above, chapters 2–4).

Moreover Prime Ministers have not always been candid when they dismiss ministers. Neither are ex-ministers always candid when dismissed. Prime Ministers have always wanted some ministers to resign because they needed their place for someone else. But this last now seems the norm to the extent that, even if one is lucky to be made a minister, about three years is the maximum one will stay one, because of the press of career politicians avid for office. The main shock of the much-criticised June 2003 re-shuffle was the scant attention paid to such aspirations. Some ministers were brought back who had had their innings, and, in Estelle Morris' case, had admitted they had failed; while another returning had even voted against the government on Iraq. Many are beginning to accept that an unfair promotion system means they will never gain, or in some cases return to, office and therefore they should make the best of what most still regard as an interesting job.

LOYALTY

What kept Labour MPs loyal? For many it may still have been hope of office. For some among ex-ministers there was the prospect of a peerage. For older members other patronage after retirement. For others there was the threat of de-selection. But for most it was memory of how disastrously Labour fared when divided; and the conviction even in 2005 that, as PM, they have the politician most likely to give them another victory, despite the doubts about him which have grown since the Iraq war. Because of a decline in trust, more MPs might rebel, but never enough to jeopardise the Labour government, unless there were a collapse in Blair's confidence or determination, or someone else can be found with enough command over Labour MPs to replace him without turmoil. Did not Japanese Liberal Democrats run a system for decades in which they combined to win elections after which they fell into factions, all bent on neutralising each other?[52]

The consequences could become worse. Almost inevitably—given that constituency business for many is their most rewarding work—the Commons will attract an increasing proportion of new MPs who like that work.[53] If Parliament's main substantive business has become the important, but mostly unexciting and largely invisible one of handling local complaints and grievances, then inevitably sooner or later most drawn to it will be those who most relish such a constituency role.

There is another danger. In the past MPs spent time with all manner of people in their constituencies. But their surgeries and their postbags may—almost without their knowing it—mean they come to know more about, and reflect more, the attitudes of those who are disadvantaged than of those who less need their surgeries or do not fill their postbags. Furthermore the increasingly overwhelming claim constituents' grievances have on their time may tend to interest candidates more with a social work or a similar caring cast of mind, or develop such a cast of mind if they do not already have it. It is good that such attitudes should be amply represented, but not that those backgrounds should deter from Parliament the numerous other kinds of people in Britain with more widely varying backgrounds and experience. Some MPs recognise this trend and make strenuous efforts themselves to overcome it, but the bias may be working its way into the system.[54]

Another consequence has been the merging of backbenchers, and to some extent, ministers, in the new rising class of political advisers and aides. They—together with their often closely-linked media counterparts—have begun to attain the glittering prizes. It was not accidental that, thwarted of their ambitions, able ex-ministers like Mellor and Portillo lodged themselves on media's slopes. Many new MPs have such a background, but there are other job opportunities that led to accusations of jobbery and crony appointments, crystallising

---

[52] I am indebted to Professor Christopher Hood for this comparison.

[53] Riddell (1998) 33.

[54] Devolution means that Scottish, Welsh and Northern Irish MPs have much less constituency work than English MPs. Those I talked to had many different ways of sharing the workload with their regional counterparts. English ministers have much more constituency work than their predecessors which must make it harder to do their ministerial job. English devolution would greatly reduce this workload.

in battles over the future of the House of Lords: over whether it might not become largely a resting-place for the same kind of people. The theory that, given power, officialdom will always aggrandise power and jobs in its self-interest, needs to be re-written with the new political class replacing the bureaucracy as having the power and the incentive to be self-aggrandisers, to multiply the jobs in the regions and London available to them.[55]

CONCLUSION

Chapter 1 argued that the paramount function of Parliament throughout modern times was holding the Executive to account. Rather than that improving in recent times to handle increasing, and increasingly complex and technical, business, it has grown worse. Though the Commons stayed representative in the primary sense that it was elected, in the more fundamental and important sense of all kinds of people, occupations, vocations, and shades of opinion being represented there, it became less representative of the electorate than ever before. But as important the quality of government statements, papers and bills presented to it was too often insufficiently objective, intelligible and complete for effective accountability.

[55] Niskanen (1971) and (1973).

11

The Spread of Grass-Roots Anarchy

We stepped out gaily on a carpet of flowers, little imagining the abyss beneath.

Comte de Segur (on the events of 1789)[1]

So the strong executive, the tradition of 'leader knows best, encapsulated in the "Westminster model", founders on the complex, multiform maze of institutions that makes up the differentiated polity. Interdependence confounds centralization. More control is exerted, but over less. Services continue to be delivered, but by a network of organizations which resist central direction.

Professor Rhodes (1997) [2]

WHILE THE DEVELOPMENTS so far described occurred in the traditional political world of Parliament, Cabinet, ministers and top officials—the focus of political history and biography—changes lower down were altering its foundations.[3] After 1979 central governments tried to centralise power. But government became more diffuse. On balance ministers lost power. Government's centre of gravity shifted downwards. In many respects it became harder to operate.

THE OLD STRUCTURE

The old structure, through which government operated, need only be outlined. There were local authorities, reorganised in various ways from 1835 to 1972; many boards and other statutory authorities with various and often ill-defined relations with central and local government; nationalised industries, often principally composed of forcibly acquired private and municipal enterprises; and other agencies for which ministers were directly responsible. In an ascending curve from the 1870s, but more after 1945, government intervened more in the economy and enlarged the public services. It required a larger civil service, many more public sector employees and higher public expenditure.

---

[1] Schama (1989) 49.
[2] Rhodes (1997a) 3.
[3] These changes in the structure and behaviour of government are described in more detail in Foster and Plowden (1996).

A less obvious characteristic of modern British government goes back to its lack of a written constitution or other formal legal arrangements defining relationships between central government and public bodies.[4] Martin Loughlin has shown how the origins of local government far precede those of central government; how its relations with the monarchy were never defined in common law; and how its powers and duties have been frequently specified and modified—first in charters, then by the courts, then by private acts of Parliament and since the late 19th century more by public statute—without the legal nature of the relationships between central departments and local authorities ever being defined.[5] Likewise the inadequacy of formal legal instruments governing relations (NOSSO in chapter 4)[6] between ministers and nationalised industries or other public bodies meant the power ministers wanted often had to be brokered through similarly informal relationships. Because of the discretion local and other public authorities enjoyed, ministers could not instruct them within existing law and did not pass laws instructing them what to do. While statutes might alter structures and so alter behaviour, they could not prescribe detailed objectives or issue detailed instructions.

This *laissez-faire approach* meant informal relations developed between them—in appearance hierarchical—through which central officials attempted to exert whatever influence the government of the time wanted.[7] Changes in their behaviour came from senior civil servants—or sometimes equally adroit ministers—moving along the *Corridors of Power*—well described by C P Snow—persuading those with discretion to do the ministers' bidding. In most circumstances the best lubricant was more public expenditure, usually available for what ministers really wanted. But by the late 1970s that lubricant had gone.

By then, the growth and stability of the UK economy was defective by comparison with many other nations. It suffered from severely distorted markets because of government intervention: for example in energy supply, transport, housing and agriculture, but in other industries also, both nationally and as between regions. Such distortions were less tolerable economically as the UK economy became more open. There were warnings from India to Russia on what happened when nations tried to operate within closed economies. The public sector could not go on as it had, simply keeping things ticking over and unconcerned with efficiency.

---

[4] David Marquand (1988) has been almost alone among non-lawyers in seeing constitutional modernisation as the key to economic modernisation and to greater political success. Ian Harden (1992), a lawyer, has criticised government's attempts to develop adequate law to govern central government's relations with public bodies. Also Harden (1992).

[5] Loughlin (1996) chapter 1; also Foster, Jackman and Perlman (1980); Butler, Adonis and Travers (1994).

[6] No statement of statutory objectives or NOSSO.

[7] Loughlin (1996) 24.

REDUCING THE PUBLIC SECTOR

In most countries there was public resistance from the late 1970s to public expenditure continuing to rise as a proportion of Gross Domestic Product.[8] It led to more determined and prolonged attempts to cut public expenditure and reduce the size of the public sector. Ministers had to accept painful cuts in their departmental budgets and force them on the public bodies they sponsored, not easy when local authorities or British Steel or British Railways persistently over-spent, despite their promises. That had to change.

In retrospect many consequences of Margaret Thatcher's determination to reduce the size of the public sector and public expenditure seem paradoxical. How did a Thatcherite process intended to roll back the state's frontiers end by multiplying the public bodies with which central government had to deal? Simon Jenkins has written well of the ideological delusion that engulfed a series of ministers, proclaiming each centralising move was a decentralising one: whether Kenneth Baker seeking more control over schools, Nicholas Ridley arguing the poll-tax would make local government more responsible to its elec-torate, Michael Howard enforcing cash limits on the police, or John Gummer describing his new government offices as 'a shift from the centre' and much else.[9] Why did similar changes in other nations accompany decentralisation while here it attempted centralisation? Political scientists, observing them closely, described them collectively as a *diffusion of power*.[10] It was a common and virtually simultaneous reaction against the centralisation of government, and its operation through large hierarchical bureaucracies in many countries: among them the United States, France, Holland, Scandinavia, Canada, Australia and New Zealand.[11] Other objectives beyond reducing public expen-diture were a desire for a public as efficient as the private sector; less bureau-cracy; more freedom to innovate; greater responsiveness to consumer needs; less domination of public services by professional and other producer interests; greater interest in outcomes than inputs; more joined-up approaches to solving social problems that cut across traditional bureaucratic boundaries; and more effective accountability throughout the public sector.[12]

For some years political scientists thought the outcomes of these changes— widely labelled the *New Public Management*—would be internationally similar.[13] One book about the 'reinvention of government' (Osborne and

---

[8] Foster and Plowden (1996) chapters 1 and 2.
[9] S Jenkins (1995) 263.
[10] Comprehensive accounts are Rhodes (1997a) and Smith (1999).
[11] Peters (2000).
[12] Hood (1991); Rhodes (1997a); Peters (2000); Butcher (2002).
[13] Hood (1991).

Gaebler) was in vogue in many countries.[14] But by the 21st century the differences were as marked as the similarities.[15] Exceptionally the Thatcher government did not aim at reducing government through decentralisation. Rather its intention was to reduce the size and scope of government altogether. By contrast right-wing American administrations had inherited a system of government with less domestic scope: much of what British central government did was already the preserve of state and local government or the private sector. Other countries' right-wing—as well as left-wing—administrations were less doctrinaire about trying to achieve smaller government, and readier to see privatisation and contracting-out as means to greater efficiency than as ends in themselves.

PRIVATISATION, CONTRACTING OUT AND AGENCIES

The straightforward method of reducing the public sector was through privatisation of public bodies where Britain led the world;[16] and by outsourcing parts of government activities through franchising and contracting-out; and the parallel requirements placed on local authorities for competitive-tendering.[17] Through these means the size of the public sector was substantially reduced; but few activities entirely removed from the scope of public policy. Within this environment, agencies, statutory public bodies, and in many circumstances private firms and voluntary bodies, operated, often in what was described as a mixed economy.[18] In all cases the legal problems of defining relations between ministers and agencies, local and other public authorities and between them all and the various public bodies were ducked, so increasing the uncertainties of power and for most practical purposes increasing its diffusion.[19] The Treasury kept control over overall budgets and pay-bills, though greater flexibility between departments and different agencies was allowed in pay scales and conditions of employment.[20] The media found a prime source of stories in fanning the public's expectation that public services should not only be as good, but the same, everywhere. Previously central departments had no greater ambition than to ensure local authorities ensured minimum standards, itself a difficult task

[14] A Cabinet secretary (Butler (1994) 263–70) pointed out how similar the principles the UK government adopted in improving government were to those advocated by Osborne and Gaebler (1992); also Moe (1994).

[15] Bevir, Rhodes and Weller (2003) 1–3 and *passim* on that issue.

[16] My own analysis is in Foster (1992).

[17] Foster and Plowden (1996) chapter 8.

[18] On the growing importance of the voluntary sector in public services, see Kendal and Almons (1998).

[19] 'Much of the alleged development towards horizontalisation of institutions and organisations—and indeed of political life more generally—has been a spontaneous and organic development which has yet to be confirmed by changes in legal and constitutional frameworks' Peters (2000) 17.

[20] Hennessy (1989) 621.

when statutes gave discretion.[21] That the public wanted uniformity in its services stimulated further ministerial intervention.

Sometimes the intention was to form a *market* or so-called quasi-market in which a regulator tried to ensure that producers behaved as if there were effective competition. But, as in varying degrees with more complex re-structurings—like those of electricity and rail privatisation and of the National Health Service—the legislation was frequently not drafted rigorously enough, or the proposed methods of operation of the institutions set down fully enough in public documents, for the new markets and quasi-markets to work as spon-taneously and automatically as intended.[22] (The attempted introduction of an internal market in the NHS ran into political difficulties and was withdrawn before it could show what it might have done.) Neither were the legal arrange-ments always strong enough later to avoid their overturn without new legislation by ministers with different ideas, as was to happen after 1997 with railway privatisation.

Yet privatisation had transferred over 50% of the public sector, or 650,000 employees, to the private sector by 1991.[23] Civil service numbers fell from 732,000 in 1979 to 520,000 in 1995, rose again after 1997 but with further large cuts again envisaged in 2004. By 1994 66% of the civil service remaining had transferred to agencies. While public expenditure had fallen by three percentage points of GDP during the 1980s, it was to rise again.

MULTIPLICATION OF PUBLIC BODIES

Margaret Thatcher came in wanting to abolish many public bodies. But a review by Sir Leo Pliatsky killed only 30 out of the 1500 he considered.[24] Instead new ones were formed—some statutory, some not—especially under Major, more under Blair. Among them were Training and Enterprise Councils, the Housing Corporation, Housing Action Trusts, NHS Trusts, Urban Development Corporations, the Highways Agency as well as bodies to regulate, inspect, monitor and audit public sector activities.[25] By the mid-1990s there were 32 major regulatory bodies, like OFFER and OFTEL. 135 more bodies regulated the public sector.[26] There were many new inspectorates. By 2004 the government's Healthcare Commission reported that 102 organisations had the power to scrutinise hospitals.[27] In addition there were European and some other

---

[21] Foster, Jackman and Perlman (1980) 21–38, 573–96.
[22] Discussed in Foster (1992).
[23] Marsh (1991) 463.
[24] Pliatsky (1980).
[25] Flinders and Smith (1998).
[26] Hood, James, Jones, Scott and Travers 'Bureaucratic Gamekeeping: Regulation of UK Public Administration', in Rhodes (2001) 80.
[27] *Times* 9 October 2004.

international bodies with similar jurisdiction.[28] By 1994 two commentators were to calculate that 5500 quangos now disposed of a third of public expenditure.[29] By 2004 the Blair government was reported as successively starting new, and ending existing, quangos, often after only a short life.[30]

Not only did those bodies have a relationship to a central department which 'sponsored' them, but often to many other public bodies, to local government, and to the private and voluntary sectors. To deliver services government used the voluntary sector more: its government income rose by 145% between 1989 and 1993.[31] Trying to get all to reflect a minister's policy change or to consult them over a bill or agree its subsequent interpretation could become exponentially more complicated.[32] While advisory committees had been supervised carefully in the past, some—as happened over BSE at the end in the build-up to that crisis—were now unsupervised long enough to have sudden, serious effects on the economy and for ministers. Relationships had to be negotiated within public bodies: for example, between doctors, nurses and administrators in settling how a hospital was to be run.[33] Hence the networks of the past grew into more complicated ones, frequently overlapping and differing from each other, not only in their functions, but according to the management philosophies and other factors current when new bodies were created. Even with privatisation—probably the best planned of these initiatives—some differences between different privatisations were capable of rational explanation, while others were not.[34]

To indicate how many relationships might need at worst to be worked through in a small policy area, Professor Rhodes gave the example of:

> the implementation structures for AIDS policy in the York-Selby area of North Yorkshire. 13 organisations plan the service and 39 organisations are involved in delivering services. There are 24 HIV positive individuals in the area and 6 have developed AIDS.[35]

LOCAL GOVERNMENT

Reducing local expenditure was most difficult of all. In 1976 the Layfield Inquiry into local government finance had identified an emerging crisis of control and accountability. The incoming Conservative government set about reducing local expenditure (though Crosland had reduced it by more than Thatcher ever did). A conviction grew that local authorities were wasteful and hard to control

---

[28] Rhodes (1997a) 137–62; Hood and James (1996).
[29] Weir and Hall (1994).
[30] S Ward, 'In the line of fire', (2004) *Public Finance,* June 25.
[31] Russell, Scott and Wilding, 395–412.
[32] In reality up to n-*factorial* since relations between every pair in the network could be germane.
[33] E.g. the discussion of the management of care by Charlesworth, Clarke and Cochrane (1996) 66–88.
[34] Foster (1992) chapter 4.
[35] Rhodes (1997b) 31–50.

under existing arrangements. Many new laws were passed.[36] Previously laws had been drafted with enough consensus for central government to use voluntary guidelines to persuade local authorities to respond to a central imperative like a sudden need to cut expenditure. However, the urgency and scale of the new cuts undermined this method. Between 1979 and 1992 143 statutes were enacted in England and Wales with a direct application to local government, 58 effecting major changes.[37] Many attempted to limit the growth of local expenditure, many also to re-structure parts of the welfare state. Some transferred local government activities to other public bodies—sometimes intended as a half-way house to privatisation—while frequently retaining a role for local government. Many functions were progressively taken from local authorities. Among the special purpose bodies replacing local government in the provision of services were Urban Development Corporations.[38] In 1988 grant-maintained schools were introduced as a device for by-passing local education authorities. Nicholas Ridley's ideal local authority would meet only once a year to open the tenders for its services, all contracted out.

Local authorities contrived to circumvent many of these new laws. Sometimes they had to, simply to pay for extra statutory burdens like *Care in the Community*, dumped on them without extra resources to pay for them. But various attempts to evade central control brought their retribution. For such behaviour the Greater London Council and the six metropolitan county councils were abolished. But again the price for their abolition was the creation of more, if smaller, public bodies to replace their activities.

Ministers' now overriding belief seemed to be that they could treat local authorities—as indeed other public bodies—as the headquarters of large private companies were thought to treat their subsidiaries. It was reflected in legislation. One official recalled the nightmare of trying to draft the bill requiring local authorities to have a referendum before they increased rates.[39] Each revision of draft instructions to counsel became more complicated as ministers changed their minds, and officials, including draftsmen, realised that what was emerging was nonsense and could not work. Eventually that bill was shelved, but many as tortuous were not.

A subtle consequence was that local legislation changed from being (1) *facilitative,* that is from *permitting* local authorities to do some things in the way they wanted, (and by implication, not others), to being (2) *instrumental,* or *instructing* them to do so: that is from legislation which provides a flexible structure enabling norms of local authority behaviour to emerge through working practices, to that of legislation designed to establish the norms and control

---

[36] Loughlin (1996) 88.
[37] Loughlin (1996) 383.
[38] Rhodes (1997a) chapter 6.
[39] Sir Geoffrey Chipperfield.

their adoption.[40] The attitude that laws conferred discretion—as of a public trust—disappeared.[41]

Their discretion was now so limited that they had little room for manoeuvre: they were in fact being instructed what to do. Possibly the first was the Right-to-Buy legislation in public housing where, despite difficulties raised by officials and parliamentary draftsmen, John Stanley as minister tried to close every loophole through which local authorities might resist selling off their stock, not unreasonably given the aims of the policy he was instructed to pursue. Contrast Crosland (above chapter 4)—persuaded there was no way he could insist on schools going comprehensive in 1968—with the 1988 Act which forced local authorities to allow schools to go grant-maintained. However, even in its own terms it turned out to be an impossible project, since the new laws were never carefully enough drafted. In conjunction with the existing law, as Martin Loughlin has said, they 'simply contained too many gaps and ambiguities to be susceptible to conversion into an instrument of command-and-control regulation.' Trust between central and local government broke down.[42] Local authorities resorted to every device to get round the new laws and restrictions on their action. Judicial review flourished. Almost invariably it found for central government because ancient custom rather than law prescribed the freedoms of local authorities.[43] The French Revolution had similarly found the then unwritten French constitution defective when relations between parts of government had dramatically come under strain, prompting a flood of new enactments and in that case many attempts at constitution writing.[44]

As we have seen with the poll-tax, consultation became perfunctory—one official referred to it as often a joke—by the end of the 1980s, the quality of explanatory documents declined.[45] Conviction politics made many ministers less keen to let their officials negotiate a wider policy consensus.[46] So as Simon Jenkins said, 'by the time a plan was presented for public consumption, it had developed a momentum . . . that made it near unstoppable.'[47] Complaints about insufficient and ineffective consultation became common. When the Hansard Society considered the matter, trenchant complaints came from bodies as diverse as the British Medical Association, the ITC, BBC, TUC and CBI.[48]

[40] Loughlin (1996) 382.

[41] Statutes conferred duties on local authorities, for example, to educate children, build houses or clear refuse but the understanding was that they had been granted in general terms by negotiation with local authorities and were not justiciable. If a citizen wanted a remedy because he believed an authority was failing in its duty, he should go to the minister, not the courts. What made much 1980s legislation instrumental, though couched in the language of duties, was the narrowing of the discretion granted and the expectation that redress would be through litigation. I am grateful to Professor Loughlin for help on this point.

[42] Loughlin (1996) chapter 3.

[43] Loughlin (1996) 170; also Foster (2000b).

[44] Schama (1989) 299.

[45] Private information.

[46] Norton in Rhodes (2001) 114–15.

[47] Jenkins (1995) 13.

[48] Hansard Society (1992) chapter 3.

Among the reasons why no White Paper set out the policy on the poll-tax, how practical and other objections to it had been overcome and how it was to be implemented, was that convention demanded such papers were circulated through the Cabinet system, not thought desirable for what might again become a contentious policy. Another was that, given all the pressures from arguments with local authorities over grants and other matters as well as drafting the bill, there were just not enough officials to write such a paper.

By such means ministers forced local authorities to reduce expenditure, but never by as much as central government wanted. By 1988, the battle was over. Central government finally won, not through legislation, but because changes to the grant-system, and the growth of universal rate-capping, reduced local author-ities' freedom almost to zero in the absolute amounts of money they could spend.[49] It proved harder to dictate to local government how it should conduct its business in detail than to executive agencies that remained constitutionally parts of a department, but by the late 1990s, many local authorities had become so reconciled to being treated as agencies that they were crying out for guidance on how they should behave.[50] A paradox remained: while central government now controlled local authorities' total expenditure, the mechanics of the grant system meant authorities still had great practical freedom in how they spent that money. But while ministers did not have the control some of them, and the Prime Minister, sought, neither did local authorities have the autonomy they once had.

In the 1990s proposals for new laws further declined occasionally into being (3) *demonstrative* that is, not—at least in their entirety—seriously intended, but promising unsettling changes in the law until local authorities obeyed. An atmos-phere was created in which legislation or just the threat of new legislation, because of the adjustments—often costly—to it needed by those affected, were less intended to alter the law, and used more as an attempt to soften the bodies concerned into compliance with what central government wanted. The process was not happy. A respected local authority leader was heard telling ministers on successive occasions when they introduced a new bill or other initiative: 'This is the blackest day for local government since . . .' the last initiative.[51] Cumulatively centralising legislation and financial controls reduced local autonomy greatly, which the *New Public Management* did almost nowhere else.[52]

LOSS OF GOVERNMENT POWER

But it was worse than that. Throughout the domestic policy areas ministers now faced local policy networks which they had complicated further by adding many

[49] Loughlin (1996) chapter 5.
[50] E.g. on how to operate the new post-committee governance arrangement. I am indebted to Philip Wood for this.
[51] Jack Smart, as remembered by Phillip Wood.
[52] Peters (2000).

extra public bodies.[53] They varied in their complexity from that required for benefits payments—still highly centralised—to cross-departmental issues, like care of the young, elderly and disabled, where numerous bodies were involved. Neither were networks on particular issues the same everywhere, partly because of pilot projects and other local experiments, but also because of diversity in the pattern of local government, itself complicated further in the 1990s. Furthermore the willingness of local networks to co-operate with each other and with central government varied, because of differences in politics, personalities and the relevance of policy initiatives to the needs of the local population as ministers perceived them.

In general ministers' ability to control these networks decreased with their greater complexity and the multiplication of public bodies. In practice the totality of change meant a diffusion of power from the centre, despite many statutes purporting to centralise power. Various attempts were made to achieve greater central control, even before 1997: for example by moving activities from elected local government to appointed bodies. But the multiplication of public bodies and the variety of relationships that grew up, even between those engaged on the same activity in different parts of the country, made central, sometimes any, co-ordination increasingly difficult at a time when public demand for such co-ordination was increasing. Moreover—while ministers had no more detailed control than they had ever had—they were still readily blamed for the shortcomings of the whole public sector, mostly by the media.

BLAME AVOIDANCE

The diffusion of power weakened ministerial responsibility. A consequence, and sometimes perhaps cause—it is difficult to be sure because such motives are readily disguised—of the fragmentation of government and diffusion of power, was that they helped ministers avoid blame. There were two polarities in their relations with their officials which—in other countries as well—ministers tried to avoid:

- Where through a convention like the British one of ministerial responsibility, ministers could be blamed for all the executives under them did, but with the understanding that officials in departments and agencies must fulfil their side of the bargain by running their activities well enough to avoid damaging parliamentary criticism;
- Where the responsibilities of ministers and officials in departments and agencies were so clearly defined—as in New Zealand—that ministers could only intervene where the contract between them allowed it.[54]

---

[53] Marsh and Rhodes (1992).
[54] New Zealand was an exception: Hood (2000).

• Rather they preferred a position where there was an apparent separation of responsibilities; but in practice, as Professor Hood puts it, ministers 'cheat' whenever they have a mind to intervene, whatever assurances have been given.[55]

Among the forms of cheating found are: covert political discrimination in hiring and firing senior civil servants and agency chiefs; blaming the bureaucracy for what is the minister or Prime Minister or their political staff's fault; putting political pressure on civil servants through ending tenure, intervening in appointments, promotion, the awarding of bonuses and performance pay; and using grants or reductions in grants to agencies, and other rewards and punishments, to serve political, rather than announced, objectives.[56]

Where ministers would once have been blamed for their departments' real and alleged misdeeds—for the shortcomings of everything from passports and trunk roads to the NHS and interest-rate policy—now the agency or other public body to which responsibility had been devolved could be blamed when matters went wrong. Or the regulator, the inspecting or the auditing body, or all of these. At the same time, as many pointed out, ministers still took credit when matters went right.

In his analysis of techniques of blame avoidance, Christopher Hood reviews many reasons why politicians, not only in Britain, adopted measures to avoid blame: among them declining trust in politicians, a greater readiness among citizens to give weight to what goes wrong than to what goes right; an electorate quicker to switch allegiances; more lawyers, insurers and political lobbies professionally involved in safety and hazard issues; and more widespread unwillingness to accept adverse outcomes as caused by fate, acts of God, or the fault of the victim or the individual worker.[57] He describes three main approaches to the avoidance of blame. One—of which no more need be said—is to devise policies reducing blame by tackling its causes. Another—to be considered in chapters 14, 15 and 16—is to shift blame by presentational means.

Relevant to this chapter is the third: agency or delegation strategies. Hood points out that they could be consistent with a sound managerialism, that is a genuine delegation of responsibility: in British circumstances, ministers could set the policy and expect to shoulder the blame for it, while the agency had the freedom to manage within that policy and took responsibility for all its actions in doing so. It would be the answer to the problem (NOSSO)—already met several times in our argument—of determining relations between ministers and public bodies: to set down for the avoidance of doubt who is responsible for what and what exactly is meant by management's freedom to manage within the constraints set by a minister's policy. In many cases—even if seen in purely

---

[55] Hood in Peters (ed) (2000); also Hood (2003a) 309–32.
[56] Hood (2003a) and (2003b) notes that officials and agencies can develop their own forms of cheating.
[57] Hood (2003b).

political terms—delegation of responsibility to a public body could be a successful blame-avoiding strategy.

MINISTERIAL RESPONSIBILITY

So no attempt was made to replace the doctrine of ministerial responsibility and the old informality of legal arrangements by more systematic, better defined, adjusted to the often new, superficially more contractual, relations between the Centre and the rest of government. When new arrangements were made such divisions of responsibility were normally fudged. So ministers could often distance themselves from criticism and blame. Sir Michael Scholar remembered being struck by an early example. Under the Banking Acts, 1979 and 1986, the Bank of England had an independent statutory responsibility for supervising banks. Yet when BCCI was closed down, the Chancellor went at once to the Commons and declared his confidence in the Governor and his actions, so revealing the independence was illusory or at best qualified. No wonder Simon Jenkins described the developments discussed in this chapter as culminating in 'Accountability to None' in his book of that name.

Attempts were made to distinguish between accountability and responsibility. Ministers were said to be accountable for all the agencies they sponsored did—in that they must be ready to give an account to Parliament—while responsible for their policy, but not for their operations for which their chief executives were responsible. Despite all the talk of independence, and of giving chief executives more freedom to manage efficiently, many ministers insisted they had the right to overrule the decisions of agency chief executives at will. The split worked while operations were not in the political limelight.

In showing the strict limits to the managerial freedom ministers would give, the classic case was Derek Lewis' sacking as chief executive of the Prisons Agency in 1995. Michael Howard and his chief executive disagreed fundamentally over their respective responsibilities with the first claiming responsibility for policy only, with Lewis responsible for operations. Not an easy distinction to understand in this and other instances since the management of prisons is an essentially operational activity and, at the time, the Home Secretary had no relevant policy advisors outside the Prison Service. As the chief inspector of prisons commented, 'if you are dividing policy and operations it means the Home Secretary is not responsible for anything at all'.[58]

Yet the Home Secretary was deeply involved. The inquiry into Lewis' sacking found he and his executives had submitted more than a thousand documents to ministers in 83 days, of which 37 contained recommendations about operational or policy matters, which it was felt necessary for ministers to see and, if necessary, decide, but without ministers finding time to discuss any of them with the

---

[58] BBC interview quoted in the *Financial Times* 19 October 1995.

agency.[59] Apparently the few prison escapes for which the chief executive was sacked—despite excellent achievement of his management objectives—the minister judged 'operations' and entirely the chief executive's fault, despite this heavy involvement by ministers in the agency, which greatly constrained the chief executive's freedom to act and, among other matters, prevent escapes completely. Or, as the sacked chief executive put it bitterly, 'you . . . invented a new definition of the word "operational" which meant "difficult".' Afterwards the public review of the Prison Service Agency concluded that its arrangements with the Home Office were not greatly different from those typical of an outlying part of a department before agencies were established:

> The Director General needs minimum political involvement in the day to day operation of the service . . . The Prison Service is a politically sensitive area and ministerial involvement is bound to be relatively high. Such a level of upward-focused activity needs to be carefully managed if it is not to interfere with the Headquarters' proper downwards supervision and control of the organisation.[60]

In other words the chief executive must face both ways at once to the detriment of operational management.

Ministers forced the chief executive of the heavily criticised Child Support Agency into defence of its ministers' policies. There were many other complaints of ministers interfering too much in agencies and preventing chief executives improving their efficiency.[61] The practical autonomy an agency had depended on the intensity of media, public and political interest in its activities. That could suddenly alter. Despite their different legal status, many statutory bodies found some ministers similarly overriding their discretion, as had happened with the nationalised industries and utilities.[62] Christopher Hood calls it *cosmetic,* not true delegation. Most seems cosmetic in Britain, certainly in the vital sense that ministers reserve the right to intervene when they believe an issue politically important—whatever the cost to efficiency and management—and in the tendency to blame a public body, even when ministers have helped cause the problem. Moreover quarrels over who should take the blame are not just between ministers and such bodies, but horizontally between them as well as between regulators, inspectors and auditors. Therefore diffusion of power in general has diffused responsibility and made it harder to apportion blame fairly. Both blame avoidance and intervention were to become more widespread after 1997, but the foundations of both had already been laid. It was another factor making it less possible for Parliament to hold the Executive to account.

But as Hood also points out, systematic blame avoidance had another consequence. Accountability frustrated can turn into vendetta. If ministers can slide

---

[59] Learmont (1995) 93. Lewis' account is in Lewis (1997).
[60] Learmont (1995).
[61] Smith (1999) 196.
[62] My first experience was a member of the LDDC in the eighties where Nicholas Ridley had stopped us mounting a programme to offset some bad social effects of redevelopment.

out of accountability for important matters, they will be held accountable for those they cannot avoid, though of no significance to the quality of government: for their sexual behaviour and even small financial irregularities. No wonder also that lawyers were found saying that since Parliament could not make such a fragmented public sector accountable to it, the courts, as in the USA, might have a better chance (chapter 19).[63]

CONCLUSION

As political scientists put it, there was a diffusion of power from the Core Executive. Rod Rhodes described it as follows:

> gone forever are the hoary clichés of prime ministerial power replaced by a recognition that power is everywhere and understood through the language of dependence, networks, governance and choice.[64]

Arguments about whether political power belonged to Parliament, Cabinet or Prime Minister were said to have become misplaced because power was increasingly based on 'dependency', that is, negotiation, not command.[65] The influence a particular actor or institution has on what happens depends on its information, legal powers, prestige, previous record of success, but also on the time it is ready to spend on a matter relative to other uses of management time.[66] No longer was government confined to the nation-state, but could involve institutions from the local to the international, many not in the public sector. Business globalisation and international political arrangements were other tendencies limiting central government control over its own national institutions. Hence government, or governance as political scientists commonly began to call it, was not about legal power, let alone sovereignty, but about influencing, guiding, steering 'without presuming the presence of hierarchy.'[67]

The outstanding question, which needs to be answered, is whether instead of such chaos, it remains possible to have a working, workable and deliberative, representative democracy in the circumstances of the 21st century, which is also well-managed and efficient.[68] These changes between them undermined ministerial responsibility and parliamentary accountability, and therefore representative democracy. What happened in politics came increasingly to depend on people's ability—from ministers to pressure groups—to lobby and manipulate the system.

---

[63] Oliver (2003) 11–14.
[64] Rhodes in Smith (1999) xv.
[65] Smith (1999) 2.
[66] Smith (1999) 4.
[67] Rosenau in Rosenau and Czempiel (eds) (1992) 14; Osbourne and Gaebler (1992).
[68] Kettl (1993).

The diffusion of power makes it harder for the citizen to know where to complain. Once one could be reasonably sure: if about traffic conditions, to the local authority; if about a driving offence to the police or at the magistrates' court; about the railways, to British Rail. Since fragmentation and habitual blame avoidance, it becomes much harder. How far is the local use of speed cameras the local police's choice, or the result of Home Office directive or pressure, or the consequence of an acute shortage of local police funds? How far is the local re-setting of traffic lights, which seems to cause so much extra congestion, a local political decision or the direct or indirect effect of intervention from on high in Whitehall? Where could one have found out the thinking and the decision-maker, preferably before it happened, and protested? Half of London's Rosebery Avenue is dug up and therefore congested for months.[69] One calls the boroughs of Islington and Camden. Do they accept authority? No. Or the police? Not their responsibility? Or the Highways Agency or Transport for London? Not theirs. Or the utility company? They say they have no responsibility for congestion, though their roadworks caused it. What about the utility's Regulator? Only at the next periodic review and probably not even then. Only when the *Evening Standard* gets interested does anything happen.

But there was another aspect to it all. Britain was about to have a Prime Minister who believed it both right and a practical necessity to instruct in great detail, if he so chose, that which any part of government and the public sector should do. Halévy, the French historian of England, had observed that because England became a centralised monarchy earlier than others, our liberties' greatest protection was not the law—absent in many areas where other nations' constitutions enshrined rights—but the inefficiency of our government institutions and processes.[70] That almost alone had stopped—and continued to stop—central government from being over-mighty.

[69] An actual example from the work of the RAC Foundation which I chaired from 1997 to 2003.
[70] Halévy (1924) 44.

PART 4

THE REVOLUTION

12

Blair's Cabinet: Monarchy Returns

You may see a change from a feudal system of barons to a more Napoleonic system.

Jonathan Powell before 1997 election[1]

Absolute power tends to corrupt absolutely.

Lord Acton[2]

B LAIR AND THE circle around him wanted as commanding a position over government as Margaret Thatcher had in her middle years, but without the weaknesses in her use of Cabinet and the Cabinet system that brought her down.[3] In Blair they had someone of equally great, but different, abilities. When his iron grip over ministers and backbenchers weakened in 2003, what returned was not Cabinet, or rather not a Cabinet system, but a talking shop reminiscent of 18th and 19th century Cabinets, though with far more to do. Power stayed with the circles round Blair and Brown. Not just Cabinet, but Cabinet's traditional functions were less important to him than to any previous Prime Minister.

PREPARATION FOR POWER

Before the 1997 election, when the Major government was about to fall, the presumption in Whitehall was that Labour ministers, out of office for 17 years, would need all help possible on how to do the job. No shadow Cabinet member—and therefore none in Blair's first Cabinet—had been in Cabinet before.[4] The only survivor of Callaghan's Cabinet was John Morris, but he was outside Cabinet as Attorney-General.[5] Gerald Kaufman re-issued his witty *How to be a Minister,* but its advice was relevant to a bye-gone age.[6] Well-wishers

---

[1] Quoted as from 'a figure then as now very close indeed to Mr Blair' in Hennessy (2000) 478; Rawnsley (2000) 27 revealed Jonathan Powell as its author.

[2] *The Oxford Book of Quotations* attributes this familiar quotation to a letter Lord Acton wrote to Bishop Mandell Creighton.

[3] On Thatcher as Blair's example: Seldon (2004) 450.

[4] A version of this chapter's argument was Foster (2004a).

[5] His most experienced ministers were John Morris and Ivor Richard who had been an EC Commissioner. Neither was ever asked for an opinion on how Cabinet or any other aspect of government might be run, or anything else outside their direct responsibilities.

[6] Kaufman (1980); new edition (1997).

engineered initiatives at Templeton College, Oxford, and in London to help new ministers learn the ropes, but their juniors and special advisers attended more than they did.[7] If collegiate Cabinet Government were to have a chance of restoration, a lesson from the past was that the centre of government—Cabinet Office and the Cabinet secretariat—must be strengthened to help avoid past mistakes. Some advice was given to Blair's advisers in opposition regarding how it might be done.[8] Its tendency was not just to re-build the Cabinet so as strengthen its executive supremacy, collective responsibility and Cabinet solidarity, but also to create a Cabinet office better able to ensure departments devised laws and implemented policies with thoroughness and practicality.

PREMONITIONS

But they were not listening. They equally saw the system needed strengthening, but largely by importing more political advisers: media handlers, policy advisers and others to handle the Party and the unions. The civil servants, who were to work with them, would do so almost entirely on their terms.

Premonitions of what was to come were that shadow ministers had been permeated by suspicion of the civil service, stimulated by folk memories of Labour failures in the 1970s, but as much by the vividness of *Yes, Minister*. Labour thought Thatcher politicised the civil service, though (above chapter 14) they were wrong to do so.[9] Many officials, expecting more change, wondered at how Tory many of their policies and attitudes were. Jonathan Powell, Blair's chief of staff in opposition, was brother to Charles Powell, Thatcher's closest and longest-serving policy aide who had observed Thatcher's great days, her fall and the first months of John Major.[10] As described above in chapter 8, Andrew Adonis, now on Blair's staff, had drawn his own conclusions from the poll tax on how policy should be made.[11] Bernard Donoghue, battered by his experience as head of Wilson and Callaghan's policy unit in the 1970s, advised on a 'more powerful Downing Street operation', not dissimilar from that adopted.[12] Peter Mandelson and Roger Liddle had written in 1996 that Blair's leadership would

---

[7] I organised a network of retired permanent secretaries, one for every designated shadow minister. Most met, but generally only once. Bower (2004) 202, reports the Templeton meetings actually increased ministers' antipathy to civil servants. Gordon Brown and his court apparently condemned Sir Terence Burns, his permanent secretary, and Alan Budd, his chief economic adviser, before entering office. For Blunkett's disdain for his civil servants, see Pollard (2005) 228 ff, 270.

[8] Peter Mandelson and Jonathan Powell invited a paper from Sir Patrick Nairne and me on *Strengthening the Centre of Government* before the election, which went through several drafts.

[9] It was also what may be called the *Guardian* view as exemplified in H Young (1989).

[10] Kavanagh and Seldon (1999), 241; 'It was sometimes difficult to establish where Mrs Thatcher ended and Charles Powell began', Sir Percy Cradock, quoted by Hennessy (2000) 406.

[11] Ironically, by 2003, Pat McFadden told Robin Cook that the No 10 Political Unit had to fix political problems for the Policy Unit because of the PU's lack of political sensitivity: Cook (2003) 249.

[12] Donoghue (2003) 334–35.

be as centralised as Margaret Thatcher's, if not as uncompromising and domineering. They hinted—more easily detected with hindsight—that an inflexible, overlarge Cabinet, composed of too many equals, would be replaced by a more personal control of government.[13] They assimilated one model from business for conducting Cabinet meetings as if board meetings: that of the chairman/chief executive who dominates discussion, takes all decisions and whose colleagues are little more than a rubber stamp. If executive members have a difference with the chief executive, they settle it outside the boardroom. Just before the election Blair told the Newspaper Society, 'People have to know that we will run from the centre and govern from the centre' which about a year later he defined as 'my office, the Cabinet Office and the Treasury'.[14]

THE TAKE-OVER OF No 10

Despite these warnings, the initial shock was great. First-time Prime Ministers had entered 10 Downing Street before with euphoria, but tentatively and with hesitation, expecting to learn on the job how it and the Cabinet secretariat worked, while plunging into immediate issues. It was doubted if Blair even read the initial briefing the civil service prepares for incoming Prime Ministers.[15] Instead, Blair and his twenty-plus aides—more special advisers than ever before and to be increased—entered as a team, knowing what relations they wanted with each other, with ministers and their special advisers and, most important, the media.[16] Though without a blueprint, they took over the pitch like a well-trained football team passing well and with many rehearsed moves up their sleeves. The Civil Service seemed to win one battle by insisting the Prime Minister's principal private secretary be one of theirs rather than Jonathan Powell, Blair's chief policy aide in opposition, but it was a Pyrrhic victory, since Powell took on the more important role of Chief of Staff.[17]

The civil servants round Blair were kept at a greater distance than before. With few exceptions, they never got to know him as well as his aides did.[18] So

---

[13] Mandelson and Liddle (1996) 232–42; as published it was watered down so as not to clash with Labour's official policy: Seldon (2004) 163.

[14] Hennessy (2000) 476–77.

[15] Private information. Seldon (2004) 416 says they stopped because the chemistry was too bad, Brown being especially awkward.

[16] Kavanagh and Seldon (1999) chapter 10; Hennessy (2000) chapter 18.

[17] By an order-in-council in 1995 special advisers had been confined to an advisory role which formalised a previous understanding that in general they were not permitted to instruct and manage civil servants. Knowing in advance that Blair wanted special advisers to head his administration, press office and policy unit, the Cabinet Secretary asked the senior parliamentary draftsman if that was consistent with the 1995 Order and was told another was needed. It formally gave special advisers this authority for the first time.

[18] Prime Ministers' principal private secretaries—like other ministers' private secretaries—had been their close confidantes and office managers, with the first role the more important. Under Blair that was no longer so. Previous PMs had generally had briefing on all matters both from the Cabinet secretariat and their private secretaries, with the Policy Unit putting in a third if it chose. The

politicised and media-fixated were their mindsets that Tony Blair was said to have judged that Robin Butler, the Cabinet Secretary who had been policy-making all his professional life, 'was unable to analyse problems and produce a delivery plan for implementing solutions'.[19] Previously the civil servants had always won out over the special advisers in the end, as under Thatcher, because sooner or later they were found quicker, less opinionated and more reliable. Now they were given no chance to show these qualities. But in breaching that previously-thought traditional, even constitutional, partnership link between minister and civil servant—as relevant to the Prime Minister (and Gordon Brown) as to any other minister—the machine was at once incapable of sustaining collegiate Cabinet Government, or co-ordinating interdepartmental activities as it had done through the Cabinet secretariat, or, equally important, as will appear, helping to ensure reasonable objectivity and truth-telling in papers and statements to Parliament and the media.[20]

THE BLAIR CABINET

The new Labour government started as it meant to continue. Blair's Cabinet was not conducted like his shadow Cabinet in opposition.[21] More like a traditional Cabinet, that had discussed policy and tactics, but what Blair and his aides had been secretive about—shadow ministers wrongly thought it incompetence rather than guile—was over who was to get what Cabinet job and how irrelevant the Cabinet was to be to policymaking after the election.[22] There were to be no Cabinet decisions. The decision to hand interest rate determination to the Bank of England was taken before Cabinet first met.[23] Besides Blair and Brown, only Prescott and Cook knew, though they had no part in the decision. When Robin Butler—still Cabinet secretary—remarked that transferring

private secretary's brief pulled it altogether and summarised the issues. It was the crux of the relationship since it provided a chance for the civil service to comment on the objectivity and truth of what reached the Prime Minister and, for example, the accuracy of statements it was proposed he might make. Now he got usually one brief from the Policy Unit, later combined with private office into the Policy Directorate.

[19] Bower (2004) 205.
[20] Up to then it had been recognised that in general because ministers had the statutory responsibilities, anything the Prime Minister said in an official capacity must be checked with the department, or departments concerned for factual accuracy and consistency with law and agreed policy. That tradition has now lapsed, as the Ecclestone affair showed.
[21] Information from Lord Richard who was in both shadow Cabinet and Cabinet; also Mowlam (2002) 75; Kampfner (2003) 14–15.
[22] Information from Lord Richard; J Jones (1999) 318.
[23] Draper (1997) 26–34; Hennessy (2000) 480–81. Unlike devaluation and other macro-economic decisions, which must be taken rapidly and secretly, there was no need for speed in this case, though this claim has been made: Draper (1997) 34. When Blair was asked if he wanted a paper on the subject, he said no: Rawnsley (2000) 32. The Treasury was even more offended that they had no prior warning that Brown at the same time told the Governor of the Bank he was to lose his regulatory functions.

monetary policy to the Bank of England was a major decision which Cabinet must be expected to endorse, Blair misunderstood the point and said, 'Don't worry, the Cabinet will agree.'[24]

When Clare Short, on resigning in 2003, condemned Blair for disregarding Cabinet, the main incident she recalled was the Cabinet discussion in June 1997 whether to abandon the Millennium Dome. Momentarily ministers thought they were asked for a decision, but it was for an expression of opinion. Blair left the room, leaving the chair to Prescott.[25] Although the majority was against the Dome, Prescott concluded the discussion by gaining agreement that the decision 'should be left to Tony'. Subsequent experience showed that the Cabinet majority was the better judge of public opinion as throughout the Dome's sorry history.[26] Thereafter Clare Short could not remember an occasion when Cabinet was asked to make, or had made, a decision.[27] The closest was when a few ministers—worsted in legislation committee—asked that bills they wanted should be reconsidered for inclusion in the legislative programme; but the decision on that, as on everything else, was taken afterwards by the Prime Minister.[28] But Blair and his immediate coterie of advisers—or Brown and his—took most, and, as we shall see, they had a different focus.[29] Moreover neither was much interested in implementation.

Without decisions or discussion of issues, Cabinet meetings rarely lasted more than an hour, sometimes less. As under Major there were no papers.[30] Short recalled only ones on the legislative programme, outlining what was to be in the Queen's speech, and none on policy. For the first time since 1916 there was no detailed agenda.[31] Blair hated formal meetings. He was not good at teasing out issues and he never seemed to be able to talk freely except to his closest advisers. Rather what was called a more 'organic discussion' developed, often hard to minute, and which Brown might ignore, ostentatiously reading papers.[32] The foreign secretary had long made an oral report on foreign affairs, a practice extended to 'parliamentary', 'economic', sometimes Northern Ireland and, for a time, also to 'European' affairs. But Cabinet now rarely discussed ministers' individual items of business. For example, the Cabinet was not involved in the early discussions of the Euro.[33] Exceptions were when there was

[24] Private sources; Rawnsley (2000) 33.

[25] Private sources; Rawnsley (2000) 54–56, 85.

[26] NAO (2000); W Jennings (2003) shows the low public support in polls from August 1997 to December 1999.

[27] Corroborated to me by Chris Smith for the first four years and by Lord Richard for the first year of the Blair administrations; also Cook (2003) 115–16.

[28] Interview with Clare Short 11 June 2003.

[29] Private information; Seldon (2004) 499.

[30] Robin Cook complained that he alone among ministers put a paper to Cabinet: Cook (2003) 63. Many excellent papers were written for Blair and Brown, and no doubt for other ministers, but were almost never made available to other ministers. Private information.

[31] Hennessy (2000) 481. Short recalls that at 'political Cabinets' at Chequers they would get papers on polling; also Cook (2003) 246–47.

[32] Draper (1997) 35; Bower (2004) 236.

[33] Rawnsley (2000) 76; Naughtie (2002) 130–32.

a crisis like BSE or the fire brigade strike was about to burst into the media, when the minister concerned might make a brief oral report. But these did not provide the occasion for discussion. The important new item was the Grid: next week's plan for the timing of ministerial announcements and for avoiding their possible clash with other political, cultural and sporting events.[34] For the first time the government's chief press officer, Alastair Campbell, regularly attended Cabinet meetings. The focus of almost all that was said—it cannot be called discussion—was on the Grid, the media and other presentational matters. Cabinet was now for chatting about next week's business, keeping everyone broadly aware of what was going on, laying down the messages on leading topics if door-stopped by the media.[35] Formal decisions were reached on the legislative programme and public expenditure, but without substantive discussion.

For a while an inner Cabinet of Blair, Brown, Prescott and Cook was thought the real decision-maker; it never was and soon stopped meeting.[36] Ministers believed Blair and Brown took the more important decisions in private.[37] Consulting Cabinet, as frequently reported in the media, became a euphemism, put out by the press office, for Blair consulting those he chose to consult.[38] Collective responsibility became a discipline he imposed on his ministers rather than based on a voluntary understanding by ministers of what was in their collective interest. It was prudent to show Cabinet solidarity, but, untested in discussion, it was often skin-deep. In 2000 he was to be openly dismissive of Cabinet Government, recalling the 1970s 'the old days of Labour governments where meetings occasionally went on for two days and you had a show of hands at the end.'[39]

Later in 2000, when the going became choppier, what Chris Smith called occasional 'discursive' discussions began.[40] Without a Cabinet paper to crystallise issues, and a few hand-written notes rather than the carefully crafted chairman's brief of the past, the Prime Minister would indicate the position on the topic as he saw it for perhaps ten minutes. Brown would follow, briefly supporting him from an economic slant, not disagreeing with him in front of Cabinet. Then the Prime Minister would ask everyone's opinion. All would chip in with their thoughts, trying to contribute something useful. Prescott was always loyal; Mo Mowlam, Clare Short and (rarely) Robin Cook might express a different view. If passionate about an issue, you could express that passion, but were nonetheless disregarded. Without papers or other preparation, and

---

[34] Hennessy (2000) 481. When Jo Moore made her fateful announcement on 11 September 2001 about putting out bad news under cover of the attack on New York, she was following one principle embodied in the Grid.

[35] Chris Smith; Lord Richard. I am indebted to Professor George Jones for reminding me that chatting about next week's business has long been an item on the Cabinet agenda, but not virtually to the exclusion of other business.

[36] Hennessy (2000) 401.

[37] Interviews with Chris Smith; Lord Richard.

[38] J Jones (1999) 119.

[39] Rawnsley (2000) 52.

[40] Interview, 8 July 2003; also Cook (2003) 166.

with it being actively signalled that disagreement was not expected, ministers were more likely to embellish rather than contradict what the Prime Minister said. The few dissenting voices he would mention only briefly in summing up, when he usually reasserted the conclusion with which the discussion had begun. As Robin Cook said, 'Normally he avoids having discussions in Cabinet until decisions are taken and announced to it'.[41]

Cook also spoke of the first Cabinet discussion on Iraq as 'a real discussion at Cabinet at last,' though Clare Short, who had demanded a discussion, remembered it as a poor thing.[42] During the immediate build-up to the Iraq war, there were 24 discussions[43] when Cabinet feeling was generally against Blair.[44] Thereafter as Blair's reputation declined and Cabinet solidarity crumbled, discursive discussion in Cabinet became more frequent.[45] Cabinet took the decision to go for the Olympics and there were heated discussions over foundation hospitals and top-up fees. No 10 used such occasions to maintain that in some sense Cabinet Government survived.[46]

But it was Cabinet without system.[47] How could systematic, post-1916, Cabinet Government return without the civil service staffwork, the preliminary interdepartmental meetings, the objective reviewing of evidence, the detailed analysis, the working up of preliminary papers and finally of a Cabinet committee or Cabinet paper in which the issues to be settled were expressed as clearly as possible?[48] A gulf lies between taking a decision, with the relevant facts carefully evaluated after good staffwork, and an unscripted discussion, when not more than one or two know in any depth what they are talking about, and unsubstantiated opinions flash across the table. An infinity of difference exists between meetings genuinely meant to test whether there is agreement based on an understanding of the issues, and those intended merely to endorse or tinker with the presentation of what has already been decided. Arguably it was worse than that. Given all their pre-occupations and other pressures, ministers often felt that they knew little more, if at all, about an issue outside their immediate policy area raised in Cabinet than any broadsheet-reading member of the public.

Except briefly in Cabinet, and then ineffectually, ministers generally saw so little of each other that there was no chance for cohesion or solidarity to develop.[49] Robin Butler's urging the use of Cabinet committees to consult more

---

[41] *Sunday Times*, 5 October 2003.
[42] Cook (2003) 212–13.
[43] Butler (2004) paras 609–11.
[44] Seldon (2004) 572.
[45] *Independent*, 1 September 2003.
[46] Private information; also Alastair Campbell's evidence to the House of Commons *Foreign Affairs Committee*, 25 July 2003, where (Q1043) he maintains 'policy decisions are taken by the Cabinet, headed, as you know, by the Prime Minister.'
[47] Butler (2004) paras 606–11.
[48] When the MP, Graham Allen, asked a PQ on when Cabinet had last discussed an issue with a paper circulated before the meeting, he was told implausibly he could not have an answer because of the 30 Year rule, Allen (2003) 89.
[49] Bower (2004).

widely among Cabinet colleagues also fell on deaf ears: 'we find the discussion is stripped of politics and lacks drive'.[50] A full range of committees was created, but most important ones met infrequently, many not at all.[51] Brown was so averse to discussion that he might not turn up, or send a deputy; if he came and chaired it, he could end discussion in a quarter of an hour, despite several weighty matters before it.

The most traditional and effective committees in the early years,[52] when constitutional reform was rapid, were those chaired by Lord Irvine, but he was replaced by Margaret Beckett on the future legislation committee after ministers indicated resentment at being asked, sometimes not unreasonably, if their many proposals for bills, almost all manifesto commitments, were necessary or, if they were, could be shorter or more clearly expressed.[53] Many resented the detail he, like Thatcher, expected, instead preferring to bargain about priority to various measures in the legislative programme, while avoiding the precision in the use of words that Cabinet and Cabinet committee papers had once demanded. They saw such clarity, or thoroughness, like 'delivery', or practicality, as a later job for civil servants, not as a joint endeavour. It was called implementation. Moreover, then and in succeeding years, that a bill was ready in more or less complete form had virtually no influence over its being preferred to others which were not; so helping continue the headlong rush—as characteristic as in the Thatcher and Major years—of incomplete and often incomprehensible legislation bewildering and tormenting Parliament.[54]

Numerous other formal and less formal committees and meetings, as well as bi-laterals between ministers not including Blair, produced policy recommendations. Unlike the discussions Blair was involved in, they could involve masses of paper, often highly technical, frequently produced by academics and management consultants. Many were devoted to joined-up government, such as policies affecting the young, the disabled, ethnic communities, the elderly and the socially excluded or poor.[55] The seminar atmosphere caused one official later to comment that the abundance of paper often seemed in inverse proportion to the importance of the subject.[56] A committee on *Improving the Public Services* might find itself discussing papers on *Leadership* and *Contestability*. These committees became an important occupation for junior ministers and contributed to the surfeit of policy initiatives at the centre.

---

[50] Kavanagh and Seldon (1999) 268.

[51] Kavanagh and Seldon (1999) 274.

[52] An exception was the Public Expenditure Committee. Initially it worked by using its members—Cabinet ministers without spending departments—to take turns putting over a Treasury brief on each department's proposed expenditure rather than resolving disputes or settling priorities. J Jones (1999) 126; Lord Richard.

[53] Andrew Grice, *Sunday Times,* 7 December 1997. On Irvine chairing a committee, see Cook (2003) 32.

[54] Private information.

[55] Mandelson was said to be a strong influence here: see John Lloyd, *The Times,* 5 December 1997.

[56] Private information.

However, the conclusions of meetings at which Blair was not present—except in areas Brown dominated—became only recommendations *ad referendum* Blair, unless he was uninterested in them, or they seemed unimportant when they would be allowed to stand, though often without much effect unless thought to have his support, or Brown's.[57] But they might be vetoed or simply disregarded by him. So ministers' relationships with the PM altered. They could be kept waiting for ages for a decision from him, or an agreement with their decision, sometimes until they found he did not intend to make one. They could occasionally get away with making their own decision, but at other times no sooner did they announce one than No 10 contradicted it.

Among those committees which never met was the Overseas Committee, not even over Kosovo, Afghanistan or Iraq.[58] However, as war in Iraq came nearer, Clare Short recalled the civil service drew attention to the need to form a war Cabinet.[59] It consisted of the Prime Minister, Alastair Campbell (on one side of the PM, the civil servant taking the minutes was on the other) Jonathan Powell (his chief of staff), Sir David Manning (his foreign policy advisor), Sally Morgan (his political director), the Foreign and Defence Secretaries, and Short. Extraordinarily, neither the Cabinet Secretary nor Sir David Omand, with whom responsibility for the intelligence services rested, attended.[60] Blair would speak several times. The service chiefs, Straw and Hoon would report, but disagreements and difficulties never surfaced and any such were handled separately in bi-laterals with the PM. Although Hoon was known to be under considerable pressure from those under him in Defence to make a stand on various points, these were not brought out in the war Cabinet where the atmosphere was wholly one of trying to please the Prime Minister.[61] Blair and a group of close associates took the real decisions on Iraq.[62]

It was at such 'sofa' meetings—so-called because they usually took place in his study round his sofa instead of in the Cabinet Room which had been normal with his predecessors, but where he was never comfortable—that the PM's

[57] Since the 1970s previous practice had been that Cabinet committee decisions were allowed to stand as if Cabinet decisions, unless the Prime Minister or the departmental minister concerned—but only with the agreement of the committee chairman—wanted to bring it to Cabinet.

[58] Neither did Cabinet meet between 25 July 2002 and 19 September 2002 while the Iraq dossiers were being prepared: P Riddell, *Times*, 18 September 2002.

[59] However it was not where the decisions were taken: Seldon (2004) 580.

[60] The most unexpected and—before Blair—unprecedented presence was Sally Morgan's, a tribute not only to her rapidly growing personal influence over him, but also to the importance now attached at every stage to judging how an issue would play out in the parliamentary and national Party, and in the unions, a role which in the past—at least for MPs—had been the Chief Whip's.

[61] Clare Short interview. A smaller group, which excluded Short, among others, without telling her, 'of key ministers, officials and military officers provided the framework of discussion and decision-making within government', meeting 25 times: Butler (2004) paras 609–10.

[62] The PM found the Overseas Committee too formal and 'insignificantly focussed' so he preferred sofa meetings with Scarlett, Dearlove, Boyce, Manning, Powell, Campbell and Morgan: Seldon (2004) 580.

decisions were often made, sometimes without another minister present, but with political advisers and selected officials. In dealing with individual ministers and their business, Blair relied even more than Thatcher on bi-laterals as his normal way of doing business: the best way for a minister to secure agreement to a policy or other decision he wanted, but only if he could squeeze a meeting into the Prime Minister's crowded and ever-changing diary, and then only if what he proposed was what Blair wanted to hear. If not, the minister might be asked to try again, often with only a confused idea of what was wanted from him, so persistent was Blair's dislike of confrontation.[63] Cook was to speak of Blair's 'immense capacity to leave the last person who spoke to him with the impression of total agreement'.[64] Substantial papers were written for him, but perhaps unsurprisingly, given inordinate claims on his time, he relied most on short briefing from his staff.[65]

In bi-laterals, ministers often found excellent Blair's ability to listen, pick up issues, and move from point to point, but sometimes found it harder to know just what decisions had been reached, particularly if there were any hint of disagreement. As he was frequently on the move making decisions as he went, the job of discovering and legitimating government decisions, and then communicating them to those who needed to know, often became fraught. There were 'running meetings' at which the subjects discussed—and people present— shaded into each other.[66] Extraordinarily at one such meeting over Dr. Kelly, the Ministry of Defence was represented by its permanent secretary, Sir Kevin Tebbitt, without the Defence Secretary turning up. Cabinet minutes and Cabinet committee minutes were generally not used to record his decisions. Ministers found Cabinet minutes among their least informative reading, less so than under Thatcher.[67] Instead, there was a constant battle with informality and many of the Prime Minister's meetings were not properly minuted.[68] Among them—it was almost a disaster—was Blair's with Bernie Ecclestone over Formula 1 and its tobacco money.[69] More seriously, because it was the crucial period in which the September dossier on Iraq was being prepared for publication, Jonathan Powell told the Hutton Inquiry that, though it 'might seem odd

[63] Richard's bewilderment over what Blair wanted him to do over Lords' Reform and eventual resignation are in J Jones (1999) 142, 146, 149, 161, 172, 191, 193–96, 250, 257, 270, 274.

[64] Cook (2003) 93.

[65] In the past the norm was that the PM received a brief from his private office and possibly one from his policy unit, merged under Blair into one policy directorate of which every member was called a policy adviser. As important had been the Cabinet secretariat brief which summarised neutrally the known views of Cabinet ministers, especially those with related departmental responsibilities. Such a brief was no longer thought relevant.

[66] *Independent,* 19 August 2003.

[67] Hennessy (2000) 482; also the *Guardian* view, H Young, (1989).

[68] Blair was not alone. The Hutton Inquiry was told Alastair Campbell's meetings on the September dossier were not minuted, *Independent,* 15 August 2003. Cook (2003) 138 said Blair was more likely to 'open up' if his meetings were unminuted.

[69] Rawnsley (2000) 93.

to people outside' (surely to most insiders too), the Prime Minister held up to 17 meetings a day during the space of a fortnight of which only three were minuted.[70]

There are three main reasons why any pretension to efficiency requires meetings to be minuted. First, that those who are to implement its conclusions can do so without any misunderstandings. Secondly, that the reasons given for such conclusions be noted. And finally so that one can know—especially if there is later to be any question of blame—what reservations, if any, were made (and by whom) to the conclusions reached.[71] The Cabinet secretariat had honed the business of keeping such minutes to near-perfection, but they were no longer present at many important meetings. Without the checks and balances such minutes provide against the misuse of executive power, not only is there no ready check on the encroachment of such power, but blame can be shifted without limit. (Brown was similar. He stopped his private office listening into his telephone calls and taking notes. Said keen to avoid blame for decisions he had taken, he avoided paper trails.)[72]

There was another way besides discursive discussion—another vestigial convention of Cabinet Government—in which the proprieties of Cabinet Government were formally maintained. Though the main Cabinet committees scarcely ever met, there was a constant and immense flurry of papers passing between ministers who, as members of the committees, were expected to sign them all off in their red boxes or at their desks. In this manner ministers were required to discharge the traditional function of collective responsibility and achieve Cabinet solidarity. In particular they were expected in this way to tell their colleagues about, and seek approval for, their policy proposals, bills and public documents, and for changes in public expenditure. Once cleared, they were recorded as government decisions in a letter from the Cabinet secretariat.

Frequently papers were moving so quickly that a minister might not have more than a couple of days to comment on another minister's business, even if of real concern to his own department. On relatively minor, non-contentious matters, involving more than one department, the system worked as indeed a similar system for lesser issues had worked in the past. But on major and controversial matters, it could make interdepartmental clearance harder than under the old system. Given the pressure the government felt itself under to 'join up government across the board', the outcome of these processes could be embarrassing, either because they moved too fast for important

---

[70] P Johnston, *Daily Telegraph*, 23 August 2003.

[71] Brown similarly had no interest in proper papers and minutes: Seldon (2004) 668. Later on more of the decisions at the PM's meeting were recorded sooner or later. But the drawback to so-called action-minutes is that they do not indicate the nature of the arguments advanced and the reasons for the actions taken, as Cabinet secretariat and more generally civil service minutes did. Private information

[72] Bower (2004) 210.

interdepartmental issues to be addressed; or because they became locked in stubborn disagreements.[73] Except with differences between those departments, which were peculiarly Brown's preserve, and might be sorted by his advisers and officials, only the Prime Minister under the new prime ministerial system had the authority to decide these issues.[74] Chris Smith remembered feeling so strongly about a proposal to disqualify asylum-seekers from working that he wrote twice to the Home Secretary about it. Getting no satisfaction, he managed to meet Blair over it who did not express his own viewpoint, but simply decided in favour of Straw. But, as often as not, the PM was too overloaded to have a meeting or form a view. So this method of simulating Cabinet Government all too often caused delays and great inefficiency. The failure to resolve such disagreements became another reason why many bills reached Parliament without underlying policy differences having been reconciled, and therefore for the poor and ill-considered bills that dogged and clogged the parliamentary process.

A further shortcoming of Blair's form of prime ministerial government was that, while its competence could be judged simply by whether decisions were taken as ably and effectively as by other regimes, its inherent absolutism suddenly seemed dangerous when deciding on war. Whose signature was on the piece of paper headed ERII authorising war in Iraq? Who authorised it? Not the Cabinet, a Cabinet committee or the war Cabinet. Not a vote in Parliament.[75] Where is that decision recorded? Though there seemed many things the Prime Minister could not achieve in practice, on matters of peace and war it would seem as if he could act on his own authority alone.

CABINET OFFICE

Since Cabinet had a lesser place in Blair's scheme of things, Cabinet Office was re-tailored to fit. Though not in name, it became a Prime Minister's Department in fact.[76] As its first effective head after the election, Peter Mandelson made its new status clear: it was '. . . to support the Prime Minister at the centre of

---

[73] Influencing the push for more joined-up, that is, interdepartmental thinking—especially active in the early Blair years—were G Mulgan (1997); Perri 6 (1997); Perri 6 et al (1999); D Wilkinson and E Appelbaum (1999).

[74] Though under constant pressure from No 10, Blunkett was usually able to get his way when he wanted to. Even then Blair—or rather, Adonis, as Blunkett believed—allegedly forced him to re-appoint Chris Woodhead as Chief Inspector of Schools against his wishes. Pollard (2005) 243, 244.

[75] Much play was made of the fact that, apparently for the first time, a government behaved as if there could be such action only after a Commons debate, but that in itself cannot be the formal authorisation needed. Presumably it was the Prime Minister's, in line with his general resumption of monarchical powers.

[76] Hennessy (2000) 485–86.

government'.[77] No longer were it, and the Cabinet secretariat, facilities whose loyalty was to the whole Cabinet. Later Jack Cunningham's brief, when Minister for the Cabinet Office, stated that changes there were designed 'to meet the corporate objectives of the Government as a whole rather than the objectives of individual departments', which implied, but left obscure, that its objectives were no longer those of the Cabinet, but of No 10.[78] The Cabinet secretariat, once a staging post for the highest-regarded civil servants, diminished in importance, no longer serviced the most important meetings, now the PM's. Units were set up in the Cabinet Office for long-term policy planning and preparation, akin to the old CPRS; to handle special cross-departmental issues like social exclusion; to advance civil service and public sector management and—increasingly important as the results of many policies were so slow to appear—to try to improve policy delivery. But though there were many bright people in its units, their multiplicity and the lack of machinery to achieve cohesion, as the Cabinet secretariat once could, often added to the difficulty of agreeing decisions and detailing policies.[79]

BLAIR AND THATCHER

By the beginning of 2002 the new way of running the Centre seemed broadly established. It depended on Blair's personality and style as much as Margaret Thatcher's had on hers. They had many similarities. Both were determined to get their way. Several even described Blair as having symptoms of being a control freak. Both drove meetings they chaired. One minister said that Blair had 'too firm a grip'. Both hated large meetings and preferred bi-laterals. Neither encouraged interruption. Blair could listen with mounting impatience to what he did not like. A minister could go to him with a proposition, or in a tri-lateral comment adversely on the proposal under discussion, and find himself talked on top of or otherwise ignored. A warning sign was when he began to tap his pencil. Levity was not easy with Thatcher unless she were in the mood. One said it was 'dangerous' to attempt levity with Blair, especially when challenging him. Neither PM took to the deliberative arguing through of positions to reach a conclusion traditional in British political life. He could for rather long see both sides

[77] Speech 16 September 1997, quoted by Kavanagh and Seldon (1999) 253. He was responsible to Blair, not to Clark, the Cabinet minister responsible for the Cabinet Office who was a cipher. Arguably, it was because a Cabinet minister's voice and vote no longer counted in Cabinet, he could be so disregarded by the Prime Minister. Mowlam (2002) 344, 356, reflected, as Cabinet minister in charge, that until its relations with No 10 were clarified, it would remain a difficult place to get results.

[78] Kavanagh and Seldon (1999) 270.

[79] A distinction needs to be drawn between those units, which were practically part of a *de facto* Prime Minister's department and were most, except for the Delivery Unit—in 2003 transferred to the Treasury—concerned with policy, and those to do with civil service management reporting in practice to the Cabinet Secretary.

of a question. Both had more than an actor's ability, not simply to adopt a script, but to wrestle with its content until it satisfied them.

The greatest difference between them was that Blair—even more Brown[80]— had nothing like her daily appetite for detail and therefore her passion for testing—as far as was possible by such methods—the thoroughness and practicality of proposals as they were developed. He could show a formidable capacity for mastering briefs before a meeting, usually an international one. If he chose, Blair rapidly absorbed detail.[81] Sometimes he would master long papers. He could appear on top of the papers through plentiful briefing. But most often, rather than the mass of papers she waded through, he wanted short briefing notes.[82] Therefore he had to rely more on his staff, who at first were mostly political advisers, rather than civil servants, though by 2003 they were mixed. Rarely did political advisers put in papers on an issue without topping it with their own opinion. Inevitably his staff came to have more influence than his ministers. It was on them that he principally relied to help avoid the perils of the past, the weaknesses that had brought about his model, Thatcher's, downfall. The most striking, some thought the only, difference in their handling of issues was between her self-reliance and the vital importance his circle of advisers came to have for him.

But there were other differences. While Thatcher was among that rare group of autocrats—like Augustus, Olivares, Napoleon and Franz Josef—who were indefatigable in their attention to detail, Blair was not, though after 9/11 a civil servant described the PM, who normally had the stamina of a sprinter, finding long-distance energy.[83] It was not just that he liked to spend time with his children around six o'clock and was a family man. While he could be immensely industrious in preparing himself for something that engaged his interest, like an overseas summit or Northern Ireland, he might not master or even read his brief, if it did not, or even resort to tricks like seizing on a paragraph half way through a paper to suggest he had read it all.[84] Moreover he could become fatigued when confronted with even major issues—particularly domestic ones—that did not interest him. Seeming sometimes extremely tired under pressure of work may appear an all too human failing, but it was a serious weakness in someone who aspires to autocratic prime-ministerial government, throwing more responsibility onto his political staff and—through the cascade principle (chapter 13)—onto his ministers.

---

[80] Both Blair and Brown disliked detail and discussing implementation. Brown hated being challenged, even over facts which were plainly wrong. He would not invite officials to his meetings from whom he expected criticism: Bower (2004) 180–81, 213, 230, 257, 272.

[81] Seldon (2004) 320.

[82] Robin Cook opined no PM had the time to read more than a two-page minute. Oddly Cook appears to have written his minute to the PM on parliamentary reform himself: Cook (2003) 142.

[83] Seldon (2004) 498.

[84] Private sources.

There were lesser, but significant, differences between them. While Thatcher frequently got her way by being peremptory, rude and abrasive, Blair was not like that, though Brown was sometimes guilty of ferocious rages.[85] One consequence was that when, despite her efforts, a disagreement erupted in Cabinet, Cabinet committee or bi-lateral, she would fight her corner with passion. He avoided such confrontations. A further consequence was that while she most often drove issues through Cabinet as with a steamroller, he preferred sofa meetings of his cronies. Neither did he interrogate people at length as she had. More important, while both could have strong convictions, she had them on everything. He had them on foreign affairs. He had strong moral convictions, but could be slow to turn them into political convictions on many domestic policy issues. He had created a machine round him which often required him to go into too much, frequently superficial, detail because making a presentation, but did not give the time to sort through the issues and decide what was important. He paid far more attention to the media and to polling, and to his staff in judging whether to accept policy ideas. Hence the indecisiveness, which often frustrated ministers when they wanted a decision from him. They found it perplexing—impeding implementation and delivery, because it slowed down the government machine—when one bi-lateral followed another on a single topic without reaching a conclusion, and then his apparently often making a decision outside a meeting. Had the right course come to him in the small hours? Or after a chat with Brown, or Campbell or John Birt or other advisers?[86]

Thatcher, like other PMs before Blair, had normally used the Cabinet Room for their meetings to give them a sense of occasion and authority. Blair did not. One observer recalled the occasion when a policy slide-show was put to them as he and his advisers lay about on sofa and chairs. Occasionally he or one of his advisers would interrupt with a comment like 'That won't play well', or ' Can't see that going down well in the tabloids'. Then at the end all that happened was no substantive comment, let alone decision, but they were enjoined to return when they had developed their thinking further. It seemed more like a TV production team pondering, not very enthusiastically, whether something was a good idea for a programme than a government. Blair was often to be heard saying, 'We must do what is right', or calling for a 'principled solution', but often that 'right' solution ran into acute presentational difficulties. The considerations that moved Blair, certainly in domestic affairs, tended to be political or presentational. The two were much the same to him. Issues of presentation featured large at all his meetings.[87]

[85] Bower (2004) 371, 415.
[86] Real decisions were taken with his cronies Seldon (2004) 499.
[87] Private sources.

THE SECOND EXPERIMENT IN PRESIDENTIAL GOVERNMENT FAILS

After the collapse in Blair's prestige at the end of 2003, Cabinet demanded and got more discursive discussions. More opinions were expressed. Blair found it harder to impose his will and therefore to impose Cabinet solidarity. But to describe it as a return to Cabinet Government was pretentious. The possibility and desire to do so was less than under Major. Gordon Brown waited, increasingly impatient to succeed. To imagine him trying to restore collegiate Cabinet Government was out of character. Moreover the possibility of restoring it was undermined by the continuing primacy of spin in the upper reaches of government; the conversion of many parts of the Cabinet secretariat and Cabinet Office into aids for the Prime Ministers rather than resources for the whole Cabinet; and by policymaking being conducted by special advisers rather than by more objective civil servants. Furthermore, as always happens with courtiers, some of Blair's best political aides left, partly a 'rats leaving sinking ship' syndrome, but more from overwork and exhaustion.[88]

CONCLUSION

Superficially, Blair's replacement of Cabinet by prime ministerial government resembled Thatcher's. But their purposes—and therefore their mechanics—were very different. She wanted to take over Cabinet's traditional function of being the Executive (above, chapter 5): the ultimate decision-maker, the initiator of important new policies and laws. Initially she knew she had to sideline Cabinet to implement her economic and union policies. But once started she did not stop, for the most part successfully, though her absolutism and arrogance got their come-uppance with the poll-tax. What made her experiment virtually unrepeatable was her indefatigability which let her replace successively departmental civil servants, the Cabinet system and Cabinet in challenging and ensuring—though not invariably—the attention to detail and practicality of new proposals. Relying on the great respect in which most media proprietors held her, and her own formidable speechmaking powers, she could generally regard news management as a secondary activity safely left to Bernard Ingham. Therefore, unlike Blair she could operate her system without surrounding herself with media and other political advisers, and without transforming the Cabinet Office. Blair also wanted to supersede Cabinet and for six years did so, but he had not Thatcher's appetite for paper or eye for detail, and his influx of advisers, individually and collectively, were as unsystematic. When Iraq under-

---

[88] By 2005 Jonathan Powell and Sally Morgan almost alone were left from the original team: Seldon (2004) 603. Able people were still coming in mid-2003. Their main purpose was characterised, post-Campbell, as finding 'new ideas', (2003) *Public Finance,* 23 September, 24, 25.

mined his ascendancy over his ministers, what returned was an unsystematic Cabinet like Major's without the benefit of Cabinet papers or other process elements of the old or Thatcher's system. The real decisions were taken by Blair—or Brown—and close advisers or by Blair and Brown together. No wonder the outcome was a succession of spun ministerial statements, ill-argued and often opaque public documents, and poorly drafted bills.

Blair's overriding priorities and purpose were quite different. Though he had strong moral convictions—influential in developing his overseas policies—he had few political imperatives. The traditional Cabinet functions of decision, policy and lawmaking were largely incidental and therefore Cabinet, which became a briefing group, was incidental to his and his associates' overriding aim. This aim was to maintain his and his party's popularity in the polls—and so maximise the chances of winning the next election through skilful, relentless, 24 hour a day, news management. To that, now the Centre's prime purpose, let us turn.

13

The Excesses of News Management

The American cause seemed our own; we were proud of their victories, we cried at their defeats, we tore down bulletins and read them in all our houses. None of us reflected on the danger that the New World could give to the old.

The Vicomtesse de Fars-Fausselandry, recalling the years before the French Revolution[1]

He's a consummate politician, brilliant at presentation, he has a wonderful style. He has a real knack for putting his finger on what people are thinking about and what they want to hear. He has gained control of his party and offered leadership.

Michael Portillo[2]

I F NOT THROUGH Cabinet, or in a meaningful, collegiate, deliberative sense through the Cabinet system, how then did Blair and those round him rule? By adapting what they knew best: the techniques needed for news management at which they were masterly, at least as long as Alastair Campbell was in charge. They affected, indeed permeated, all government did.

NEWS MANAGEMENT

Blair and his campaign team learnt from US presidential elections what to copy and from observing his predecessors—Michael Foot, Neil Kinnock and John Smith—what to avoid. For six years triumphant news management—and economic success—gave Blair the backing of public opinion and overwhelming support within the Labour Party. Successive Labour defeats had taught Blair and his press chief, Alastair Campbell, that winning the election required the most carefully worked-out media strategy to stop the media exploiting divisions of opinion within the Party. A daily succession of good stories—with many exclusives—was needed to keep the public, but also reporters, feature-writers and proprietors, favourable.[3] Clinton and his aides had taught them to be proactive, foreseeing and shaping to-morrow and the next day's stories, not reacting on the back foot to to-day's; to computerise masses of information for

---

[1] Schama (1989) 49.
[2] BBC Radio 5, 17 November 1997, quoted by Rawnsley (2000) 52.
[3] Some thought the frequent granting of exclusives not always distinguishable from a form of corruption since it could be a reward for a newspaper giving favourable coverage to an earlier item.

instant access; and to give air time to those among ministerial hopefuls with the readiest and safest ability for sound-bites, while blocking awkward questions. In technology and efficiency, Labour's Millbank news operation—with its Excalibur computer and instant rebuttal unit—was unprecedented in British politics. It contributed hugely to winning the 1997 and 2001 elections. Frequent polls and focus groups kept their thinking popular and persuaded the media that the People were on their side. Realising that what some media proprietors most wanted was attention to their commercial interests, Millbank supped with a long spoon and persuaded them that they would not lose from a Labour government. The greatest previous personal experience of most around Blair was in the media. Used to the loose but competitive management techniques of television, ministers, including the Prime Minister, were like presenters. Their media handlers and other advisers were like directors and producers. Heavily influenced in every respect by American, and particularly by Clinton's, campaigning, Blair's team built up the strongest camaraderie and trust between each other, more important to them for electioneering than comradeship and trust between would-be ministers.

These attitudes, and ways of relating to each other, persisted after the election. Their intention was to fight a permanent re-election campaign. Not until the Hutton and Butler Inquiries did the public get a glimpse of how central 24 hour a day news management was to everything they did. Moreover the collegiate feeling, which wise Prime Ministers had encouraged in Cabinet, now belonged to the aides round Blair,[4] while Cabinet became a briefing group. Alastair Campbell got the authority and resources to centralise news management[5]. The senior ranks of the civil service—aware the media had undermined the Major administration by picking off Cabinet ministers—could only agree to its desirability. Hence a strategic communications unit was formed. Ones judged friendlier to the government, and in many cases thought Labour supporters, replaced most departmental press officers.[6]

Campbell and those round him built up and projected the Prime Minister's public image. What was new about that? Many factors have long made Prime Ministers more than first among equals in gaining public attention. After the suffrage was extended in 1867—shooting that Niagara of democracy—and the subsequent rise of political parties, the public importance and visibility of Prime Ministers greatly increased. The thousands who tramped tens of miles to listen to Gladstone orate for hours in the open at railway stations, were not responding to the chairman of a committee. Disraeli, Lloyd George and most others were great public figures to those who listened to them on the stump, or read them in the newspapers at far greater length than now. The order of magnitude

---

[4] The Hutton Inquiry was to show that camaraderie and trust buckle, as Campbell's staff seemed to undermine Campbell's testimony.

[5] The No 10 resources devoted to news management about doubled from before the 1997 election to 2004: *Times*, 25 March 2004.

[6] Ingham (2003) 141–46; N Jones (1999) 66–71, 133–36.

difference between then and now has become that modern Prime Ministers since Churchill—and television—must dominate election campaigns and, once elected, be visible every day, utter an opinion on every event. There seems no place in modern politics for the quieter, less ostentatious and charismatic, but effective Prime Ministers of the past like Asquith, Baldwin and Attlee, the last of that kind allowed to be supremely effective, as Alec Douglas-Home's failure shows. The demands of office, and invasions of their equally publicised private life, became punishing, as they were not before Anthony Eden.

New after 1997 were not only the scale of the resources devoted to promoting the Prime Minister, but until 2003 Blair's near domination of government relations with the media. Blair was first-class material. Peel, Palmerston, Gladstone, Lloyd George and Thatcher may have been as able to rouse and enthuse their audiences, but there was always at least a large minority who strongly disliked what they said. Perhaps Churchill at war alone had a similar charismatic ability to unite people as Blair had until the Iraq war. Blair had an astonishing, for more than six years endlessly refreshed, ability to intuit what people cared about. He had as strong a moral vision and certainty as Reagan. He was intelligent, sure-footed, an exemplary family-man without the flaws of a Clinton or the rough edges of George W Bush, in public apparently inexhaustible, able to move effortlessly between audiences and topics with the shuffle of a script. His failures, as once when barracked by the Women's Institute, were conspicuous because rare. The worse the corner he found himself in—as several times over Iraq—the more resilient he was. Still journalists were surprised to find Alastair Campbell ordering the Prime Minister around—to do or say this and not that— at press interviews and conferences.[7] He could peremptorily instruct the Prime Minister not to mention prayer in a speech about Iraq: 'We do not do the God thing.'[8] But it was as part of presentation. It would be wrong to read into it more than close relations between a presenter and a producer. Blair had a genius not only for presentation, but also for positioning what he had to say so as to disarm criticism and gain maximum acceptance. Neither was he a puppet. He controlled the substance.

To keep the PM in the limelight and popular, the No 10 news operation was ruthless. It did not hesitate to blanket stories critical of government by contriving a flashier story of its own, or regularly—as Jo Moore admitted in a famously disclosed e-mail[9]—using some major media story to slip out bad news stories unobtrusively. As long as it remained a monopolist controlling all government stories that mattered, it could subdue many journalists, rewarding favourable stories with exclusives and better stories, conversely punishing those it thought hostile. It was also ruthless with ministers. Ministers were at first inclined to compete for the attention of the media as Major's ministers had done. No 10

[7]   N Jones (1999) 44–48; also R Harris quoted by Abse (2003) 293.
[8]   *Sunday Telegraph*, 4 May 2003; *Sunday Times Magazine*, 19 May 2003.
[9]   Sir R Mottram's statement, *Times*, 26 February 2002.

quickly moved to reduce the number of ministers' appearances and ensure the acceptability of their content. All speeches must be cleared with No 10. All lunches ministers and senior civil servants had with journalists must be reported to them too.[10] Yet Campbell took about a year to reduce off-the-record briefings by ministers, not under his control, to a trickle. A media-obsessed world saw the requirement that ministers clear their speeches with Campbell as the true end of Cabinet Government. Peter Riddell was provoked into commenting, 'Good-bye Cabinet Government. Welcome to the Blair presidency.'[11] But it was needed to check the destructive leaking of ministers against each other in the Major years. It too worked for some six years.

Ministers knew their standing in Parliament and their ambitions depended on the celebrity the media alone could give them. The better a minister appeared in the media, the more they wanted that minister. Yet with the PM dominating the media, and their own appearances controlled, such celebrity could be hard to come by, except for those few—like Brown, Straw and Blunkett—who were celebrities before 1997. After the exit of Charlie Whelan, Brown's impact on the media was generally through carefully prepared—and previously trailed— speeches, rather than through daily contact with the media.[12] Others made occasional important speeches, but only after painstaking clearance with Campbell, who could order them around.[13] Or, as had always happened, they were designated to tell bad news or explain away blame. Otherwise, unless unable to escape the limelight, some, having become ministers, sought fewer media opportunities because of the dangers. Yet insufficient agility with sound-bites was still a main reason for ministers and MPs not being promoted and for some ministers going. The time ministers and their advisers took preparing for the media was often the most important call on their time.

MEDIA OBJECTIVES

In broad terms No 10's media objectives, largely achieved in the first six years, were:

- To ensure the Prime Minister and Labour remained high in the polls;
- To that end to build the image and popularity of the Prime Minister by maximising his favourable exposure and identifying him with good news;
- To ensure no one else, not even his wife or Gordon Brown, impaired that popularity or crowded him out;

---

[10] V Elliott, *Times*, 13 March 1998; Draper (1997) 96.

[11] *Times*, July 1997, cited by Hennessy (2000) 483. The reference was to the revised *Ministerial Code* (Cabinet Office (1997) para 88). Also Peter Riddell, *Times*, 28 November 1997; 5 January 1998.

[12] Blair's doubts over whether to let Brown appoint Whelan, Whelan's mounting ability to irritate Campbell by spin-doctoring for Brown, and No 10's final ousting of him are well told in Rawnsley (2000) 20, 21 and *passim;* N Jones (1999) 273–79.

[13] N Jones (1999) 208–12.

- To dominate departments' PR, both because the media would otherwise play one minister off against others and because No 10 believed it alone had the expertise to do major PR effectively.

Not expected of them was to get a clear account of a decision or proposal, and the reasons for it, into the media.

THE PRIZES WON

Blair's and Labour's poll ratings, and victory in 2001, long showed how successfully these objectives were achieved. Until mid-2003 there were almost no occasions when his or the government's popularity fell substantially. Almost the only time was because of the Fuel Duty Protests in 2000, a classic example of a highly-focused media operation failing to see a major new issue coming up fast, though given ample warning.[14] Other slight ups and downs in Blair's popularity did no real harm. Some could be regarded as tactically wise: to help avoid politics becoming boring. Or letting the media score until Blair made a comeback or switched attention to another issue. With their genius for presentation, Blair and Campbell, until Iraq, always escaped from an issue before it became threatening. By winter 2004, Blair's popularity with voters had fallen, but was still ahead of other party leaders' or Brown's.

Above all, the dramatisation of news management into a contest between government and the media prevented opposition parties from gaining much beyond passing, often derisory, attention. While William Hague as opposition leader frequently had the better of Blair in the Commons, that fact was eclipsed by the Prime Minister's evasions in answering questions and Hague's poorer performances on radio and television.[15] By the time Iain Duncan Smith and then Michael Howard became Tory leader, Prime Minister's Questions had, as already noted, become a weekly gladiatorial bout, watched by as many MPs as could crowd into the Chamber, by which the victor raised the spirits of his side to fever pitch. For a while, when Howard became Tory leader, he was the more frequent victor. But though marvellous for morale, it was hardly a rational contest. Did not the Prime Minister overcome, at least for a time, doubts about his June 2003 re-shuffle, and the lack of depth of thought underlying the constitutional changes he then proposed, by gibes about those who wanted to keep wigs, women's tights and 18th century clothing? Rather than by showing he had given serious consideration to the knotty problems raised by the separation of powers? Yet, as almost always, he had judged his audience well. This stratagem, like others he and his advisers used, for a time disarmed the opposition.

---

[14] Particularly by the RAC Foundation, of which I was then chairman, which communicated its concern several times, both to No 10 and to the Department of Transport.

[15] M Parris, *Times*, 15 January 1998; M Chittendon, *Sunday Times*, 1 February 1998.

While this news management was long effective in its own terms, it had several disadvantages for the quality of government which eventually undermined its achievements and popularity:

(1) Truth-telling

One downside to this centralised, strategic news management, was a developing realisation among the public that the PM and No 10 did not always tell the truth. An early example of a new attitude to the truth was Brown rather than Blair. The Treasury's permanent secretary was content for Brown's press aide, Charlie Whelan, to come in as special adviser but resisted his becoming the Treasury's press secretary, stressing the importance of a civil servant giving out statistics and other factual information, so as to preserve as far as possible its reputation for accuracy. No sooner had Brown overruled him on this than Whelan was reported telling the media several untruths about the departing Conservative Chancellor, Kenneth Clarke, for example that he had left behind him a black hole in the public finances, that inflation was heading for 4% and that his correct prediction that unemployment would fall was a 'massaged' statistic.[16] One must be sensible about this. Occasionally the truth cannot be told. Callaghan could not about the government's intention to devalue.[17] Otherwise the markets would have forced devaluation before the authorities were ready for it and made a killing. Similar prospects were always good reasons for budget secrecy, since those to whom its measures were prematurely and selectively disclosed could gain financially.[18] Matters of war, security and commercial confidentiality may prevent the truth being told.[19] But occasions when these, rather than political embarrassment, are valid reasons for avoiding the truth are rare. Moreover they can usually be met by the old stratagem of not telling the full truth—by being economical—rather than by telling an untruth.[20]

Given the importance of both truth-telling and objectivity for the effectiveness of representative democracy, several safeguards under the British system

---

[16] Bower (2004) 204–7.

[17] Callaghan, when questioned by Robert Sheldon in the Commons, while not admitting the truth that devaluation had been decided, went to the greatest lengths to avoid telling Parliament an untruth, but his evasions unsettled the market. Devaluation was announced two days later: Morgan (1997) 272–73.

[18] Now that what were budget secrets are regularly disclosed before the Budget is presented to Parliament, it remains important that they are disclosed universally if there is a chance that more limited disclosure might make anyone money.

[19] Many defence and security secrets can be handled by the old device of disclosing them to opposition leaders under their Privy Councillor's oath.

[20] Within reason, it is sensible for a minister to want to delay making a statement until ready to do so. Hence the well-established practice in such circumstances of responding to such a question by saying that it was speculative or saying 'I have no plans for X'. For one civil servant a new day dawned in the 1990s when a minister, told that a reason for proceeding with a large infrastructure project was untrue, accepted that was so but simply said he would take the risk of telling that untruth to the media and Parliament.

severely limited lies being told successfully, habitually or even often, both about what really mattered and less important topics:

- Collegiate Cabinet Government itself, in that Cabinet colleagues found it difficult, even if they were so minded, not to be straight and tell each other the truth;
- The closeness of ministers, including the Prime Minister, to their civil servants among whose duties was at all times to remind ministers what was true and objective;
- Habitually setting matters down on paper, carefully drafted, to be sure the words had the meaning they were meant to have, so that all, who needed to know at every stage in its progress through the system until publication, knew that meaning;
- The convention that policy and changes of policy should be announced first to Parliament so that MPs or peers should have the chance to assess and test their meaning;
- The convention of ministerial responsibility, which meant that, because a minister was responsible for whatever his officials said and did, both risked condemnation if the truth were not told.

Unchecked by Cabinet colleagues, civil servants, Parliament and the media, this British government told untruths as an aspect of news management, not always, not systematically, often chaotically, and usually when under pressure, sometimes because of spin, sometimes because of the rushed reactions needed for 24 hour a day news management. Richard Sambrook, the BBC's director of News, said the BBC had given up accepting Campbell's assertions—with which he said Campbell bombarded them long before Iraq—that various stories about the government they carried were untrue:

> It is regrettably true that in recent years some denials have been modified when information came to light.[21]

The 'modified denials' he mentioned as changing their policy of accepting government denials were:

- Martin Sixsmith said to have resigned when he had not;
- Cherie Blair found having had more dealings with Peter Foster than at first conceded;
- The time it took to discover the real facts about Lakshmi Mittal's £150,000 donation to the Labour Party and Blair writing a letter to the PM of Romania recommending Mittal's firm for a contract, even stranger because it was not a British firm;
- How long it took for the facts to emerge about Blair's phone call to Romano Prodi, then Italian PM, to try to advance Murdoch's business interests.

---

[21] *Independent*, 26 August 2003.

The compelling arguments for the PM, his aides and other ministers telling the truth, whenever they can, need not be primarily moral. Or that it has long been a convention that even on minor matters ministers must tell Parliament the truth, as John Profumo found to his cost. Rather it is prudence and a require- ment of democracy. The chances of the truth eventually being found out— through leaks, whistle-blowers and inquiries—are often high, as the Blair government discovered. Neither is a lost reputation for truth-telling easily regained, as Blair also found. But democracy cannot work at any level if a rea- sonable approximation to the truth is not told, as all discovered when the true position about weapons of mass destruction—even as known at the time with- out benefit of hindsight—was revealed. But there were many lesser, but not unimportant, examples.

Ecclestone

An early example under Blair of the difficulties caused by the erosion of these safeguards—particularly when under severe pressure from hostile media—was over his accepting the first, and considering requesting a second, million pound donation from Bernie Ecclestone to Labour Party funds.[22] In writing to Sir Patrick Neill, then chairman of the Committee of Standards in Public Life, No 10 did not want to reveal it had already accepted the first million—the Party funds were still in substantial deficit from the election—when it was asking whether it should accept a second million.[23] Neither did it want to reveal that, having already received the first million, Blair told Frank Dobson, then Secretary of State for Health, to exempt Formula 1 racing from the proposed ban on tobacco advertising. But it all came out.

The Wallpaper

Another departure from the truth was over the Lord Chancellor and the expen- sive and total refurbishment of his House of Lords official house. The Pugin wallpaper alone was to attract much public attention. When the facts hit the press, a furore ensued for months. Irvine on taking office had been more than keen on the refurbishment; it should be complete; there should be no economis- ing and indeed no expense spared. Lord Richard, the leader of the House of Lords, had repeatedly, but without avail, urged Irvine to be less lavish, if only for prudence' sake and to save the reputation of the Labour Party. He knew it would leak, as it did.[24] The defence decided on by Irvine and No 10 was that the

---

[22] Rawnsley (2000) 91–105; also Seldon (2004) 535; Oborne and Walters (2004) 216–17. A differ- ent instance was Cook asserting that British Aerospace seemed to have the key to No 10 garden-gate. He never knew No 10 come up with a decision against their interests: Cook (2003) 73; also Kampfner (2003) 14–15.

[23] P Riddell, *Times* 17 November 1997.

[24] The story is extensively told in his wife's memoirs: J Jones (1999) 76, 88, 90, 91, 94, 151, 159, 160, 179, 180, 181–83, 185, 189, 237.

expenditure was part of a planned refurbishment of the Houses of Parliament settled before the election. The difficulty was that it was not true, as No 10 knew and a 'killer minute' by Black Rod, General Sir Edward Jones, showed. Richard intimated to the Commons' Public Administration Committee that it might ask Black Rod about the minute, but it decided Lords' housekeeping was not its business. Thereafter Black Rod believed it would have 'demeaned the House of Lords to get involved in a slanging match with the Lord Chancellor.'[25] It was not his duty to volunteer the truth. He would have revealed it if asked, but he was not. Irvine in agreement with No 10 then asked for his version of the story to be disclosed to the Lords in a statement, but the Clerk rejected it as untrue, having seen Black Rod's minute. Despite its untruth, it was issued through No 10 as a government press release.[26]

The Wanless Report

Gordon Brown asked Derek Wanless, who had been Chief Executive and then Chairman of the NatWest Bank to report on the state of the NHS, which he did, concluding that by most criteria British healthcare was worse than elsewhere in Europe and that serious reform was needed. On his car radio Wanless was astonished to hear Brown misrepresenting his report in the Commons as largely justifying how the NHS was run and managed.[27]

Mandelson

Another example was over Mandelson's second resignation. A story in the media said the Cabinet Secretary had recommended his resigning, but the Hammond Report made clear later that Sir Richard Wilson had not believed Mandelson could be shown blameworthy.[28]

The Iraq dossiers

A far more serious example was the allegation that No 10 had tampered with, edited, and thereby falsified, information from intelligence sources on the existence of weapons of mass destruction in Iraq, to be discussed in chapter 17.

(2) Too Many Initiatives

The untruth, or doubtful truth, of some stories No 10 (and other government media-handlers) relayed—some important, some less so—were not the only

---

[25] Jones (1999) 181–82.
[26] Lord Richard.
[27] Bower (2004) 378–83.
[28] Hammond (2001).

adverse consequences of intensive, unrelenting news management The media had an inexhaustible appetite for stories. More than their predecessors, the PM, Campbell and his staff hunted for new policy initiatives as the best source of good news stories. However, for the media and No 10, a new idea or scheme reported in the media was as good as done. By the time actual implementation was needed, the story had become old and of little interest to the media and therefore to No 10. Before then another, sometimes conflicting initiative on the same topic might appear in the media. But more than few had not really been intended and had simply been invented to impress the media, some even becoming law.[29] Other policy ideas flowing from select committees and other sources in Parliament, and from working groups of junior ministers and others within the Cabinet system, added to the confusion caused those working in the public services, or otherwise affected.[30]

As a consequence the centre of government, departments and Parliament spent in-ordinate time generating sometimes conflicting proposals rather than choosing and developing one policy, filling in the detail, consulting over it, assuring themselves that what they wanted to do was practical and was well reflected in regulations or a bill.[31] Too many laws were too soon replaced by new initiatives. So many initiatives confused Parliament, the public and the media, but above all public bodies and those they employed, undermining their ability to meet their targets and improve the services they gave. Frequent policy initiatives make media copy, but are inimical to better services.

(3) Objectivity and Intelligibility

Further shortcomings of news-managed government were mainly responsible for the unintelligibility which MPs now expected from most white papers, green papers and other public documents (chapter 10):[32]

- The requirement they be submitted to No 10 for editing or re-writing which often had the effect of making them more obscure, evasive, illogical and jazzed up;
- No 10's unwillingness to sanction a statement of policy until polling or the media—which always engaged in generalities—indicated that it already had wide public support, a support which often required ambiguity;

[29] Parliament was recalled in August, 1999, after Omagh, to pass a bill with penal powers to deal with terrorism, which seems never to have been activated.

[30] So Mo Mowlam was to complain of too many cooks over drugs policy: Mowlam (2002) 324–25.

[31] On obsession with media, squeezing out thinking about the medium and long-term: Seldon (2004) 437–50, 463, 610–12.

[32] The public documents cited are among the more meaningful. An example of an almost entirely vacuous and therefore unnecessary White Paper is DEFRA, June, 2002. The annual reports on its total activity the Blair government thought it should provide were also vacuous: see P Riddell, *Times,* 19 July 2000.

- Unclear and ambiguous forms of words hiding unresolved and sometimes unrecognised disagreements;
- No understanding of the need for clear and detailed information—and forecasts—in public documents, rather than propaganda, if policies were to be understood, challenged, improved in the light of past practical experience and therefore capable of proper implementation.

Controlling ministers' speeches and other public appearances meant more than might at first appear, since among these pronouncements were ministers' statements on policy, now almost invariably made first to the media, not Parliament. In vetting their public appearances, No 10 had machinery in place of Cabinet, which once had that role, for vetting their expressions of policy, whenever it wanted.[33] It did so about anything it judged important, particularly when it was the focus of media scrutiny as most significant policy statements, white papers and similar public documents were. It was true at two levels: at the departmental level where a spin doctor, rather than an impartial civil servant, was likely to put a gloss on a document or press release. Second because, if important, that document or press release would be gone over and altered at No 10, that is, at one further remove from departmental or agency officials knowledgeable enough and motivated to check its truth and objectivity. One BBC journalist, closely involved, gave his opinion that the greater involvement of special advisers and other political media handlers made it harder to check the truth of government statements with departments.[34] Departmental officials observed that the changes No 10 so systematically made or incited were concerned not with truth and objectivity, but with political saleability.[35] Moreover it was not just a question of particular untruths. The news handlers, especially at No 10, could so alter the content as to alter the policy, subtly or not, consciously or subconsciously, with or without reference to the PM.[36] Or they might want to give contradictory messages to different parts of the media as when an enthusiastic pro-Euro Blair interview in the *Financial Times* appeared on the same day as an anti-Euro one under his name in the *Sun*.[37] Furthermore they might wish to delay such a document until they thought time was ripe, or exclude what they thought difficult or not immediately popular material.

The outcome was, more often than not, either no relevant document or unintelligible, unhelpful, or—even if in some respects good—seriously incomplete documents. For example John Prescott's 1998 *Transport Policy White Paper* produced a superficially attractive vision of a transport future in which traffic growth could be switched to public transport without road pricing to manage

[33] John Lloyd (2004) lays most blame on the media for driving governments towards superficiality but it seems to me equally No 10's intention, given their priorities and comparative lack of interest in policy development.
[34] N Jones (1999) 72–73.
[35] Private sources.
[36] Private information.
[37] Naughtie (2002) 145.

demand and therefore little or no road construction would be needed, but without the quantification and analysis needed to show it was feasible.[38] If that had been undertaken, its objectives would have been shown to be infeasible.[39] John Prescott's 2000 *Transport Plan* was welcome in that it undertook the analysis to help show the scale of investment needed in road and rail, nationally and locally, but did not address the fundamental question of how one justified the almost equal investment in road and rail—later to become more disproportionate—given that 85% of the traffic went by road, 6% by rail, an issue that became crucial as public expenditure suddenly became constrained, while rail costs, and therefore the need for rail subsidy, soared.[40]

The *New NHS: Modern, Dependable*, 1997, and *Our Healthier Nation: A Contract for Health*, 1998, set out a Third Way of running the NHS, transcending old methods of state management and the market, but bore little relation to what happened;[41] the Energy White Paper, *Our Energy Future: Creating a Low Carbon Economy*, set out the problem to be addressed excellently, was supported by first-class analyses, but did not bring the argument together in any meaningful form.[42] In particular the conclusion that such a low carbon economy could be achieved by growing dependence on renewable energy rather than on nuclear, depended on the unargued, indeed hidden, and implausible assumption that its cost, financial and social, could in some unspecified way be brought down to the level which made that feasible. The Pensions White Paper, *New Ambitions for our Country: A New Contract for Welfare*, 1998, was uplifting in its Third Way language, but neither it nor its successors, though they set out the problem of security and pensions in an ageing country, answered the hard questions that needed to be addressed.[43]

Finally, the papers which sought to explain why we needed a Supreme Court and the abolition of the Lord Chancellorship after a thousand years, were rushed out after the decisions had been made and announced in the context of the 2003, summer Cabinet re-shuffle. Ill-argued, their case turned on vapid appeals to modernisation and the separation of powers, with no recognition that that principle was alien to the British constitution and, if extensively adopted, would have more far-reaching consequences, as will appear.[44]

[38] See Foster in Seldon (2001).
[39] As was demonstrated by a far from roads-dominated group I chaired in *Motoring Towards 2050* (RAC Foundation, 2001).
[40] C D Foster, *Observer*, 3 August 2003.
[41] Department of Health (1997) and (1998); also Newman (2001) 43–46.
[42] DTI (2003). Here is not the place to elaborate the point but the classic form of a White Paper is that of an investment appraisal. Its components need to be: a description of the problem; a projection into the future if things go on as they are; description and evaluation of the options considered, including a projection if the preferred option is adopted. Crucially the evaluation and any detailed second projection were omitted. See Foster in McLean and Jennings (forthcoming).
[43] Department of Social Security (1998).
[44] In 2003, the Lords referred the relevant bill to its committee on the Constitution, chaired by Lord Richard on which the Lord Chancellor, Lord Falconer sat as a member. With more than 400 amendments, it did the work the government had failed to do to get the proposals into workable shape.

It is hard to think of one document, which reached the standards of comprehensiveness, evidence marshalling, and reasoned intelligibility, far from uncommon in the bluebooks and White Papers of the past.[45]

AVOIDING EXCESSIVE NEWS MANAGEMENT

The best safeguards against misrepresentation is that any editing of such information should be only, if at all, to make such documents clearer; and done only by an impartial official, not by someone like Campbell, as a special adviser presumed to be motivated by political interest and indeed hired to make political capital out of presentation. That the preparation of material relevant to a decision on whether we should go to war should be processed by something called the Iraq Communications Group overseen by a political adviser, rather than by a politically impartial official—like the sexing up of virtually every other policy document—was a new development since 1997 and not one calculated to inspire confidence in the probity of the outcome. At the Foreign Affairs Committee Sir John Stanley twice asked why the Cabinet Secretary had not been involved in the process.[46] Campbell seemed not grasp the significance of the question, saying he could see no reason why the Cabinet Secretary should be involved, and that in any case he had someone from Cabinet Office on this Group, though he could not remember his name. This response to Stanley's questions could not be a more telling witness of the extent to which the safeguards—and objectivity—of Cabinet Government had declined.[47] The significance of Campbell's omission—and explanation of his incredulity—was twofold:

- It used to be among the Cabinet Secretary's duties to ensure that relevant members of Cabinet—here, certainly the Overseas Committee and War Cabinet, but probably, given its importance, full Cabinet—had the opportunity to read, comment on and approve, or disapprove, all public documents;[48]
- It was also among his duties to verify that, in their passage through the Cabinet system, they had attained the standards of consultation, rigour, and

---

[45]   There were also examples of almost total vacuity: eg DEFRA (2002) and SRA (2003).

[46]   Seldon (2004) 13, 24.

[47]   When Blair demurred from sacking Geoffrey Robinson himself, but asked the Cabinet Secretary to ask Gordon Brown to do so instead, Brown not only refused, but was reported as having refused to speak to Sir Richard Wilson for three years: Bower (2004) 282–83. In past times the Chancellor refusing to talk to the Cabinet Secretary would have been seen as a serious obstacle to conducting government business.

[48]   Turnbull's role as Cabinet secretary had changed to being head of the public sector. But he still attended Cabinet. Was his doing so now only symbolic? Had he any responsibilities to Cabinet? As would not have happened in similar circumstances before, he had no role before the Hutton or the Butler inquiries.

then objectivity and truth required of such documents as Cabinet papers presented to Parliament.[49]

CONCLUSION

Blair for long had an almost unassailable instinct for what the people wanted and therefore for what was politically expedient. But the belief that the best way to win the next election was to ensure the PM headed every poll, led too often to extreme short-termism and a failure to realise longer term goals. No 10's thoroughness and resourcefulness in feeding the media 24 hours a day were long remarkable, but frequently dominated everything the PM did, too often settling his priorities and delaying other important business.

By another irony, as the years passed, but especially when preparing for elections, No 10 was heard wishing Blair had had more time to develop a better-worked up, more comprehensive set of policies.[50] But that frustrated hope reflected yet another aspect of news management: the wish to come forward with an American style all-embracing acceptance speech and election manifesto, not only crafted to appeal to as many as possible, but also, once the election was won, able to settle policy arguments in the PM's favour whenever they arose.[51] But the notion—despite the media for their purposes regarding it as necessary for contesting general elections—that one can have a policy blue-print once every few years rather than let policies develop in response to often unexpected events, careful examination of the evidence and genuine consultation among those affected seems as much the antithesis of good government as endlessly making policy part of 24 hour a day news management.

[49] It also raises the issue of how Dr Kelly might have been better handled. If a permanent secretary was faced with an allegation that one of his officials had been over-stepping the mark in talking to the press, he should have been able to handle it much as follows: 1 He would have asked his PEO 1 what authority Kelly had had to speak to the press, in what terms, and where it was written down; 2 What previous problems, if any, there had been and, for example, if he had diligently minuted all those conversations, sending them to his superior; 3 What he had, or believed he had, said in these instances; 4 What public statement might clear the matter up and 5 if he advised that Kelly's instructions should be altered. He would then have seen Kelly—did Tebbitt?—with his line manager and PEO, to go through the position; if necessary, deliver a reprimand and secure Kelly's agreement to any change in instructions. He would probably have told his secretary of state, before and after, what he was up to. He might advise him, as Tebbitt advised Hoon, that it would be unwise to let Kelly go before the FAC. If Hoon or the PM, Campbell or Powell tried to overrule that recommendation—particularly if at the same time saying it was a decision for MOD—he might have gone to the Cabinet Secretary who, if persuaded, would have taken it up with the PM. If the PM had persisted in putting Kelly in front of the FAC, it would have been minuted as his decision. Sir Paul Lever, who had been chairman of the JIC, said he would have remonstrated with Campbell that he should not be asked to re-write the dossier on the grounds that intelligence was better expressed in the words the intelligence services used with all the qualifications left in. If Campbell had insisted, he would have gone to the Cabinet Secretary. If that had failed, he would have seriously considered whether he should resign.

[50] Seldon (2004) 437–39, 656. The 1997 and 2001 manifestos were too lacking in detail: Seldon (2004) 453.

[51] There was also jealousy that Brown and his advisers seemed better able to work up ideas, helped by their control of the spending reviews: Seldon (2004) 463.

After Iraq, Alastair Campbell's successors could not as easily control the media or ministers. The end of his tight discipline over journalists and ministers led to relations between them more like the Major government's. Journalists found ministers again approaching them directly, less fearful of No 10's retribution should they step out of line. Some journalists heralded it as the collapse of presidential government, which it was, and as a return to Cabinet Government. But it was not that in any meaningful sense for reasons given in the last chapter. The media were learning their own tricks, were far more numerous, attracted the best brains, started to score more points against the government. The government was more frequently out-manoeuvred in the press. The media had had secured many ministerial scalps in recent years. Now it saw the chance of a prime ministerial one.

However from the public's point of view—a public which included not only people as electors, citizens, consumers and producers of public services, but also their representatives in local authorities and Parliament—a still more important development was that government information—from soundbites to its public documents—could no longer be relied on to be intelligible, or, if intelligible, well-argued and approximately true.

Perhaps the most important development from this government's standpoint was that, increasingly, the public became aware of, and resistant to, spin, displaying declining trust in both politicians and journalists. Blair several times declared an end to spinning.[52] But attempts not to spin could seem like spinning. When one's whole expertise, working methods and style derive from a lifetime's experience of news management—when they have been so successful in propelling Labour back to power and keeping it there, since first adopted in 1994—how does one teach ageing dogs new tricks and what on earth would they be? Besides, people are not fools. Ultimately they judge a government, not by what it says, or by what it says it might do, but by what it does.

But there was still more to the influence of spin-doctoring on government. Blair's intention from the start had been not just to triumph in the polls, but to change his party, his country and then the world. Their methods, their spin-doctoring, not only gradually undermined people's belief in the truth and objectivity of much of what they were saying, but permeated their whole approach to government.

[52] E.g. *The Independent*, 1 September 2003.

14

Ministers' Diminished Standing

> The punk pundits have said everything is run from the Centre and on this evidence the punk pundits seem to be right.
>
> *Andrew Marr* (2003)[1]

Despite their both being presidential, there were great differences between Thatcher's and Blair's administrations. As well as Blair's concentration on news management, other features made for its greater confusion; and for most ministers' lowered status.

UNDER THATCHER

AT FIRST MANY of Thatcher's ministers did not share her convictions. It was an able Cabinet. Whether wet or dry, Biffen, Carrington, Gilmour, Heseltine, Howe, Joseph, Prior and Walker were powerful characters, many brimming with ideas, many relishing it when officials challenged them in the time-honoured way and most decisive when they felt discussion should stop. Some replacements both shared her convictions and, like Ridley and Lawson, welcomed fundamental challenge of those convictions, agreeing that their ideas might be improved by it, but confident they would not be knocked off course. Others, less patient, still welcomed challenge on the detail and implementation of their policies. Some, lacking self-confidence, avoided discussion, seeming keenest to reflect whatever they believed she wanted. Ministers could sometimes change her mind, but only after a blazing row and only then if she believed they shared her fundamental convictions. Those who stood up to her, and would not submit, could occasionally insist on doing what they, not she, wanted, but not persistently. Kenneth Clarke developed the art of doing what he wanted by keeping issues away from her. After the Falklands War gave her the prestige to fashion the Cabinet she wanted, Margaret Thatcher as Chief Executive came to expect her ministers to hold convictions which mirrored and did not clash with her own. By the end, few, perhaps only Howe and Lawson—both close to her once—had too much political standing for her to sack if they disagreed with

---

[1] As a comment on Geoff Hoon, the Defence Secretary's, evidence to the Hutton Inquiry, the *Today* programme, 28 August 2003.

her. So she manoeuvred them into semi-detached positions where they could not be as effective and became, she hoped, less threatening to her.

She insisted ministers were on top of the detail, even minutiae, of their policies. They could no longer survive by extemporising from an official brief they had not mastered. Had they absorbed their brief, she was not pleased if they had swallowed their officials' line, especially, but not only, if she were against it. Indeed she and Keith Joseph were explicit in their wish to break down consensus and replace it by new thinking. So most ministers acquired, if they did not already have it, a distrust of the departmental store of wisdom on most issues. In an excellent book based on interviews with officials and ministers, Campbell and Wilson put it that:

> In the 1980s ministers were very anxious to please the Queen-Empress in Downing Street by forcing the wayward tribes of Whitehall to amend their thinking.[2]

Often this change of approach meant replacing the old Whitehall practice of studying the problem, and then consulting over what could be done before reaching a solution, by a radicalism based on theory, often that of right-wing economists like Friedman, Hayek or Niskanen, or on presumed business practice.

Influenced by, though not experienced in, management, the mantra of management became her powerful tool as Chief Executive, but open to various interpretations. Bringing Derek Rayner from Marks and Spencer into Cabinet Office was one route by which ministers were persuaded of the importance of managing their departments.[3] Another was Michael Heseltine's own experience and passion for it. But there was a different, apparently related meaning she gave management which became of greater daily importance. As the years passed Margaret Thatcher's passion for detail developed into a relentless quasi-managerialism in which ministers were required to meet every division of their department and amass quantities of information about all, which no one, especially no minister, could digest.[4] The No 10 Policy Unit fed Margaret Thatcher briefs for her 'judge and jury' sessions with ministers when she would interrogate them on their policies and performance. These meetings became a feared and hated part of ministers' lives.[5] Many felt they did little to improve delivery of their policies, which, in practice, most left to their officials; let alone management of their departments, which all left to officials.[6]

Rather, under the guise of reviewing the management of their business, such meetings enabled her to intervene in policy development to ensure it was to her

---

[2] Campbell and Wilson (1995) 57. An invaluable source of civil service opinion.
[3] His work was carried on by Clive Priestley and Michael Beesley.
[4] Campbell and Wilson (1995) 127.
[5] Hennessy (2000) 424.
[6] Heseltine showed an unparalleled interest in discovering how every part of Environment spent its time and altering it to reflect his usually justified view of what mattered: Heseltine (2000)190–94; Heiser (1994) 16–17.

liking.[7] They reinforced the arrogation of power to her, secured by her use of the Cabinet system. They also encouraged her wish that most ministers should concentrate on their own department's business and not stray into that of others, though she allowed more latitude to Whitelaw, Ridley and, early on, Lawson whom she saw as on her side. Ministers' most immediate accountability came to be to her, not Parliament. For reasons only partly explained by changes within Parliament (chapter 10), making a statement there or answering parliamentary questions became less demanding and daunting experiences for ministers than appearing before her.

To achieve a political unity of purpose within their department, most ministers met their junior ministers and political advisers at least once a week. Most worked harder than in the past to keep their teams of ministers and special advisers united, though in a few departments, senior departmental ministers found junior ministers harder to control. The Scott Report found junior ministers from several departments—but not the Foreign Office where the Foreign Secretary seemed to supervise them better—not just administering but also making policy on the hoof for a complex export licensing scheme, apparently not controlled by their departmental heads.[8] Alan Clark was pursuing his own policy at variance with Tom King, his departmental boss. But his diaries reveal he believed Thatcher had put him into Defence as a junior minister to spy on and change King's policies.[9] However, in this belief as much else, he may have been inaccurate.

Though the quality of Cabinet ministers remained generally high during the Thatcher years, they were struggling to cope with increasing departmental workloads with fewer senior officials. While their functions remained as all-embracing as in the past, how they carried them out was altering. Their freedom for manoeuvre was declining for reasons as various as Europe, and the doubling of the workload of legislation, to Margaret Thatcher's greater domination of policy formation, but also the media's increasing demands. Ministers must be instantly ready to defend whatever they and their departments were doing both to the media and her. Before 1979 few thought they must work out every word they would say before meeting either Prime Minister or media. After 1979 most felt they needed to rehearse and, where possible, keep to an exact script in front of both. Only the most confident still felt they could choose their words on the spur of the moment.

To meet all those demands, but especially those of conviction politics, ministers insisted power shift back to them from their officials. But too much was going on for that power to return to them in the old way through their own immersion in the processes of policy preparation right through to legislation. To

[7] Yet some doubted if ministers should bother to find out why one division in their department had 4 higher executive officers when others had three.
[8] Foster (1996) 583–86.
[9] Clark (1993) 249ff.

satisfy her, they had to be on top of policy formation, but the pressure of work meant they increasingly left implementation, and thinking about implementation, to their officials.

UNDER BLAIR

Before considering the still more diminished position of ministers under Blair, there are two further factors—additional to the marginalisation of Cabinet and the pervasiveness of news management—which need discussion: relations between Blair and Brown; and the cascade principle, both adding to the haste and confusion with which this government frequently operated.

BLAIR AND BROWN

Peter Riddell had suggested that the relation between Prime Minister and Chancellor was like that between the chairman and chief executive of a holding company.[10] But that model was hardly tenable—except possibly towards the end of Blair's second administration in 2004—given Blair's hands-on interest in overseas issues, and his insistence on intervening in anything whenever he and his advisers believed news management required it. As media attention and public concern built up, he took over the management of delivery problems in education, the NHS and the railways (later extended to include roads), as if CEO of these subsidiaries, too.[11] Nevertheless important economic and other domestic policy decisions depended on the personalities of the Prime Minister and Chancellor, and on relations between them.[12] Brown operated in some secrecy in his relations on most issues with Blair, but with the might of the Treasury behind him in economic and public expenditure policy. That might at times was reported as one motive in making Blair and his advisers try to rival the Treasury by building No 10 and Cabinet Office into a Prime Minister's department.[13] Each had strengths the other lacked, without seemingly much sympathy for each other. Brown's expectation that he would succeed Blair, and his knowledge that

[10] Riddell, *Times,* 4 December 1997; Ed Balls was said to have pushed the analogy: Seldon (2004) 671.

[11] The vehicles were his fortnightly meetings with Michael Barber's Delivery Unit on each. One outcome was that some of the agencies involved were readier to push their case and, if requested, disclose information to the PM than to the secretaries of state whose statutory or other executive responsibility they were. David Blunkett, first at Education and then at the Home Office over crime and disorder was more resistant to central micro-management.

[12] One Brown biographer believes that despite disagreements and tension, their relations remained good until spring, 2002: Bower (2004) 395. Discussed at length in Peston (2005).

[13] A Bevins, *The Independent,* 19 January 1998; R Sylvester, *Daily Telegraph,* 9 February 1998; S Jenkins, *Times,* 29 July 1998.

he was intellectually superior, were said to cause tension.[14] But many issues were settled between them at their bi-laterals or over the telephone.[15] Just what they said to each other was frequently among Whitehall's mysteries, since their outcome was often imperfectly communicated.[16] The media were frequently awash with tales of their disagreements, said to be particularly great in autumn, 2004.[17]

DIARCHY: AN EXPERIMENT IN MINISTERIAL DISCUSSION?

But though their power relationship held government together, their distinctive approaches could be divisive and confusing. For example, Clare Short's resignation speech stimulated some ministers to want Cabinet to discuss if there should be a referendum over the Euro.[18] Instead of a full Cabinet discussion, there were tri-laterals, Blair and Brown with each Cabinet minister in turn. Brown, like Blair, hated large meetings, although in this instance Brown could probably have dominated Cabinet with his superior expertise and knowledge as he normally could a public meeting or the Commons. However, a full Cabinet discussion could have got out of control. Instead Brown insisted that each minister read the 25,000-word Treasury briefing over the weekend. They were not to use their civil servants to précis it or brief them on the issues.[19] Given that Blair wanted to leave open the chance of joining the Euro more quickly; that most ministers were pro-European; and that Blair had more public persuasive power than Brown, it was plausibly a Brown tactic to redress the balance of power in his favour.[20] As a highly intelligent man with Thatcher's appetite for digesting academic papers, he knew them inside out.

But to stop officials briefing ministers was extraordinary. Since the Treasury papers were not only long, but technical, this attitude signified that Cabinet Government had ended in another sense. Its essence had been that Cabinets constantly reached decisions on matters on which most ministers were not

[14] Articles, even books, were written about them: how Mandelson had decided, to Brown's mortification, that Blair was the better bet to win an election; and how they had drawn up a pact to define relations between them before and during their period in office, as well as promising the reversion of the Prime Ministership to Brown at some undisclosed date.

[15] Early on Blair and Brown were to said to have met face-to-face or telephoned 4 or 5 times a day: Bower (2004) 223.

[16] After a difficult start, their meetings were generally minuted, but their circulation excluded many, who would have been expected to receive them under previous regimes on a need-to-know basis. Brownites said Heywood's minutes—an experienced Treasury official and long Blair's principal private secretary—bore no relation to what had happened at PM/GB meetings: Seldon (2004) 669; also Peston (2005).

[17] D Scott (2004).

[18] Eg *Sunday Telegraph,* 11 May 2003.

[19] *Times,* 16 May 2003; *Telegraph,* 17 May 2003.

[20] However two of Blair's aides, Liddle and Scott, were reported as saying they couldn't detect where Blair stood on the Euro: Rawnsley (2001) 74. But see Peston (2005).

expert. That ministers had different experience, skills and personalities, made it likelier they would reach a balanced conclusion. They did so based on summaries and analyses which officials had the skills to prepare. Not many chancellors—let alone his Cabinet colleagues—would have digested 25,000 words on any issue at one time, even one so important, and as well-argued as these papers were. Not even Crosland—with his formidable intellect and gifts of comprehension—would have mastered as much paper in a few days. Indeed his tendency to demand a week or more to understand and test a major policy document was what helped make his period at DOE less productive than it should have been (above chapter 6).

Collegiate Cabinet Government depended on civil servants being trusted to be objective and impartial when boiling issues down to the minimum length for satisfactory decision-making. Its replacement by the notion that government should be by experts and near-experts—acting within a discipline imposed by special advisers, media experts, pollsters and outside academics—was a transformation. No longer were Cabinet ministers valued as highly as were Blair and Brown's policy advisers and Blair's pollsters. Not for their political judgement or skills; nor for their knowledge of public, party or other political opinion. Nor for any other expertise or experience. Though there were exceptions, Blair's special advisers tended to be media specialists and academics. Brown's Treasury—special advisers and the rest—were increasingly professional macroeconomists. Except for Brown himself, who had acquired a considerable understanding of economics, though not an economist, almost absent now were the economic generalists whose job it had been to make the department's policy proposals intelligible to Cabinet, Parliament and the public.[21]

There was more to how these papers were used. Policymaking is not just producing descriptions, explanations and predictions of the consequences of a given policy, in this case joining the Euro. That falls into the trap, of which David Hume warned—and which many have fallen into before and since—of trying to derive 'ought' from 'is'. A rational policy decision requires the further factual exercises of identifying the gainers and losers from a change, giving some attention to enumeration of the benefits and costs to each—if at all important, and certainly in this case, doing it numerically—and in many cases considering the distribution of those costs and benefits through the community.[22] The necessary normative or political weighing of the pros and cons of the options under review could frequently be done qualitatively, as was long consistent with their presentation in Cabinet papers under the British system. But not only in an instance like this one, ministers might have been glad of a formal and, as far as possible, comprehensive cost-benefit analysis, which would still have allowed

---

[21] Peston (2005) saw it as unique, not understanding the constitutional oddity of not letting economically literate officials translate economics into terms ministers could actually understand.

[22] One ex-minister told me he thought that the best approximation to such a deliberative approach was to be found in the Cabinet Office's Better Regulation unit.

Cabinet to reach a variety of political decisions depending on the weight given to all the various considerations.[23] Here Blair and Brown drew their conclusions, apparently without such analysis, at least a comprehensive one, and without exposing their rationale in doing so.

But there was still more to the issue, since Blair himself, unlike Thatcher, was no expert reader of papers. Though he could digest a mass of papers before a European summit, he was no terrier like Thatcher, no critical reader of papers put to him, except insofar as he liked or disliked their overall tendency or tone. Therefore, as we have seen, he depended on concise briefing from his Policy Directorate.[24] Revealed was a clash of styles between the two men, who in a diarchy at the heart of government, largely determined its policies.[25] Blair's was instinctive, dependent in his decision-making on how the media and public opinion were judged to react, and on outside experts, real and presumed. Brown's was expressed through the medium—mostly economic—of evidence, analysis and models (though often fatally not carried through so far as really to grip the problems of implementation).[26] It had spread from macro-economic policy to being the life-blood of what became Treasury control over domestic policymaking, especially evident during its periodic public expenditure reviews.

THE CASCADE PRINCIPLE

A further source of confusion was that who decided what depended also on what the PM had the time, energy and inclination for. If *subsidiarity* is the principle that decisions be taken by the lowest level of government with the resources, expertise and powers capable of doing so, Blair's government now operated by its reverse, that is, by what might be called the *cascade* principle. Except for those Brown made, decisions were taken at the highest, the prime-ministerial, level, but only to the extent No 10 wanted or could cope with them. No 10 invariably believed it could cope with more than it could. As we have

---

[23] Professor Richard Layard of the LSE was the foremost British academic economist behind much of Brown's thinking on how to reduce welfare dependency. He warned him not only that many issues of implementation were unsolved, but that a cost-benefit analysis was also needed: Bower (2004) 241–42.

[24] In August 2001, the PM's private office and policy unit were combined into his Policy Directorate, the previous heads of each—Jeremy Heywood, an official, and Andrew Adonis, a special adviser—becoming joint heads. All the private secretaries were re-named policy advisers, a subtle indication of a change of function: J Sherman, *Times,* 18 August 2001.

[25] Blair was said to show lack of interest in policy compared with Brown. Rather, the difference was that Brown had thought everything through. However like Blair he showed no interest in 'proper papers, discussion and minuted records' according to one official: Seldon (2004) 666–68. The papers Brown preferred were by academics and other outsiders and were generally light on problems of implementation. Hence the often over-complicated tax and benefit proposals which required excessive resources to implement (private information).

[26] E.g Bower (2004) 180–81; 211–13, 234–35, 242–43 (tax credits); 238, 257 (tax breaks for savings); 293–94 (working families' tax credits); 309 (ILAs); 335 (NHS targets); 369–72 (the transformation of the Revenue into a Benefits department).

seen, there were times when Blair, using Michael Barber of the Cabinet Office Delivery Unit as his agent, seemed to be overseeing the NHS, education, crime and the railways single-handed.[27] It was even said that 9/11 knocked the PM off course from improving the public services.[28] Moreover under the daily stresses of news management what No 10 believed it must decide was constantly changing. Administrative detail could blow up into something it was thought the PM must settle. If sooner or later, it became clear the PM could or would not deal with them, then the departmental minister might. If ministers had not the time or inclination, it might trickle down to civil servant or agency, complicating further the problem of knowing—and legitimating—what had been decided and by whom.

Blunkett—along with Brown—became unique in that he had the independence to announce endless initiatives at the Home Office whatever No 10 thought. Other ministers must reveal their intentions to the Policy Unit through constant interrogations, and to other ministers through correspondence. Ministers found that how best to do what they wanted was to keep those intentions as concealed as possible in the hope they might not be noticed. But while some ministers may not have wanted the Centre to know what they were thinking, more did not appreciate, at least at first, the misunderstandings which can arise if agreed decisions are not written down and communicated clearly to those who must implement them.[29] Few Cabinet ministers were as lucky as Clare Short, able to do a good job because No 10 took virtually no interest in what she was up to. Many, at least for a time, found a quiet corner where they could make some decisions. But inevitably, it was a fragmented, not collegiate, and in many respects inefficient, even chaotic government.

Blair's failing grip over his ministers from 2003 meant he had to spend more time with them over the most newsworthy issues and had still less time for other important issues, so more was cascaded to departmental ministers and the vagaries of resolving disputes between them by correspondence. Such complicated and shifting patterns of responsibility further strained Cabinet solidarity, since it made it hard to report on all that was going on in a short Cabinet and hard for anyone, even the PM, to remember all of it. How will one know if Hoon—and for some reason Cook—but apparently not the PM, knew the weapons the Iraqis could launch in 45 minutes were only battlefield ones, unless such an important fact is written down in a Cabinet paper or otherwise recorded in a minuted discussion?

By the end of 2004, it seemed neither a presidential nor Cabinet, but chaotic, government in which who led on what often seemed a matter of chance. Outsiders contacting No 10 might be told the PM indeed wanted something they

[27] At the end of July, 2003, at a press conference at which Blair expounded again his vision for improving public services, Barber was exposed to them as the first item. The news people present could at times find the management jargon he used utterly alien, *Sunday Telegraph*, 3 August 2003.
[28] Seldon (2004) 483.
[29] J Jones (1999) 198, but 156.

wanted, but was stopped by the departmental minister or Brown.[30] Was it the truth or subterfuge?

MINISTERS' FUNCTIONS

A casualty of Blair's method of operating government was that almost all ministers lost importance and status. Legally ministers still had the statutory functions, but practically Blair—and to some extent Brown—tried taking them over as and when they chose.[31] No 10 special advisers could be found chairing meetings of ministers.[32] Ed Balls, Brown's *de facto* Deputy Chancellor and permanent secretary was said to be openly disdainful of the PM.[33] No 10 now required contrary qualities from its senior ministers: impressiveness to enhance the government's public and media reputation, but also subservience, a willingness to do what the Prime Minister (or Brown) wanted, a willingness, too, to yield to them any credit when it was going, but to shoulder the blame when that was needed. But it was not always easy to find ministers that docile, or, if they were, they could have other failings, like Stephen Byers and Estelle Morris.

No 10 did not want ciphers. The media, and the Prime Minister, still expected ministers instantly to know about and correct everything they raised a fuss about. That expectation encouraged a process by which departmental ministers, senior and junior, were turned into the chief operating officers (COOs) of subsidiaries, obliged to correct, that is, change, what was going on beneath them. It wanted COOs who would pursue the objectives given them with imagination, energy and relentless attention to detail. Until deterred by Commons' resentment, Blair appointed some with business experience, whom he made peers, to ministerial and quasi-ministerial posts, though he did not use those with the most relevant business experience—Lords Haskins, Simon, Sainsbury and Birt—as COOs.[34] However, nothing in most ministers' previous experience had prepared them for this role. Even among Conservative MPs, Heseltine and, later, Archie Norman were rare birds with substantial business experience. Moreover, especially where the chief executive is not omni-competent and tireless, chief operating officers need—and usually are given—the freedom to manage within the broad parameters laid down, while ministers and other heads of delivery units mostly were not. The notion—central to the Prime Minister's conception of his role, and by delegation that of his ministers—that they should intervene in the day-to-day working of any part of government or the public services whenever news management seemed to justify it—without

[30] Private information.

[31] The major exceptions were those decisions—eg planning—where ministers had to go through statutory processes.

[32] As Adonis apparently chaired meetings with Robin Cook and Gareth Williams: Cook (2003) 51–52.

[33] Seldon (2004) 671, 677.

[34] Apparently he would have liked to: Seldon (2004) 436.

reckoning the cost—was the antithesis of good management and not conducive
to improved efficiency.

LAWMAKING

Lawmaking remained as difficult and excessive as it had been in the previous 25
years. Because many issues remained undecided for too long by the Prime
Minister or by ministers at a lower level, different ministers—too long pursuing
their own preferred attitudes to policy—were another reason why white papers
were botched or avoided; and why bills, when introduced into Parliament and
sometimes long afterwards, were found still straddling unreconciled and sometimes conflicting points of view (above chapter 10).

DELIVERY

Once policy was decided, even if only in sound-bites and press-releases, the
Prime Minister, and at times other ministers, spoke as if the implementation and
delivery of policy was for 'them'. Hence the urge to turn ministers and civil servants into managers. Brown's new approach to public expenditure planning
was at the heart of public sector improvement. In many respects a sensible adaptation of an enlightened private sector model, it could have provided an assured
policy framework within which departments and agencies were given managerial freedom to spend their money and meet their targets, subject to monitoring,
but only to intervention when something went seriously wrong. But there were
several reasons why it did not.

It was not helped by confusion between Brown's two roles—as Chief
Executive and Finance Director—and Blair's. It was as if ultimate authority in
BP or Tesco lay with its Director of Communications. Since Blair and Brown do
not behave like past PMs and chancellors, clarity was lacking over their job
descriptions. Once there were said to be some 6000 targets, an impossible number for effective management and often arbitrarily initiated by the Treasury
without proper consultation with departments and agencies. Gradually many
poorly-specified targets were eliminated or replaced. But even after seven years
many remained ill-defined, or gave perverse incentives, or made presentational
rather than management sense.[35]

An insufficient recognition of a fundamental difference between private and
public sector vitiated the process. Making a greater profit is the private sector's
only objective. Every intermediate target can be seen, and evaluated in terms of
the contribution it is expected to make to a firm's profit.[36] Little attempt has

[35] T Travers in (2003) *Public Finance,* 22 August.
[36] An exception may seem to be when a firm has to meet a legal obligation—for example over
safety and the environment—but it will still aim to meet the obligation at the least possible cost.

been made to develop similar single-valued non-profit objectives for public bodies.[37] Almost all public bodies have multiple objectives. Working out the trade-off between them is inevitably a political process, either done internally or imposed from without.[38] Whichever was the norm, public bodies were at the mercy of central or departmental policy initiatives altering those trade-offs and so affecting their ability to achieve their targets. Imposing trade-offs between multiple objectives and targets from above is inconsistent with management freedom and efficiency.

The fragmented public sector, which Blair inherited (above, chapter 11), meant networks of public, and sometimes private and voluntary, bodies must often co-operate if each were to realise its targets. Too frequently—especially if reporting to different departments—they had conflicting targets and incentives. Making such networks operate as one often presented insuperable problems. If the public sector is to become efficient, complex networks must be disentangled into simpler stand-alone bodies; or each and every part of them must be given clear objectives and financial frameworks consistent with every other part, a formidable task.

Furthermore the outcome was an encouragement to influence-peddling which cut across normal channels of democratic accountability. The main argument behind John Prescott's urging that the North-East should vote in a referendum for a regional assembly was that it would gain One Voice—to set against all the other voices—to lobby in the corridors of Whitehall.

Many bodies in these networks were inspectors, auditors or regulators, often independent enough for their policies—which could also change unexpectedly—to clash with government policy and prevent public bodies realising their targets. Blair's government created even more public bodies, many also with poorly defined objectives, responsibilities and indistinct boundaries with neighbouring bodies. Ministers and officials could spend endless time trying to overcome the consequences of these perversities.

Neither did ministers try to determine the legal, or even conventional, relations between government, its agencies and other public bodies. The formal ability of departments to instruct a public body—never the Centre which formally had no such ability—varied from agencies which ministers could instruct—because departmental off-shoots—to statutory bodies and local authorities over which they had no, or limited, legal powers. The Centre was constantly complaining that departments were using their 'default powers'—

---

[37] On one such attempt for the NHS (the Qly). another for public transport (passenger-mile maximisation per £ subsidy), and more generally on the problem of setting targets, especially where there are multiple objectives, see Foster (1992) 243–47, 362–65; also Foster and Plowden (1996) 161–64, 198.

[38] An important hidden issue here (see Chapter 16) was how ministers imposed these trade-offs. Did they do it openly by publishing explicit numerical criteria? Or did they insist on the right to intervene in a hidden and underhanded way as the independent rail regulator, Tom Winsor, found when Stephen Byers told him he would rush a law through Parliament if Winsor did not do what Byers wanted (Winsor) (2004a, b and d).

that is, the fact that any legal powers, which existed to enforce compliance, belonged to them—to dawdle or otherwise avoid doing what the Centre wanted. Public bodies could also use their default powers to procrastinate or bargain with departments. But the more the Centre interfered, the more those in the field complained of being overwhelmed by bureaucracy.[39]

While public expenditure seemed abundant, it was used to induce compliance and make policy networks work. Special grants were invented, prizes awarded, other financial inducements contrived. Some were given more money because they were good and thought able to spend more, some were given more because they were bad and needed more to catch up.[40] But how would similar compliance be achieved if, as seemed increasingly likely from 2004, a shortage of public expenditure meant there was no longer the additional money to do so? Already sticks as well as carrots were quixotically used to motivate more compliant behaviour. But how does fining a hospital a million pounds help it do better, when it has done well against all its targets, except shortening its waiting list?

A further perversity was that ministers still tried to interfere more while avoiding blame. Often because of the exigencies of news management and parliamentary questioning, ministers were constantly being interfered with, as they in they turn wanted to interfere with their agencies or associated public bodies, including local authorities. But the reasons for central intervention in public bodies were seldom to help them meet their targets or otherwise improve their efficiency.

The commonest came from the daily problems of news management. No 10 frequently interfered with departments, public bodies and even private firms supplying the public sector, or substantially dependent on public money like the rail companies, when they were in the public eye. Whenever a complaint, or a crisis, blew up, either No 10, if it were a media sensation, or the departmental minister would intervene. Frequently the outcome of such interventions was a policy change or other requirement which affected a public body's ability to improve or deliver.

This hyperactivity reinforced a blame avoidance culture in which responsibility for something going wrong was shuffled onto someone else. With moderate care ministers could always protest that what went wrong was someone else's fault.[41] Scapegoats, when needed, were now commonly officials, even when responsibilities were poorly defined and, through interference, they had not the managerial freedom to be truly responsible. David Blunkett was among those particularly apt to blame his officials, or judges, or the police, or someone else, when anything went wrong.

---

[39] Private information.

[40] Brown was often persuadable that the public expenditure allocated to a department could be vired providing he could be assured that the targets laid down could be met.

[41] For examples of the length to which Brown allegedly went to avoid blame, see Bower (2004) 210, 255–59, 294, 360–61, 337, 390.

Policymaking—once ministers' characteristic role—became a job for No 10 or No 11, involving ministers as junior partners. The Centre had the last word. The role of ministers in central policymaking became, in general, that of implementing what had been decided above them, a top-down rather than a bottom-up process[42], except in so far as the cascade principle gave them freedom. But those at the Centre did not have the time to engage in the sustained iterative process needed to demonstrate policy coherence or the thoroughness and practicality of what was proposed, nor the time to find a more practical alternative, either before the decay of Blair's power in 2003, or after, when policymaking became more chaotic[43].

However, the cascade principle meant Cabinet ministers took other, generally less important, decisions off their own bat. They did so without the political and interdepartmental testing to which the old Cabinet system had subjected significant changes in ministerial policies. Perversely a government, which had come in wedded to promoting more interdepartmental initiatives—more joined-up working—for this reason found interdepartmental co-operation harder. Another reason was that without Cabinet solidarity; with a less collegiate sense of a common interest; and with No 10 advisers regularly going behind their backs to junior ministers and officials to check what was up, ministers became more reluctant to allow officials from different departments to consult each other and sort out difficulties in advance.[44] On their own, some ministers could even run foul of the law, as Stephen Byers allegedly had when criticised for illegal handouts to private firms.[45]

Because usually so little involved in developing their bills or consulting over them, ministers frequently had little detailed knowledge of them (above, chapter 10). In the past (above, chapter 4) ministers had had to defend them, and the policies on which they were based, to many interest groups, as part of consultation. Instead officials could be found explaining and defending all sorts of policies to many kinds of audience, which almost inevitably made it difficult for them not to appear politicised.

The government prided itself on the extent of its consultative processes along policy networks, but there was nothing like the steady, iterative processes of the past. Ironically the processes of consulting on proposed new legislation took more time and resources than ever before, but consulting tended to be over detailed policy points only: not over the rationale of the whole policy or the demonstrable practicality—after consultation—of its implementation.

---

[42] When minister at the Cabinet Office, Mo Mowlam found 'more and more decisions taken without consultation with the relevant secretaries of state': Mowlam (2002) 356.

[43] Sir John Coles, Permanent Under-Secretary at the Foreign Office until late 1997, has described the parallel decline in attention Cabinet ministers gave foreign policy making and particularly to thinking ahead. They spent much more time on it in the 1950s and even into the 1960s, but thereafter progressively less: Coles (2000), *passim*.

[44] Mowlam (2002) 356; private sources.

[45] *Sunday Times*, 30 April 2000.

Moreover there were often widespread doubts over how much ministers were listening, particularly since government had lost the habit of producing a White Paper which reviewed substantive comments and argued why they were accepted or rejected. Consultation often seemed to be regarded as the legal necessity it was, rather than as a way of improving legislation or other policy initiative and making it more practical.

MINISTERS AS MANAGERS

Ministers' principal function became that of progress-chasers, spending a substantial proportion of their time—like the chief operating officers of sub-sidiaries in business—on the telephone, demanding to know from agencies or local government why this, that or the other, had or had not been done. Departments had to submit returns by which they could be monitored either to the Treasury or in the four problem areas selected by Blair—health, education, crime and order, and transport—to Blair himself. Their regular meetings with him and the Delivery Unit—often falling by the wayside because of other pressures on his time—became ordeals for ministers, and exasperating occasions for him, as he struggled to overcome the non-delivery of their, or rather Blair or Brown's, plans.

Therefore, while power was centralised, it was perhaps unsurprising that those at the Centre complained they still had not enough power to modernise government and establish their policies. The Prime Minister rebuked departments: they were not ready enough 'to think outside the Box'; they were too prone to think everything must be 'incremental'. Despite theirs being all the statutory powers, Blair overrode ministers when, and wherever, he wanted. That became harder from 2003. Even before then, departments and agencies were said by the Centre to use their 'default' powers to impede. They did not show enough initiative. Above all they did not 'deliver'. They were too slow. Departments found that the Centre simply did not understand the complexity and slowness of the processes that had to be gone through to persuade people to do what they did not want to do. One very senior policy adviser was puzzled it did not seem as yet possible to write a Manual detailed enough to set out exactly what everyone should be doing in every operation.[46] Or the density of regulations required to implement the detail the Centre was ready to go into in specifying just what was needed to avoid a postcode lottery—as with curricula or waiting lists—if the demand were to be lawful. Somehow the Centre seemed to think some user-friendly slideshow could magic doubts away and inspire enthusiasm. They did not appreciate that while it may be possible to drive single-objective private firms, by issuing instructions from above and using fear to secure their implementation—however, never a wise and sometimes a fatal

[46] Private information.

policy in place of leadership—one cannot run multi-objective public organisations in that way. They require good communication up and down the line, leadership and more management freedom than single-objective bodies do.

While public expenditure was abundant, ministers could go far in persuading local authorities and others to obey the Centre, though it remained almost impossible to aspire to uniformity of service provision, given the plethora of public, private and voluntary bodies—often varying locally in their configurations, abilities and attitudes—which were involved in delivery (above, chapter 11). But, even then, surely opposition to the reforms imposed would dissolve, if only agency chiefs and their managers at all levels had half Blair's presentational skills? Meanwhile No 10 did not hesitate to brief against ministers, often long before the PM sacked them, seldom giving a reason beyond saying he wanted their place for someone else.[47]

In the private sector unless the business is exceptionally simple or its every detail can be reflected in a computerised blueprint, it is unwise to assume that its operations can be laid down, even more altered, simply by instructions issued on high. A leadership that listens is fundamental to better delivery. Even the Japanese rightly argue the greater wisdom of not being too mechanistic and of involving the workforce by giving them room to shape and improve what they are doing. People do not perform best as cogs. All the more so in the public sector where virtually all bodies have multiple objectives. One cannot expect good policies, even more satisfactory implementation, unless they are given well-defined and observed management freedom, as well as protection from too many policy changes and other interventions from on high, many prompted by news management and blame avoidance. Neither must there be inappropriateness or cronyism in making senior appointments. Blair's methods made substantial improvement of most public services impossible except by expenditure of more public money.

CONCLUSION

The fundamental flaw was to expect ministers to be subordinate media handlers, but also managers. There has long been controversy over whether management was sensibly among their functions, while in practice few ministers even tried to be managers, despite the pressure Thatcher put them under to take management seriously. Prime ministerial, like presidential, government may only have use for managers. If so, that normally means they should be businessmen or others with experience of managing large organisations, not politicians. If management was to be their prime function, then there were other places, as in the USA, one would look, not to MPs almost all of whom had no appreciable experience of it. Ministers are on a hiding to nothing if they are no more than

[47] Mowlam (2002) 352–56; Ingham (2003) 187.

spokesmen under orders, managers and progress-chasers, as Estelle Morris admitted when she resigned as secretary of state for education.

If ministers are to be a necessary part of a well-functioning government—whether prime ministerial or collegiate—they must do what they can do best which traditionally has been decision, policy and lawmaking as well as explaining and defending those activities to Cabinet colleagues, Parliament, the media and the public. One man—or a diarchy—cannot sensibly attempt these functions. They will become grotesquely overloaded. Who decides what will be hidden by the erratic operations of the cascade principle. Their political courts will quarrel and disagree. There are other dangers of absolutism. As the poll-tax showed, government need more than one overwhelming politician, the Prime Minister. Moreover without Cabinet Government one cannot provide the roles and experience to enable his or her potential successors either to fall by the wayside or develop the knowledge and skills to occupy the highest positions in the state.

However, there is another factor. Comparing the quality of ministers over the generations is not easy. My own belief (chapter 10) is that there is no reason to suppose contemporary MPs—though impoverished by their lack of non-political experience—intrinsically les able than those I knew in the past. As well as the way they are used diminishing them, the other main reason for their lower public standing is that they are no longer boosted, as their predecessors were, by the support (above, Chapters 2, 3 and 4) close partnership with their officials once gave them.

15

Civil Service: End of Northcote-Trevelyan

... it is not fanciful to say that the constitutional textbooks are truer now than they have been for some time ... Officials ... have been brought obediently to heel by the mighty hand of three successive democratic mandates ... What we have lost and are in danger of losing forever is institutionalised scepticism.

Hugo Young (1990)[1]

Disoriented and destabilised by a decade of almost continuous change, many civil servants are now uncertain about what the future holds both for themselves and their profession ... Fifteen years ago the importance of the civil service would have seemed self-evident and beyond question.

William Plowden (1994)[2]

SOMETIMES IT IS suggested Thatcher and Blair regarded civil servants similarly, but it was not so. Thatcher narrowed the scope within which they could challenge ministers, but they were still treated as partners. Blair treated them as subordinates and excluded them from central policymaking unless ready to be politicised.

THE CIVIL SERVICE UNDER THATCHER

Most senior officials found the Thatcher years strenuous, often fraught, but usually exhilarating, preferable to the previous frustrating decade. There was important and interesting work to do and a dawning realisation that Britain was emerging from its economic troubles at last; and that they were part of that process. The sense of shame lifted, which Nicholas Henderson had felt, when Ambassador to France, in representing a nation stumbling from one crisis and failure to another.[3] But some changes affecting ministers' relations with their officials had lasting effect.

---

[1] Hugo Young quoted in Campbell and Wilson (1995) 60.
[2] Plowden (1994) 1.
[3] Henderson (1994) 271–72.

Margaret Thatcher had a visceral distrust of corporatism and therefore of large institutions. She distrusted the civil service as such an institution, and thought it responsible for past failures—alongside many ministers, Tory and Labour—and an unworkable system.[4] Her distrust led to early spats with permanent secretaries and the sidelining of the head of the Treasury, Sir Douglas Wass, for doubting her economic policies. Her antipathy crystallised at a disastrous dinner with permanent secretaries meant to clear the air, but leaving her surer than ever that their intention was to criticise rather than support her.[5] A year later she asserted her ascendancy by closing down the Civil Service Department and forcing the head of the civil service, Sir Ian Bancroft, into early retirement.[6]

As an inducement to cut waste, Thatcher imposed a target of cutting civil service numbers in departments by 1984 by more than 100,000 from their 1979 level of 732,000. This target was achieved. By 1990 another 70,000 had gone.[7] Most senior civil servants agreed there was overmanning, some civil servants doing jobs which investigation proved unnecessary. Her motives were not only to reduce the size of government and achieve public expenditure cuts, but also a doctrinal presumption based on Niskanen, an American economist's, view—Keith Joseph recommended his book to his officials—that bureaucrats used their power to increase their numbers in their own self-interest.[8] However, the introduction of information technology into large clerical operations in the Inland Revenue and Social Security was most responsible for the fall in civil servant numbers, though policy change sometimes saved jobs. Geoffrey Howe's abolition of the reduced rate income tax band saved 1400 Inland Revenue jobs.

Top jobs were most cut back, especially specialist professionals. In the long run it was perhaps the most serious cut of all since it greatly reduced departments' ability to keep abreast of all scientific and social science developments in their field as well as to engage in their own research and analysis. Between 1979 and 1990, grade 1 to 3 jobs, that is, from permanent secretary to under-secretary, were cut by a quarter. But legislation and top officials' other work about doubled. Growth in numbers in the two grades below under-secretary entailed 'delayering' which in practice meant less experienced officials, less supervised by those with greater experience, more often making submissions directly to ministers. Reducing the opportunities for promotion was also demotivating. Yet with so much more legislation, the activity associated with it and more other policymaking activity, the workload on ministers and senior officials shot up.

Margaret Thatcher's suspicions of all professions as vested interests and her conviction politics meant that she, and those ministers who thought like her,

[4] Hennessy (1989) chapter 15; Kavanagh and Seldon (1999) chapter 6.
[5] H Young (1989) 230–31.
[6] There were other reasons for it, e.g. mismanagement of labour relations, leading to a civil service strike in 1981: Campbell and Wilson (1995) 44–45.
[7] Willman in Kavanagh and Seldon (1994).
[8] Chapman (1979) reinforced Niskanen's views. Also Dunleavy and O'Leary (1987).

influenced her hostility to the old civil service traditions of deliberation and consultation, followed by testing and adjusting policies to achieve consensus. She professed she did not understand why some ministers needed so much civil service help.[9] She and many ministers saw established civil service practices and procedures as often delaying the process of getting things done. Furthermore Niskanen suggested officials had not pursued them for their own sake, but to put politicians off the scent while officials went on maximising their power and budgets.[10] Such theories influenced her suspicions. She disliked consensus-seeking or appealing to the public interest. She and 'dry' ministers wanted less deliberative officials, less likely to question ministers' commitments and convictions, set out options, engage in lengthy consultation, or delay basic policy decisions by calling for statistics, analysis or research. Officials found that members of her Policy Unit were warning them the advice they gave ministers did not reflect her policies, an approach consistent with Nicholas Ridley's characterisation of her as Chief Executive with overall responsibility (above chapter 7), but at odds with the traditional convention of ministerial responsibility.[11]

But was it wrong for Treasury officials to set out the arguments against a rapid dismantling of exchange controls in 1979; or Sir Douglas Wass the arguments in favour of an expansionary budget in 1981? Or Education officials to warn against the difficulties of replacing student grants by loans? Or Heseltine and Heiser to argue against replacing rates in 1981? Or DTI officials against the abolition of regional development grant? Or DOE officials to try to persuade Patrick Jenkin of the disadvantages of introducing rate-capping, or abolishing the GLC and the metropolitan counties?[12] Was it better when, from the mid-years of her rule, such challenges were actively discouraged? Would it not have been better if more attention had been given to officials' reservations over the poll tax? Did everything have to be done in such a hurry that haste trumped thoroughness and practicality? Certainly civil servants could be wrong. So could outside interests. But policy and legislation will improve if serious reservations are weighed and overcome.

She and her ministers wanted and got a generation of civil servants who, without challenging ministers' convictions, still challenged every aspect of the implementation of those convictions and who worked hard, and with commitment, to implement their policies. Officials had plenty to do marshalling the evidence; getting the facts right; challenging policy detail and how policies were best implemented; drafting public documents and preparing bills; selecting and supervising the teams of consultants who now came to be used to work up methods of implementation. Why persevere with the traditional duty of challenging the bases of policy when, with the passing of years, fewer ministers

[9] Prior (1986) 134.
[10] Niskanen (1973) 6–8. A good, brief discussion is Mueller (1989) 447–73.
[11] Campbell and Wilson (1995) 257–58.
[12] Berberis (1994) 38.

appreciated it, and never the Prime Minister? Ministers became readier to assert that, because they were elected, not only could they overrule the advice they received in making the final decision—which had always been true—but they were readier to be peremptory in disregarding it earlier, as over the poll tax.

CIVIL SERVICE APPOINTMENTS

Another sign that the balance of power had swung back to ministers, most particularly to her, was Thatcher's unprecedented influence on the selection of the most senior civil servants.[13] Ministers in the past had been asked if they accepted the civil service nomination to senior posts in their department, but expecting they would do so. An old man wanting familiar faces, Churchill demanded Norman Brook back as Cabinet secretary, not the just appointed Tom Padmore, but his was a rare insistence. However, Thatcher wanted senior posts filled by 'one of us', by which she did not mean the politically sympathetic.[14] A Commons committee reported her preferences were considered when short-listing for senior posts;[15] but an inquiry was to absolve her of the 'politicisation' of such appointments.[16] However, that was to define the issue narrowly.[17] She was not interested in their politics. Some officials thought how they dressed mattered more. Conviction politics meant officials must conform to and work within the political convictions ministers held and not challenge those convictions, or question if they had identified the problem correctly, or ask what they were really trying to achieve.[18] If they did, they might find themselves not promoted or even in early retirement. Some did not make the transition from consensual to conviction politics. Donald Derx, a high-flier, was tipped to become permanent secretary, but was unwise enough to ask her to her face, 'Prime Minister, do you really want to know the facts?'[19] He did not get the job. It was not so much what he said, but the bluntness with which he said it. Only within those constraints did she want independence of judgement, objectivity and 'speaking truth to power'. Candidates for top jobs could be passed over if not in that sense Thatcherite, though thought politically conservative, as Sir Anthony Rawlinson was for the Treasury. However, neither she nor other ministers picked individuals as was to happen after 1990. She simply made known

[13] Campbell and Wilson (1995) 64–66, 262–65; Smith (1999) 141; Dowding (1995) 124–25; HC Debates 92, 1985–86, vol 1, 157; vol 2 Q 728; Lawson (1992) 267.

[14] Campbell and Wilson (1995) 262–63; Plowden (1994) 94–95.

[15] House of Commons Treasury and Civil Service Committee (1985); (1986) 'Civil Servants and Ministers', vol 2, 154; Callaghan said he took no part in senior appointments, HC Debates 92, 1985–86, vol 2, Q 728; Richards (1997).

[16] RIPA (1987).

[17] House of Commons Treasury and Civil Service Committee (1993) 'The Role of the Civil Service', vol 1; Hennessy (1989) 630–34.

[18] Campbell and Wilson (1995) 65.

[19] Prior (1986) 186. Prior, his boss at Employment, described Derx as among the best and most dedicated officials he had.

what she thought the qualifications should be. Her influence over the top appointments seeped down to lower ranks who soon learned the qualities needed for promotion.

Her general distrust lasted until as a consequence of her influence a new, but still non-politicised, type of civil servant emerged at the top of departments, sometimes called a 'Can-Do' type, but misleadingly, because there were many 'doers' in the past and both Peter Carey and Frank Cooper were such among those she inherited.[20] When Peter Middleton unexpectedly succeeded as head of the Treasury in 1983, he was called a 'trouble-shooter.'[21] Some officials of a thoughtful, intellectual, deliberative, but more sceptical, cast of mind, or less pushy—who, one believed, would have reached the top in the old days— marked time, not suited for conviction politics. There were more casualties on the way up. But there were plenty of Can-Do types to succeed. And plenty for them to do.

An irony was that Margaret Thatcher found the civil servants in No 10 hard working, agile and just what she needed.[22] While initially advised to surround herself with political appointees, she soon found the civil servants more reliable, loyal and useful. She was not sad for long when John Hoskyns and Norman Strauss from her first Policy Unit decided to go.[23] Even she acknowledged to the Scott Inquiry that she could not read all papers coming to her. Rather her civil servants did.[24] She was kind and considerate towards them, not trying to rule them by fear, as she did ministers and civil servants not in her circle. She built up such a circle of officials and some, Ingham and Powell, she kept past normal civil service practice. She found the CPRS tiresome, rather than useful, and abolished it. The number of special advisers around her declined during her years in office, as they did also in the departments, where their job returned mostly to speech-writing and party contacts.

At the same time most ministers developed good relations with their officials. The 'companionable embrace'—close partnership between ministers and their officials—remained, unimpeded by special advisers. New legislation had increased the ministerial decisions to be taken. Most were still made in the time-honoured way by officials in their name, referring specimen or unusual decisions to ministers for approval. The Carltona principle of organic unity of minister and official still held in decision-making. Ministers still needed officials to carry through new policies, implement legislation and otherwise play the Whitehall game, especially over public expenditure.[25] Most ministers appreciated their civil servants.[26]

[20] Richards (1997).
[21] Lawson (1992) 268–69.
[22] Kavanagh and Seldon (1999) 145–86.
[23] Hoskyns (2000) chapter 18.
[24] Campbell and Wilson (1995) 24.
[25] Tebbitt (1988) 182.
[26] Norton in Rhodes (2001) 112–13.

DECLINE IN PUBLIC INTEREST AND CONSENSUS-SEEKING

However, there were several ways in which the standing and influence of officials were undermined. With reduced numbers and conviction politics, pressure of business meant that from about 1983 official consultation of outside interests often became unsystematic. Conviction politics, shortage of time and fewer policymaking officials, made some ministers less willing to allow civil servants to consult with the interest groups relevant to a bill, though ministers varied in this.[27] Regularly lunching out began to seem self-indulgent and time-wasting, rather than a necessary programme to update officials' outside contacts. Senior civil servants more often found themselves eating a sandwich lunch at their desk. By the early 1990s, unthinkable a decade earlier, a senior minister told me it had not occurred to him to consider his civil servants the main source of information about what the various pressure groups, trade associations and experts thought.[28]

Another, but invisible, factor in the decline of civil service robustness before ministers was the frequent deterioration of the departmental information bases. Protected by the 30 year rule, historians do not realise how much harder it will be to reconstruct how governments work.[29] Pressure of work in departments meant the filing was no longer as systematic and comprehensive as had been standard. That decline eroded the collective memory and undermined the assurance civil servants had that they could easily access virtually all the administrative precedents, the law, the latest interest-group opinions and other knowledge relevant to the areas for which they were administratively responsible. The failure to develop the use of IT adequately—expenditure on this was cut—in lieu of staff cuts made during the 1980s and 1990s helped undermine the filing systems and in many areas further weakened the authority and knowledge of civil servants. (Not everywhere. The BSE inquiry found Ministry of Agriculture files as meticulous as ever.)[30]

A further factor was that conviction politics had less time for research, particularly in the social sciences. Instead of professional staff being built up—which would have been a godsend after 1997—and made more use of in policymaking, in some but not all departments less money was spent on them and less use made of internal and external research. The running down of many departments' professional staffs in undermining their command of research and other knowledge, relevant to their policy areas, and so their ability to support and challenge, cannot be underestimated.

[27] Norton in Rhodes (2001) 114–15.
[28] John MacGregor.
[29] Unless ready to trawl through mounds of fragmented, ill-related and often incoherent e-mails.
[30] Although it proved possible to reconstruct most of the files needed for the Scott (and the Legg) Inquiry, in the first case it took time and there were some omissions in both. The files, to contain all the papers that led up to the decisions on the poll-tax, never were reconstructed with completeness, private information.

STANDARDS

A permanent secretary at the end of the 1970s and early 1980s later recalled a significant change.[31] When a minister's private secretary, he could not recall the permanent secretary consulting the minister before appearing before the Public Accounts Committee. Rather the permanent secretary assumed his whole duty was to be objective and tell the truth, however uncomfortable, when challenged about departmental finances. When asked what the policy was within which the department was operating, he would make a plain statement about it, not expecting to be tripped up. Because of media interest in departmental detail and greater partisanship in Parliament, both absent before, he found himself in 1979–81 consulting the minister in advance before the PAC on the policy aspects of his evidence. It was a subtle recognition of how objectivity and truth-telling to Parliament were yielding to deference to ministers as the leading official duty and also that plain expressions of ministerial policy might be less readily found in the public domain.

Later accusations that civil servants were being politicised took the form of allegations that sometimes they were forced to help in writing political speeches or be complicit when ministers told untruths. A civil servant, Clive Ponting, was so troubled by the government planning to mislead Parliament about the circumstances in which the Belgrano was sunk in the Falklands War that he went public about it, was dismissed and prosecuted. In apparently concealing government policy over sales of arms to Saddam Hussein, some officials were tainted with the charge of no longer insisting on telling the truth or being objective.[32] There were also worries about the authenticity of unemployment figures after changes made in the 1980s, allegedly for political reasons.[33] Under Terry Burns, a political appointee as chief economic adviser to the Treasury, and later still widely regarded as one when he became its permanent secretary, there were concerns that the government economic forecasts were being politicised in that they were criticised as giving too rosy a view of economic prospects, again to meet political requirements.[34]

In the Pergau dam affair Sir Timothy Lankester, permanent secretary to the Overseas Development Administration, had requested a ministerial instruction to make a much publicised loan to the Malaysian government to build that dam which he judged to be an imprudent and uneconomical use of aid money.[35] The

[31] Sir Patrick Nairne.
[32] Foster (1996).
[33] Campbell and Wilson (1995) 254.
[34] Campbell and Wilson (1995) 206, 221. Government statistics had rarely been so questioned before. By 2004 the Statistics Commission, the relevant watchdog, was calling for a statutory code of practice regulating official figures and misleading presentation or spinning of them, *Times*, 4 May 2004.
[35] *R v Secretary of State for Overseas Development ex parte World Development Movement*.

Public Accounts Committee upheld his view.[36] The courts later decided the loan was also unlawful. The government had to fund the project from outside the aid budget.

Bancroft's forced resignation, when the Civil Service Department was abolished, was a shock. Many officials wondered what next, if someone—among the best of the old school of civil servants—who was so shrewd, intelligent, perceptive, lucid, even if deliberate, in discussion and on paper, and kindly, could not be forgiven the blunt expression of opinions, which earlier ministers had welcomed.[37] What then ultimately mattered other than deference to ministerial convictions?[38] Under these pressures many officials became concerned whether they could always perform their duty to give objective, impartial advice, or advice on what was lawful, fair, truthful and not misleading, or to exercise what they saw as instrumental duties which by their nature they cannot share with ministers: to decide what options to bring and not bring to ministers; how summarily or in how much detail to give their advice; how far to simplify it by drawing analogies between one situation and another; when to reveal differences of opinion within the department where they existed; and how long to persist when a minister, inadvertently or deliberately, ignored their advice and yet they believed it vital.[39] Such difficulties arise only because ministers' decisions were often made in a rush and compromises must be made. Since no law prescribed such duties, the dilemma now took the inconvenient form of asking if officials had a duty above and beyond that to ministers, for example, to the Crown. Robert Armstrong gave an answer to that question in a considered statement:

> Civil servants are servants of the Crown. For all practical purposes the Crown in this context . . . is represented by the Government of the day . . . . The Civil Service as such has no constitutional personality or responsibility separate from the duly elected government of the day.[40]

It was intended to reinforce the convention that officials had no accountability or responsibility to Parliament except through ministers. So it seemed a reaffirmation of the traditional doctrine.[41] Yet the overwhelming tendency of the Armstrong memorandum was to imply there were no circumstances in which civil servants have duty superior to that they owe ministers, as long as they acted within the law. It is understood ministers make decisions bearing in mind the

---

[36] The Pergau case helped establish a new convention of reporting ministers' instructions over expenditure to the PAC.

[37] Wilson hard tried hard to rid himself of Sir Lawrence Helsby as Head of the Civil Service and failed. Private information.

[38] I remember Sir Peter Lazarus, when a deputy secretary in the 1970s becoming uncommonly fussed over the fate of tied cottages and atypically for him going on and on about it. Crosland was at first amused, then exasperated, but treated it as an aberration in an otherwise superb civil servant.

[39] Chipperfield (1994).

[40] Armstrong (1985).

[41] Private information.

advice given them. But again, suppose they disregard aspects of that advice or act only on the advice of political colleagues or outsiders?[42] Or reach their decisions inconsistently or unfairly or without considering the public interest first, or even unlawfully?

Armstrong was seen as undermining the positions of civil servants in such circumstances, even though such situations remained largely hypothetical. Part of the problem was that a Head of the Civil Service, who is Cabinet secretary as Armstrong was, and Bancroft was not, cannot as easily distance himself from daily political turmoil. From one standpoint Armstrong's words did not surprise civil servants, but threw into relief what some saw as a decline in the values they and ministers had once shared. Once a mere mention that something was not true was enough to dissuade a minister from saying it. Or, if they believed an important piece of advice was disregarded, they could filter it back to ministerial attention up the hierarchy or through the Cabinet system. Now under-supervised junior officials were found by Scott apparently trimming the truth to what they thought would be their minister's liking when drafting answers to PQs.[43] To some it seemed little more than poetic justice—perhaps unfairly—when Armstrong found himself in the *Spycatcher* case before an Australian court, defending ministers, come what may, and being tied in knots over Edmund Burke's phrase, 'being economical with the truth', it being interpreted as a euphemism for lying.

DENIGRATION

What most threatened to undermine officials' professional confidence was that the denigration to which they were subjected seeped into their souls.[44] If so bright, why were such intelligent people hiding in Whitehall when they could be in the real world earning real money?[45] In what they did, their deliberateness and absorption in procedure—in protecting legality, consistency, fairness and other values—were not widely appreciated by ministers. It was contrasted with the decisiveness and rapidity in action presumed characteristic of captains and lieutenants of industry. Though most ministers had no more knowledge of business than their officials, they were forced to adopt that model by the political and public reputation of business, and by their much hated business meetings with Thatcher. She frequently behaved as if Derek Rayner, not Ian Bancroft, was Head of the Civil Service in her eyes.[46] The role of permanent secretaries became more management, less policymaking, starting that slide towards

---

[42] Plowden (1994) 102–9.
[43] Foster (1996)
[44] Willman in Kavanagh and Seldon (1994) 73–74.
[45] See the backhanded compliment in Heseltine (1990) 44, who blamed the machine as unworthy of the people.
[46] Hennessy (1989) 630–35.

officials being required to do that for which they had not been trained rather than that for which they had.[47] Ministers became readier to take outside business advice on how their departments were run and their policies implemented. Much quoted was John Hoskyns' remark that civil service morale remained 'too high'.[48] The Rousseau of this revolution in the 1980s—its forerunner, entertainer, emotional charge—was *Yes, Minister*, which portrayed officials as comic, fussy, devious, obstructive—but manipulative and always with their own agenda—though in different episodes they came out morally on top as often as ministers. Because funny and not unfriendly, it succeeded in developing ministers' suspicions of officials' excessive power and therefore of its adverse effects upon ministers' freedom to act, as it was to arouse similar suspicions among Blair's ministers. Ministers, shadow ministers, officials, other politicians, the general public and Margaret Thatcher alike watched it. The effect of all this denigration was to undermine many officials' self-esteem.

Because of that, and the disdain with which they were treated, some of the best left for jobs elsewhere, tempted by money, greater challenge and more opportunities for advancement.[49] One ex-civil servant going into the City recalled overnight doubling his salary in a less demanding job. Some left the service who would have risen to the top in the 1990s and 2000s. Deryck Marghan, a high-flier as Douglas Wass' private secretary saw the signs and left to rise to become CEO of Salomon Brothers worldwide. The civil service did not fill its quotas for graduate recruits throughout the 1980s.[50] There were concerns about the amount and the content of training given officials, which seemed too much rooted in the needs of the past, far from able to provide the skills the new state needed. Much more management and other private sector skills were needed in the new world of contracting out.[51]

UNDER MAJOR

The lack of collegiate spirit and solidarity, which soon overtook some ministers in the Major government, weakened partnership relations further. The Man from Whitehall no longer knew most, let alone best.[52] Most ministers still listened when their policies were challenged in the traditional manner by civil servants, but often seemed less responsive. For ideas on policy ministers were readier to use think-tanks; and to go outside the civil service for specialised advice.[53] Civil servants were no longer the only source of advice, which we have

---

[47] Berberis (1994).
[48] Hoskins (2000) 20, seems to attribute it to Norman Strauss.
[49] Plowden (1994) 10, 11.
[50] Plowden (1994) 4.
[51] Plowden (1994) 31.
[52] Campbell and Wilson (1995) 50–53.
[53] Campbell and Wilson (1995) 67–68; Plowden (1994).

argued generally beneficial, but not always even the final source of advice. Worse, it became harder with some ministers to ensure consistency, fairness, objectivity and legality in their decision-making. Hence the increase in judicial review that ministers like Michael Howard in the Home Office had to face.[54] That change undermined officials' constitutional position upon which the Carltona principle was based (above chapter 3).[55] A price for failing to be thorough was paid in decisions increasingly challenged in the courts and legislation sometimes so ill-considered that, as we have seen, one law after another on the same topic found its way onto the statute-book, also frequently creating a need for more judicial interpretation. As one senior official said:

> . . . this lot are even worse than under Thatcher. At least she had an instinct for self-preservation we could appeal to; this lot don't even have that.[56]

Civil service morale fell.[57] Many ministers still worked well with their officials, but Sir Geoffrey Holland resigned as permanent secretary because he found his advice was not listened to.[58] Sir Peter Kemp had to resign because his effective implementation of government policy in creating Next Steps agencies was too single-minded for Waldegrave, his new minister. Major started a habit, increased by Blair, of appointing more permanent secretaries from outside a department so that their knowledge of, and ability to command it, could be much reduced.[59] Most ministers continued hard-working, but when officials went to one minister on business, he habitually continued to watch cricket on television.[60] Relations were not improved because the government argued for putting all civil servants on short-term contracts.[61] Meanwhile, with a weak Prime Minister, some departmental ministers in effect started selecting their own senior officials when there were vacancies. One minister moving to a new department went round bargaining with candidates for the permanent secretaryship, which he saw as in his gift.[62]

A senior civil servant in the early to mid-1990s, looking back over the battlefield since 1979, could reflect with some satisfaction that the service had just about met the requirements of its post-1979 masters and that their personal relations were generally good, but with dismay that the strong sense of loyalty to the Crown, of mutual respect between ministers and officials and of deference to professional excellence of all kinds, had gradually been replaced by a more

[54] Riddell (2000) 39–61.
[55] Freedland (1995) and (1996).
[56] 1993 interview, Campbell and Wilson (1995) 63.
[57] Willman in Kavanagh and Seldon (1994); Plowden (1994).
[58] Campbell and Wilson (1995) 63.
[59] The old practice was that most permanent secretaries came from the department, with an occasional one from the Treasury, sometimes to ginger up a department but also to find posts for Treasury second secretaries.
[60] Private information.
[61] Cabinet Office (1994).
[62] Private information.

self-seeking culture, as ministers struggled for power and officials for position, in a climate where their promotion increasingly depended on ministers.[63] At the same time with fewer civil service numbers—there was a cut of about 25% in senior posts in the years immediately before 1997, itself the worst preparation for the increased activity to come—many ministers were less interested in what civil servants still had to offer. Officials were supplying a less well-evidenced, challenging and professional service than had once, with all its faults, been available. Even so, the creation of departmental select committees, which, despite their virtues, started questioning officials about their minister's policies—requiring them in practice to defend them, lock, stock and barrel—could put them in positions where they seem politicised. How could they state publicly any private reservations they might have? In that and other ways, the breaking down of the convention of ministerial responsibility, and the inclination of ministers to avoid blame in the wake of an unintended fragmentation of government, were pushing some officials more into the limelight to be accountable for their—or sometimes for ministers'—actions, never to receive credit, always to blame. What was weakening was a conception of central government as a set of intricate, interlocking processes—not stately, but rapid—driven by the pressure of events, but handled as far as possible with due regard to values appropriate to democratic government.

UNDER BLAIR

What government wanted from civil servants changed. Under Thatcher and Major, with more work, but with fewer at the top to do it, officials felt less able to challenge ministers, but still essential. After 1997 ministers seemed not to know how to use, certainly not to get the best from, them. Ministers disregarded the constitutional conventions by which they were expected to take all decisions openly with them. Many ministers developed closer partnership relations with their special advisers. Civil servants felt manoeuvred out of work for which they had been trained: not just policy work, but writing Cabinet papers, public documents and careful minutes of ministers' meetings and telephone calls and ensuring factual accuracy in ministerial statements, and both that, and reasonable objectivity, in published documents. They were for the first time treated as simple subordinates with little or no recognition they had a constitutional function of institutional scepticism, of speaking truth to power; of helping ministers to ensure fairness in their decision-making, of legitimating that decision-making; of helping them achieve objectivity and truth in their public statements and documents. They were no longer allowed to make 'full submissions' challenging and appraising ministers' policy ideas or suggesting alternatives that might be more practical. However absurd, redundant or administratively

63 Or the Prime Minister.

flawed, whatever was in the election manifesto, or later emanated from No 10 or No 11, was beyond criticism, as never before.[64] Most senior civil servants saw far less of ministers. No longer did the two work in partnership.

The most important and interesting policy work moved to No 10 and the Treasury, to special and outside advisers.[65] Suggestions circulated that only young officials should expect to be involved in policy work, usually under the wing of special advisers.[66] The more senior ones, if allowed to be involved in policy, were expected to see what they were doing as politically—and media-focused—as the special advisers did. They were often for practical purposes 'politicised', though civil servants tried to find solutions to political problems in the areas, still extensive, where it was allowed them. The crafting of public documents passed to, or was heavily influenced by, spin-doctors with very different values, except for the multitude of consultation documents—a pallid substitute for the blue-books and white papers of the past—and some plans and technical annexes. So officials were set up as specialists on implementation. As such they found themselves blamed for the complexity of regulations and tortuousness of bills, mainly forced on them by political imperatives and changes of mind, and by Europe. Suddenly, the Cabinet Secretary was no longer regarded as the apex of a machine serving ministers: in some sense the counterpart of the Prime Minister, a counsellor to him on the greatest matters of state and a watchdog to ensure the interests of Cabinet, and the individual ones of other Cabinet ministers, were not disregarded. The Butler Review noted that his new exclusion from security and intelligence matters—suddenly true of most policy issues after Turnbull succeeded Wilson—was, for the senior officials concerned, 'to weight their responsibility to the Prime Minister more heavily than their responsibility through the Cabinet secretary to the Cabinet as a whole'.[67] Rather he was a mechanic whose job was by hook or by crook to get that machine to do what ministers wanted. He still attended Cabinet, but only for old time's sake.[68]

Officials found their salaries substantially increased, especially at the top.[69] But they were under the cosh, more at the mercy of ministers who either did, or were thought to, put pressure upon them through awarding or not awarding bonuses; agreeing or not agreeing appointments and promotions. One minister, returning in 1997, and remembering relations with permanent secretaries as a junior minister in the 1960s and a senior one in the 1970s, was dismayed to find he was expected to assess the performance of his senior officials with an impact

---

[64] Brown apparently would not invite officials to his meetings if he thought they would be critical. Similarly, he could take ministerial colleagues' criticism as a personal affront: Bower (2004) 210, 277.

[65] Peter Riddell, *Times,* 25 February 2004.

[66] Private information.

[67] Butler (2004) paras 607, 608.

[68] Private information.

[69] 'Top civil servants to get £200,000', *Times,* 29 August 2001.

on their bonus.[70] The ridiculous requirement that almost all posts were open to competition meant that succession planning—which sensible businesses rely on, bringing in inevitably less well-known outsiders only when there is no suitable internal candidate—was impossible. Simply because they could not win a competition for another post, competent officials could languish in a post past the date when they had anything new to bring to it. Civil service morale did not rise, though the Treasury flourished because of a renewed sense of being at the centre of action. Both Defence and the armed services prospered while they enjoyed success in the field, but again with the sense that ministers were readier to spend time on cultivating the media before going to war than on taking decisions that meant the troops were as well-prepared and equipped as possible.[71]

Ministers developed stronger views on appointments. No 10 urged more outsider appointments. The commonest excuse was that existing officials failed to deliver. There were less efficient and ineffective officials; but ministers never seemed to consider how far their methods of working—their news management, endless initiatives, interventions and faulty laws—were responsible for 'the Delivery Problem.' Moreover officials, rather than their political principals, were blamed, often unfairly, for failures to deliver. More edicts went out. Many were sacked or threatened with sacking. Of course officials should go if lazy or otherwise incompetent. Of course they must acquire new skills, many similar to those in the private sector, but comparisons between public and private sector can be facile.[72]

THE CIVIL SERVICE AND THE PRIVATE SECTOR

Civil servants felt that Northcote-Trevelyan had been undermined, and indeed before the end of 2003 the Cabinet Secretary had excluded policymaking from the list of aptitudes civil servants needed.[73] One heard from those close to ministers that many more heads must roll, especially at the highest level, and be replaced by people from business or local government, before the civil service became fit for purpose. Meanwhile public expenditure rose throughout the

---

[70] John Morris, who had been in Callaghan's Cabinet, recalls his astonishment that as Blair's first Attorney-General he had to write a chit recommending the Treasury Solicitor for a bonus.

[71] Or planning the peace: Seldon (2004) 453. However, the US State Department, the Foreign Office and Overseas Development had done their own good planning only to have it have it overturned at the top, principally from last-minute initiatives of the US Defence Department (private information).

[72] My own ideas of the skills needed—not all private sector—is in Smith Institute (1999) in the report of a group I chaired on which Shirley Williams, Lord Haskins and two ex-permanent secretaries sat.

[73] Cf Sir Andrew's letter and paper, 'Improving Leadership Capacity in the Senior Civil Service', 22 August 2003, just after becoming Head of the Civil Service, in which, with virtually no mention of policymaking or other traditional functions, he describes the more action-oriented skills required of them in future. By autumn, 2004, all parties were promising huge culls of the civil service. The most senior were said to be arguing for salaries comparable to those earned by chief executives in the private sector if that were to be their future role: *Independent*, 22 September 2004.

seven years after 1997 without the expected improvement in the public services. Among the reasons for it were increasingly complicated and frequently changing initiatives; the creation of more regulatory, inspecting, advisory and other public bodies; more attempts to co-ordinate the work of different public bodies; huge increases in the volume of private and public sector regulations; and more—often lawyer-driven and therefore time-consuming and expensive— inquiries into what went wrong. All required more civil servants. They were high among the reasons why the civil service increased by 55,000 between 1997 and 2004. The Prime Minister in February, 2004, called for senior civil servants to become 'skilled specialists in the improvement of services' and Whitehall to be 'run like the private sector.' When the PM at the same time, then Gordon Brown in his 2004 budget, announced a reversal and reduction of 40,000, followed by the Conservatives and the Liberals, one wondered if the government— or any other political party—understood the administrative simplification required.[74] But several obstacles lay in the way of their achieving this ambition.

- Multiple and complex objectives often prevented public bodies being run as single-mindedly as private firms, as did complex co-ordination requirements between bodies and sometimes intensive involvement of high-level professional skills (above chapter 14).
- Public accountability standards—ultimately to Parliament, but also to many intermediate auditing, inspecting and regulating bodies—are more onerous. Habitual blame avoidance, which stops ministers immediately accepting responsibility when something administrative goes wrong and promising to do better, means equally habitual special investigations and inquiries throughout the public sector, taking people away from frontline activity, but complicating the management task and adding to the resources needed, as do the ever increasing volume of ministers' and MPs' questions, most prompted by constituents' concerns which public bodies are expected to have the people to handle. These are among the reasons—along with the sheer complexity of many tax, benefit and other new initiatives requiring more staff—why civil service numbers rose by 55,000 since 1997. What simplifications in accountability procedures and working practices will permit the 40,000 fall promised in the 2004 budget?
- The Rule of Law in most circumstances means setting down in regulation what officials are to do on their behalf. Underlying this requirement is that the Rule of Law requires ministers and officials to act *consistently* and *fairly* so that as far as possible, for example, different benefit claimants receive the same treatment in similar circumstances. If further justification were needed, it is that a private firm's customers can usually go elsewhere if disliking its product or service. Public bodies are normally monopolies in what they

[74] *Financial Times*, 25 February 2004; Peter Riddell, *Times*, 25 February 2004; *Public Finance*, 19 March 2004. Later *Public Finance* was full of articles questioning the thought that had gone into these proposed culls: eg 25 June 2004; 30 July 2004; 10 September 2004.

provide. Reading that the handling of asylum-seekers in one part of the country was rushed over a period, and many normal checks aborted, apparently to meet targets, prompts the thought whether the resulting discrimination was unlawful. In more general terms a clash may be apparent between the Rule of Law and the wish to run the public like the private sector, and to cut civil servant numbers.

• What at its senior levels also distinguished government from private sector was the special constitutional relation of partnership between ministers and their civil service advisers. It could not, and did not, survive in the new world with incalculable consequences for the objectivity and reliability of statements and documents. If the relationship of partnership cannot be revived, then another way needs to be found of ensuring we re-achieve the minimum standards needed for democratic government.

CONCLUSION

The Northcote-Trevelyan tradition became narrowly defined as political impartiality, a trait the Centre had no objection to among its executives.[75] But there had been much more to the Carltona principle and close partnership with ministers than that. It was an attempt to ensure that two sets of people, with different motivations, unable to influence each other's promotion prospects, worked together on everything of importance, to ensure enough truth and objectivity for ministers' decisions, policies and bills to be as open and carefully explained as to make their underlying reasoning, and the evidence for it, reasonably transparent and clear. But the new purposes were replacing the old without public discussion and were not all appropriate for retaining a representative democracy.

---

[75] As is largely true of the definition used in the Committee on Standards in Public Life: Wicks (2003) 5–6, 32 and Appendix E.

16

Nadir of Government: The Railways

The problem with the railways is that they are not quite important enough. Hospitals? Important. Schools? Important. They're the things governments are judged by. 'Will I die? Do I know anything?' Those are real questions. 'Can I get there?' Not quite the same thing, is it? Not quite.

David Hare (2003)[1]

WHAT BEST ILLUSTRATES the failings of Blair's news-managed kind of government? Some would judge the Iraq war as his and Bush's greatest failure. Others would broaden it to Blair's propensity to go to war: five times, or more than any other Prime Minister.[2] Still others the failure to improve the public services. That admirable fortnightly *Public Finance*—the *New Statesman* and *Spectator* of the public sector—catalogues some successes, but many such problems, in each issue, reflecting what seem to have become the endemic problems of the public sector: muddle, confusion, unceasing new initiatives and insufficiently informative public documents.

But as indicative as any—and one I observed closely—was the mess the railways became.[3] Rail privatisation could have been better done (above, chapter 9). But the greatest political failures, which made the railways a disaster, came after 1997. Transport ministers less hostile to privatisation, and a PM less obsessed with news management, could have helped the railways overcome privatisation's teething problems and expanded the rail system successfully by encouraging a rational approach to safety; setting clear industry objectives and insisting on developing a defensible, operationally and financially viable investment strategy for the whole industry.

---

[1] Hare (2003) 7. I have been helped in this account, as in the section on railway privatisation, by comments from, or conversations with, John Armitt, Chris Bolt, Sir Patrick Brown, Chris Castles, Vic Cocker, Jim Cornell, John Edmunds, Professor Andrew Evans, Lord Freeman, Professor Stephen Glaister, Sir Robert Horton, Edmund King, Ian McAllister, Lord MacGregor of Pulham Market, George Muir, Aidan Nelson, Nigel Ogilvie, David Rayner, Andrew Smith, John Smith, John Swift, John Welsby, Tom Winsor, Christian Wolmar and Philip Wood. As always, my use of their comments is my responsibility.

[2] Kampfner (2003).

[3] I was John MacGregor's non-political special adviser from shortly after the 1992 election until Railtrack was formed, where I became a non-executive director, retiring a few months before Hatfield.

EARLY SUCCESS

Despite the failure to rectify initial flaws and several setbacks, the industry could remain optimistic until the Hatfield crash in 2000. Safety continued to improve and at a somewhat faster rate than under BR.[4] Even including the 31 killed at Ladbroke Grove, fewer were killed in the 1990s than in the previous or any earlier decade.[5] After a period when traffic had been flat since the end of the Second World War, passenger traffic rose by 36%, freight traffic by 50%, in part stimulated by more effective marketing.[6] But a downside was that many trains and some routes became overcrowded.[7] After privatisation some train companies had been unwise to reduce driver numbers, thoughtlessly cut middle management and other supervisory staff, and take other cost-cutting measures with adverse effects on overall train companies' punctuality; but in 1999/2000, reliability overall was higher than it had been in 1995/6.[8] And higher than when the railways were nationalised.[9] After Hatfield it became, and in 2004 was expected to remain, worse than under BR for another 5 or 6 years.[10] Moreover there were improvements in operating efficiency: unit operating costs were lower until Hatfield than they had been in the 1980s.[11] BR productivity improved overall from the mid 1980s until Hatfield when it became lower than for about forty years.[12]

A persistent Blair government strategem has been to blame the failings of the present on the supposed sins of (a mostly Tory) past.[13] However, Roger Ford has shown how misleading it is to claim—as the Blair government repeatedly did—that the railways were starved of money for maintenance and renewals in the 1980s.[14] BR had spent around £2bn a year on maintenance and renewals from 1975 to 1991/2, an average rate by European standards.[15] Then BR and a not yet privatised Railtrack reduced maintenance substantially for two years,

[4] Evans (2004).

[5] Rail Safety and Standards Board (2003) 23–24; also A Evans (2003); J Smith (2003) para 38.

[6] There had been strong cyclical growth in the late 1980s to a highpoint in 1988. Comparing the later 1990s with 1988, there had still been a substantial extra increase in passenger traffic of 29%.

[7] A rough attribution is that 20 percentage points of the passenger traffic increase was due to economic upturn, 15 to fares policy and better marketing. The political decision to hold fares down increased congestion on many routes.

[8] SRA (2003/4) 1st quarter trends. See also A Smith (2004) 40, whose series on reliability goes back to 1975 with an average of about 89%.

[9] Pollitt and Smith (2002); A Smith (2004).

[10] Ford (2003) 18.

[11] Pollitt and Smith (2002). Allowing for scale effects they were arguably 13% lower in 1999/2000 than they had been in 1992/3.

[12] A Smith (2004).

[13] E.g. Glaister (2004) 28, 44–45.

[14] Ford (2003). Ford quotes several such claims. Darling claimed it again in his 2004 White Paper. Andrew Smith has pointed out to me that there may be problems in the interpretation of these numbers, mainly because of changes in accounting policy. However, if, the government or Network Rail believes these figures conceal under-investment, theirs is the need to demonstrate it.

[15] Shown in a series of unpublished UIC studies in the mid to late 1990s.

caught by a fierce Treasury ban on spending more money.[16] Under Railtrack renewals expenditure did not immediately increase enough to reduce that shortfall, but after a year or so it began to, so that maintenance and renewals expenditure just about reached BR levels by 1997/8 and had risen much higher since Hatfield.[17] By 2000 the Rail Regulator judged RT needed to increase its spend to £3bn a year on operations, maintenance and renewals. By 2003 Network Rail wanted £6bn a year, the Regulator conceded £5bn.[18] By 2004 Network Rail's costs were two to three times BR's equivalent costs.

Costs must be reduced. Consider how devastating it would have been for the railways and rail travel if the recent more than doubling of Network Rail's operating costs had had to be met by the rail-user. Ticket prices would have to rise by some 65%. (To cover the full increases since privatisation when most fares were frozen they would have to have risen about as much again, probably a self-defeating policy since so much traffic, and therefore revenue, would have been priced off the system.) Unless costs fall dramatically—much more than at present planned[19]—experience suggests taxpayers will eventually rebel, given the mounting cost of the NHS and all the other claims on public expenditure.

INVESTMENT

Compared with operations, major investment after privatisation soon became and stayed a mess. The original idea had been that, as soon as the Office of Passenger Rail Franchising (OPRAF) had let the first franchises, it should immediately prepare for the next round of franchises seven years later. In that context, and in collaboration with the secretary of state and Treasury, it would determine the services to be provided and the investment needed. Because of complications arising when several companies used the same track, the need to minimise disruption and to have effective project management, it was thought essential to build the investment proposed in each franchise area into the next set of franchise bidding documents, so that both the incumbent franchisee and any would-be competitors would have known what they were expected to do.[20] Any profitable investment—as most renewals would have been, provided

---

[16] Until flotation or sale, the government determined the amount of money available to the various parts of what had been BR. In BR's last two years and Railtrack's first two years, when it was still subject to government-imposed limits on its expenditure, there were much reduced maintenance and renewals for four years. Also A Smith (2004).

[17] *Financial Times*, 25 July 2003.

[18] There would seem some doubt between Ford, and Smith and Pollitt, over how far maintenance unit costs went up before Hatfield, in part because unit volume data on maintenance activity was not systematically collected under the fixed price contracts in place after privatisation. No doubt but that they have done since.

[19] Department of Transport (2004) 4.2.6, suggests only by 31% below 2004 levels, to be achieved over five years.

[20] Section 54 of the Act intended as the basis for OPRAF providing public money for investment outside franchise rounds was used once: to get Railtrack away in 1996.

on-going subsidy levels were maintained—would be funded as appropriate by the rolling stock companies, the train companies, and Railtrack.[21]

But, as a loss-making industry, almost all substantial investment to increase railway capacity, also being unprofitable, would require additional subsidy. Any such investment, for which it could secure Treasury approval, OPRAF would help fund as in the public interest, even though unprofitable. Moreover any large investment, which entailed major disruption to the extent that train companies received large-scale compensation, should have been avoided through negotiation if this second franchising process had been well conducted.[22] Whether such a procedure would have worked on the West Coast Main Line, used by 13 train companies, is problematic, but it should have worked in other franchise areas.[23] All incumbent parties in each case would have had to co-operate to produce a bidding document, acceptable to all concerned, which made clear the levels of operation, investment and subsidy proposed, as well as how they should co-operate in effecting planned major investments.[24]

That interpretation of the legislation did not survive the election. Confusion over the two regulators' roles had been a flaw in the original privatisation (chapter 9), but became worse after 1997, when John Prescott appointed two unusually adversarial people—Tom Winsor and Alastair Morton—to the two posts:[25] Christian Wolmar describes very well how, to the despair of the rest of the industry, when Morton became head of the *Strategic Rail Authority*—as OPRAF was re-named after 1997—he refused the role of providing an investment strategy or similar detailed, complete bidding documents. This role was not properly described in a White Paper and not adequately reflected in legislation, and neither he nor John Prescott seem to have seen it as part of his job description. If anything destroyed the privatised rail industry's ability to grow and continue taking on increasing traffic, it was this inaction, made worse in July, 1997 by an amendment to Railtrack's licence, effectively splitting responsibility for determining investment between the two regulators, the Rail Regulator acquiring powers to determine the correct level of operating and

[21] In this curious, heavily subsidised, but privatised industry, one must be careful what one means by 'profitable' investment. If a franchise gets the subsidy to let it invest in renewals or enhancement, it should be profitable to the franchisee—and to agents of that investment like Railtrack—while being 'unprofitable' to the government. BR would equally have invested in truly profitable investment not requiring subsidy.

[22] The bidding documents would not only have settled the investment to be undertaken in the franchising period, but at least in rough outline programmed it and built the possessions thought necessary without provision for compensation unless those possessions were exceeded. They would have incentivised all parties to undertake the investment as co-operatively as possible and with minimum public disruption.

[23] Railtrack had hoped it could use satellite signalling to keep costs low. When that proved technically impossible within a reasonable timescale, costs spiralled.

[24] On the serious inadequacies of the bidding process, Helm (2002) 12; not one re-franchising had been completed by the end of Sir Alastair's term at the SRA.

[25] On how much better regulation was structured and achieved in the water industry, see J Smith (2003).

maintenance costs as well as renewal investment requirements. After 1997 the notion that ORR determined what maintenance and renewals, but also enhancement, Railtrack did, was built into the system. What was idiotic was that this task was not given to the government, or the Strategic Rail Authority as its agent, but to ORR as the economic regulator.[26] The direct consequence of this error, not changed until 2004, was that Tom Winsor, as rail regulator, could force the government to spend far more on Railtrack (by now Network Rail) than it would have chosen, despite this arguably being an infringement of parliamentary control over public expenditure. This split responsibility in deciding investment, between the SRA for enhancement and ORR for renewals, made no sense. The industry's disastrous failure to develop an adequate, financially and operationally viable investment programme follows directly from it. As late as 2003, Tom Winsor was reported as chiding the SRA for not having a clear strategy.[27] But the damage went further than that: without a financially viable strategy for the industry, no separate part of it could have its own coherent business plan with which to approach the City for a Rights Issue or any other application for funds.

RISING DEMAND EXHAUSTS CAPACITY

Underlying this was another source of confusion. From the start privatisation was expected to result in some, generally modest, traffic growth: through filling trains, especially off-peak, on the more heavily-used, but not on the chronically under-used, routes; and by running more trains on busy routes where there was enough capacity and demand for it. But the ability to run more trains, and the cost of providing more capacity where existing capacity was full, varied enormously. At worst, by 1999 the routes into all London termini from Liverpool Street southwards and westwards round to Victoria were so busy that any further increase in traffic required their by-passing by new underground lines intersecting them at inner suburban stations at huge cost. (The most significant, Cross-rail, was endlessly promised, but postponed, as again in 2004, because of its great cost.) Indeed as a generalisation, by then increased traffic, where the demand existed—that is, generally on the busiest lines—could only be met by massively subsidised infrastructure improvements. In many cases any expansion was physically or environmentally impossible. Far from letting the public know

---

[26] For one regulator to determine franchises and regulate Railtrack's licence was held to entail a conflict of interests. I do not believe that the sensible way to design regulatory functions. If Railtrack believed the subsidy OPRAF/ SRA provided insufficient to operate the network, ORR could have mediated and there could have been a right of appeal to another body like the MMC, now the Competition Commission. As water regulator, Ian Byatt engineered a process by which price, cost and quality were traded off. Including safety, a similar process could have been devised for the railways.

[27] As well as exceeding his powers *Daily Telegraph,* October 2003. See also the comments of Rana Roy (2003).

the truth about these matters—both as to cost and feasibility—the government, thinking any mention too sensitive—went on behaving until 2004 as if it were just a matter of time before all these capacity constraints would be overcome and that first investment, then increased traffic, would materialise on every route, relieving road congestion as it did so. Even then it did not come clean on the matter.[28] Rather many half promises for major rail investment were quietly dropped.

A related confusion was over investment criteria, which OPRAF had been directed to provide so as to be able to evaluate both economic and non-economic investment, but which neither it nor the SRA ever did. The railways had been unprofitable for an eternity.[29] Since very few new investments would be profitable, the case for more rail subsidy to finance additional investment must be that additional social benefits made extra subsidy worthwhile. Franchising should have enabled OPRAF/SRA to determine the social worth of that extra subsidy in terms of reduced congestion on the roads and environmental benefits for each extra £ of subsidy. However, the distinction between profitable and unprofitable investment was blurred by confusion over what was profitable or unprofitable for individual traincos, or Railtrack, and for the industry as a whole; as well as by the SRA's failure to assess social benefits rigorously, and even more by a failure to distinguish between what was profitable, and what could be privately financed if there were *de facto* an implicit, but unacknowledged, taxpayers' guarantee. Thus nobody knew what the investment criteria were, a failure which in 2004 still prevented the emergence of a rational investment strategy whose benefits could be compared with those of investment in road. Furthermore the failure to publish expected returns from rail enhancement investments obscured the fact that returns from road investment would almost invariably be much higher, even when environmental and other social factors were taken into account.[30]

DIFFICULTIES

The crisis after the Ladbroke Grove crash was to start undermining much of the hard-won operational improvement. As Christian Wolmar has said, after Ladbroke Grove the government was keen to protect John Prescott from blame in the media for the accident.[31] While in opposition, Prescott had repeatedly

---

[28] Department of Transport (2004).

[29] Constraints on closure, and the public's expectation of continuing service on existing lines, still makes it hard to apply the same criteria to the retention of services even where traffic levels are very low. MPs are influencial here. Private information.

[30] Affuso, Mason and Newbery (2003).

[31] From my own experience as a non-executive member of the Railtrack board, corroborated by Gerald Corbett, the Chief Executive, *Daily Telegraph*, 3 September 2004, who said Railtrack suffered constant gibes from the government that it was putting 'profits before safety'. Also Glaister (2004) 38.

called for ministers to resign when anything went wrong. The Conservative party conference was on when Ladbroke Grove happened. From it came calls for Prescott to resign. No 10 quickly spun blame onto the railway industry so as to focus adverse attention on the industry and its executives instead of the blame falling on him.[32] For Prescott to have been blamed would have been absurd in reality, though apparently Blair thought he should have been ready with legislation and improvements before Paddington and Hatfield struck.[33] Fatally, the industry was branded a 'national disgrace' when, as noted, safety and performance had improved significantly. As had not happened at earlier major train accidents, the trackside became a police scene of crime. No one would attribute to human error what had happened at a signal which had been passed safely thousands of times. The railways were not allowed, as had been usual, to deplore what happened, promise a careful investigation, state the intention to learn from the experience so as to continue improving rail's safety record. Instead Railtrack board members were vilified, their home addresses displayed in the press, their wives and children door-stopped, as indeed were the wives and families of signallers and other staff. Yet safety held up, but morale began to sag.

Most fatally, John Prescott also made the dire statement that 'safety would be improved whatever it costs'. So the government fuelled the expectation that it would fund any increase in costs to meet safety, however poorly prioritised and poor value for money. Both the Southall—still sitting when Ladbroke Grove happened—and Ladbroke Grove accident inquiries were thereby encouraged to recommend massively expensive measures irrespective of cost,[34] though experience was to show that a sustained trend of simpler and inexpensive measures like better training and attention to detail were largely behind the overall improvement in rail safety which continued despite Hatfield.

2000: HATFIELD

Hatfield was the watershed, or more specifically actions taken in its aftermath. There was suddenly a changed mindset within the industry. In an instant and insufficiently considered reaction to the broken rail that caused that crash, every metre of track was inspected for gauge-corner cracking.[35] Railtrack's Chief Executive, who had just relinquished, and not replaced, his two most senior engineers, acted in great haste. Engineers, throughout the contractors and Railtrack, slapped on speed-restrictions. Once imposed, they no longer—not so in the past when more was left to engineering discretion—could be lifted

---

[32] Wolmar (2001) 116.
[33] Blair blamed him for failing to deliver in the first term, despite an impossible timetable. More reasonably Blair criticised him for being anti-car: Seldon (2004) 41–46.
[34] Wolmar (2001) 151–52.
[35] Now called rolling contact fatigue.

without Health and Safety Executive approval. Because of re-organised safety arrangements the government had initiated, what had been guidelines interpreted with engineering discretion, turned into requirements with the force of laws. In consequence, incidents reported took much longer to resolve.[36] All led to delay and extra expenditure, even though no other rail was found in a condition approaching that which caused Hatfield.[37] Indeed broken rails peaked at 4 per million train-miles in 1979; they fell to 2.2 in the mid-eighties.[38] They increased in the 1990s, peaking at 3.1 in 1998. They were already on the way down before Hatfield and by 2002 were back to pre-privatisation levels at 2.3.[39] The most plausible cause of the 1990s' increase was the four years' reduction in maintenance and renewals expenditure, which, as we have seen, started 2 years before privatisation, and of the subsequent improvement, the increased in track renewals and grinding rails from 1997.[40] But this concentrated attention to detail was misplaced. Broken rails elsewhere have caused few accidents. Like Southall, and Ladbroke Grove, Hatfield was caused by human error. What went wrong at Hatfield, and was subsequently put right, was a serious management systems failure.

Much of the huge increase in expenditure on the network since Hatfield has gone on such practices as: reducing the lives of rails and other assets, in some cases by about a third; using long-welded rail where it was never in the past thought necessary; discontinuing the time-honoured and safe practice of cascading used rail after some years from intensively to less used routes; and to pay for the reductions in productivity of maintenance and other operational activities caused by Health & Safety requirements previously thought unnecessary.

Responsible for this massive increase in costs after Hatfield, which was to be the railways' undoing, was the huge increase in risk aversion among rail employees at all levels so as to avoid the jail sentences urged by survivors' groups and others. After Ladbroke Grove many railwaymen not unreasonably assumed that, and all the talk about criminal proceedings, was meant to encourage them to be extremely risk-averse. Yes, there may be cases where negligence justifies prosecutions. But there will also be unforeseen accidents and human error. To encourage a mindset in which the reaction to any accident is to try to track down the supposed criminal responsible does not strengthen the judgement of those involved. Rather it induces, as it has, extreme risk aversion. Not true safety, but the hammering a barrister may give one in court, becomes the test of what it is reasonable to spend. Not only the huge increase in costs, but also the fall in reliability is a casualty of risk aversion.

[36] Roy (2003).
[37] Broken rails have caused two other fatal accidents since Hither Green in 1978: Ulleskelf in 1981 and Elgin in 1983.
[38] Rail Safety and Standards Board (2003) 169.
[39] Rail Safety and Standards Board (2003); A Smith (2004).
[40] Private information.

Railtrack management also lost confidence after Hatfield, which led to a multitude of re-railing initiatives and temporary speed restrictions 'just in case' anything should be wrong, rather than continuing, even intensifying, the pre-existing and successful programme based on rational top-down criteria.

Costs also increased because of the government's multiplication of rail safety authorities—put right only in 2004—whose complex interrelationships delayed action and the restoration of service after an incident, and the return of a ' cost-plus' or 'begging bowl' attitude towards government, by which bidding up spending needs became a permanent occupation of senior managers in the industry, replacing rigorous financial analysis.[41]

Government putting Railtrack into administration undermined all incentive to contain costs,[42] further compounded by the equally crass government action of replacing it with a quasi-nationalised company, Network Rail, engineering driven, which had no motivation to resist cost increases.[43] Ironically Andrew Adonis, now in the No 10 Policy Unit—who we have seen (above, chapter 3) believing he had learned from studying the poll-tax that policymaking should be more politicised to avoid such political disasters and who was among those who helped Blair achieve that outcome—was among the advisers at the Centre who pressed Stephen Byers to put Railtrack into administration before replacing it by Network Rail.[44] Utterly unclear, its Statement of Objectives gave no indication of how it was to strike a balance between the interests of present and future customers, employees, the taxpayer, those who lent to it and the wider public. When challenged on this issue at its AGM by members of its 100-strong government-appointed board, they were told their duty was to do whatever was in the best interests of Network Rail.[45]

But the damage went much further. Because the whole railway system became risk averse, encouraged by the perception at all levels that managers might be sued, or worse, criminally prosecuted, in the courts, reliability plummeted. It soon recovered somewhat but has remained low ever since. In 1998–2000, an average of 88% of trains were on time. That average fell to 78% in 2001/2. Even in 2003, Network Rail promised no less than 7 years to return to pre-Hatfield standards of reliability, but only then at vastly increased cost which was already by the beginning of 2004 making rail investment for less worthwhile than road investment by any rational criteria taking into account environmental impacts and congestion.[46] Richard Bowker, SRA chairman, was troubled by this and urged Network Rail to do better without apparently realising how much the government's interventions in safety policy were the prime cause of the

---

[41] See Glaister (2004) 13, who also pointed out the 2004 White Paper proposals further encouraged this.

[42] Such an increase in costs also happened when the BR financial regime broke down in 1973/4 and was to that extent foreseeable.

[43] Also Glaister (2004).

[44] Private information.

[45] Glaister (2004) 43.

[46] Affuso, Masson and Newbery (2003).

railways' new unreliability and much higher costs.[47] Moreover it was unclear by now who thought themselves in charge: Richard Bowker who sent directives from the SRA; Darling, the secretary of state for transport, who did not hesitate before getting into such detail as ordering that there should be one person in each area deciding what happened when any incident threatened reliability; or the Prime Minister issuing instructions at his regular meetings with Richard Bowker and the Delivery Unit. The resulting mess was replaced in 2004 by Darling proposing his Department of Transport take over the supreme command, and that London and other regional authorities should all have a role in the strategic direction of the railways, by all precedent a recipe for even more frequent political interference in the railways whatever the government protested.[48] Darling claimed that, despite the more than doubling of costs, which he expected to reverse by only a third, the railways remained of great social and environmental benefit: unhappily an ever more tenuous proposition which he did not try to demonstrate quantitatively.[49]

WAS PRIVATISATION TO BLAME?

Christian Wolmar wrote a well-written and useful book on rail privatisation. However its overall thesis—like that of David Hare's play, *The Permanent Way*—is that the present dire situation of the railways is almost solely the consequence of privatisation. To refute it one needs to unpick the proposition because several issues lurk here. Was privatisation flawed? I have already argued that it was (Chapter 9). For political reasons too much was attempted too quickly. In particular regulatory responsibilities were poorly assigned and the outsourcing of maintenance and renewals should not have been done, or should have been postponed, or done carefully over several years. In addition significant traffic growth was not anticipated. So the performance regime did not provide for it. But these flaws did not prevent a general improvement in the railways' traffic and performance until after Hatfield. Moreover with goodwill, instead of latent hostility, the incoming government could have remedied these faults. Between them, ministers and regulators had made as great post-privatisation adjustments to help other privatisations: for example, telecommunications, gas and electricity.

---

[47] The RSSB suggests £1.5m per fatality served as a not unreasonable assumption for planning investment and other measures to improve safety. A Smith (2004) estimates that a value of £152m, or about ten times as great, is needed to validate the increase in costs since Hatfield. Far more lives could have been saved for the same expenditure on improving the NHS or even the roads. If Network Rail, the prime culprit, argues that the prime objective of its cost increases was not risk aversion, and therefore directly or indirectly, improved safety, it needs to show what it was aimed to achieve and how that may be justified economically.

[48] Glaister (2004) 53.

[49] Department of Transport (2004) section 2.5. No significant investment to increase capacity appreciably can be justified at anything approaching cost levels. Costs need to be cut back to pre-2000 levels.

To argue, as Wolmar does, that virtually everything which has gone wrong on the railways is the consequence of privatisation, one has to go further than is reasonable. For example, he devotes a whole chapter to each dreadful accident at Southall, Ladbroke Grove and Hatfield. He mentions that each was the result of human error and observes, as has happened, that each was most readily remedied by comparatively simple measures like greatly improved training and maintenance oversight procedures. But Wolmar—though he says other accidents might have occurred—then goes onto consider many ways by which in other circumstances each of these accidents might have been avoided if this, that and the other had not happened, so building up a picture of endless mishaps and errors. In virtually every case he supposes old BR would have avoided those mishaps and mischances because of what he repeatedly characterises as 'Fat Controller' dictatorial management from the top. But this is to get the issues out of proportion. Abundant evidence shows that BR had far from perfect management in the old days. Even in the Golden Years of Bob Reid I and John Welsby, there were human errors, accidents, problems with reliability and with investment.[50] In 1988 and 1989 serious accidents at Clapham Junction, Purley and Bellgrove followed each other in quick succession. There were management and other human errors. Moreover no managerial regime in any industry stands up to the criticism that every possible thing needs to be done to prevent anything going wrong. Neither should it, because it would be an extravagantly expensive policy: whatever one does, one cannot eliminate all risks, only ensure that all reasonably practical measures have been taken to ensure a reasonably safe, reliable and cost-effective operation, valued by its consumers. So one comes back to basics: there was no underlying discontinuity in the improvement in railway performance until after Hatfield. Rather, overall it went on improving. So did safety even after Hatfield.[51]

Therefore one cannot blame Hatfield on privatisation. By that time maintenance relations between Railtrack and its contractors should have been improved, helped by ministerial or regulatory intervention. What went wrong was really something quite different and there is no sound reason to suppose it would not have happened even if the railways had remained nationalised. Because of Hatfield, close media attention, the treatment of crash scenes as scenes of crime, the intervention of lawyers, lawyers chairing inquiries, who were encouraged by ministers to disregard cost in recommending measures to reduce accidents, and the threat of criminal proceedings against individual managers, all suddenly combined to increase risk aversion, reduce reliability and

---

[50] See Professor Andrew Evans' criticism of Wolmar's book in Evans (1999) x.

[51] Incidents continued to decline in 2002/3, though fatalities rose that year, not because of Potter's Bar, but because of an upward blip in other fatalities. I am indebted to Professor Andrew Evans for this point. The railways' improving safety record is excellently shown in Evans (2003). If by any dreadful mischance—for which there is no current evidence—fatalities were to continue to rise it would be hard to exempt recent changes in policy and organisation from being part of the explanation.

was overwhelmingly the main cause of increased operating costs. In addition risk aversion made it harder to get and use track possessions efficiently and effectively for renewals and other investments.

Can one suppose that a Southall, Ladbroke Grove, Hatfield or Potter's Bar would not have happened if the railways were still nationalised? Equivalent incidents did happen. The increase in British litigiousness had nothing to with privatisation, as NHS experience shows. Would media attention not have been as great, intrusive and demoralising after Ladbroke Grove and the other 1990s accidents? It was not caused by privatisation, but by a changed attitude within the media driven by an imperative urge to raise sales and TV ratings, and therefore exploiting the fact that privatisation was politically contentious, not least under a Labour government. The nationalised railways would not have avoided these problems. They cannot be resolved by re-nationalisation. Or by putting Network Rail, or the train companies in such an ambiguous position, it is not clear whether they are private or public, how far under government control, how far financially motivated.[52]

LESSONS

Rail privatisation exemplifies many failings of modern British government:

- Under Major privatisation was too complicated and disputed to be satisfactorily completed in five years. Furthermore such fundamental institutional changes are unwise unless one is confident enough about winning the next election to let them bed down, or that the opposition is—probably tacitly— sympathetic enough to the change to make the best of it; or—like Thatcher and her changed economic and union policies—one believes them essential for the national well-being. The argument for fundamental institutional and organisational change being discussed and prepared to secure bi-partisan agreement is strong. At no stage was the policy comprehensively explained, and shown to be practical, to the public, those expected to implement it, or Parliament. Indeed the bill was an enabling bill allowing privatisation to be varied substantially after the law was passed, as it was. So there could not be proper publication or scrutiny of what actually happened, and to change ministers several times during development of a major policy is a recipe for discontinuity and trouble.
- Under Labour a more sympathetic government—ready to consider in detail how the defects of rail privatisation might be put right, rather than follow doctrinaire and media-driven policies—could have overcome its initial shortcomings. Rather a rigid commitment to the manifesto did not allow what was in it to be challenged, or in any depth thought through, by the industry and other parties affected, or by civil servants. John Prescott's 1998 White Paper foresaw traffic growth being diverted onto rail and other public transport.

[52] Department of Transport (2004); Glaister (2004).

Modest quantification and assessment of the limited capacity for growth that existed on most of the network would have quickly shown how impossible that was: 92% of traffic (pass-km) was by road; not much more than 6.5% by rail; the 35% increase in rail traffic experienced was but a year's growth on the roads; 85% of motorists said they never used rail.[53]

There are many lessons to be learned from this.

- Do not waste scarce administrative and legislative time turning one body into another—here OPRAF into SRA (and then a few years later abolishing it)—when the apparent object is to give the re-named body spurious, ill-defined extra powers to be a 'tough regulator' and, equally spuriously, to be seen as at a greater distance from government when the only real concern appears to have been ministerial blame avoidance.

- Don't bad-mouth an industry or the people in it to save a minister's skin.

- Don't appoint unsuitable people, moreover without a well-defined relevant job description. Often their greatest claim was that they had in some way served the party or a politician before the election.

- After Ladbroke John Prescott repeatedly called what he called 'summits' of the industry at which he spoke as if he had as much right to give orders as he must have believed he had when they were nationalised (so distant had memories of NOSSO become), and spoke, too, of re-negotiating the contracts, while having no legal basis for doing this.[54]

- Since Hatfield, unit costs have gone through the roof, principally because government did nothing to dissuade, and plenty to persuade, people that money should be spent on almost anything that might conceivably improve safety, however cost-ineffective, and whatever the consequential fall in reliability.

- Again, don't let an agency—here the Health and Safety Executive—introduce so much law and regulation into its operations, as greatly to increase its costs and unreliability, without a tangible equivalent benefit, here in safety, and do not think ministers can long get away with ducking the hard decisions—here about how one strikes a balance in the use of resources in consumers' interest between safety, reliability and new investment—which once were thought what ministers were for, and could make or unmake their reputation.

- Moreover the superficial and erroneous belief that recent accidents and current unreliability were caused by privatisation, has led to a superficial and thoughtless sloganising belief that the answer is to revert to nationalisation where possible: putting Railtrack into insolvency, creating Network Rail as a kind of mutual, it taking maintenance back indoors.

- A further lesson is to not set up a system in which financial incentives and competition are meant to drive efficiency, and then undermine it by bailing out loss-making parts of it when they get into difficulties.

[53] Department of Transport, (2003); RAC Foundation (2001) using a cross-modal team—not the government—did the relevant analysis; King and Liebling (2004).

[54] Tom Winsor was particularly pungent about ministers' repeated threats and actual breaking of the law: Winsor (2004a), (2004b). See also his (2004c) and (2004d).

Despite all the Treasury's talk of the importance of contracts and financial incentives, the industry was largely reconstituted on a cost-plus basis with residual risk taken by the taxpayer. There and in other respects the discipline of financial incentives was undermined.

- Because the government has given insufficient thought to how one motivates the various parts of the industry now, more and more orders and exhortations travel down from the top. Under the 2004 changes that is likely to increase. The demand for returns and other red tape grows. At the same time ministers' and MPs' endless queries need unprecedented resources to answer.
- The government should not have created and then worsened a situation whereby an increasing number of safety and economic regulators with unclear powers interact with each other and the industry, distracting management and adding to cost without arguably as such improving safety or efficiency.[55] They should not complicate and confuse investment and operating criteria so that an industry does not know how to establish its priorities.
- At no stage, not even in the 2004 White Paper, has the government published—and almost certainly not made—any clear, thorough analysis of the worsening problem, formed a reasoned view of its causes and set out its solutions with enough precision to be intelligible.[56] It is yet another PR document for the media rather than an objective public document. If ministers cannot or will not set out their policies in well-argued, clearly stated white papers—if they do not themselves engage in proper consultations and show they have met valid objections raised, it can only end in misunderstandings and disaster;
- You should not ask an industry to suggest how to solve its own problems. Consumers will be ill-equipped to argue their case while private and public sector interests involved will press their self-interest, possibly by trying to create cosy, cartelised arrangements, or by seeking to ingratiate themselves by recommending what they believe the government wants, since it is the source of their funds and profits in a subsidised industry.
- Furthermore, do not purport to solve the problems of an industry by writing as imprecise a white paper—and with as many loose ends—as happened in 2004.[57]
- But above all heed the charge made by Stephen Glaister, a great expert on the industry and on privatisation. If over 7 years a government repeatedly takes steps to frustrate the effect competition and financial incentives have had in improving performance in other privatised industries, expect to get and retain an inefficient, poorly performing and demoralised industry, unable to respond to the Department of Transport, the Treasury and No 10's dictating.[58]

[55] Despite promising simplification, Department of Transport (2004) remains imprecise over this as over many other details.
[56] Glaister (2004) 50, rightly calls it 'this rather vague document proposing remarkably little fundamental reform'. Its only pretension to one was abolishing the SRA, the only body Prescott had created.
[57] C Wolmar 'No sense of Direction', (2004) *Public Finance,* July 30th.
[58] Glaister, makes this case powerfully. He sees the 2004 White Paper as ineptly arguing against contracts being used to secure relationships between parts of the industry, saying that they must be replaced by something else, but giving no indication of what they might be, Glaister (2004) 54–63.

CONCLUSION

Fundamental re-thinking is needed because the overall effect has been to undermine, not improve, the railway industry.[59] In particular, how do we get people throughout the industry to concentrate on value for money in safety improvement rather than risk aversion? How do we get rail costs down to a level where substantial parts of it can compete economically with road—and with sensibly quantified allowances made to reflect differences in their impacts on safety and the environment? How do we re-engineer the right incentives? Not through creeping re-nationalisation, but by attention to detail, better and, I would argue, more sensibly incentivised management, as well as less adversarial relations throughout the industry, whatever the form of ownership.

More widely, how do we achieve government supervision of this industry and of other parts of the public sector, which is informative, intelligible and constructive?

[59] For a view on what is needed, see Foster and Castles (2004); also Glaister (2004).

17

Summarising the Revolution

When a great entity like the British Constitution has continued in connected outward sameness, but hidden inner change, for many ages, every generation inherits a series of inapt words—of maxims once true, but of which the truth is ceasing or has ceased . . . An ancient and ever altering constitution is like an old man who still wears with attached fondness clothes in the fashion of his youth: what you see of him is the same; what you do not see is wholly altered.

Bagehot[1]

No one rises so high as he who knows not whither he is going.

Oliver Cromwell[2]

WHAT SUPPORTS THE judgement that the years after 1979 were not another example of successful adaptation, but of constitutional and administrative revolution?

THE NATURE OF THE REVOLUTION

First, what does one mean by a revolution? Plainly not one marked by bloodshed, as were the mid-17th century English, the American, French, Russian and many other revolutions. But neither has it been a sustained period of political evolution like the 25 or more years from the early 1860s, when Gladstone and the political classes made many changes to the working of the political system to make it safe, as they saw it, for democracy, despite more constitutional changes between 1997 and 2003 than for 300 years. Nor do I claim it a revolution in any epoch-making sense, as the product of inexorable social and economic forces, though changes in external circumstances have been important.

A distinguishing characteristic of political revolutions is that, whatever deep grievances or other upsets cause them, they get out of control. One unplanned, unpredicted development follows another so that wherever it ends up, it is not where anyone initially expected. Usually increasingly chaotic events end in an autocracy: in an Augustus, Cromwell, Napoleon or Lenin. Cromwell was an outstanding general and administrator (though a wordy and often rambling

---

[1] Bagehot (1997) 1.
[2] Tanner (1928) 146.

speaker). Where he was like Blair was that he did not have the vision, the genius, to make a lasting constitution, though he tried often enough. However, an exception was the Glorious Revolution of 1688.[3] It was a revolution in that the Marquess of Halifax, and others who precipitated it, put themselves at William III's mercy when they invited him to replace James II. They were lucky because William was too busy fighting wars on the continent to impose many demands on the new settlement which was also revolutionary—that is radical—in its outcome, but remained benign in its effects on the English constitution, as judged by the standards of the time.[4] The American revolution, while even more radical, was fortunate—as almost no other revolutions have been—in that three of its founding fathers wrote in *The Federalist,* the most amazingly reflective and thorough work expounding the principles and solutions adopted in the American constitution, showing how unusually well thought-through that constitution was.[5]

If without bloodshed and mayhem—and also without a blue-print as both the Americans and Halifax and his colleagues in broad terms had, though theirs were not as ambitious, well-argued and ingenious as *The Federalist*—how does one know we have already gone through a revolution? Because, as this book has argued, we have—since 1979, but most since 1997—gone through an extended series of changes in the structure and working of the British political system, moreover ones which have no coherence and have achieved no constitutional stability.

But even more by its outcome. British government is not working as it should. Its component parts do not perform the functions they once did. Above all it is less democratic and the checks and balances on the executive are less effective.

CONSTITUTIONAL CHANGES

The seriousness and greater significance of the more fundamental changes, which first Thatcher, and then Blair and his advisers made, were hidden by more publicised, dramatic and overt constitutional changes. Well-discussed elsewhere, not much need be said about them here.[6] They were not the outcome of sustained, reflective thought as permeated *The Federalist*. The prime motivation

[3] Less often called The Glorious Revolution now because many concerned, including William III, are now seen to have had self-seeking motives: Rose (1989); Claydon (2002). But it remains glorious in the sense that England changed from a state in which relations between king and Parliament were often turbulent to one in which the Crown recognised restrictions on its absolute power, all without much bloodshed and helping achieve much greater political stability.

[4] Oborne and Walters (2004) 167 compared Blair's constitutional changes with the Glorious Revolution. Graham Allen, MP, wrote of them as justified as a move towards Montesquieu and the United States constitution: Allen (2003) 13.

[5] Madison, Hamilton, Jay (1992). Originally written as a series of articles in various New York journals (1787 and 1788).

[6] For example in the many excellent publications of the Constitution Unit at University College, London.

behind most was to solve an immediate political problem. So they suffered from short-termism:

- *Devolution* was principally the response to a need to beat the Scottish National Party at the polls, a necessity fuelled by deep Scottish—and Welsh—indignation at Thatcher's ability to impose Tory policies on a nation with few Conservative seats at the start and, because of those policies, none by 1997.[7] Its importance has been great for Scotland, Wales, Northern Ireland and—to a limited extent—Greater London, but not for the United Kingdom and England.[8] However it was poorly thought through and most needs rectification (below, chapter 19).

- *Proportional representation* had to be promoted to appease the Liberal Democrats whose support Blair thought he might need if he had a smaller and more Left-inclined majority. It was adopted in voting for legislatures other than Westminster where its main consequence for subordinate governments—as in Europe—was to make coalition more likely. But it was in Westminster that the Liberal Democrats most wanted it to secure a share in power.[9]

- The media, whose support had to be won to win the election, were influential forces wanting greater *Freedom of Information*. But David Clark's attempt to have a far-reaching act was undermined because of determined and successful opposition, principally by Jack Straw and other ministers, but also by most officials who saw the undesirability of governing if all government's thinking was conducted under media spotlights.[10] The full effect on the workings of government of the *FOI Act* that emerged, has yet to be seen but will be to encourage further the use of still more informal, less written down, methods of administration, because of fear of exposure.[11]

- *Abolishing the House of Lords*—not only an anachronism, but always a Tory stronghold—seemed safe socialist manifesto material. Before 1997 Blair proclaimed he wanted it elected, but gradually changed his mind. Ostensibly the dispute over its future became about how far it should be elected; but an important issue was patronage and how it should be exercised: by the PM, either by direct appointment of peers, or less directly through their election from those on a party list, or through a less easily influenced appointments commission. An irony was that, because ministers, as late as the 1970s, introduced decent, well-explained, complete bills into Parliament, the disappearance of the Lords, mooted in the 1970s, would have been no functional loss to the British constitution. By the end of the century,

---

[7] Irvine chaired a secret committee in 1995 looking at various devolution options. Brown, Cook, Dewar, Robertson, all Scottish MPs—made it clear it must not be dropped: Seldon (2004) 205.

[8] So far the single achievement of the London mayoral experiment has been the successful introduction of congestion charging. Otherwise it only restored some of the powers that belonged to the old Greater London Council.

[9] Seldon (2004) 265–77.

[10] No 10 so disliked his proposals that they spun against him as a bad minister: private source; Oborne and Walters (2004) 155.

[11] The Hutton Inquiry website showed just how much was revealed about a single episode.

as we have seen, the Lords had become a necessity. Another irony was that its partial reform had increased its legitimacy and therefore its ability to stall and improve government legislation, but sometimes in ways No 10 did not mind.[12] Its lasting shape, but not its function, was still unresolved in 2003.[13]

- In June 2003, a further constitutional proposal was that the Law Lords should be separated from the Lords and a *Supreme Court* set up.[14] Advocated as achieving a separation of powers, there was no discussion of why it was necessary to introduce—as was argued in chapter 1—such an alien doctrine into the British constitution. In recommending the establishment of a Supreme Court separate from the House of Lords, there seemed no longer any recognition of the strength it had derived—as indeed had the Commons—from the presence of distinguished lawyers; no understanding of the strength the British constitution had always gained from the joining together in Parliament and Cabinet people who indeed had separate powers, but deliberated together. The Lords gained greatly from the presence of the Law Lords in their corridors and from their contributions from debate.

Each was a major change. If done carefully—even more if thoroughly discussed in Cabinet and Parliament—each would once have been the main business of a Parliament. But the new Prime Minister and most ministers had little interest in them.[15] Indeed Blair has shown no obvious interest in constitutional issues, conventions or principles.[16] Yet, significant though those constitutional changes were, they did not constitute the revolution.

THE REAL REVOLUTION

The changes, which are the essence of the revolution, are more fundamental, though they are less clear-cut and owe practically nothing to statute. As argued in earlier chapters, they have been in:

- *The Commons*, whose ability since 1997 to hold the Executive to account has worsened, and to pass clear, effective laws has not improved. It is now composed almost entirely of career politicians increasingly drawn from those with a media or political background and a deep interest in constituency business. Though many able people still become MPs, their previous experience is

---

[12] No 10 was opposed to several measures—e.g. on hunting—to which a majority of Labour MPs were wedded. Rather than stand up to these measures, it could rely on the Lords to dilute or send them packing.

[13] Dawn Oliver, who was a member of the Royal Commission on the Lords, shows how hard it was to get good media and therefore public discussion of the issues: Oliver (2003) 189–202.

[14] Department of Constitutional Affairs, *CP* 11/03, July 2003; also Department of Constitutional Affairs, *CP* 10/03, July, 2003; also Bingham (2003).

[15] Hennessy (2000) 508–12.

[16] When the Scots would not follow the rest of Britain in charging higher university fees, Blair protested to Paddy Ashdown that 'Scotland cannot do something different from the rest of Britain.' Reminded this was what devolution was about, the PM responded 'I am beginning to see the defects in all this devolution stuff': Ashdown (2001).

narrower, their ability to acquire subsequent experience diminished, and their contacts with the outside world also narrowed, if only because of the weight and nature of constituency business and the unintelligibility or irrelevance of much else they are expected to do;

- *The Lords*, whose reform became a shambles and descended into farce, but which now, as never before, is an essential revising chamber. However, while they clarify the often muddled bills reaching them and reconcile them with existing law, the outcome is no better than the underlying policy which all too often is hasty, ill-thought out, untested for its practicality and soon overtaken by another policy initiative and another law.

- *Cabinet and the Cabinet system*. The Cabinet no longer exercises executive supremacy, though the fiction is doubtfully maintained that the Prime Minister's decisions are Cabinet's. Similarly there is no longer any real attempt to achieve collective responsibility and Cabinet solidarity by disciplined and rigorous discussion among Cabinet ministers, only through a discipline imposed on them and, since that collapsed, discursive discussion unsupported by enough staffwork to be rigorous.

- *No 10 and Cabinet Office*. Modelled increasingly on the White House, effective executive supremacy and collective responsibility have passed to it. Acquiring so much responsibility made the Prime Minister overloaded beyond his capacity. The new court of political advisers was not as able on his behalf to moderate prime ministerial overload as the civil service once had. Moreover, as was endemic in courts round monarchs, there were many dissensions among them. No 10's working methods largely reflect those thought appropriate to handle the media 24 hours a day. It almost seemed as if Blair, and some around him, were so obsessed by the media that they saw other functions of government—the traditional ones of Cabinet—as a job down the line for someone else. A quirk of the Blair government—since it is so dependent on the personalities of Prime Minister and Chancellor of the Exchequer—but currently fundamental to its operations, is the anomalous creation of a diarchy between them. Diarchy further complicates and slows down the often-chaotic working methods of the Prime Minister, the chancellor and their close advisers.

- *The Opposition* finds it far harder to make an impact and therefore to play its traditional role. It is not just because of personalities or fissures within the Conservative party. How can opposition be effective confronted with slippery, evasive, non-objective ministerial statements and public documents? Evidence to the Hutton Inquiry reinforced the view that the Blair centre saw the media, but especially the BBC, as more its opposition than was the Conservative party. An obsession with the media and therefore with news management served the Blair government well for six years, keeping it high in the polls; but as the public became more aware of spin, people became disillusioned by government without developing enthusiasm for the opposition.

- *The status of Cabinet ministers* declined to that of agents of the Prime Minister or Gordon Brown without resolving the question of how that is consistent with their retention of most statutory powers. Because they have these powers they are often seen as blocking what the Centre wants and not satisfactorily implementing its policies. The freedom which they once had to initiate policies and take decisions now depends practically on the adoption of the cascade principle: they do what the Centre does not choose or have time to do, or more recently, the ability to insist on doing. The boundary is rapidly variable.

- *The relationship of partnership between ministers and civil servants*—important for the effective despatch of business and constitutionally in helping ministers protect their integrity—has been replaced by close relationships between ministers and a new, unelected political class who are no longer just advisers, but powers.[17] Though there are exceptions, relations between ministers and their political advisers at all levels are more important for policy and decision-making than those with their civil servants. Moreover the relations that matter most on a day-to-day basis for departmental ministers, senior and junior— more than those with their own advisers—are with No 10 and the Treasury.

- *The end of the Northcote-Trevelyan tradition* in which senior members of a politically impartial civil service chosen by merit had worked in close partnership with ministers. They had been selected and given enough independence to speak truth to power. Because distanced from policy and decision-making in No 10, they are no longer as able to practise their 'institutional scepticism'; to challenge the good sense and practicality of policy issues; or to argue for objectivity and factual accuracy in ministerial statements and public documents, especially, but not only, in those originating from or vetted by No 10, as most important ones now do.

- *An increase in the number of public bodies of all descriptions*, which have experienced a great reduction in the discretion they once had to manage their affairs as if a public trust, but without that custom being replaced by well-defined legal relationships. Rather they are treated as independent and responsible when required to shoulder blame, but the Centre interferes with and tries to override them whenever it wants. Moreover they are over-regulated and inspected by too many scrutineers.

- *The growth a new political class of MPs*, special advisers and other temporary political appointments, politically appointed lords, members of the European, Scottish, Welsh and Northern Ireland Parliaments, and of local authorities, together with their closely-related counterparts in the media and the lobbies. Their numbers have increased rapidly enough in recent years as to invite the

---

[17] The idea that Jonathan Powell and Alastair Campbell were exceptional in getting powers to order civil servants around by Order in Council has been shown to be misleading, as the case of Jo Moore showed: any adviser can order an official if he has the backing of their minister and many, post-1997, have done so.

Niskanen gibe which Margaret Thatcher aimed at the civil service (chapter 15): that they use their power to increase the jobs available to them.

IRAQ

The public might be readier to accept these usually less visible shortcomings of its government if it had remained competent; but by 2004 prolonged disappointment over public service improvement and the Iraq war were undermining that confidence. We have maintained there are many reasons why government—organised as it is now—is unlikely to solve the problems of the public services (chapters 14–16). The hearings before the Hutton Inquiry and the report of the Butler Review provoked great unease at what they revealed about how government was carried on at the highest levels. In the run-up to Iraq, too many decisions seem to have been taken by the Prime Minister without in any meaningful sense consulting and involving the Cabinet. Two closely-linked episodes show the failings that affect one of the most important matters of state: spin rather than objectivity; reliance on cronies and courtiers rather than Cabinet; civil servants' diminished ability to maintain standards of objectivity; and the reduced ability of the Commons to hold the Executive to account.

THE SEPTEMBER 2002 DOSSIER

As serious as possible an example of not telling the truth was the allegation that No 10 had tampered with, edited, and thereby falsified, information from intelligence sources on the existence of weapons of mass destruction in Iraq. As so often it was easily, and perhaps deliberately, confused with other important, but distinct, allegations: whether the intelligence information was itself reliable; or, insofar as it was reliable, was it sufficient to substantiate the government's arguments for going to war? Moreover, did it seem reliable—was it sufficient at the time—even if not with hindsight? Such questions raise the most important matters of political judgement, as for previous Prime Ministers in similar circumstances. But they are distinct from the allegation, which concerns our argument, that the first, September 2002, dossier had been altered or edited—and the second, February 2003, dossier, indeed written by No 10 spin-doctors, but its status misrepresented—to the extent that for a time this misrepresentation helped persuade Cabinet, most MPs and most public opinion of the military necessity of going to war, if Iraq were not to use weapons of mass destruction to threaten world and Middle East peace.

This Iraq affair raised a further issue, hard to explain to those whose experience was in the media. Their work was always being edited, shortened and their words changed by editors and sub-editors, if only to compress it into the time or space available. A running argument during Alastair Campbell's appearance before the Commons' Foreign Affairs Committee—and later between him and other participants in the Hutton Inquiry, and for the Butler Review—was over the extent to which he had altered the presentation of the September dossier of which the Joint Intelligence Committee provided the substance.[18]

Campbell protested his innocence to the FAC and to Hutton. He told Hutton that he had no influence on the contents of the September dossier. But events, and the Hutton inquiry, showed that he mis-spoke himself about this.[19] Shoals of comments were made on versions of the dossier, many by his own staff.[20] When asked, he denied responsibility for his own staff doing this, observing that, if they had done so, they were operating above their 'pay-grade'. After comparison of the versions it went through showed that its presentation was altered so as to strengthen the argument for war, Campbell's contention changed: the responsibility was not his, but John Scarlett's, chairman of the Joint Intelligence Committee who had taken full 'ownership' of the dossier.[21] Scarlett acknowledged he had. Hutton accepted that this fact—and that he, Hutton, was persuaded the dossier told no actual falsehoods—absolved Campbell and the PM from any misrepresentation caused by 'sexing up'.[22] Subsequently, however, it was reported that some in the intelligence services believed the final version of the dossier seriously misrepresented their views.[23] Later, the Intelligence Services Committee and the Butler Review compared successive versions in which the intelligence services' caveats had been dropped.[24] Whether it amounted to 'sexing up', or whose was the re-writing, were red herrings.[25] Neither does it matter—we do not know because minutes do not exist to show it—if the PM directly brought pressure to bear, or Alastair Campbell, or others among his close aides, for whose actions the PM cannot but be fully responsible. The plain fact is that under No 10 influence the Joint Intelligence Committee did not include what Butler called the 'normal caveats and warnings, which the intelligence material contained,[26] and therefore Parliament was

[18]   House of Commons Foreign Affairs Committee, 25/7/2003, Uncorrected Transcript, 4, 5, 6, 31, 34, 5, 39, 41, 44, 54, 62, 77.
[19]   *The Independent*, 20 August 2003. Campbell told the FAC he had first chaired a meeting on the dossier on 9th July and had not seen a version without reference to Iraq's 45-minute capability. Later it emerged he had forgotten he had chaired a meeting on 5th July: *The Independent*, 13 August 2003. On that day a draft was available for Jonathan Powell, who observed that it needed a substantial re-write to make a convincing case for war: *The Independent*, 19 August 2003.
[20]   *Times*, 20 August 2003.
[21]   Confirmed by Butler (2004) paras 320, 462. The Hutton Inquiry was later told that No 10 took over 'ownership' of the dossier in the last few days before its publication, *Times*, 5 September 2003.
[22]   'Sexing-up' was far from the only ambiguous phrase which made Andrew Gilligan's notorious, 29 May 2004 broadcast so misleading: Lloyd (2004) 2–9.
[23]   *Times*, 4 August 2003; also B Jones, *The Independent*, 23 July 2004.
[24]   Butler (2004) paras 330 and 334ff, and Annex B compare versions. The Annex seems to imply the PM's foreword—which contained the firmest reference to weapons of mass destruction being capable of being fired within 45 minutes—was not in the JIC's versions of the dossier, but was added later.
[25]   Butler (2004) para 310, says there was no evidence of 'embellishment'; or, para 315, that it was intended to make a case for war; or, achieve any other policy objectives in relation to Iraq.
[26]   Butler (2004) para 467.

misled. Butler found it 'a serious weakness that JIC warnings were not made sufficiently clear' in the dossier.[27]

On a matter of such importance, if no minute were found instructing the deletion of the caveats, one would have expected that Hutton, the ISC and Butler would have discovered a minute on the files from Scarlett, or a member of his team, stating that his advice had been that the caveats should be included in the published dossier, but that he had been over-ruled. No such minute was found. Rather in saying that he took full responsibility for drafting the dossier, the implication was that Scarlett had not discharged the time-honoured civil service function of speaking truth and objectivity to political power. The omission of the caveats had as powerful a consequence as the inclusion of an untruth would have done.

Civil servants must not be open to the accusation they are blocking a policy which ministers have chosen and which they are ready to defend in Parliament. But they depart from the role expected of them, if they do not inform ministers what their advice is, how reliable it is and in particular where in their opinion the facts—also possibly the law—do not justify the minister's view.

The Scott Report had found junior civil servants bending the truth to please junior ministers.[28] In this case a similar tendency seems to have reached the highest levels of the civil service and on an issue that could not have been more important.[29] This admission inevitably raised the question—hard to prove one way or the other—how stalwart even senior civil servants might be in standing up for truth in this new Whitehall world, where the most senior civil servants were, or thought themselves to be, subject to ministerial favour for their bonuses—which had since 1997 become a much greater slice of their expanded pay packets—and promotion prospects.[30] In practical terms, did it mean that Scarlett—and indeed other officials allowed to join the charmed, but *politicised* and highly media-focused, circle round the PM—had *de facto* joined the ranks of special advisers, leaving behind them the integrity, impartiality and objectivity expected of a civil servant? In January, 2004, Sir Roderick Braithwaite, a past chairman of the JIC, made the significant observation that past chairmen had filled this post as their last before retirement.[31] So they were immune from career pressures, but Scarlett's career was not at an end. Ahead of him was the possibility of a more senior post—dependent on the PM—indeed of becoming head of MI6, as a year or so later he did.[32]

[27] Butler (2004) para 464–65.

[28] Foster (1996).

[29] It might be argued that Scarlett was a member of the SIS, not the civil service and therefore not to be judged by its standards. But members of the intelligence services did show the greatest concern in upholding the dossier's objectivity. If that were still thought a problem, it reinforces the Butler recommendation that the JIC chairman should be a civil servant.

[30] *Independent*, 21/8/03.

[31] Also Butler, (2004), para 597. Butler backed the view that the JIC chairman should be in his last post before retiring.

[32] Butler, (2004), 597, explicitly recommended that the chair of the JIC should be 'someone with experience of dealing with ministers in a very senior role and who is demonstrably beyond influence,

THE JULY 2004 IRAQ DEBATE

A striking example of the decline in the ability of the Commons, led by the Opposition, to hold the Executive to account was Blair's victory in the July 2004 Iraq debate. During the previous 25 years, and despite the increased range and complexity of ministers' responsibilities, partisanship had arguably made it easier for them to escape criticism, even in matters of security. James Prior, and his junior minister Nicholas Scott, argued their way out of resignation over the Maze prison break-out.[33] William Whitelaw offered his resignation when an intruder invaded the Queen's bedroom and when defeated over an immigration bill, but in neither case was it accepted.[34] Neither did Lord Young resign over the Barlow Clowes affair, the House of Fraser take-over or the Sale of Rover.[35] Nor did Kenneth Baker over the Brixton Prison escape[36] (though Derek Lewis had to resign for a prison break-out as chief executive of the Prisons Agency when it had taken over direct responsibility for prisons from the Home Office).[37] Despite a magnificent speech, Robin Cook could not shake one minister into resigning after the Scott Report. If Kinnock had performed well over Westland, Margaret Thatcher's position would have unwound, but he failed to deliver the killer blow. On these occasions the minister survived, but it continued to be recognised that the parliamentary test[38] was still the moment of truth.

Nevertheless there were still great parliamentary occasions when ministers were effectively called to account and subsequently resigned. Carrington resigned over the Falklands. John Nott did not, though arguably he was as culpable by the classic theory of ministerial responsibility for the lack of military preparedness as Carrington was for the preceding foreign policy; but his attempt to justify the sinking of the Belgrano was a disaster and he resigned soon after.[39] Leon Brittan's failure to please anyone as Home Secretary, when commending capital punishment for terrorists but for no one else, contributed to his demotion to DTI not long after, and soon after Westland he left the Commons.[40] Above all was Geoffrey Howe's great speech which brought down Margaret Thatcher.

By July 2004, it was manifest that the Commons had been misled over the case for invading Iraq. But was it done deliberately? Did it happen because Blair did

---

and thus probably in his last post', a recommendation not followed when Scarlett's successor was appointed.

[33] Woodhouse, (1994), 124—134.
[34] Whitelaw, (1989), 276–82, 291–7; Woodhouse, (1994), 136–143.
[35] Thatcher, (1993), 679–80; Woodhouse, (1994), 143–153.
[36] Baker, (1993), 458–61; Woodhouse, (1994), 153–161.
[37] Lewis, (1997), 164–205.
[38] Carrington, (1988); Cosgrave, (1989).
[39] *Hansard*, 3/4/1982, 664–8; Dalyell, (1987), 14, 5; John Nott maintained he resigned because he had enough, Nott, (2002), 316–21.
[40] *Hansard*, 13 July 1983, 885–95; private information.

not ask the right questions? Or did he avert his eyes? The Intelligence Services Committee and then the Butler Review had shown that he—or those immediately round him, for whom he was directly responsible, responding to his wishes—had influenced the chairman of the Joint Intelligence Committee— what other reason could he possibly have—to the extent that he dropped the caveats from the intelligence reported in the September 2002 dossier (above chapter 13).[41] Whether that amounted to 'sexing up' the dossier is a red herring. If the dossier had reflected the intelligence's original caveats, it is unlikely the House would have supported the war: it would have insisted the inspectors be given more time to find weapons of mass destruction. The Attorney-General will have told him that his underlying reason for going to war, regime change— as disclosed in his 23rd June speech—was unlawful and could not be used.[42]

Rather than address these issues in any systematic way, the PM, allowing himself to be constantly interrupted, relied on a series of skilful disconnected soundbites to rally the emotions of his supporters, rather than a reasoned defence. Even so he wiped the floor with his opponents. Thereafter—though supposed to be in the greatest peril defending his conduct over the war—he did not stay for more than a few speeches. (For a long time no minister was present.) While there he was reported as frequently chatting to Jack Straw beside him, not listening.[43] What mattered to him was the media's reception of his own speech and, to a far lesser extent, that of his principal opponent. He was helped by the fact that for many years the media had increasingly frequently, and recently once or more a week, called for a minister's resignation. These calls had become so devalued that ministers became readier to ignore them and gain their party's support in doing so.

No wonder many MPs became discouraged from speech-making. There were many fine, pointed speeches in that debate, as in the two earlier Iraq debates.[44] But what impact could they possibly have when staying in power had become so much more important than the PM truthfully presenting the case for going to war? It was not as if the government had to fall. In not dissimilar circumstances, Chamberlain had given way to Churchill, Eden to Macmillan. Part of the problem was that with so many fewer opportunities for other ministers to shine, and to show and develop their qualities, in Cabinet and Parliament, it was less obvious who were the best candidates for the succession. Blair's method of government had made identifying a good successor much harder (chapter 18). So Blair again showed how unimportant Parliament was to him, since he could control it enough to ensure a favourable vote whatever many, even among his own MPs, thought privately.

---

[41] House of Commons Intelligence Services Committee (2004) compared successive versions of the dossier; Butler, (2004).

[42] Butler, (2004), para 379.

[43] Kampfner, *New Statesman*, 20 July, 2004.

[44] Among the excellent speeches unreported in the media were ones by Charles Kennedy, William Hague, Tam Dalyell, Alex Salmond, Marsha Singh, Michael Meacher and Tony Wright. Anthony Sampson, present at the Commons' debate after Suez and at the 26/02/03 Iraq debate, believed the Iraq debate to be of the higher quality, Sampson, (2004), 15, 6. But at Suez the government had been listening.

PART 5

WHAT NEXT?

18

Resilience or a Third Presidency?

HENNESSY: do you think there is a degree to which we ought to worry about excessive . . . creeping prime ministerialism? BUTLER: I do not think so . . . the instruments are all there for, if a Prime Minister gets off the leash, doing something about it. What could illustrate it better than what happened in the Margaret Thatcher case . . .? The deal is that you give people very considerable power for five years, then they can be thrown out, and, in the meantime, if things get bad enough there are ways of getting rid of them. That is the deal of our constitution.

Peter Hennessy and Robin Butler[1]

MIGHT NOT CABINET Government be restored by a much reduced parliamentary majority, or by a change of Prime Minister, or by a change of attitude in an existing Prime Minister? But after nearly 25 years of revolutionary turbulence the necessary resilience may have been lost and may not easily be regained.

In August, 2003, Blair's out-stripped Attlee's as the longest-serving Labour government. Given the purposes of this narrative, it does not matter whether Blair stays, or is replaced by Brown or another from the Labour party. Or the electorate's disillusion and weariness put a Conservative, Liberal Democrat or coalition government into office. Sometimes it is suggested that Blair, or any other PM, must govern differently if the next election meant a majority as small as Callaghan or Major's became, or indeed if it were under 50: that a sharp loss of power over MPs would make this Prime Minister or a successor revert to something like collegiate, effective Cabinet Government. But would it?

THE FLEXIBILITY OF THE BRITISH CONSTITUTION

Commentators, who were at first inclined to see the Blair administration as yet another example of the adaptability of our unwritten constitution to the personality of a new Prime Minister, questioned the fundamental or lasting nature of his assumption of Thatcher-like methods of operation.[2] Had not the power of previous Prime Ministers in Cabinet varied greatly? Had not Aberdeen, Campbell-Bannerman, Asquith, Baldwin, Attlee, Douglas-Home and Major

---

[1] Hennessy (2000) 6.
[2] Kavanagh and Seldon (1999); Hennessy (1999) but not (2000).

appeared little more than first among equals, chairmen of a committee? Did not many ministers complain of the imperious, even 'imperial', behaviour of other Prime Ministers and called them 'autocratic' or 'dictatorial', as Harcourt did Gladstone; as Bonar Law, Austen Chamberlain, Montagu[3] and Curzon called Lloyd George; as many judged Churchill; and at times Crossman, Castle and Benn even stigmatised Wilson, especially after losing an argument in Cabinet, still more if their party lost the election soon afterwards? Furthermore had not Salisbury in his first administration and Heath dominated Cabinet because of their colleagues' comparative lack of talent? Had not Palmerston, Disraeli, Gladstone, Lloyd George, Churchill, Thatcher mastered Cabinets with many talented ministers in them, though never absolutely, and often ending in tears?

Undoubtedly the modern British Prime Minister has long had important powers, not in law but by convention, setting him above his Cabinet, which have increased over time. Among them are powers Blair, too, was to use: to call an election, appoint and dismiss ministers, set Cabinet agendas, summarise its conclusions and legitimate its decisions.[4] And he was to add to them by central-ising into his own hands other once royal prerogatives which had descended to Cabinet[5]. Margaret Thatcher may often have crushed opposition in Cabinet. Blair's unique contribution was to take its executive supremacy away by no longer letting it be a decision-making body. Collective responsibility dwindled into all ministers being required in effect to agree to stand by all his decisions, however limited or non-existent their awareness of them: if they disagreed openly, not to be surprised by the sack. Cabinet solidarity was no longer a requirement because the Prime Minister, and those around him, had developed other methods of controlling ministers through the parliamentary and national party. Did not ministers for the first time appear much less important than his political advisers? Though checked by the stubbornness of some ministers, Blair behaved for the first time among Prime Ministers as if his—or Brown's—were the right to direct how secretaries of state used many of their statutory and prerogative powers.

THE LIMITS OF PRIME MINISTERIAL POWER

But could not all this still be reversed? Lloyd George emerged from the First World War with such prestige that his power was thought presidential.[6] He could rebuff a protest by 370 MPs in April 1919 by declaring that, if they continued with it, he would ask their constituencies to settle the matter by not

[3] Mackintosh (1962) 363, 393.

[4] His admitted functions and powers have changed over time. For a more recent account see Hennessy (1995) 86–92, also (2000).

[5] R Brazier,'Constitutional Reform and the Crown' in Sunkin and Payne (1999) 350–54. Using prerogative as a general ministerial ability to take decisions within law, he, rather than Cabinet, laid down the policy when he cared to do so.

[6] Jennings (1959) 297–301.

re-electing them.[7] But then his mainly Conservative Cabinet suddenly over-
threw him. His so-called Garden Suburb was a coterie of special advisers, but
was banished and not replaced as soon as Bonar Law succeeded him. Churchill's
wartime power at times became almost presidential in that it grew into a position where he appeared almost the sole source of executive authority.[8]
However, such developments were novel and arose from the understandable
belief that drastic measures were needed in war. Moreover Attlee ended them.

The Prime Minister always determined some issues alone or in conclave with
a few colleagues. Since the Second World War, progressively more were, but
while Cabinet ministers collectively felt able to disagree with the Prime Minister
and win whenever an issue seemed important enough, the Cabinet retained
supreme executive power which it could be presumed to have no more than
sometimes delegated to the Prime Minister. Margaret Thatcher had taken some
years to develop her handling of Cabinet, and increase her power over ministers,
so that she could usually, but far from always, flatten them with impunity. The
Blair administration's abandonment of a collegiate Cabinet and Cabinet
system—though disguised by ambiguities and equivocations—was instant. But
that need not make it irreversible by a new Prime Minister.

Crossman only had to look back to Eden running Suez with a hand-picked
inner group of ministers for evidence of what he metaphorically called presidential power.[9] Later, his diaries—not always reliably—report Wilson, though
usually a stickler for Cabinet consultation, contriving decisions which by-
passed or bounced Cabinet. Similar practices are found in earlier and all subsequent governments. They can be helped by a Prime Minister's conventional
powers, but can still have far reaching consequences as did Gladstone not con-
vening his Cabinet for months on end; Asquith asserting that Lloyd George's
attack on landed interests in his 1909 budget had Cabinet approval when the
majority was against it;[10] Callaghan delaying fatally the 1979 election against
the views of a majority of his Cabinet;[11] and Margaret Thatcher driving decisions through Cabinet without seeking a majority there. This said, Prime
Ministers—even Thatcher—had always practised some restraint for fear of
strong reaction or even revolt from Cabinet colleagues: the fact they could
sometimes, even often, get their own way, did not make it wise to behave as if
they could always dominate their colleagues. Several, among them the greatest,
learned that lesson too late.

[7] Mackintosh (1962) 371.
[8] Never in domestic affairs which he left almost entirely to others where unrelated to the war effort.
[9] Crossman's introduction to Bagehot (1963); also Butler in Herman and Alt (1975) 202–3; Hennessy (1996) 210. An extraordinary example is Churchill, as first Lord of the Admiralty, mobil-ising the fleet in 1914, despite a Cabinet decision that morning against it and the Prime Minister not committing himself—but the Germans had declared war in between: quoted in Mount (1992)120–1.
[10] Walker (1970) 27.
[11] Morgan (1997) 639–48.

A REVERSION TO CABINET GOVERNMENT?

So one can never rule out that revolt among ministers, as in 1990, or among backbenchers, might lead to the revival of a collegiate Cabinet Government with or without a new Prime Minister. Cabinet ministers could still overturn the Prime Minister as Margaret Thatcher's experience showed.

In 1999 I concluded that Cabinet Government would not end unless Cabinet, Parliament and a political party's power, relative to the Prime Minister, declined to the point he or she could regard Parliament no more than as a store from which he or she can draw ministers at will and dismiss any of them without retribution.[12] While that possibility remained implausible—whatever the appearance of presidential power and though operationally the old Cabinet system had gone—we did not yet have a presidential or prime ministerial system, furthermore not one in law.[13]

But if Cabinet ministers could not stand up to the PM, if MPs were to become so keen to gain or retain office; or acquire a peerage or other patronage from the Prime Minister; or to avoid losing their seat at the next election; or risk deselection, what then? If Cabinet ministers felt they had not backing enough in the Commons to withstand a Prime Minister—who could dismiss them, however important the issue—the Rubicon would have been crossed.

THE BELITTLING OF MINISTERS

Subsequently, there have been several indications that this might have happened. All Prime Ministers have had various weapons to shore up their power. But the pre-dominance of the career politician made their systematic use more feasible. Instead of the personal fear Thatcher inspired, disciplining Cabinet and other ministers became systematic. Under Thatcher ministers learned that, if they opposed her too often, they would be dropped. Blair, helped by his control of the party apparatus, could also use this threat. Indeed it seemed easier than under Thatcher for the Prime Minister to dismiss many Cabinet and junior ministers, principally because of the press of others anxious to take their places, but also because the qualities the Centre most required of ministers had become diminished almost to their being safe pairs of hands when it came to sound-bites before the media, and progress-chasers. Here the contrast with Thatcher was complete. She may have bullied her ministers and often cowed them into submission, but many of her ministers did not always toe her line; as in different circumstances Major's ministers did not.

---

[12] Foster (1999).
[13] Hennessy (2000) 482–8.

By contrast few Cabinet ministers in 1997 had their own independent public standing. Robin Cook's was removed from him almost at once by his loss of face over his divorce to the point he could not or would not stand up to his subsequent demotion. John Prescott could not resist being marginalised after the 2001 election, always supported Blair in Cabinet, and did not try to stop the dismemberment of the department created for him in 1997. Jack Straw's considerable independent personality and reputation was undermined almost as soon as he went from a congenial post at the Home Office to one overshadowed by the Prime Minister at the Foreign Office.[14] Clare Short for a time maintained a more independent stance, because of her erstwhile popularity and because Blair's retention of her seemed to show his tolerance. Moreover her department was at one remove from his central interests: she and it were the government's conscience. Besides Brown, perhaps David Blunkett alone achieved and retained the standing to have his own way at Education and then at the Home Office, but the price was that neither the Centre nor his own officials—let alone Cabinet, as once would have happened—could curb his wilder flights.

More ministers went or changed posts after the 2001 election than at any previous election not involving a change of government. It became common to hear it remarked that most MPs could expect no more than a spell of about three years as a minister, taking their turn with others before returning to the backbenches. By 2003, only three of the 1997 Cabinet were in their original posts.

PARTY DISCIPLINE

By 2004 the increasing number of ex-ministers in the Commons, particularly the angry and effective resentment of Cook and Short, might seem to threaten Blair's control over his parliamentary party.[15] However, more than any previous PM, Blair presided over a powerful party machine inside and outside Parliament. To wage war under Kinnock against Militant, the leadership had gained a control over the Party at its conference and in the constituencies which it had never had before. As over Iraq, immense efforts were made to secure a majority in the Commons. As well as the threat of de-selection, the prospect of a peerage, or some other job after an election, another inducement was the carrot of office. In the past many ministers, though chagrined by defeat, welcomed the chance to spend more time on their other careers, and sometimes to repair their fortunes. Career politics now meant that most were never as financially well off as when ministers. Around the turn of the century ministers' and MPs' salaries and expenses went up substantially in part as a kind of compensation,

[14] Subsequent evidence has suggested Straw and the Foreign Office were far less persuaded than the PM that war was advisable, or preparations for reconstruction adequate, *Daily Telegraph*, 18 September 2004.
[15] Mandelson seemed to be tilting against these when he criticised some MPs for undermining the PM because they did not care if Labour stayed in power, *Times*, 12 February 2004.

but further increasing the comparative pain from loss of office. (Though if their career prospects became so dim and truncated—if being a minister had become such a subordinate and short-lived role for most—how long would the strivers stay who famously had seen Parliament as the stage for a glorious career?)

The pressure of those eager for promotion, the size of the parliamentary majority and party discipline—the fact even that he brought back some dismissed ministers or gave them advisory posts—meant that those ministers opposed to Blair over Iraq could not look for sufficient support from the parliamentary party to defeat him. That was despite the belief that enough Labour MPs were privately against war for him to lose, though supported by the votes of the Conservative opposition. So Blair and his circle maintained their supremacy over Cabinet, ministers and Parliament.

But the greatest inducement to conform was the memory of the effect disunity had had in keeping Labour out of power for 18 years. After mid-2003 Labour ministers and backbenchers might feel freer to rebel and reject government proposals, but there were limits on how far they would go: they would not threaten the government's staying in power. A new dialectic developed over foundation hospitals, top-up university fees and several subsequent issues through which government and backbenchers jockeyed to find compromises saleable both to the median voter and more leftish backbench Labour opinion. So while a much smaller parliamentary majority or even less confidence in the Prime Minister might make back-benchers readier to challenge government on particular measures, it seemed unlikely they would go so far as to risk its future. Had not 1990 shown that ministers could overthrow a Prime Minister? But the difficulty the Tories had in finding a worthy successor, and their period in the political wilderness that followed, did not make that example encouraging.[16] What was not achieved in 1990 was more ominous for the future than what was.

But is not the proposition that, even if a particular PM does not fall, as Thatcher did, British government always reverts to collegiate Cabinet Government, proved by what actually happened after Blair's loss of prestige in 2003? No, because like Major's, but to a greater extent, it did not recapture the solidarity and effective collegiate processes of the past which had enabled most Cabinets to be effective most of the time. It was more like a 19th century Cabinet trying to cope with the modern flood of work. Moreover many around the PM were tired. Many of the best were gone or going. Blair seemed at times a lame-duck Prime Minister, though at others fired with a great burst of energy, but without a fixed four-year, or any other, term election to force closure.

---

[16] Michael Portillo was interesting and insightful over these issues of loyalty, *Sunday Times*, 16 May 2004.

SUCCESSION

Blair's position was strengthened by the absence of an obvious successor except Brown. Gordon Brown seemed the marked-out successor as much as Chamberlain or Eden or RA Butler had been. But was he the right person? While none doubted his great intellect and ability to generate policy ideas, many wondered if he had the public and presentational skills to lead them to another victory. Moreover, though his presidential style would be different, he would surely try to be as presidential as Blair.

But who else? Indeed who might succeed Blair? What reason to suppose him or her better from any standpoint? The trouble is that Blair's form of government—and the media—no longer give ministers and would-be ministers the chance to shine and prove themselves as they once could in Cabinet, shadow Cabinet and Parliament. It is not accidental, when anything except being PM is less prestigious and politically rewarding than it was, that some of the best material in the Tory party—Michael Portillo, Ken Clarke or William Hague—are either leaving Parliament or hiding in its shadows. Neither is it accidental that fewer US presidents now came from the Senate—unless by mischance or death through the Vice-Presidency—but from state governorships which give them a more prominent public platform. Perhaps the only position in Britain, giving an aspiring politician a similar jumping-off position, where he could demonstrate the presentational skills marking him or her out as a great electoral asset, was as yet that of the London Mayor. (Indeed the style of the Blair prime-ministership and the Livingstone mayoralty were strikingly similar—a small coterie of trusted advisers; informal, often *running* meetings, that is ones with an indeterminate agenda and time-table; with focus on the big picture and on policy dominated by presentation.[17])

The Prime Minister must have remarkable, inexhaustible presentational abilities to win media battles time and again. He has also inherited enormous power. But the experience of the Blair prime-ministership raised the further possibility that the kind of person who is brilliant at political presentation rarely, if ever, has the qualities of steadiness, chairmanship, and inspiring trust among his colleagues—or the understanding of people or otherwise the ability to get things done—needed to drive a great government machine.

So, more than ever, the choice of a party leader—from whatever party—will be a leap in the dark. The chances are that any party's candidate for PM will be chosen and drilled to have as far as possible the presentational qualities which made Blair great. But what chance would MPs or the electorate have to know if he or she had the other qualities needed for a good Prime Minister? And if, much more than in the past, his colleagues—many with more ministerial experience

---

[17] Private sources. Livingstone's one outstanding success—London congestion charging—owes its practicality to the thorough previous work done by Derek Turner and his team under Livingstone.

than he had—were jostling, even conspiring, against him for the top job as the only one that mattered, what chance of shadow or future Cabinet solidarity?

Moreover, one will find nobody—not Thatcher—with all the skills needed by a presidential British Prime Minister. If one could, one would still fear the consequences of one person's inevitable gross overloading, and his or her absolute power. So how does one get some rigour, system and focus on non-presentational aspects into the use of that power? How re-construct the checks and balances against its misuse?

THE ROLE OF THE UNELECTED POLITICAL CLASS

Furthermore what is needed for reversion to collegiate government is not only the replacement of one person. The Blair project, unlike Thatcher's, depended on the build-up in opposition of an unelected political class with its own ideas on its political future, individually and collectively. Must new candidates for Prime Minister now always build their own coteries to win the media battles necessary to gain office? Will they always expect to share power with them at the expense of his ministers and civil servants? What other inducements could he hold out to them after victory if Cabinet Government replaced coterie government? The resources needed to win a general election seem to force a would-be Prime Minister to promise gainful employment to his media-handling and policymaking allies after he has won: the promise of a British White House seemingly inconsistent with Cabinet Government, a high standing for Cabinet ministers and a capable, supportive, but challenging civil service.

Neither should one underrate other difficulties. The revival of quality Cabinet Government will require first-rate civil service staffwork. The resurrection of Cabinet Government in its old, let alone an improved, form means basing it on habits and conventions gone from ministerial memories and fast fading from civil service ones. In 1997 no Cabinet minister had any idea of what being in Cabinet meant. By 2005 just enough, but a rapidly diminishing band of officials knew how it was run.

A MORE PRESIDENTIAL GOVERNMENT

Another reason why no attempt might be made to restore Cabinet Government is that Blair, or a successor, might draw a different lesson from recent history. Cardinal Wolsey, and then Henry VIII, may have attempted to create a modern unified—and, by the standards of those times, centralised—state, but that did not exist until Thomas Cromwell created the administrative machinery for it to be possible.[18] Blair believed he had learned the need for even greater centralisa-

---

[18] Elton (1959) 6–8 and *passim*.

tion and politicisation of decision-making to avoid repeating Thatcher's mistakes and her ultimate downfall. So Blair or his successor might conclude Blair's fault was that he had not gone far enough to secure effective prime ministerial government. The public reaction to Clare Short's resignation speech in 2003 showed that, while many reacted with sympathy to her accusations of Blair subverting Cabinet, at least as many, if not more, saw centralised government as the natural order of things, even in its domination of the government majority in Parliament.[19] The second British try at presidential government may have failed, but most would-be successors might want to try again. While many in the public sector front-line—and others indirectly dependent on public funds—had been complaining of ever more intrusive administrative dictatorship from the Centre, people at the Centre protested that frequently they had not power enough to overcome opposition to their reforms from ministers to grass roots.

To overcome such opposition a subsequent government could attempt a more comprehensive prime ministerial or presidential regime. Indeed thus far the replacement of Cabinet by presidential government in Britain has been a metaphor, as much a misnomer and oversimplification under Blair as under Thatcher. Among the reasons for saying so are that Blair did not introduce any of the institutions, including checks and balances that characterise the American, French or any other democratic presidential government. He would have needed new law to do so. Instead, all the institutions of Cabinet Government survived. How they worked depended almost entirely on convention, not laws. Public attention, which has been limited, has concentrated on the changes in law—devolution and the rest—and to a limited extent on changes made in Parliament or Cabinet. The crucial changes were not only there, but elsewhere, as earlier described. Their combination has made them revolutionary, but the most important were achieved without much legal or institutional change.

MORE AMERICANISATION

The easiest route might seem further Americanisation of the British constitution, but it could be as facile as the instant move in 2003 to set up a supreme court. A temptation—itself readily seen as another implication of the rigid 18th century doctrine of the separation of powers—might be to copy the United States by replacing Cabinet and other elected ministers drawn from Parliament by business and other prime-ministerial appointees without them having to be in Parliament, so putting them and the chiefs of the more important agencies in a similar relationship of dependency on the Prime Minister. No statute bars such a development.[20] Surely then, the Centre would have the power it needs? But to

---

[19] *Guardian*, 13 May 2003; *Evening Standard*, 13 May 2003.

[20] By convention only ministers who are peers or MPs can introduce public bills. So either such ministers would need junior ministers who were in Parliament or, on the US model, would need members of Parliament to sponsor their bills. These are not insuperable problems.

reflect on the implications of such a measure to overcome lower level executive intransigency shows new problems would be created.

At first Blair had tried to infiltrate a number of peers as ministers, or high-level quasi-minister advisers, mainly ones with outside established business experience, like Lords Simon, Sainsbury, Macdonald, Haskins and Birt. Not in most cases obviously politically successful, backbench MPs, who saw their career opportunities blocked, resented their appointment. When Baroness Amos replaced Clare Short as Secretary for International Development, Labour back-benchers in the Commons were indignant, though she was black, a woman and of some proven ability.[21]

If political appointments from outside Parliament were to become the norm—with or without peerages—what checks would a Prime Minister accept on cronyism or the fallibility of his knowledge of suitable people? They would need to be at least as strong as the checks the US Senate imposes on such appointments.

Even so, as American experience shows, it is not always easy to find qualified candidates. Moreover, copious experience shows that even when presidents place their appointee in a job, they often develop a mind of their own, about which in practice presidents can do little.

But other more fundamental issues would emerge. If MPs no longer had the inducement of ministerial office, how would one attract as good people to the Commons? Would one reconcile MPs to the end of their ministerial ambitions by allowing them yet higher salaries and expenses? Or through accepting that constituency will attract most MPs in future work and that they will tend to be the kinds of people most interested in such social work? But already Scottish and Welsh MPs have lost much of that work because of devolution. English devolution ought to diminish the importance of that work among English MPs. But what other significant functions would the Commons have left (above chapter 7)?

Another possibility is that we might adapt further to the American pattern by turning Parliament into a true legislature or Lawmaker. Laws in congress not only must be introduced by members of congress, but are habitually re-made in committee. If so, the role of the British Executive would be very different. It would greatly limit the Executive's past and present ability to make laws[22]. (An interesting question is whether a legislature, as independent of the Executive as congress is, could be relied on to interact with the EU so as to fulfil its obligations under European law.)

It would also—to judge by American experience—much enhance the ability of industrial and commercial interests to influence the content of those laws

---

[21] Information from interviewing MPs.

[22] As was observed in chapter 2 a few Scottish law officers, and occasionally others—generally Commonwealth statesmen in wartime—have not sat in Parliament but they have not introduced legislation. One can imagine a non-parliamentary senior minister delegating legislation to junior ministers in both Houses. It is hard to see how the Commons would tolerate it as a norm.

through what in Britain, but not America, would be called corruption: payments to help senators and congressmen meet their election expenses.[23] Some, but far from all, would welcome this Americanisation as a means of giving more power to economic interests to prevent the tendency democracy always has to re-distribute wealth to an extent that may damage the economy, or even lead to its corruption, and so lead to less wealth for all or almost all. As a means by which plutocracy can temper the redistributive tendencies of democracy, they might see it as preferable to the murky shadows of letting such interests attempt to exert their influence by dominating consultation exercises and—it will always be believed—through contributions to party funds.[24] But others would challenge the wisdom and good sense of giving business such an assured influence over legislation.

Would British governments accept other checks and balances which limit federal power? Would they be ready to *devolve* most aspects of domestic policy, giving much more to the private sector, the states and local government, all of which have much more scope and independence of central government than in Britain? Another safeguard of personal freedom against US executive tyranny is the much greater protection given by the Law. Because ours is a bi-partite 17th century constitution—though informally made tri-partite from the end of the 19th century by the constitutional role of the civil service—the vital relationship—that of accountability for responsibility—is between Parliament and the Executive. Would that Executive permit ours being turned into a tri-partite constitution in which the Law and a new supreme court, with expanded constitutional powers, were at least as important checks on executive power as Parliament? [25]

As a corollary, would it concede that departments and agencies, though under heads appointed by the Prime Minister, must work only within regulations strictly supervised by the courts, as occurred in the United States during the 20th century (chapters 2 and 19)? [26]

SHORTCOMINGS OF THE US MODEL

Moreover the workings of the US model are imperfect. The American political scientists, Campbell and Wilson, compared Whitehall with presidential decision-making, especially as practised in the USA.[27] They stressed how hard it was to achieve coherence and consistency in the US presidential system which the

---

[23] Foster and Plowden (1996) chapter 2.

[24] See, for example, *Sunday Telegraph*, 7 September 2003.

[25] Though it will inherit a few constitutional functions, especially in relation to devolution, it will remain an appellate court, not a constitutional one in the sense of interpreting and applying a written constitutional document. That is why Woolf LCJ called it a second-rate Supreme Court, *Daily Telegraph*, 4 March 2004.

[26] Greatly strengthened since the Administrative Practices Act, 1946: Breyer (1982).

[27] Campbell and Wilson (1995) 148–61.

Blair government saw as its ideal and model. As Hobbes said, a single individual should find it easier to know his mind and therefore be more coherent and consistent than a Cabinet.[28] But modern US presidents, like Blair, have often become too overloaded to act coherently and consistently, and too dependent on their staff. Their staffs often do not themselves agree on what should be done, or with departmental, agency or external advisors, interested in the same problem. Blair's working methods could not bear the weight of attempted centralised decision-making. They were a recipe for delay, indecision, changes of mind often masquerading as changes in presentation, and inconstancy. But the similar characteristics are found in US presidential government. Bush has been as much criticised over Iraq for ill-judged and coterie decision-making as Blair. There is no reason to suppose a more presidential Prime Minister would be less overloaded or overwhelmed by decisions he must make, behave any the less arbitrarily and with insufficient thought, unless positive steps were taken to make him less inclined.

CONCLUSION

The greatest danger from more presidentialisation is that an Executive, believing in its powerlessness, will adopt from America the expedients it believes will increase its power without introducing the checks and balances which in the United States—and in other democratic countries—restrain its use. It will diminish the influence of lawyers and the law diminish by excluding top lawyers from Cabinet and Parliament without establishing a real supreme court or equivalent safeguard of our rights.[29] Yet over the last 60 years, but especially the last 20, centralisation of power has gone as far as it can in Britain—some might say further—without raising fundamental issues about the nature of the society we want to live in and the form of government most suited to it. Improvisation—the speedy following of one change by another—has marked the course of our revolution. The tendency of those changes—not surprisingly given virtually all were at the instance of the Executive—has been to centralise and politicise power. Unchecked one must expect that tendency to continue, whether or not it tries to look more like presidential government. The likelihood that government introduces checks and balances limiting its use of power seems remote.

---

[28] Hobbes [1651](1996) 130–34.
[29] The government made it clear it was not to be a constitutional Supreme Court, as in the US and many other constitutions, Banner and Deane (2003) ch 2.

19

A More Legal Constitution

To inquire into the best form of government in the abstract, as it is called, is not a chimerical, but a highly practical employment of scientific intellect; and to introduce into any country the best institutions, which, in the existing state of the country, are capable of, in any tolerable degree, is one of the most rational objects, to which practical effort can address itself.

J S Mill (1861)[1]

BY A MORE legal constitution I mean one where some constitutional conventions are replaced by laws—as well as some poor constitutional laws by better laws—so that our constitutional arrangements are clearer and, when necessary, legally enforceable.[2]

Broadly there are two variants. The more pragmatic argument is that more law is needed to sort out particular muddles and shortcomings. For example, the next chapter considers how our traditional constitution could be strengthened and modernised. The changes suggested could rely on convention—which has the great advantage of an easier adaptability to changing circumstances and as such worked well for about 300 years—or on new law. The tenor of our argument throughout has been that the more we can rely on convention, while re-gaining constitutional stability, the better.[3] Nevertheless this chapter first considers two inter-related issues—ministerial responsibility and devolution—where the case for more law is particularly strong, and a third—ministerial decision-making—where it is also strong, unless the constitutional role of the civil service can be restored.

A more extreme position, then considered, is based on such disillusionment with the present political system that—certainly in its more thoroughgoing forms—it wants it largely replaced by legal process. In its less extreme forms it foresees a future in which extended human rights legislation and the courts transform our political system. But it would be the end of democracy and, if really preferable, a tremendous indictment of our ability to reconstruct our political system to acceptable standards.

---

[1] Mill (1910) 181–82. Burke said much the same: Burke (1845) iii, 82.

[2] A related comparison in approaches to constitution-making is between British Hobbesian and American rights-based: Marshall (1971) 2.

[3] I do not consider whether we need special constitutional or entrenched laws and a constitutional supreme court. I hope not, for all the reasons argued in this book; but it is too complex and detailed a matter to argue here.

RESPONSIBILITY AND ACCOUNTABILITY

The heart of the British political system is the notion that the Executive is accountable to Parliament. But, as has been argued, the convention of ministerial responsibility no longer adequately defines who is responsible for what. Given the complexity of modern government, and its fragmentation, we cannot return practically to relations between its various parts being regulated by convention. Even before fragmentation, the problems here labelled NOSSO caused serious difficulties. Because the convention of ministerial responsibility has broken down irretrievably, accountability cannot be effective unless it is made clear what every part of government is responsible for and to whom they are accountable.[4]

If individual civil servants, or parts of departments, agencies and agency chiefs are to shoulder blame, one needs to know what responsibilities can be attributed to them; and what right Cabinet or ministers—or any other bodies— have to override their discretion, and in what circumstances. It may be unavoidable that a public body can be instructed by several ministers or other public bodies—and be accountable to different elected bodies for different purposes— though there should be as little of this as possible. But what there is should be clear. In other words, the long-standing problem must be resolved by which the extent of ministerial powers over public servants and public bodies was left vague. Once it helped protect their autonomy, but progressively since the 1980s it has become an instrument subordinating them to central power. Otherwise the muddle, inefficiency and blame avoidance culture which has undermined parliamentary and, for that matter, media accountability, will not end.

It is not unreasonable for higher levels of government to call in the activities of lower levels if they do not achieve a minimum level of performance; but such intervention must be based on sound evidence. Inspectors, auditors and regulators are among those who need their functions, the limitations on their freedom and accountability more carefully defined. Disputes between parts of government and the public sector seem inescapably destined for the courts even if political decision, policy and lawmaking reign within each part's competence.

A model might be the work of the Haldane Committee after the First World War which in some ways similarly had seen a rather chaotic, though more limited, upheaval in government institutions.[5] Another concerted effort is needed to suggest answers to three questions simultaneously:

---

[4] Another important implication is for ministerial responsibility. A minister cannot expect as frank, open advice from officials who are independently responsible to Parliament. They must be expected to put that duty first. A difference must be expected between civil servants working close to ministers, who do not have independent responsibilities, and the heads of public bodies who in modern circumstances need to have such responsibilities, and for them to be written down.

[5] Haldane (1918).

- What minister, department or other public body is responsible for every public activity and to what elected body—Parliament, regional assembly or local authority—are they accountable?
- What law or regulations determine the powers and duties of every public body; fix the management freedom and other discretion they have; and determine the powers ministers and superior public bodies have to instruct them?
- What are the sources of finance to be for each public body, and the rules governing expenditure, so that higher levels of government are not able to override the independence of lower levels of government by manipulating the purse-strings? One cannot sensibly determine structures and legal relationships without specifying financial relations as well. An issue of some difficulty is whether some laws should be entrenched by being made harder to change, for example by requiring more than a simple majority.[6]

DEVOLUTION

Our devolutionary arrangements also require clear—and related—specification. Further devolution is essential for the good working of a competent government system to avoid the overload and gridlock which brought our old regime down in the 1970s.[7] But do we not already have overload-reducing machinery in the regional devolution already completed, as well as that in prospect within England? Cannot it provide such an agenda for better government?

The Blair Scheme

Devolution could have been the most significant constitutional change of the Blair government; but it is imperfect because insufficiently thought-through. Moreover it contains the seeds of its own destruction, and should be revised as soon as possible. Its best current defence is its popularity in Scotland and Wales; but that may be because it is as yet at an early stage of development. So far it only affects the 15% of the population. More ominously, it has as yet only had to contend in Scotland and Wales with circumstances in which the same political party has been in control—or has been leading a coalition—in those regions as controlled by Westminster.

The issues devolution raises are complicated and specialised. Some of the strongest arguments, as Simon Jenkins reminded us, go back to de Tocqueville and are to do with good citizenship rather than administration: to provide active and interesting local politics to persuade people not to 'withdraw from public

---

[6] There are disadvantages in giving laws a special entrenched status and therefore made hard to change, if only because of the likelihood we will not get all right first time and need to make subsequent adjustments.

[7] On other, theoretical, arguments for devolution, see Foster and others (1980).

affairs into their private concerns'.[8] We can only outline the difficulties.[9] Different models have been adopted for Scotland, Wales and Northern Ireland (and London and the English regions). Set aside Northern Ireland as a special case: when an ordinary democratic government becomes electable, it will need a new constitutional framework. Meanwhile the principal problems seem these:

(1) Welsh devolution turns on a distinction between secondary legislation, which Wales can legislate for, and primary reserved to Westminster. But it is an artificial distinction: statutes vary greatly in their secondary-legislation making powers. Some have none. Others have little else. And the discretion they allow varies. So what the Welsh Assembly can do depends on how particular laws were drawn up which bears little relation to what interests it. The Assembly has tried to persuade the UK government to pass primary legislation to increase the scope of the secondary legislation it can make; and alter its nature; but Welsh priorities rank low in Whitehall and few such laws have been passed. Moreover the government has produced UK bills, some aiming to centralise power. It is a constant battle to ensure UK bills, primarily meant for England, give the Welsh Assembly scope for its own secondary legislation.[10] Furthermore nothing can stop a future government— particularly if a different political party from that governing Wales—from introducing bills drawn so tightly that Wales gets no delegated powers, or loses some it has.

No wonder the Welsh Assembly has repeatedly asked—and in 2004 the Richard Commission recommended—that Wales should have the same primary legislation powers as Scotland.[11] At present the government shows no signs of agreeing; but if it did, there would be further problems already found in Scotland.

(2) As we have seen (above chapter 10) there has been a large increase in constituency business among English and—to a lesser extent, because only secondary legislation is devolved—among Welsh MPs. Most issues that interest the Scottish electorate are devolved to its Parliament. While that could mean Scottish MPs having little constituency business—and therefore much less to do in total than other MPs—in practice the fear many Scottish MPs have of being cut off from their grass-roots, and of becoming as little known locally as MEPs, leads to many *ad hoc* arrangements for dividing

---

[8] S Jenkins (1995) chapter 14.

[9] For facts, though not conclusions, I am indebted to the Constitution Unit's annual volumes tracing the development of UK devolution: Hazell (2000); Trench (2001); Hazell (2003); Trench (2004); also Sandford (2004).

[10] A further unsettling quirk is an understanding between Whitehall and the Welsh Assembly that when Westminster legislation proposes Henry VIII powers—power to amend primary legislation through secondary legislation—they shall apply to Wales if of limited extent or effect. As long as a piece of string, indeterminate in its consequences, it reinforces the argument the system is inherently unstable.

[11] Richard (2004).

constituency business between them and the corresponding MSPs. They may even compete for it, especially when national and regional constituencies do not share boundaries, even more when MPs and MSPs come from different parties. No wonder that Welsh MPs are foremost in resisting devolving primary legislation for fear of being similarly cut off from their constituents' main interests. What would happen if English regions followed suit? Might that mean all MPs would find it harder to keep close to their constituents? What then would be the basis of their power and influence?[12]

(3) Another anomaly arises over Westminster voting. A few Scottish MPs follow Tam Dalyell and do not vote on 'English' bills, but that principle cannot always be followed since many England and Wales bills have some UK clauses which as such necessarily apply to Scotland. So Scottish MPs have a good reason for voting on them. The 2003 bill on Foundation Hospitals, whose essential clauses did not apply to Scotland, had a few UK clauses. It would not have passed without Scottish votes. A similar situation can always be engineered by which bills principally applying to England and Wales—even if the majority of their MPs are against—are passed by Scottish MPs to whose constituents its main clauses have no application.

(4) Finance is another source of future conflict. Scotland has limited tax-raising powers, so far unused. Wales and Northern Ireland have none. In practice the only freedom they have to resource different services, or levels of service, comes from the higher *per capita* grant they receive under the Barnett formula, initiated in completely different circumstances in the 1970s. However the difference between *per capita* grant levels has over time already been almost completely eroded in Wales and Northern Ireland, and soon should be in Scotland. It is hard to see how the Barnett formula can be re-negotiated to the satisfaction of all parties—English devolution may bring this issue out—or substantial tax-raising powers given Scotland, Wales and the English regions which enable them to finance services and policies markedly different from English ones. Until then, to spend more on something, they must spend less on something else, unless they can persuade the UK Treasury to finance it. Thus the UK government can exercise strong influence over how the regions spend their allocated money, as it does over English regional and local government. So far different parties have not been in control in London and the regions. When that happens, the regions' inability to raise money will make political differences between them and London harder to resolve. Furthermore it is an uneasy and unstable compromise which make this antiquated financial straitjacket stop Scottish policies and laws (and Welsh secondary legislation) diverging as much as from English ones as those regions would like. What has eased financial tension between Whitehall and the regions so far has been relatively strong economic performance and generous public expenditure provision.

[12] Worst if choice of candidates followed a party list system since that would give party leaders stronger control of their parties.

(5) A further problem for the future is that nothing bars Westminster over-riding present arrangements by passing primary laws which overturn Scottish legislation or neuter Welsh secondary legislation. Since devolution the UK Parliament has passed many UK laws applying to Scotland by so-called Sewell amendments by which the Scottish Parliament voluntarily agrees to be bound by UK law. One reason given is the shortage of policy-making time in Scotland, but Sewell amendments are facilitated by a Labour, or Labour-led, government there, being readier ideologically to accept Labour measures drafted in London.

(6) We have seen how the distinction between primary and secondary legislation is artificial and in practice highly variable.[13] Equally, so is what primary legislation is devolved.[14] Here, too, are the seeds of future conflict. Experience of devolved government elsewhere shows that clear-sightedness is needed over what is best done at each government (or administrative) level, or pushed outside government altogether. While some matters can be wholly reserved to one level—e.g. foreign policy and defence at the national level—and some safely devolved to the most local level, public opinion generally expect some matters—like education, health, industry, social benefits and many others—to be considered at more than one.

The distinction needed, say between national and regional levels, is between higher and lower policy decisions, or between setting a policy framework at national level and giving lower levels discretion within it, or sometimes between policy and administration. In health, education and other matters, the nation remains concerned, one imagines, that every region attains at least minimum standards, and probably in some other respects does not wander far from the national norm. In transport, energy and the environment, the fact that much transport, and some energy and pollution, crosses administrative boundaries—however drawn—means that some split between national, regional (and local) policymaking, but also co-ordination between them, seems inescapable. Experience in the USA, Germany and other federal nations shows the subtlety needed to ensure a workable federal system and that it requires institutions joined together by political and financial, as well as legal, mechanisms. In Germany the federal government can legislate wherever uniform rules are deemed needed, though the Länder have concurrent powers of legislation. The Länder, however, receive most of the tax revenue and have strong representation in the Upper House.[15] In the USA, the states are represented in the Senate and federal grants may be legislated which let Washington influence state policies, but also lets the

---

[13] The many forms of secondary legislation are discussed in Baldwin (1995).
[14] Interaction with the EU also creates its problems: agriculture is devolved in Scotland. But it is of major concern to the EU, which holds the UK government responsible for implementing its EU responsibilities.
[15] Schmidt (2003).

states refuse to comply if they refuse the grant. In short, workable devolution—especially when different political parties rule and when the same parties develop their own identities and interests—requires far greater and more subtle attention to detail, as was attempted here in 1978, but not in 1997. Moreover long-run workable devolution will surely require similar, symmetrical, treatment of regions.

(7) Furthermore—and it is what matters most in this book's context—Blair devolution was not designed to reduce central government overload and has not done so. If one lesson above all emerges from the post Second World War history of government in Britain, it is the extreme desirability of reducing Cabinet, or more recently prime ministerial, overload. History shows how often the consequences of not doing so have meant poor, rushed decisions and laws and, as in the 1970s, gridlock. The aim should be that the Executive at every level should take on no more work than it can do competently; take decisions which can stand up to parliamentary—or legal—scrutiny; formulate policies which have been thoroughly researched and consulted about; and draft bills or other legislation, which are complete, well explained and demonstrably workable. If that guiding principle means that a Prime Minister has no more time than broadly to do well what a US President does, so be it. Better than attempting too much if Prime Ministers confine their attention to foreign, European and defence policy, inescapable macro-economic issues and certain policies, like those towards asylum-seekers and other immigrants—a long list—which cannot be devolved since they must be uniform across the nation.

(8) Not only regional devolution matters. What that needs, if properly done, is only part of a programme—of which re-assessing ministerial responsibility is another part—needed to re-define responsibilities and accountabilities generally.[16] What, and in what terms, should be devolved to:

1. Local government?
2. Regional government?
3. Statutory bodies or networks of bodies interacting with each other in ways which are clearly and statutorily defined as internal markets might have been?
4. Administration by officials, made more autonomous by ministers relinquishing some decisions—previously made in close partnership with their own officials—to officials and agencies accountable to the courts or a similar institution, so that ministers are no longer responsible and accountable to parliament for them?

[16] Oliver (2003) 62–66. Wheare (1963) 10, the great authority on federalism, distinguishes between federal devolution, where the constitution defines each level's powers, and non-federal where it does not. On this analysis the EU is not federal. Because of the common law sovereignty of Parliament, Britain cannot be federal: Oliver (2003) 245. I believe a more useful distinction is between a system where the powers are defined in law, but not necessarily entrenched law—which Wheare would call quasi-federal—and one where there is no such certainty.

5. European government by relinquishing some policy areas to European authorities, though transferring powers to Europe has always increased, not reduced, ministerial burdens, because of increased negotiation?

6. No one, except possibly the market or other autonomous private decisionmakers, by withdrawing from some areas of government intervention altogether, so making government smaller (as happened with exchange controls in 1981 and interest rates in 1997)? And in doing so accepting that some problems which most taxed governments until the 1980s, would not have been soluble, even if ministers had been less loaded, in which case perhaps they should not have tried to solve them;[17]

7. Individual consciences, by re-adopting some such moral *laissez-faire* principle, like John Stuart Mill's that government interferes with people's freedom to do what they like only when that does demonstrable, objective, not merely subjective, harm to others, so reducing the scope of government through greater toleration of minority opinions and behaviour?[18]

Despite several different devolution schemes, the reality is that ours is a machine with two gears. Except for matters wholly reserved to the UK, Scotland can legislate as it pleases, and the UK government has no legal or political power over it. Scotland to most intents and purposes is already a separate nation. Blair may have believed he could still maintain substantial political control over devolved policymaking in part through his powers of persuasion and budgetary control, but, as in Northern Ireland, that seems unlikely to survive long in Scotland. Elsewhere—whether by manipulation of what constitutes secondary legislation, or in England through central government's financial and other powers (above, chapter 5), Westminster and Whitehall can rule when they want to; for example, Blair could have stopped London introducing road pricing.[19] In practice there will be endless wrangling over the scope of primary and secondary legislation for Wales. Moreover the question whether there should be English devolution as well raised further difficult, largely unthought-through, issues. What principles would determine what an English region could do, or would devolution be a cover-up disguising the fact that English regional authorities were as much agents of central government as local authorities have become? The present mess surely cannot last without putting our political institutions in great jeopardy.

---

[17] E.g. King (1975).

[18] 'On Liberty' in Mill [1859] (1910) 72–73.

[19] I spent some time helping persuade the PM and others not to stop Livingstone in his tracks. To make the case for pressing on with road pricing was a prime purpose of RAC Foundation (2001). It has been said to me that the secretary of state for Wales has more actual power than the elected Assembly First Minister.

EXTENDING JUDICIAL REVIEW

As long as civil service independence and a close partnership relationship broadly corresponded to reality, it was hard to find a tag on which to mount an application for judicial review of ministers' decisions, rare until recently.[20] Early examples of judicial review were successful because, like *Padfield v Minister of Agriculture*, ministers were found to have acted contrary to official advice.[21] In the 1960s the courts stopped being deferential to ministers when ministerial decisions were challenged, though the grounds for allowing a challenge remained narrow.[22] In the 1970s the judges became readier to challenge government decisions, when they believed them defective, made easier from 1977 by various technical process changes in judicial review.[23] But judicial review remained rare until it shot up in the 1980s. In an extraordinary development, applications for it rose from 149 in 1980 to 2753 in 1997.[24] As the courts became more experienced in judicial review, they have been readier to engage in it.[25] By the turn of the century an Administrative Court division of the High Court had to be created to handle the workload. However, though the number of applications against ministers rose similarly, they were only a small proportion of the total of which three-quarters were against the Home Office, followed by Health and Social Security.[26] Particularly the Home Secretary has been challenged by the judges, who are able to halt a ministerial decision to a greater extent and more effectively than in the House of Commons; but with less political and public effect than he would have been to subject to if the major complaints against him had been effectively debated in the House. However, most departments received no more than one or two a year.

As it happened—surprising some officials—what emerged from judicial review was that the principles judges expect to be obeyed are similar to those of *natural justice* or *fairness* and *consistency,* which it was traditional for civil servants to help ministers uphold (above, chapter 3); but more restrictive, less able to concentrate on the merits of the decisions, and less sensitive to political and policy issues. British judges, unlike American ones, confine themselves to legal, largely procedural, criteria. They do not pronounce upon the merits of ministers' decisions as public policy as judges do in the United States. However,

---

[20] To an earlier version of this argument in Foster and Plowden (1996) Daintith and Page objected that rules did exist affecting relations between ministers and officials and that therefore we had underestimated their importance: Daintith and Page (1999) 387–88. All I can say is that in most circumstances they were in the bottom drawer, never referred to.

[21] I am indebted to Professor Loughlin of LSE for this point. Also Schwarz (1987).

[22] Riddell (1998) 55–74.

[23] Law Commission (1976).

[24] Treasury Solicitor (1994) 3. See Appendix (1)—to end October 1998 only. I am indebted to Sir Henry Brooke for this table.

[25] See Jowell and Oliver (1988).

[26] Flinders (2001) 54.

the greater frequency of judicial review in the 1980s shocked ministers—and officials—into a realisation of their need to be careful. The pamphlet, *Judge Over Your Shoulder,* helped them do this and checked the growth of judicial review, but only temporarily, as the increase in applications for it to about 5000 in 2003 showed.[27]

This far higher level of judicial review was variously attributed to the effects on the judges of the arrogance of a party in power for such a long period; the unconservative, radical nature of New Right conservative governments; the expansion of European law and the influence of continental traditions of legal interpretation; a greater readiness by public groups and other public bodies to challenge government; as well as to more arbitrary ministerial behaviour even to the extent of ignoring legal constraints; the decline of parliamentary debate and committee scrutiny of Bills; and the failure of departments to discuss legal issues or take advice from the Treasury Solicitor, their own or other lawyers as much as was desirable. Whatever the weight given other factors, what was most responsible for this increase was the decay of the disciplines with which ministers and civil servants in partnership had been able to surround departmental decision-making.

To get fairness, consistency and other aspects of the rule of law back into government decision-making, one must either again implement the Carltona doctrine (above, chapter 3) or move to what was there called Woodrow Wilsonianism: a system in which the courts play the primary role. Where stands that legal principle now when so many decisions are taken without that advice? When many policies under which officials operate do not have a clear and coherent cabinet or ministerial policy to guide them? When officials seem under pressure not to challenge ministers and their advisers? At the end of the Second World War, the new German constitution—so as to strengthen civil servants' ability to stand up to their masters—symbolised it by laying down that their loyalty was to the Constitution. That was a deliberate echo of the British position where civil servants are servants of the Crown, instead of that fact being played down as it was by Robert Armstrong (above, chapter 15). When the safeguards against ministers taking decisions on their own are disappearing, and incidentally therefore against the entry of corruption, can one be sure that eventually there will not be corruption? Furthermore what do those shortcomings, if unrelieved, imply for the proper scope of judicial review?[28] A Civil Service Act is

[27] Treasury Solicitor's Department (1995).

[28] Among the cases suggesting something improper was the allegation that Keith Vaz, when minister responsible for immigration, personally overturned official recommendations for 50 visa applications, *Observer,* 18 March 2001. Also House of Commons (2001). Was he consistent and fair in these overturnings? Did he recognise the important distinction made in chapter 3 between a minister not being able to alter such decision, even though he disagrees with it and going through the necessary processes to change a policy, which may involve going to Cabinet and then, having changed the policy, having to follow it until another equally processed policy change? Similarly, if the allegations reported were true, how could Beverly Hughes, when she was immigration minister, justify as fair and consistent the different treatment of asylum-seekers apparently depending on where they were in Britain and the length of the backlog that justified this? *Times,* 31 March 2004.

needed which makes clearer where civil service loyalties lie and what principles and standards they are expected to observe.[29]

FROM A POLITICAL TO A LEGAL CONSTITUTION

In her admirable exposition of what a more written, or more accurately legal, constitution would entail, *Constitutional Reform in the United Kingdom,* Dawn Oliver shows how much more of our political system could be *juridified* in the sense that increasingly more of what those engaged in the Executive did— ministers and officials, all public bodies—would be subject to law, their discretion reduced, and therefore subject more to judicial review by the courts, not only over the procedures they used in decision and lawmaking, but over the merits of those decisions, so requiring ministers always to explain and justify their actions as a protection against review.[30] That broadly is the position in the United States since 1946 and in many other countries.[31] To help such review— whatever its precise form—judges would be aided by being able to appraise what they were reviewing by reference to various legal norms or rights. The European Convention on Human Rights is already an important set of norms to which all public decisions and laws must measure up. But these particular rights have little relevance to many areas of government. So similar conventions might be established to cover other aspects, for instance by establishing equivalent economic and social rights. It is no part of my brief to attempt a detailed critique of attempts by lawyers—and to some extent by the Blair government, though largely fortuitously—to advance the legal constitution. Still it could readily be built up into a powerful protection against ministers being arbitrary, unfair, not giving reasons for what they do, acting in their own electoral interest rather in the public interest as well as disregarding whatever are held to be basic rights.[32] Some more of it is bound to happen given the power of European law, adherence to the ECHR and some ministers' increasing disregard of the law.

However, while there are arguments for preferring such legal protection to the current situation, it has many disadvantages compared with what used to be:

• Civil servants and the cabinet system can, or at least could, influence ministers before they made up their minds, while judges can only intervene afterwards;

---

[29] In the author's opinion one that goes further than the Commons' Public Administration Committee suggested in January, 2004.

[30] Hutton was widely criticised for not being even-handed between the BBC and the government in apportioning blame for the death of Dr Kelly; but while much of what the BBC did could be judged unlawful as infringing its charter and regulations, so much of what the government did could not, because of the informality of its procedures and the absence of relevant regulations.

[31] Breyer (1982).

[32] Irvine was reported as favouring a 'rights' view of the relation between law and politics. Blair was said to be less liberal and more authoritarian: Seldon (2004) 210. Also Pollard (2005) 284 9.

- Judges rarely have much professional understanding outside the law and generally shy away from foreign policy, defence and even from economic and commercial policy, which make up so much of government activity. Very few of our judges have first degrees providing relevant experience outside law, while roughly half the judges in the USA have first degrees in economics or business studies. The more judges pass judgment on the merits of ministers' decisions, the more problems they will meet in ensuring they have the knowledge to make their opinions worthwhile;[33]
- Such judicial review comes long after the event, is normally long drawn out, costly and demanding of time, most accessible to those who have money or a formidable burden for legal aid. Only a small proportion of decisions will be reviewed, while Cabinet system and civil service procedures provided a discipline for all decision-making;
- Such extension of review will promote a compensation culture. Courts ordinarily disregard the consequences for public expenditure when deciding what is lawful;
- As John Griffith observes, do we really want a system of government where so much ultimate power belongs to the upper and middle class kinds of professional people which by background and education judges are almost bound to be?
- Depending on how much ministerial decisionmaking is juridified, and in practice passed, or heavily constrained, by judges, those few lawyers like Professor Griffith and Jeremy Waldron—actively dissenting from a more legal constitution—are surely right that it might mean a catastrophic diminishing of the scope for political decision-making to the point where it would hard to call us still a democracy;[34]
- All legal decisions have to be openly reached on the basis of the relevant law and evidence. Similarly most political decisions and policies were capable of reasoned explanation to Parliament. But just occasionally disagreements are so profound that there had to be fudge to save the day. A classic case, already mentioned, was Lloyd George's 1922 achievement in hoodwinking all parties concerned into signing an agreement over Ireland which kept peace for fifty years.[35] Politics can achieve such occasionally necessary stratagems, but not the law.

One could erode ministers' roles still further. Dawn Oliver's legal constitution has much to say about laws, and how they may be restricted in their interpretation by fundamental laws, laws about rights and by judges' interpretation of them. The minister's lawmaking role then might become that they have the

---

[33] The classic case of judges making asses of themselves through not understanding the issues was over Ken Livingstone's policy of subsidising London buses in the early 1980s.

[34] Griffith (1991); Waldron (2001). Stevens (2002) has many examples of the problems that arise for judiciaries when judges find themselves taking what are seen to be political decisions and in so doing appearing politicised.

[35] McLean (2001).

ideas which germinate into law. As the recipients of grievances, concerns and policy ideas from a mass of sources, their job is then somehow to outline new policies and introduce new bills, which may well continue confused and other-wise bad.[36] Thereafter judges knock them into shape, making them compliant with previous law and pre-determined norms or 'rights'. It is not impossible that such a division of labour may seem all too attractive to a government locked in daily battle with media to maintain its poll ratings, searching for the right sound-bites and press releases, and with little time for more. But what if the policy idea is bad one, which reasonable scrutiny would have shown? What if the too hasty decision is one about peace or war? What if the public services still do not improve?

Some of what permeates the thinking of lawyers—quite the most energetic we have—about our constitutional future sees that as that of a participatory democracy, in which Parliament slides into the shadows, and where public opinion is consulted in surveys and focus groups before being reflected in new laws, which are then tested by the courts to ensure they are consistent with other law and do not infringe rights. If they are inconsistent or infringe primary rights, then the courts adjust them accordingly. Such an approach all too easily casts into the background several important matters.

How do we ensure that the processes of discovering public opinion are not themselves manipulated in their own interest by the politicians presiding over them? Already using polls and focus groups raises difficult questions about the weight to be given to different opinions; to popular, but possibly less informed, opinions contrasted with that given producer and other worker interests, and others directly involved; on how polls and focus groups are set up; what questions are asked; and what safeguards adopted to ensure defensible procedures are used and questions asked.[37]

How do we compensate for the fact that few, if any, members of the public have the time or the interest to understand fully the facts and opinions relevant to an issue before they make up their mind? Besides, there are just too many issues for the public not to require a filter or filters to act on their behalf: ministers, Parliament, officials, outside experts and the media. Unbridled participatory democracy reinforces policy 'initiativitis', bad laws and regrettable decisions.

Such tolerance pays virtually no attention to how one best ensures that politicians go through decision-making and policymaking processes in ways which are constructive, evidence-based and likely to be implementable, perhaps because all necessary tidying up is seen as a job for the courts.

Since the legislative role of Parliament under such a legal constitution is not much more than that of sending ill-considered laws on their way, unsurprisingly

[36] Oliver (2003) 360–63.
[37] Direct democracy can be criticised because it can mean manipulation by the lobbyists who make the most noise; also because of the effect of referenda in bringing California to bankruptcy: see Sutherland (2004) 27–28.

some extreme legal thinkers question the need for such an irrational body as a legislature.[38] Let the judges straightway take the policy ideas, and using previous law and a battery of norms, or rights, shape the legislation into the form needed. More juridification of the relations between different parts of the government and public sector is needed, but the further one goes in this direction, the less scope there is for representative democracy in making political decisions. As our constitutional arrangements have become more complicated, and ministers less careful in observing the law, more encroachment by the courts on politics has become inevitable, but to throw up one's hands and find a legal alternative to political decision and policymaking where possible, seems neither feasible nor wise.

CONCLUSION

One possibility would be to move further from our political to a legal constitution. As this chapter argues there are areas where this already seems right and proper, and areas where, while inferior, unavoidable unless the impartial, objective and independent status of the civil service can be restored. But how far should we go? As the ability of civil servants—or of ministers within the cabinet system, off their own bat or briefed by officials—to challenge or otherwise criticise the prime or other ministers, has declined, so lawyers have increasingly argued that such tasks should be taken over by them.[39] Lawyers principally have three sorts of task in mind:

- One—already under their aegis through judicial review and by other interpretation in the courts—focuses on some ministers' tendency to break or disregard the law;
- The second is the realisation—mainly by comparison with the United States—that the courts cannot challenge much of what the PM and other ministers do—less than in almost every other advanced democracy—because based on convention, not law, and on devices like the royal prerogative;
- The third is the growing and correct impression that too many ministerial decisions are now slapdash—taken by the PM, or another minister with little scrutiny of the evidence or weighing of pros and cons; or, after Iraq, taken by nothing more rational than by the votes of inadequately briefed Cabinet ministers. The culminating example was the decision to set up the Supreme Court, and abolish the Lord Chancellorship in 2003, as part of a cabinet re-shuffle. Voting has a bad name in jurisprudence. Rather lawyers expect, as they should, that decision-making, policymaking and the preparation of legislation tend 'to be associated with reason and rational thinking, with the ability of an enlightened mind to cut through the accumulated layers of'

---

[38] The view of the Oxford jurist Joseph Raz: Waldron (2001) 34–35.
[39] Waldron (2001) 184–85.

evidence, argument and local usage.[40] But to hand more than is absolutely essential to the courts is to lose faith in the possibility of democracy. It is the decline in the Cabinet system and in the influence of the civil service which has brought ministers to this pass. It is there—and in Parliament—that remedies should be sought before abandoning hope for democracy.

[40] Waldron (2001) 47; also 26, 91.

20

Restoration

A state without some means of change is without the means of its conservation. Without such means it might even risk the loss of that part of the constitution which it wished the most . . . to preserve.

Edmund Burke[1]

AMONG THE ADVANTAGES of reviving what we have, rather than developing a more presidential, or a more strictly legal, constitution is that we do not have to start from the beginning. We can work on our institutions to make them fit again for democratic purposes. But we cannot simply go back. Too much has changed. The modern world is a different place. People expect more from government. Innovations like information technology and much improved accounting systems can transform the mechanics of government, if properly introduced, as they rarely have been. We can only revive our own system and make it fit for purpose by being determinedly radical and thorough about it. However, in a work which repeatedly makes a virtue of thoroughness, the reader will appreciate that this one chapter can only outline what is needed.

ACHIEVING BETTER GOVERNMENT

We now have a situation in which the supreme executive—currently the Prime Minister—may have improved its efficiency in news management, but in most other respects its ability to progress work with reasonable thoroughness, practicality and success is less, for three main reasons:

- The decline in Cabinet which means too much responsibility falls on the shoulders of the PM;
- The PM's disregard of Parliament which allows government decisions, policies and bills presented there, not to be objective or intelligible, and therefore often incapable of being properly scrutinised; and
- The decay in close working relationships with officials which once let ministers achieve so much more than they now can, or are allowed to, do.

---

[1] Burke [1790] (1845) vi, 40.

A first change required is to reduce the flood of new policies for which we have already given other good reasons. As an approximation it should be possible to halve the number of new bills—judging by how short an effective life many statutes now have—and reduce public expenditure by greater thoroughness in policy and bill preparation and by curbing pointless policy initiatives. The diet of new initiatives, which Alastair Campbell and his successors demanded to feed the media with enough stories, is not compatible with good government.[2] The last chapter also argued that, whatever the form of government, workable accountability requires a systematic mapping of responsibilities and accountabilities throughout government and the public sector, as well as enough devolution of both so that neither executive nor Parliament have more than they can do reasonably thoroughly.

But more change will be needed than that to restore Cabinet, Parliament and the efficiency and constitutional role of the civil service. Or else the case for a more extreme legal constitution will be strengthened.

THE CABINET

Among the reasons for preferring Cabinet to prime-ministerial or presidential government are:

- A Cabinet, if not too large, can transact much more business than one person, provided ministers have enough Cabinet solidarity to forge between them collective responsibility for government policy and performance, and for their relations with Parliament and the media;
- A well-functioning Cabinet should limit prime-ministerial overload, enabling the PM to stand back and oversee what is going on, resolving difficulties and differences with the detachment that comes from not being involved in settling every policy and deciding every issue, while reserving his or her energies and leadership for a few issues agreed to be of the greatest importance;
- It should check any tendency the PM may have to arbitrary decisions or absolute power. The media-obsessed processes of politics in every country may—more than in the past—select as political leaders people who are actors, demanding of popular adulation, self-absorbed and, at least sometimes, without practical wisdom or remotely relevant previous experience: therefore dangerous, if unchecked by Cabinet colleagues;
- Until recently a brilliant device, Cabinet showed enormous potential for evolutionary development, and for adapting to different personalities, as well as to changes in circumstances, like peace and war. Devolution ought to be the means by which its business can be reduced so that it can become thorough again;

[2] *Sunday Times*, 26 September 2004, reported departmental directors of communications in conference complaining that No 10 was still endlessly demanding new stories about policies to feed the media; and that therefore policies were announced long before they had been worked on long enough to be ready.

• The different motivations needed to secure balanced decisions—and probity—should come from the fact that ministers—unlike special advisers and
  other courtiers—are not all cronies, or in any narrow sense hand-picked by
  the Prime Minister.[3] Better if they reflect different strands of opinion within
  the party, and if they have different expertise and experience, and therefore
  different ways of approaching problems;
• Cabinet Government gives other ministers the chance to show their quality
  and some to emerge as possible successors to the PM. Prime-ministerial
  government does not allow Cabinet ministers the same opportunities.

Therefore Cabinet, not the Prime Minister, should again have supreme power
so as to reduce the dangers of both overload and absolute power which arise
when executive power continues to be concentrated in one person and his or her
unelected political advisers. Political advisers, appointed by him and able to be
dismissed by him, cannot be expected to be robust in speaking truth to power as
Cabinet colleagues can, provided most have independent political standing.

A return to Cabinet Government must not mean that all important decisions
come to full Cabinet or an inner Cabinet. History has shown both to be impracticable. Rather a variable number of Cabinet ministers—but always more than
one—should understand and collectively approve each significant decision.
Therefore there is a place for Cabinet committees of some formality and
permanence, and for legitimating significant government decisions in Cabinet
minutes.[4] But Prime Ministers should not be able to handpick those they consult
so as to get the decision they want.[5]

It is not enough to go back to the Cabinet system of the past which ultimately
proved a failure. Reducing overload by devolution will make it more workable.
However, more change is needed to meet the strains and stresses of modern government. If one cannot find a means of detaching ministers—including the
Prime Minister—from too much daily absorption in the media preventing them
progressing the real business of government, we cannot have a genuine representative democracy which works. Neither can we unless public documents
are well argued, intelligible and properly evidence-based.

(1) Strengthening the Cabinet System

If Cabinet and the Cabinet system, rather than the PM and his aides, or judges,
are to be the engines ensuring good government, the apparatus needs strength-

---

[3] Since the 18th century few have been dominated by Yes-men.
[4] Including the convention that Cabinet committee minutes stand as if they were Cabinet minutes unless further discussed in Cabinet. If the PM, the Chancellor or any other minister hold bi-laterals or other informal meetings, their decisions should be recorded with similar formality.
[5] Ensuring that committees consider most measures—whether formal or *ad hoc*—are composed
of ministers with the greatest departmental interest in a matter, should help.

ening. One might take a leaf from the German constitution, which since the Second World War—as a protection against recurrence of Hitler's arbitrary, rushed and over-personalised decision, policy and lawmaking[6]—requires the German Cabinet to have a Cabinet paper before it whenever it takes a decision, except in the most urgent circumstances. It must have been discussed previously with the relevant departments and secured their approval that the issues are well set out and explained, and their viewpoints reflected. The Cabinet secretariat, acting neutrally for Cabinet, needs to have the capacity do this rapidly and well. So it should be possible for Cabinet to re-achieve the collective responsibility for policy, executive activity and presentation to Parliament it once had.

To which may be added overall responsibility for presenting and co-ordinating government's relations with the media. The greatest challenge is whether Cabinet Government can handle the media as effectively as Blair did in his early years, but more honestly and objectively.[7] Modern government requires first-class news management which, as the Blair administration found, needs central direction and co-ordination. But while the Prime Minister should be the spokesman on many matters, there are more where other Cabinet ministers should lead on their own departmental business. If so, the central news management team—perhaps under a senior Minister for Information—were better responsible to the whole Cabinet, not just the PM. Therefore it should be in Cabinet Office, which, in this as in other respects, should no longer be a Prime Minister's department in disguise, but should again act for all the Cabinet.[8]

Media statements and press statements are important—and can be available 24 hours a day, though to attempt instant reactions to issues which have not been thought through courts disaster, as recent experience shows. However, other audiences matter, including Parliament and those who will implement new policies and legislation. To help achieve clarity, comprehensiveness and objectivity, civil servants should be responsible in the first instance to departmental ministers for drafting all authoritative policy and other official statements whether published or not. But important new policies should be tested through the Cabinet system. Therefore the Cabinet Office needs strengthening so that Cabinet can do more business thoroughly, by establishing a part of the secretariat whose job in dialogue with departments is to check the adequacy and intelligibility of the substance and explanation of every proposed white, green or other consultation paper, bill or other major policy change from the first stage of proving it desirable to its final approval and presentation to Parliament.

---

[6] Kershaw (2001), where relevant in his narrative, records these deficiencies in unsparing detail. M Beloff, *Times,* 9 December 1999, went to the extreme of making a basis for comparing Hitler and Blair's methods of governing.

[7] John Lloyd (2004) argues that the British media must improve if they are not to continue to undermine our politics. He has excellent ideas on what might be done.

[8] The experience of having ministers of information has not been without problem as Sir Edward Osmotherly has pointed out to me. But the idea that a senior minister presides over a mix of official and political press officers at the Centre and can oversee and co-ordinate PR elsewhere in government seems right in principle.

Preparing these so that they are objective and intelligible are among the skills they have been trained to have. It should always be clear which is the authoritative statement on a matter whether a White Paper or other public document, or a ministerial statement in Parliament. Presided over by a senior minister[9] and a strengthened Legislation Committee, its model might be the French *conseil d'état* and *conseil constitutionnel*.[10]

(2) Binding Ministers Together

Solidarity is an important characteristic of a well-functioning Cabinet. While Cabinet ministers must recognise that practicality does not permit all to be involved in every Cabinet decision, all need enough involvement and trust in the system not to think they are being misled. They need special advisers ready to advise them on the political aspects, and officials capable of advising them on other aspects, of Cabinet papers which interest them either because they affect their own departmental business or because personally interested in the topic.[11] Another requirement for solidarity is that Cabinet must not leak. Leaking has weakened and in some cases brought down many modern Cabinets. A Cabinet that has insufficient understanding of its collective interest not to leak will sooner or later be destroyed. Is it too much to suggest for its own preservation that a Cabinet—even when a shadow Cabinet—should develop a solidarity, camaraderie and culture which bans mischievous leaking? Almost all PLC boards—though the issues before them are generally not as publicly interesting—develop such a culture. Until some advisers at the Centre let each other down at the Hutton Inquiry, the closeness of those around Blair was such that they seldom leaked, except intentionally.[12] If a court can develop such solidarity, cannot a Cabinet?

---

[9] A variant of Churchill's overlord experiment with more chance of success since these ministers would form a matrix of departmental ministers with power and resources: the Chancellor of the Exchequer to oversee all financial and economic implications; a minister of information to ensure media contacts work well and are co-ordinated; a senior political lawyer—the Lord Chancellor, if still around—to ensure only bills likely to make good law reach Parliament; perhaps a minister of regulation to ensure new secondary and tertiary law is necessary and passes a cost-benefit test.

[10] Oliver (2003) 202.

[11] Departments cannot provide experts on non-departmental matters, so both special advisers and officials must again be able to interrogate their counterparts in other departments.

[12] Bad habits are catching. Blair's principal economic adviser Derek Scott was, by past standards, shockingly disloyal in what he revealed about Blair and Brown to the disparagement of both: D Scott (2004). But so was Sir Stephen Wall, who had been Blair's principal adviser on Europe until he believed the PM had perhaps irretrievably mishandled entry into Europe, when he left and went into print against his once political masters on policy as no senior civil servant had previously done, *Daily Telegraph*, 25 September 2004.

PARLIAMENT

A strength of the British constitution has always been that the Executive is drawn from, but still sits in, Parliament, so that ministers may be held accountable, face-to-face, by people who have an opportunity to know them well and who have different motivations because they are drawn from different parties, come from different backgrounds and have—or at least had—continuing different outside experience. It enabled much government business to be transacted with reasonable accountability.

(1) Re-Establishing Parliamentary Accountability

But the complexity of modern government has long limited the scope of parliamentary accountability. Reasons have been given why recently the Commons has dwindled in effectiveness, even within that limited scope. The media's holding to account—though of great importance—is sporadic and fitful. Something more is needed. The system will not work unless ministers are frequently in the House so they may be known and also listen to what is said there. That may not be achieved until Parliament, rather than the media, again becomes the first forum for policy announcements and for discussions of performance. At a more mundane level, it probably requires going back to evening sittings so that broadly speaking ministers may again spend the day on Cabinet and departmental business, the evenings in Parliament. Unless they spend adequate time in both Parliament and their departments, they cannot do their job properly. Far harder to imagine how to do it, but Parliament would be more effective if most MPs again had as wide a variety of non-political careers first and as MPs were again involved in non-political activities to broaden their knowledge and understanding.[13]

Furthermore the alternative idea, which has grown since Thatcher, that the real accountability of the Executive is to the PM has many drawbacks: the pressures of overload; the PM's inevitably strong political and defensive motivations; and the fact that almost all public activities are national or local monopolies. It is another instance where the analogy between business and government breaks down.[14] A chief executive sensibly demands strong internal accountability reporting to him. If he does not, he will be weakened, and possibly destroyed, through the pressures of competition. Not so public activities. The only practical alternative to Parliament—or devolution of accountability to elected regional Parliaments or local authorities—which in any meaningful

---

[13] A logically related, but utterly impracticable, idea is that MPs should be chosen by lot in the traditions of Greek democracy, so freeing them from party influence: Sutherland (2004) 124 35.

[14] Another view is to make use of a wide range of accountabilities, including to officials' professional bodies: Day and Klein (1987) but this does not solve the problem of parliamentary accountability.

sense can be called accountability to the People, though of an utterly different kind, is to increase accountability to the Law through a legal constitution. If we cannot improve Parliament's ability to hold the Executive to account, that alternative, legal accountability, almost certainly will, or perhaps should, take over to an increasing extent as it has in the United States.

(2) Better Parliamentary Machinery

Accountability, which makes for effective government, is not just about getting stories into the media, inevitably more interested in personalities than substance. Parliament greatly needs to improve its machinery for holding the executive accountable, principally by strengthening its support staff—not of policy wonks and social workers—but also of lawyers, accountants and other experts, bound together and interpreted by generalists, able to penetrate masses of information and interrogate as remorselessly as happens in congress. The Executive will not like it, but what is needed for effective accountability in modern times is to expand and extend the availability of NAO or similar resources from the PAC to all departmental and other select committees, not to generate new policy ideas of which we have too many.[15] Rather it is to make sure ministers—and all others assigned public responsibilities for which they are accountable to Parliament—can understand, explain and defend what they, and others for whom they are responsible, are up to, both new proposals and past actions.[16] Moreover all significant executive activities need to produce enough routine, standard form paperwork for this to be possible. Neither, as argued in the last chapter, is it sensible for public bodies to be accountable for the same activity to different elected bodies with varying requirements and standards. If an activity is responsible to an elected regional or local authority it should not normally be accountable to Parliament.

THE CIVIL SERVICE

The third efficient secret, whose importance this book has stressed, was the close partnership which developed between ministers and officials in departments and in the Cabinet system. It was the principal reason why ministers became able, with reasonable efficiency and probity, to do so much more than their counterparts in other countries. Least appreciated by the public is the decline in the position of the civil service. We have argued that decline has led

[15] Michael Heseltine's invention of the Audit Commission, on which I sat in its first years, was excellent, but it is misguided for it to be used as an instrument of the Executive. Better it had been an instrument of parliamentary accountability like the NAO. Should they be merged? Someone whose basic discipline is economic, will always prefer competition, even among auditing bodies.

[16] I have further set out my own ideas on how this might be done in Foster (2000a).

to a precipitate decline in ministers' efficiency, certainly in their ability to get lasting things done with thoroughness and practicality. The extent of that decline has been largely masked by a misguided misunderstanding of the so-called 'delivery problem' which shuffles the blame onto anyone else but ministers, to whom in substantial part, it has also been argued, it should belong. The Blair government is stopping most officials from being policymakers, except for the few who *de facto* become special advisers. Rarely are they any longer able to exercise their traditional constitutional functions of challenging political policies, questioning their need and sense, suggesting alternatives, ensuring that ministerial statements to Parliament and public documents are objective, do not tell untruths, and are intelligible and reasonably comprehensive.

(1) Speaking Truth to Power: Probity

But the traffic was not one way. Close partnership meant political judgements were more readily reflected in administrative action. Moreover, the civil service, because always there, was the best safeguard of probity for the mass of everyday business, much more so than the judiciary can ever be, since judges can only investigate *ex post* when a matter is referred to them. As a legal principle—the Carltona doctrine—ministers and officials were presumed such an organic whole that officials' decisions reflected ministers' policies and ministerial decisions could be assumed to have been taken with official advice.

(2) Restoring Impartiality and Objectivity

What is the remedy? The cornerstone of *The Federalist*'s argument on this point—Gladstone's generation produced no comparable analysis, but similar thinking was implicit in the Northcote-Trevelyan reform of the civil service—was that no part of the constitution should be unduly able to affect appointments, promotion, dismissal or otherwise control the behaviour of any other. Recent developments which have given ministers undue influence over civil service appointments, bonuses, promotions and early retirements, are as much an undermining of civil service independence and impartiality as they would be of the judges', on whom in Britain the probity of ministers as yet depends rather less.[17] Here ministers have been deceived by another mistaken analogy with the private sector, only relevant if the sole civil service objective were efficiency. Incentive schemes and other measures are needed to promote official efficiency, but the separation of powers—rightly understood—means that, whoever controls them, ministers must not, if the reality or suspicion of improper influence

---

[17] Among possible solutions may be both restricting the role of political appointees and requiring the Leader of the Opposition's approval for all civil service posts above a certain level.

is to be avoided.[18] Whether it makes sense to turn civil service appointments into short-term ones raises many considerations, but whatever the outcome, it must not be an excuse for more ministerial, that is politicised, appointments.[19]

(3) The Power of Appointment

More generally, safeguards over appointments are needed to ensure that no one element in the constitution is subordinate to another, but that as far as possible they work well together rather than being rigidly separated into different institutions. That also holds for the judges. Both in Parliament and the Cabinet, as Lord Hoffmann has said, good development of the law depends on effective partnership between Legislature and the Judiciary, and, one might add, the Executive.[20] In Cabinet the presence of eminent lawyers among other ministers has helped ensure laws were better-devised through on-going discussion. Similarly, in the past many lawyers of high quality in the Commons as well as the most senior judges in the Lords, as well as all the other experience and expertise represented there, made for more informed discussion and better laws. In Cabinet further checks and balances were secured by ministers having the opportunity to challenge and over-ride the Prime Minister as well as their having the spread of backgrounds and the staff which helped them question each other effectively.

The Federalist—and no doubt Gladstone's generation—was well aware of the necessity of separating as far as possible how people were appointed to the separate parts of the constitution. In order to create effective checks on the Executive, it must not choose the Legislature and the Judiciary. Hence different systems of election for president and the two parts of Congress, while the independence of the US judiciary was preserved by giving members of the supreme court such security of tenure that no one president could plausibly change its political complexion. In Britain the methods of securing checks on the power of the Executive were more complicated, but as real. Formally a Prime Minister chose his ministerial colleagues, but in practice was limited in the choices he could make by the need to reflect different shades of opinion within the party. Though in modern times the PM was an MP, elected like other MPs, he had little influence over those chosen to be his supporters in either House. Neither did he and his ministerial colleagues have any power to select, promote, appoint to particular posts, or sack, the civil servants with whom they must work. But these checks seem in danger of being eroded by several developments:

• The much more considerable subordination—especially in the Labour Party—of the party machine to the party leader and the far greater influence he or she has in selecting and deselecting parliamentary candidates;

---

[18] It may be right also to separate the personnel management systems within which senior officials close to ministers work, from those in agencies and other executive activities.

[19] Times, 7 January 2004.

[20] Hoffmann (2001) 141.

- The greater influence the Prime Minister has in the choice of peers which could be still greater if either a system of election or political appointment were adopted;
- The apparently almost complete ability a Prime Minister has developed to appoint or sack ministers without bothering about opposition within the party;
- The distancing that has taken place between ministers and their senior officials, in part by the intervention between them of unelected advisers; but
- Most important, the tensions created because of the influence ministers now have on what top officials are paid, the jobs to which they are appointed and their early retirement. Politicians' ability to subordinate them is being increased by their effectively being put on short-term contracts.[21]

What might restore these checks and balances? Some possibilities are:

- To introduce a popular element into the choice of parliamentary candidates, perhaps analogous to US primaries;
- To secure that ministers have little or no influence in selecting peers, whether elected or appointed;[22]
- To ensure once again that ministers cannot advise on who should be appointed to senior civil service positions—only on the qualities required—and have no influence on their individual remuneration.[23]

But the issues, which these and alternatives measures raise, need far more discussion than there is here space for, especially if they, or equivalent measures, are to be shown to be practical.

CONCLUSION

Many recommendations have been made in this and previous chapters. Their effective implementation will depend on a Prime Minister and Cabinet, or their shadows, seeking to gain, or retain, office, who will adopt these governance policies:

[21] *Times,* 10 January 2004.

[22] If peers are selected by an appointments commission, who selects its members? If elected, who selects the candidates, whether chosen by a party-list or any other system? Thatcher, as we have seen in chapter 12, was persuaded by Niskanen to believe officials were aggrandising their numbers and promotion prospects. But now the hypothesis should be re-formulated in terms of the political class whose number in the Lords, regional assemblies, the European Parliament, and as media handlers and special advisers, is increasing all the time.

[23] A corollary might be the separation of the executive civil service in agencies and other bodies from the civil service in departments advising ministers. Business-like methods of choosing, promoting and remunerating the first are more appropriate, though the analogy cannot be complete because of multiple objectives in the public sector. Senior civil servants may well be subject to bonus. There may well be a place for more outside appointments and late entrants. But the crucial point is that in these respects they should not be under political control if this cause of excessive executive power is to be avoided.

- To work constructively with Parliament so as to strengthen its ability to hold the Executive to account and to that end to ensure that everyone may know in law who is responsible for what—and subject to what override—in every part of government and the public sector, as well as to whom each is accountable, whether Parliament, local government or some other elected authority;
- While accepting that Cabinet can no longer collectively consider and decide all government policy business, to use it and Cabinet committees to re-establish genuine collegiate Cabinet Government, able to exercise again collective responsibility for policy and executive action. In particular to secure that the most important decisions, like those about peace and war, do not depend on the opinion of one person supported by unelected advisers, who are his appointees and so ultimately his creatures;
- The flow of Cabinet decisions, policy approval and legislation should be reduced to a level no greater than ministers working within the Cabinet system can process effectively;
- Except for rapid action in response to emergencies, important policy decisions should be preceded, first by a white paper—approved by Cabinet—to state the problem, the options to be considered and the consultation process to be adopted; and then by a second white paper, or explanatory memorandum, also approved by Cabinet, which reports on the outcome of the consultation, and presents the solutions to be adopted, in particular why they are judged practical, perhaps even setting out the milestones and targets selected for monitoring implementation; and finally, where relevant, a bill approved by Cabinet as complete enough to present to Parliament;
- Ministers and officials should again work together closely enough for ministers' decisions, and those made by officials on their behalf, to be consistent with government policy, as well-based on as much evidence as time allows for, while being fair, reasoned and defensible as in the public interest;
- There is a role for political advisers as aides to ministers to help with policy advice, political liaison and speech-writing, but they must not usurp the role of elected ministers or have executive authority.[24]

The often subtle, surreptitious consequence of those changes we have called a revolution has been a vast, but deceptive, accretion of power to the Prime Minister through erosion of traditional checks and balances to the point where the greatest protection of our liberties is not the law or the constitution but the inefficiency of our government processes. In reviving, while modernising, the potential for better government, and the checks and balances on the Executive, which Parliament, Cabinet and the civil service can provide, the best future for government lies.

---

[24] Not easily solved by a provision in a Civil Service Act. The problem is that a special adviser, who is close enough to a minister to be accepted as an *alter ego*, will be regarded as having that minister's authority.

Conclusion

Where Do We Go From Here?

People will not look forward to posterity, who never look backwards to their ancestors.

Edmund Burke (1790)[1]

ONSET OF REVOLUTION

IN SPITE OF widespread pretence until very recently that little has changed, we are at an intermediate point in the greatest changes in our constitution since 1688. They are certainly *revolutionary*. So far they have not been glorious. The most visible and discussed changes since 1997—such as devolution, Lords' reform and the extension of PR—are not the most important elements in what is going on, which has been on its way for twenty years. Though not unimportant, they could still be seen rather as a smokescreen for the vital changes, except that implies too deliberate a strategy.

Because poorly thought-through and precipitate one can summon up again all the wrath of Edmund Burke against the French Revolution—his foresight largely backed by its most recent historians—and of a modern conservative, Michael Oakeshott, over our recent preference for leaps into the dark rather than slow organic change; but for two factors. The first is that we do now have enough understanding of the ways in which governments work, and of political economy and politics, to have planned many of the consequences of constitutional change. Therefore we could have engaged in moderately rational social engineering of which the outcome should have been reasonably predictable, so as to have modernised without tears. Second, because of irreversible changes inside and outside government, institutional and economic, we have no choice now but to go on, somehow steering the canoe of state through the rapids to calmer waters, one hopes, beyond. New forms are now needed to meet the objectives of good government. If not, we could end up in a state with a government which not only pleases no one, but a Weimar, whose mixture of political turbulence and arbitrary, ill-thought-out political power could be a staging post to worse government. What form that worse government will take, we cannot say, but it could involve lost economic prosperity through corruption

---

[1] Burke [1790] (1845) 18, iii, 52; Oakeshott (1962).

and even lost democracy. While there is truth in it, we must also contest the exaggerated argument that politics is a less important activity than it used to be. But how we are governed matters, even if in a well-governed state most do not bother to pay much attention to it.

Nothing is easier to suppose than that we can go on much as we are. In modern British politics parties do not gain power by winning elections. Incumbent administrations lose them eventually through the accumulation of problems and from exhaustion. So politics becomes locked into a series of cycles. To win power to-day a party has to let, even encourage, one person to build up a dominant position in the eyes of the media. To help that person do so, she or he must form a coterie of media advisers, pollsters and others aides for whom the prize is power at the Centre of government. Each new administration enters office determined to avoid its predecessors' mistakes and centralise power more effectively, so as to continue to dominate the polls by presenting as co-ordinated and cohesive a front as possible to the media. For a time their followers in Cabinet, Parliament and the party are so pleased with electoral success that they allow them to behave as if they had presidential powers more extensive than those of the US president. But the first call on the Prime Minister's time is in daily contest with the media with its appetite for sound-bites and ceaseless new policy initiatives. For much of the public, for the media and the political classes, politics is part of Entertainment. So the quality of new policies, laws and public sector management initiatives remains poor. Mistakes are made, perhaps even as serious as over the Iraq war. Suddenly the political world wakes up to realise that the Prime Minister's power—dependent as it is on popularity rather the law—has drained away. The cycle is ready to start again.

The position of British Prime Minister is still sufficiently attractive, and prominent at home and on the European and even world stages, for a succession of outstanding people, some arguably political geniuses, to make the attempt, first to challenge successfully at Prime Minister's Questions, then in the media and the polls, and finally in a successful election campaign. Within the main parties successors wait and fret, hoping to persuade their party and then the electorate that he or she has the qualities to be a presidential Prime Minister. Few past Prime Ministers would have had the media qualities now needed, certainly not Attlee—often judged the most successful postwar PM—not Macmillan, Harold Wilson or Callaghan. One wonders if Churchill with his idiosyncrasies and mood-swings would have had the patience to deal with a relentless media. Perhaps Lloyd George would. Would Gordon Brown, given his personal absorption in the detail of policymaking, show the rapid resilience and lightness of touch a modern Prime Minister needs? There must be doubt whether a PM, who has the qualities to be, and wants to be, endlessly conspicuous, will have the judgement and other qualities needed of a leader.

Moreover, except in the most superficial terms of swings between presidential and Cabinet Government—from Thatcher to Major, from early to late Blair—the dominant pattern in recent British politics has not been cyclical.

Rather this book has argued that we have been going through an unfinished, turbulent, though peaceful, revolution in British government, reasonably called one because of the accumulated magnitude of the changes of the last 25 years or so. Power has drained from Parliament, Cabinet and civil service into the PM and those around him. That has had many consequences. The most worrying are paradoxical. The checks and balances on the power of the Executive—first forged in the battles between king and Parliament in the 17th century, but developed in the three centuries since—have worn very thin. The three most powerful—Parliament, Cabinet and an impartial and objective civil service— have lost effectiveness. Local authorities no longer have the freedom they had to adjust their policies to reflect the wishes of their electorates. The Centre wants other public bodies to be its agents. The courts have made some ground as a check on executive power at all levels of government, but far from enough to offset the decline in other checks and balances.

The paradox is that under our constitution the PM's use of this greatly centralised power depends on consent, principally upon his Cabinet ministers' and backbenchers' willingness to concede him the authority to wield that power. When that consent is withheld—as it eventually was under Thatcher and Blair, more quickly under Major—the British presidential system does not work. However, that is not the same as saying we then revert effectively to Cabinet Government and parliamentary democracy. We do not. Over the last twenty years how our government system has been hollowed out means that it can only respond if a presidential Prime Minister with a court exercises power. At present we do not have the machinery—which needs to be more powerful than in the past—to entrench presidential power or revive good Cabinet Government or parliamentary accountability.

But there is a further paradox. Prime-ministerial overload, and the intensity of his pre-occupation with the media, seemed to prevent Blair gripping many problems, as it had not with Thatcher; though both Thatcher and Blair suffered from another flaw inherent in presidential systems, the ability, even certainty of making bad mistakes, hers the poll-tax, his most serious, but not only one, being Iraq.[2] Yet the further paradox is that what also limits the Executive's unbridled power has been Britain's increasing ungovernability over the same 25 years. To assert this point is not to deny the Prime Minister largely controls our foreign policy, where he has too much power, even apparently that of deciding whether we should go to war. British government has also recently seemed able to pursue an effective macro-economic policy. The problems mostly arise in other domestic policy areas. Britain is not ungovernable in the sense that at times threatened in the 1970s when, occasionally and for short periods, the lights went off, garbage was not cleared from our streets and even corpses stayed unburied. Rather in a less inflammatory, but insidious way, while the government tries to control everything as if from one railway signal box, many levers pulled do not

---

[2] I would put the railways in almost the same category, though smaller in scale.

work. Nothing much happens. Or what does is seldom what was intended. Certainly the promised improvements in public services are slow to arrive. Does the inefficiency of our processes still protect our liberty, as Halévy, the historian, once said? Not really, because those who run our services on the ground are so beset by new laws, new initiatives, paperwork, demands from the media for instant answers to complaints and interventions from on high, that they are greatly constrained in their freedom to do what they think best. Similarly, private firms complain against the growing burden of excessive, ill-thought-through regulation. Cumulatively organisational changes of the last twenty have greatly reduced the real power of the Centre without freeing up public or private sector to develop their potential.

So can we go on as we are? I doubt it. Each administration will come in determined to learn from its predecessors' mistakes, which may mean attempting further centralisation of power. There is no saying where that will end. At the same time—and there is a connection—public interest in politics and government—measured by the proportion bothering to vote—will continue to fall. The public is turned off in the long run by politics as media entertainment. People differ in their ideas over what constitutes effective government and good public services, but that is what they want. Muddling on will not achieve it.

But some will say that the conclusions urged here—this emphasis on thoroughness, practicality and intelligibility—is wholly unrealistic. It does not get to grips with the nature of modern politics, which is inevitably about winning a host of daily battles in the media. Press and TV are filled ceaselessly with what the government wants. Otherwise they will turn to the Opposition, or more to non-political stories, to sell copies and raise ratings. It is through the media that governments are re-elected. Modern politics is about good news management, not good government which, if habitually in the forefront of ministers' minds, might bore the media. What actually happens—by way of foreign policy, new law or public service improvement—are means to an end. Indeed bad stories about lawmaking and the public services—because they gain more media attention—can help, more than hinder, ministers who regularly shift blame somewhere else and suggest yet another initiative to put matters right. To call for more considered government is to whistle in the media wind.

If true, the consequences will be immense and disastrous. But one would never say about a new aeroplane or a car that all that matters is its public presentation, not whether it is safe and works well. The spread of litigation reflects consumers' increasing insistence that they are protected against such risks. Advertising matters, but ultimately what the public wants is a safe and reliable product or service. In the NHS and other public services, if compensation is paid rather more often than the underlying causes are put right, the public prestige of politicians—and the percentage voting—will go on falling. The sad recent history of the railways shows what can happen when politics and news management are put before the measures needed for sound operational management. There have been many historical periods when the ruling classes—

now the media classes—have been far more absorbed in battling each other than in thinking about the effect of their wars on the people. Armies going about their own business have laid cities and the countryside waste or at best lived off the land without doing much good or harm. All one can suggest to those who believe the superficiality of news-managed government inevitable is that the ultimate cost will be great.

WHAT NEXT?

I have described the strengths and weaknesses of the old system, the reasons why it began to fail, and the characteristics of what has replaced it. In those contexts, I outlined—and frequently referred to—the features I believe a political system needs if it is worthy of being called a representative democracy and works. I agree many systems of government have, or could be developed to have, those features, though I note that even the American form of democracy is under strain. No modern government system is exemplary.

One possibility is further Americanisation of our constitution. Responding to the lure of more presidential government, to some extent we have already been doing this piecemeal. But there is much further we could go. Where do we stop? An American president in some respects has greater power than a British Prime Minister. In particular he does not have to—indeed cannot—appoint his Cabinet from congress, but chooses whom he wants. But it is power within a far narrower compass. Many matters, for which a British Prime Minister is responsible, are for the states or local government. Since the president does not control congress, he is less able to get laws passed. The courts much more constrain what his appointees to government departments and agencies can do. In sum, there are many more checks and balances on his power. I have argued, moreover, that creeping Americanisation is more likely to lead to greater centralisation of power than to checks on that power. It is up to those who believe in greater Americanisation to make their case and show that the outcome will be at least as consistent with representative democracy, and as able to produce effective decisions, policies and laws, as their US model is.

However, the most active and coherent thinking in Britain about the future of government is among judges, barristers and academic lawyers. It is greatly influenced by experience of interpreting European law and by judicial review in the courts; by knowledge of the American constitution, often based on postgraduate courses in the USA; by the growing frequency of meetings and conferences where judges from many nations compare their work; and, in a few instances, by being brought up in South Africa when civil liberties were imperilled. Its strength is that this thinking is based on wide, international experience of the ways in which government activities may be juridified and political decisions disciplined by courts. Among its difficulties is that the development of this thinking has been almost entirely by lawyers to persuade lawyers; that it tends to be sceptical of the value and redeemability of politics and politicians; and that it concentrates too exclusively on lawmaking and the courts as the instruments needed to contain and control the Executive. In that last sense their opinion is that legal accountability should replace parliamentary accountability and is already on the way to doing so through means as various as judicial review; the deployment of the European Convention on Human Rights; the growing need to observe treaty obligations to other international bodies; and the availability of the Judicial Committee of the Privy Council to settle disputes between national and devolved levels of government in Britain.

But the issue of how to reconcile these developments with democracy remains as problematic as a presidential future. Lawyers have much less to say about government policymaking and decision-making, and how they may be well done, which has been much of the focus of this book. There is a danger that lawyers see politics as being of secondary importance: as well achieved by the complex—and, as here maintained, often misleading and possibly fraudulent—processes of participatory democracy as through Parliament. But as has been argued, the complexities and uncertainties of participatory democracy place a still greater responsibility on ministers when they try to evaluate all the opinions they receive before deciding on a new policy, unless instead—as to some extent is already happening—they introduce a hash and a muddle leaving it to the House of Lords and the courts to sort out. If that were to become the norm, politicians and politics might still jostle for space in the media, but leave little of substance behind them.

Despite Blair's emphasis on delivery, he has not found a form of government superior to that of past governments. Rather its attempted grounding in the centralisation needed for news management has produced new weaknesses. Therefore a need remains to find a more satisfactory form of democratic government than has evolved in recent years. It needs to have the checks and balances necessary to avoid the perils of absolute power. Hence the perhaps unexciting conclusion that we are most likely to rescue our democracy if we reconstruct, while modernising, what we have, than if we go on lurching in a fundamentally thoughtless way, first in one direction, then another. But it is most unlikely to happen without planned forethought and needs to be achieved without a constitutional crisis.

FOURTEEN PILLARS OF REPRESENTATIVE DEMOCRACY

A way of summing up the contentions of this book is not to dwell on changes to our political institutions; or to summarise the arguments for and against future directions of reform; or to consider to what extent laws might usefully replace constitutional conventions; but to fasten on various principles—all discussed earlier in the book—which together constitute the necessary pre-conditions and safeguards of a representative democracy. Indeed they can be argued to provide a working definition of it, whatever their institutional and legal expression.

Some qualities governments require seem common sense and apply in all its forms. Government should be politically successful, stable between administrations and retain public support. Its functions should be performed economically, efficiently and effectively. Politicians and officials should be competent and well trained, formally or through experience and example. They and their officials—however the distinction is drawn between them in different regimes—need to work well as teams and be able to access relevant information, research and analysis, so as to reach decisions, most of which are appropriate, publicly acceptable and in some sense work. Governments need to deal with the routine, but also be ready to meet overseas and civil emergencies as well as a multitude of unexpected events. Politicians must be able to communicate effectively with each other and the public. These considerations are important for all governments, even the worst democracies and absolutisms masquerading as democracies.

But more should be expected from—is indeed implicit in the notion of—a representative democracy.

(1) Its first and fundamental requirement is one of *accountability,* which in a democracy must ultimately be to the People through election, but must in practice be mediated through elected representatives. Every part of government and the public sector must be accountable to Parliament, or another elected body.

(2) Accountability will not work unless it is clear throughout government and the public sector who is *responsible* for precisely what. In Britain the convention of ministerial *responsibility* once determined that ministers were responsible for all government did. The decay of that convention, and habitual blame avoidance, normally now means one cannot actually assign responsibilities.

(3) Moreover responsibilities cannot be discharged meaningfully by a Prime Minister or any other part of government that is grossly overloaded. Satisfactory accountability therefore pre-supposes *effective devolution.* What each level, and indeed every part of government is responsible for, should be no more than it can discharge with reasonable thoroughness and practicality.

(4) Another requirement is resolution of the problem of *supremacy,* sometimes called sovereignty, though that word is better reserved to the Crown-in-Parliament to which legal sovereignty belongs. Some body or someone must have the supreme power within government. It used to be the collective responsibility of Cabinet to which was attributed the responsibility for all that was done officially by individual ministers and therefore by all government.[3] If it is to be replaced permanently by prime ministerial supremacy—or diarchy—that needs to be known and probably expressed in law, though

[3] Jennings (1959).

it does not seem consistent with the requirement of effective devolution. Furthermore, the complexities of the modern political world (above, chapter 11), not forgetting Europe and our hitherto confused experiments with devolution, mean that one needs to know more than who or what is supreme. One needs to know what discretion, or 'supremacy', every part of government has and in what circumstances, and by whom, it may be over-ruled.

Two more requirements are in a sense more straightforward, though no less important.

(5) *Legitimacy* was secured—to know who was responsible for each significant decision so that it might be revealed if parliamentary accountability required it—by careful minuting throughout government. The most important decisions were recorded in Cabinet minutes. Now many such decisions are unminuted to an extent that one sometimes cannot know who took them.

(6) *Legality* was scarcely ever a problem. Present at all their decision-making, civil servants could warn them if in danger of being unlawful. The distancing of officials from ministers, and the growing complexity of the law, makes this more problematic as the growth of judicial review shows. Yet a government which disregards the law cannot be democratic.

Further requirements concern ministerial and official behaviour.

(7) Of the greatest importance is that it should not be *corrupt*. Corruption in this context means a decision taken with personal or party financial advantage—as through a contribution to party funds—in view. Virtually by definition such behaviour serves other masters than the People.

(8) A related requirement was the notion that every policy proposal and decision should be argued through sequentially with officials, ministerial colleagues and in Parliament as in the *public interest,* not in terms of electoral or personal political advantage. That has given way to a determinedly political and presentational approach to issues which often side-steps the public interest or leaves it obscure.

(9) *Consistency* and

(10) *Fairness* in decision-making are important aspects of the rule of law. Like should be treated alike. As far as possible they were ensured by bureaucratic procedures, many now decayed, to ensure ministers' decisions were consistent with government policy and fair between individuals.

(11) A further sensible democratic requirement to preserve national unity is that policies and decisions should not be simply majoritarian, but where possible shaped by attention to the concerns of all affected. *Consensus-seeking* was done through consultation procedures which tested how a policy proposal might affect the interests—especially producer and such external interests as those relating to safety or the environment—of those concerned. Modern consultation procedures are frequently perfunctory, gone through only because a statutory requirement.

(12) *Solidarity* is the more political or managerial aspect of collective responsibility. One reason for Cabinet solidarity is the good sense and practical benefit ministers feel from being part of a team. Another relates to party and personal loyalty. When loyalty in Parliament was more fluid and members readier to change their support for a government, it was practically necessary for a Prime Minister to have within his Cabinet, representatives of all those bodies of opinion among MPs whose votes he hoped to command so as to maintain a majority. Prime Ministers have found it prudent to have some Cabinet colleagues whose loyalty they believed unwavering. With the rise of tightly knit parties, it developed into the equally prudent practice of ensuring most, if not all, elements within the party were represented within the Cabinet. It became essential within the Labour party, given the strength of the elected National Executive within the party and the further requirement that the first Cabinet of an administration should be drawn from elected shadow Cabinet members. But there was another practical reason for Cabinet retaining enough solidarity to support the government's actions: a Prime Minister needed sufficient commitment from Cabinet members to ensure the cohesion of government and to avoid ministers publicly contradicting each other. At the highest level the Prime Minister must ensure that he keeps enough goodwill in Cabinet for its members to provide effective and cohesive corporate authority for all its decisions, however processed within the Cabinet system or whatever replacement is designed to co-ordinate Cabinet activities. To achieve it, the Prime Minister (or people on his behalf) must be able to settle which decisions can be taken bilaterally, which at committees of various types and which must be squared with the full Cabinet, whatever means of doing so is adopted—around the Cabinet table or otherwise—so that business is as expeditious as is consistent with Cabinet solidarity. But he must use this agenda-setting power wisely. If he believes the Cabinet will accept decisions, say, over nuclear policy made in secret by a small committee, then he will do so, as most Prime Ministers have done. If he believes he can get away with decisions taken in ad-hoc committees, packed as Margaret Thatcher did to get the outcome she wanted, he will be tempted to do so as Margaret Thatcher did for a time until the Cabinet rounded on her and forced her to go by withdrawing their support. As the political scientist, George Jones, has said, 'A Prime Minister who can carry his colleagues with him can be in a very powerful position, but he is only as strong as they let him be.'[4] Ferdinand Mount, the second head of Thatcher's policy unit, said the criteria for what requires Cabinet discussion depend ultimately on what colleagues will tolerate.[5] What ensures solidarity now? However solidarity is not only needed at the top. There always be internal differences

[4] G Jones in King (1985) 216.
[5] Mount (1992) 133.

of opinion—often constructive—but a department or agency will not be efficient, effective or responsibly accountable unless it has enough unanimity—solidarity—of purpose and cohesion to overcome internal differences, and unless those who discharge its responsibilities are comfortable enough with what they are doing to speak up for it.

However, a government may meet all these requirements and still not be effectively accountable.

(13) *Not lying* means that as far as possible in a democracy untruths should not be told. While recognising some information cannot be disclosed because it is secret or commercially confidential, most can.

(14) *Objectivity and openness* require that when an argument is made, it should be logical, and that the relevant evidence should be presented with an assessment of its relevance. What different audiences—other ministers, Parliament, those directly affected, and the general public—need to make an honest and well-based assessment for their own purposes will and should vary. That approach is utterly at odds with the notion that government statements and papers should be spun, or have little more content than is needed to gain a good, and avoid a bad, story in the media.

Without these safeguards the contention of this conclusion, indeed of this book, is that representative democracy must be something of a sham, deceiving the electorate.

Appendix

THE AUTHOR'S RELEVANT EXPERIENCE

A S A YOUNG Oxford academic I was encouraged by the then chairman
of London Transport to do a cost-benefit analysis of the social case for the
Victoria Line to overcome the Treasury argument that it would be financially unprofitable. I was then asked to head a unit at Oxford on regional and
urban issues, funded by the Ministry of Transport. In 1965 I became a part-time
adviser on regional affairs at the Department of Economic Affairs, suddenly moving as special adviser and chief economist to Barbara Castle and subsequently
Dick Marsh at the Ministry of Transport, building up a cadre of special advisers,
mostly economists, in size second only to that in the Treasury. I was asked to join
the CPRS in 1971 by Victor Rothschild to work on nationalised industries, but,
though a fascinating challenge, it was against my political allegiance. Besides I
had a new job at LSE where I was to have a chair in urban economics and to
develop a strong interest in local government finance[1]. In 1974 I became a part-
time special adviser on it and on housing and land taxation, to Tony Crosland—
whom like Barbara Castle I came to know well—John Silkin at the Department
of the Environment and briefly to Peter Shore. I then found myself, while still at
LSE, directing an American-style think tank, the Centre for Environmental
Studies, which was killed off by Michael Heseltine, the Conservative Secretary of
State for the Environment, for political reasons.[2] At the same time I was a non-
executive member of the Post Office board and chaired an inquiry into road
haulage for Bill Rodgers, when he was Secretary of State for Transport (Foster
1978). In 1978 I was invited to lead the Economics and Public Policy Group at
Coopers and Lybrand (where eventually I was to become a board member until it
started on successive mergers). I found myself leading a number of studies for or
in relation to many departments and for the No 10 Policy Unit. I worked for and
got to know many Conservative ministers. I was an adviser on the ill-fated Poll
Tax to Kenneth Baker and William Waldegrave. For several years my main work
was on privatisation: airports, telecommunications, and electricity.[3] (I left
Coopers and Lybrand for two years to be on the recently privatised BT executive

---

[1] It resulted in a book: Foster, Jackman and Perlman (1980).
[2] He had every justification. Under my predecessor it had been run as a left-wing commune,
though funded mostly with Ford Foundation money, with every researcher doing his or her own
thing. Though, having mastered a strike, I believed I had tamed it, the price Heseltine demanded,
as a price for continuing it after the election, was that it would work on a housing policy for a conservative government beforehand. Our housing specialists refused.
[3] It, too, resulted in a book: Foster (1992).

board with responsibility for helping control its budget and for relations with its regulator). During this time I was on the Megaw Committee on Civil Service Pay, the Audit Commission, the ESRC and London Docklands. For some years I was chairman of the NEDO committee on the construction industry and then of its private sector successor. In 1992 I was again at the centre of a Whitehall department as non-political adviser on railway privatisation, (later becoming a non-executive board member of Railtrack until 2000). That experience made me realise what a revolution there had been in how ministers and civil servants operated from the Whitehall I had known in the 1960s and 1980s and eventually triggered this book.

I was invited to write a memorandum by Peter Mandelson on how to cope with entering government before the 1997 election and tried to help in other ways to ease the passage. As a private individual I have done my best to keep in contact with what was going on in Whitehall and have developed a close interest again in transport policy as chairman of the RAC Foundation, an independently funded body devoted to defending the interests of the responsible motorist, who also wants good public transport and a good environment. As such I sat on my last government quango, the Motorists' Forum, until 2003 and chaired and published—drawing in more independent voices—the kind of argued, reasoned and evidenced White Paper on Transport Policy—in the old blue-book tradition—which it was once the privilege and pleasure of ministers to present to Parliament, but, for reasons discussed in this book, is so no longer[4]. It has been well, indeed enthusiastically, received in public among others by the Prime Minister and the Transport Secretary.[5]

I should say something about my own political leanings. I do not believe they have influenced my work for Conservative ministers as my own interest in government and policy has always been technical rather political. On sick leave from school I was Oliver Lyttelton's dogsbody during the 1945 election, carrying his speeches, taking down his instructions and driving around from one election meeting to another with him and his wife, Lady Moyra, in their Daimler, unfolding the car steps for them to descend and helping look after her dog. At Cambridge, after a brief spell of jungle warfare and fired by some doubts about our colonial policy in Malaya, I became a Labour voter, joining in various Labour preparatory work before the 1964 and 1974 elections. Since then I have remained a Labour voter, always of the moderate left, except for two elections in the 1980s when I voted Social Democrat. As it happens, despite all my strictures on what they are doing to government in the wake of their predecessors, I remain a supporter of the intentions behind many Blairite domestic policies.

[4] RAC Foundation (2002).
[5] Blair to the Liaison Committee of the House of Commons (2002) and Alastair Darling in a speech to a conference on *Motoring Towards 2050: On Making it Happen*, 26th November, 2002.

Bibliography

ABSE, L (2003) *Tony Blair: The Man who Lost his Smile* (Robson Books)

AFFUSO, L, MASSON, J and NEWBERY, D (2003) 'Comparing markets in new transport infrastructure: Road vs. Railways', *Fiscal Studies,* 24(3) 235–315

ALDERMAN, G (1973) *The Railway Interest* (Leicester, Leicester University Press)

ALLEN, G (2003) *The Last Prime Minister* (Imprint Academic)

ALMOND, G and VERBA, S (1980) *The Civic Culture Revisited,* (London, Sage)

AMERY, L S (1953) *Thoughts on the Constitution,* (London, Oxford University Press)

ANNAN, N G (1995) *Changing Enemies* (London, HarperCollins)

ANSON, W (1908) *Law and Custom of the Constitution,* (Oxford, Oxford University Press)

ARMSTRONG, R (1985) *The Duties and Responsibilities of Civil Servants in Relation to Ministers: Note by the Head of the Civil Service,* (London, Cabinet Office)

ARMYTAGE, A H G (1951) *A J Mundella: 1825–1897* (Ernest Benn)

ASHDOWN P (2001) *The Ashdown Diaries: Vol II: 1997–9,* (London, Penguin)

AYLING, S (1988) *Edmund Burke* (London, John Murray)

BAGEHOT, W, [1867] (1997) *The English Constitution,* (Sussex, Academic Press)

BAKER, K (1993) *The Turbulent Years* (London, Faber and Faber)

BALDWIN, R (1995) *Rules and Government* (Oxford, Clarendon Press)

BANNER, C and DEANE, A (2003) *Off with their wigs,* (Imprint Academic)

BENN, T (1990) *Against the Tide: Diaries 1973/6,* (London, Arrow Books)

BENTHAM J, [1776] (1948) *Fragment on Government,* (Oxford, Blackwell)

BERBERIS, P (1994) 'Permanent Secretaries and Policymaking in the 1980s', *Public Policy and Administration,* vol 9, 35–48

BEVIR, M, RHODES, R A W, and WELLER, P (2003) 'Traditions of governance: interpreting the changing role of the public sector', *Public Administration,* v 61, no 1

BINGHAM OF CORNHILL, LORD (2003) *Ditchley Foundation Lecture*

BLAKE, R (1966) *Disraeli,* (London, Eyre and Spottiswoode)

BLUNTSCHLI, K (1898) *The Theory of the State*, trans, D G Ritchie (Oxford, Clarendon Press)

BOWER, T, (2004) *Gordon Brown,* (London, HarperCollins)

BRAZIER, R (1999) ' Constitutional Reform and the Crown' in Sunkin and Page (eds) *The Nature of the Crown: A Legal and Political Analysis* (Oxford, Clarendon Press)

BREYER, S (1982) *Regulation and its Reform* (Cambridge, Mass, Harvard University Press)

BROWN, R G S, and STEEL, D R (1979) *The Administrative Process* (London, Methuen)

BUNBURY, H N (1957) *Lloyd George's Ambulance Wagon* (London, Methuen)

BURK K and CAIRNCROSS A (1992) *Good-Bye Britain: The 1976 IMF Crisis,* (London and New Haven, Conn, Yale University Press)

BURKE, E, [1790] (1845) *Reflections of the Revolution in France,* in *Works,* iii (Rivington)

BUTCHER, T (2002) *Delivering Welfare,* (Buckingham, Open University Press)

BUTLER, D, ADONIS A, and TRAVERS, T (1994) *Failure in British Government: The Politics of the Poll Tax* (Oxford, OUP)
—— and KAVANAGH, D (2002)*The British General Election of 2001,* (Basingstoke, Palgrave)
BUTLER, R (1994) 'Reinventing British Government', *Public Administration,* vol 72, Summer, 263–70
—— (1999) *Cabinet Government,* Attlee Lecture, 18 March 1999
—— (2004) Chairman, *Review of Intelligence on Weapons of Mass Destruction,* (HC 898, The Stationery Office)
BUTLER, R.A (1975) 'Reflections on Cabinet Government' in Herman, V, and Alt, J A, *Cabinet Studies* (London, Methuen)
CABINET OFFICE (1991) *Citizen's Charter,* Cm 1599 (HMSO)
—— (1994) *The Civil Service: Continuity and Change,* Cm 2627 (HMSO)
—— (1997) *Ministerial Code,* July
CAMPBELL, C, & WILSON, G K (1995) *The End of Whitehall* (Oxford, Blackwell)
CAMPBELL, J (1994) *Edward Heath,* (London, Pimlico)
CARLYLE, T, [1867] (1899) *Critical and Miscellaneous Essays, vol 5,* (London, Chapman and Hall)
CARRINGTON, LORD (1988) *Reflect on Things Past* (London, Collins)
CASTLE, B (1984) *The Castle Diaries: 1964–70*; (1980), *1974–6,* (London, Weidenfeld and Nicolson)
CHANDOS, LORD (1962) *Memoirs* (London, The Bodley Head)
CHAPMAN, L (1979) *Your Disobedient Servant* (London, Penguin)
CHARLESWORTH, J, CLARKE, J, and COCHRANE, A (1996) 'Tangled Webs? Managing Local Mixed Economies of Care', *Public Administration, vol 74, Spring, 67–88*
CHESTER, D N (1975) *The Nationalisation of British Industry: 1945–51,* (HMSO)
CHIPPERFIELD, G (1994) *The Civil Servant's Duty,* Essex Papers in Politics and Government, No 95
CHISHOLM, A, and DAVIE, A (1992) *Beaverbrook: A Life,* (London, Hutchinson)
CLARENDON, E, [1648–73] (1826) *History of the Rebellion,* (Oxford, Clarendon Press) vol 6
CLARK, A (1993) *Diaries,* (London, Weidenfeld and Nicolson)
CLAYDON, T (2002) *William III: Profiles in Power,* (Harlow, Longman)
COLES, J (2000) *Making Foreign Policy,* (London, John Murray)
COLVILLE, J (1987) *The Fringes of Power: 1941–55, vol 2* (Sceptre) *Commission Representing the Public Interest in the Health Service,* http://www.achcew.org.UK/Commision/report/html
COOK R (2003) *The Point of Departure,* (London, Simon & Schuster)
COOK, J (1995) *The Sleaze File,* (London, Bloomsbury)
COSGRAVE, P (1989) *Carrington: a Life and a Policy,* (London, Dent)
CRAIG, P P (1994) *Administrative Law,* 3rd edn (London, Sweet and Maxwell)
CRICK, B (1964) *The Reform of Parliament,* (London, Weidenfeld and Nicolson)
CROSSMAN, RHS (1975) *Diary of a Cabinet Minister: Minister of Housing: 1964–6,* (London, Hamish Hamilton)
—— (1976) *Lord President and Leader of the Commons: 1966-70,* (London, Jonathan Cape)
CURRIE, E (2002) *Diaries: 1989-1992,* (London, Little Brown)
DAINTITH, T and PAGE, A (1999) *The Executive in the Constitution* (Oxford, OUP)

DALE, L E (1941) *The Higher Civil Service* (Oxford, OUP)

DALYELL, T (1987) *Misrule,* (London, Hamish Hamilton)

——, (1989) *Dick Crossman* (London, Weidenfeld & Nicolson)

DAY, P, and KLEIN, R (1987) *Accountabilities: Five Public Services,* (London, Tavistock)

DEFRA (2002) *Foundations for our Future—DEFRA's Sustainable Development Strategy,* June 2002

DELL, E (1997) *The Chancellors* (London, HarperCollins)

Department of Constitutional Affairs (2003) *Constitutional Reform: a new way of appointing judges, CP 10/03, July 2003*

—— (2003) *Constitutional Reform: a Supreme Court for the United Kingdom, CP 11/03, July 2003*

Department of the Environment (1977a) *Housing Policy: a Consultative Document,* June; (1977b) *Technical Volumes,* vol, 1, 2, 3

Department of the Environment (1981) *Alternatives to Domestic Rates,* Cmnd 4741

Department of Health (1997) *The New NHS: Modern—Dependable,* Cmnd 3807

—— (1998) *Our Healthier Nation: A Contract for Health,* Cmnd 3852

Department of Social Security (1998) *New Ambitions for Our Country: a New Contract for Welfare,* Cmnd 3805

Department of Trade and Industry (2003) *Our Energy Future: Creating a Low Carbon Economy,* Energy White Paper

Department of Transport (2003) *Transport Statistics*

—— (2004) *The Future of Rail, Cm* 6233, July 2004

DICEY, A V, [1889] (1959) *Introduction to the Study of the Law of the Constitution,* 10th edn (London, Macmillan)

DIPLOCK, LORD (1985) Exposition of the Powers and Principles of Judicial Review in cause of the *Civil Service Unions v Minister for the Civil Service*

Dod's Companion (2004)

DONALDSON, F (1962) *The Marconi Scandals,* (Hart Davis)

DONOUGHUE, B (2003) *The Heat of the Kitchen,* (London, Politico's)

DOWDING, K (1995) *The Civil Service* (London, Routledge)

DOWNS, A (1957) *An Economic Theory of Democracy,* (London, Harper and Row)

DRAPER, D (1997) *Blair's 100 Days,* (London, Faber and Faber)

DUNLEAVY, P and O'LEARY, B (1987) *Theories of the State,* (Basingstoke, Macmillan)

—— and RHODES, RAW (1990) 'Core Executive Studies in Britain' *Public Administration,* vol 68, 3–28

DUNN, J (2000) *The Cunning of Unreason,* (London, HarperCollins)

EHRMAN, J (1969) *The Younger Pitt,* (London, Constable)

ELTON, G R (1959) *The Tudor Revolution in Government,* (Cambridge, CUP)

EVANS, (2002) 'Review of Christian Wolmar: Broken Rails' *Political Quarterly,* Vol 79, No 2, 244–6.

—— (2003) 'Fatal Mainline Train Accidents on Britain's railways: 1946–2002', Centre for Transport Studies, University College, London, June

—— (2004) 'Rail Safety and Rail Privatisation in Britain,' Inaugural Lecture. Imperial College, July

FLINDERS, M (2001) 'Judicial Accountability', *Parliamentary Affairs,* vol 54, no 1, Jan

——, and SMITH (1998) *The Politics of Quasi-Government,* (Basingstoke, Macmillan)

FORD, R (2003) 'BR Infrastructure Maintenance Spend Shock', *Modern Railways*, August

FOSTER, C D (1963) *The Transport Problem,* (Blackie)

—— (1971) *Politics, Finance and the Role of Economics* (London, Allen & Unwin)

—— (1978) Chairman, *Report of the Independent Committee of Enquiry Into Road Haulage Licensing,* (HMSO)

—— (1992) *Privatisation, Public Ownership and the Regulation of Natural Monopoly,* (Oxford, Blackwell)

—— (1996) 'Reflections on the Scott Report', *Public Administration,* vol 74, No 4, Winter

—— (1999) *The End of Cabinet Government*, Public Management & Policy Association, January

—— (2000a) *Two Concepts of Accountability: Is a Bridge possible between them?* Public Management and Policy Association

—— (2000b) 'The Encroachment of Law on Politics', *Parliamentary Affairs,* vol 57, 2, April, 328–46

—— (2001) *The Corruption of Politics and the Politics of Corruption* Public Management and Policy Association

—— (2004a) 'Cabinet Government in the Twentieth Century', *Modern Law Review,* 67(5) 752–70

—— (2004b) *The Economics of Rail Privatisation* (Bath, Centre for Regulated Industries)

——, and CASTLES, C (2004) *Creating a Viable Railway for Britain: what has gone wrong and how to fix it.* Submission to the Secretary of State for Transport, July

——, Jackman R A, and Perlman, M (1980) *Local Government Finance in a Unitary State* (London, Allen and Unwin)

—— and Plowden, F J (1996) *The State Under Stress* (Buckingham, Open University Press)

FOSTER, R F (1981) *Lord Randolph Churchill* (Oxford, Clarendon Press)

FREEDLAND, M (1995)' Privatising Carltona: Part II of the Deregulation and Contracting Out Act, 1994, *Public Law* 21–6;

—— (1996) 'The Rule Against Delegation and the Carltona Doctrine in an Agency Context', *Public Law,* 19-30.

GARDINER A G (u/d) *The Life of Sir William Harcourt,* (George H Doran)

GILMOUR, I (1992) *Dancing with Dogma,* (Pocket Books)

GLAISTER, S (2004) *Competition Destroyed by Politics: British Rail Privatisation,* (Bath, Centre for the Study of Regulated Industries, University of Bath)

GRABSKY, P (1997) *I, Caesar* (London, BBC Books)

GRANT, W (2000) *Pressure Groups and British Politics,* (Basingstoke, Macmillan)

GRIFFITH, J A G (1963) 'Comment', *Public Law,* 401-2

—— (1991) *The Politics of the Judiciary* (Glasgow, Fontana)

GRIGG, J (2002) *Lloyd George: War Leader,* Penguin: Allen Lane

HAILSHAM, LORD (1978) *Dilemma of Democracy* (London, Collins)

HAINES, J (2003) *Glimmers of Twilight,* (London, Politico's)

HALDANE, R B (1918) *Report of the Machinery of Government Committee: Ministry of Reconstruction* Cd 9230 (London, HMSO)

HALEVY, E (1924) *A History of the English People in the 19*th *century*, v 1 (Benn)

HALIFAX, MARQUIS OF, [1688] (1704) 'The Character of a Trimmer' in *Miscellanies by the Late Lord Marquis of Halifax* (London, Rogers)

HAMMOND, SIR A (2001) Review of the Circumstances surrounding the Application for the Naturalisation of Mr SP Hindooja in 1998, HC 287

HANSARD SOCIETY (1992) *Making the Law,* (Hansard Society)

HARDEN, I (1992) *The Contracting State,* (Buckingham, Open University Press)

HARE, D (2003) *The Permanent Way,* (London, Faber and Faber)

HARRIS, J (1997) *William Beveridge* (Oxford, Clarendon Press)

HARRIS, K (1982) *Attlee* (London, Weidenfeld & Nicolson)

HAZELL, R (2000) *The State and the Nations,* (Imprint Academic)

—— (2003) *The State of the Nations,* (Imprint Academic)

HEADEY, B (1974) *British* Cabinet *Ministers,* (London, Allen and Unwin)

HEALEY, D (1989) *The Time of My Life,* (London, Michael Joseph)

HEISER, T (1994) 'The Civil Service at a Crossroads?', *Public Policy and Administration,* vol 9

HELM, D (2002) 'A Critique of Rail Regulation', in C Robinson (ed) *Utility Regulation and Competition Policy* (Cheltenham, Edward Elgar)

HENDERSON, N (1994) *Mandarin,* (London, Weidenfeld and Nicolson)

HENNESSY, P (1989) *Whitehall,* (London, Free Press)

—— (1995) *The Hidden Wiring* (London, Gollancz)

—— (1999) *The Blair Centre: A Question of Command and Control,* Public Management Foundation

—— (2000) *The Prime Minister,* (London, Penguin)

HERMAN, V and ALT, J A (1975) *Cabinet Studies* (London, Methuen)

HESELTINE, M (2000) *Life in the Jungle,* (London, Hodder and Stoughton)

HEWART OF BURY, LORD (1929) *The New Despotism,* (London, Benn)

HEYWOOD, P (1997) *Political Corruption,* (Oxford, Blackwell)

HIBBS D A (1987) *The Political Economy of Industrial Democracies,* (Cambridge, Mass, Harvard UP)

HOBBES, T, [1651] (1996) *Leviathan,* (Cambridge, CUP)

HOFFMANN, LORD (2001) *Separation of Powers,* The Combar Lecture 2001.

HOOD, C, 'Relations between Ministers/Politicians and Public Servants', in Peters, B G (ed) (2000) *Governance in the Twenty- first Century,* McGill-Queen's University Press

HOOD, C (1990) 'De-Sir Humphreying the Westminster World of Democracy' *Governance,* 3, 2.205–14

—— (1991) 'A public management for all seasons?', *Public Administration,* vol 69 Spring, 3–19

—— (2003a) 'Control, Bargains and Cheating', *Journal of Public Administration and theory,* vol 12, No 3 July, 309–332

—— (2003b) 'Institutions, Blame Avoidance and Negativity Bias: Getting to Grips with the Blame Culture', All Souls College, Oxford (unpublished)

——, James, Jones, Scott and Travers, 'Bureaucratic Gamekeeping' in Rhodes, RAW (ed) (2001) *Transforming British Government,* (Buckingham, Open University Press)

HOOD, C, and JAMES, O (1996) *Bureaucratic Gamekeeping: the Regulation of UK Public Administration,* Discussion Paper 1, LSE

HORNE, A (1989) *Macmillan: 1957–1986,* (London, Macmillan)

HOSKYNS, J (2000) *Just in Time,* (Aurum Press)

House of Commons: Expenditure Committee (1977) General sub-committee. Eleventh Report, *Eleventh Report,* 'The Civil Service' 1976–77, HC 535 (HMSO)

House of Commons: Liaison Committee (2002) *Annual Report for 2002,* HC 558

House of Commons, Foreign Affairs Committee (2003) Uncorrected Transcript, 25th July
House of Commons, Intelligence Services Committee (2003) *Iraqi Weapons of Mass Destruction,* Cm 5972, 9th September
House of Commons, Committee on Standards and Privileges, *Complaints against Mr Keith Vaz,* House of Commons (9 March 2001)
House of Commons (2004) *Parliamentary Debates,* Hansard, 20th July
House of Commons, Treasury and Civil Service Committee (1985) *Seventh Report: 1985–6,* vol 2
House of Commons, Treasury and Civil Service Committee (1986) 'Civil Servants and Ministers', *First Report* 1986–7, HC92 (HMSO)
House of Commons, Treasury and Civil Service Committee (1993) *Sixth Report, 1992–3,* HC 390, 1 (HMSO)
HOWARD, A (1987) *R A B: The Life of R A Butler* (London, Jonathan Cape)
—— (1990) *Crossman* (London, Jonathan Cape)
HOWE, G (1992*),* 'Managing the Statute Book', *Statute Law Review,* 165, 8 May
—— (1994) *Conflict of Loyalty* (London, Macmillan)
—— (2002) 'Whither the Law Officers?', *The House Magazine, October 7, 72*
HUNT OF TAMWORTH, LORD (1993)' British Civil Service Ethics', *Business Ethics,* vol 2, no 3, July
INGHAM, B (2003) *The Wages of Spin,* (London, John Murray)
JAMES, R R (1963) *Rosebery,* (London, Weidenfeld and Nicolson)
—— (1970) *Chips: The Diaries of Sir Henry Channon* (Harmondsworth, Penguin)
JAMES, S (1992) *British Cabinet Government,* (London, Routledge)
JEFFRYS, K (1999) *Anthony Crosland* (London, Richard Cohen Books)
JENKINS, R (1988) *Asquith,* (London, Collins)
—— (1991) *A Life at the Centre* (London, Macmillan)
—— (1995) *Gladstone,* (London, Macmillan)
—— (2001) *Churchill* (London, Macmillan)
JENKINS, S (1995) *Accountable to None,* (London, Hamish Hamilton)
JENNINGS, W (2003) 'Blame Management in Two Public Celebration Projects: the Australian Bicentennial in 1988 and the Millennium Dome', Feb (unpubl.)
JENNINGS, W. I, (1959) *Cabinet Government* (Cambridge, CUP)
JOHNSON, N (1980) *In Search of the Constitution,* (Oxford, Pergamon)
JONES, G (1975) 'Development of the Cabinet' in Thornhill, W (1975) *The Modernisation of British Government,* (London, Pitman)
—— (1985) 'The Prime Ministers' Advisers' in A King, *The British Prime Minister*, 2nd edn (Basingstoke, Macmillan)
JONES, J (1999) *Labour of Love,* (London, Politico's)
JONES, N (1999) *Sultans of Spin* (London, Victor Gollancz)
JOWELL, J, and OLIVER, D (1989) *The Changing Constitution,* (Oxford, Clarendon Press)
——, and —— (1988) *New Directions in Judicial Review* (London, Stevens)
JOY, S (1973) *The Train that ran away,* (Ian Allan)
KAMPFNER, J (2003) *Blair's Wars,* (London, Free Press)
KAUFMAN, G (1980,1997) *How to be a Minister,* (London, Sidgwick and Jackson)
KAVANAGH D, and SELDON, A (1994) *The Major Effect,* (Basingstoke, Macmillan)
—— (1990) *British Politics: Continuity and Change,* (Oxford, OUP)
——, and SELDON, A (1999) *The Powers Behind the Prime Minister,* (London, HarperCollins)

KENDALL, J, and ALMONS, S (1998) *The UK Voluntary (Third) Sector in Comparative Perspective,* PSSRU, University of Kent

KERSHAW, I (2001) *Hitler: 1936–45,* (London, Penguin)

KETTL, D F (1993) *Sharing Power: Public Governance and Private Markets,* (Washington, Brookings Insitute)

KIDD, J A (1987) *The Beaverbrook Girl,* (London, Collins)

KING, A (1975) 'Overload: The Problem of Governing in the 1970s' *Political Studies,* 23, 162ff.

—— (1981) 'The Rise of the Career Politician in Britain and its Consequences', *British Journal of Political Science,* Vol 2, No 3, July

—— (1985) 'Margaret Thatcher: the Style of a Prime Minister' in A King, *The British Prime Minister,* 2nd edn (Basingstoke, Macmillan)

—— (1988) 'Margaret Thatcher as a Political Leader' in Skidelsky, R, *Thatcherism* (London, Chatto and Windus)

KING, E, and LIEBLING, D (2004) *Commuting and Travel Choices,* (RAC Foundation)

LAFFONT, J J, and TIROLE, J (1993) *A Theory of Incentives in Procurement and Regulation,* Cambridge, Mass, MIT Press)

LAUGHRIN, D (1996) *Swimming for their Lives: Waving or Drowning?* (Cabinet Office, Office of Public Service) March

LAW COMMISSION (1976) *Report on Remedies in Administrative Law,* No 73

LAWSON, N (1992) *The View from No. 11* (London, Bantam Press)

LEARMONT, J (1995) *Review of the Prison Service in England and Wales and the escape from Parkhurst Prison on 3.1.95,* Cm 3020 (HMSO)

LEIGH, D, and VULLIAMY, E (1997) *Sleaze: The Corruption of Parliament,* (London, Fourth Estate)

LEWIN, H G (1936) *The railway mania and its aftermath: 1845–52. The Railway Gazette*

LEWIS, D (1997) *Hidden Agendas* (London, Hamish Hamilton)

LLOYD, J (2004) *What the Media is doing to our Politics,* (London, Constable)

LOCKE, J, [1690] (1924) *Of Civil Government,* (Everyman)

LONGFORD, E (1972) Wellington: *Pillar of State,* (London, Weidenfeld and Nicolson)

LOUGHLIN, M (1996) *Legality and Locality,* (Oxford, Clarendon Press)

LUBENOW, WC, (1971) *The Politics of Government Growth,* (Devon, David and Charles)

MACKENZIE, WJM, and GROVE, JW (1957) *Central Administration in Britain* (Harlow, Longman)

MACKINTOSH, J P (1962) *British Cabinet* (London, Stevens)

MACMILLAN, H (1938) *The Middle Way,* (London, Macmillan)

MADGWICK P J. (1975) 'Resignations' in Herman, V, and Alt, J A, *Cabinet Studies,* (London, Methuen)

MADISON, J, HAMILTON, A and JAY, J [1787/8] (1992) *The Federalist*

MAITLAND, F (1908) *The Constitutional History of England* (Cambridge, CUP).

MANDELSON, P, and LIDDLE, R (1996) *The Blair Revolution,* (London, Faber and Faber)

MARQUAND, D (1977) *Ramsay Macdonald,* (London, Jonathan Cape)

—— (1988) *The Unprincipled Society,* (London, Fontana)

—— (2004) *Decline of the Public,* (Oxford, Polity)

MARR, A (1995) *Ruling Britannia* (London, Michael Joseph)

MARSH, D (1991) 'Privatisation Under Mrs Thatcher', *Public Administration,* 69, Winter, 459–80

MARSH, D and RHODES, RAW (1992) *Policy Networks in British Government,* (Oxford, OUP)

MARSHALL, G (1971) *Constitutional Theory,* (Oxford, Clarendon Press)

—— (1989) (ed) *Ministerial Responsibility* (Oxford, Clarendon Press)

——, and MOODIE, G C (1964) *Some Problems of the Constitution* (London, Hutchinson)

MATTHEW, H C G (1986) *Gladstone: 1809–1874* (Oxford, OUP)

—— (1995) *Gladstone: 1875–1898,* (Oxford, OUP)

McLEAN, I S, and FOSTER,C D (1992) 'The political economy of regulation: interests, voters and the UK Regulation of Railways Act, 1844', *Public Administration, 70, 3,* 313–32

McLEAN, I (2001) *Rational Choice and British Politics* (Oxford, OUP)

—— and JENNINGS, C (forthcoming) *Applying the Dismal Scheme: When Economists Give Advice to Governments* (London: Palgrave)

MIDDLEMASS, K (1979) *Politics in Industrial Society* (London, André Deutsch)

MILL, J S (1910) *Utilitarianism, Liberty and Representative Government,* (Everyman Library)

Ministry of Transport (1966) *Transport Policy,* Cmnd. 3057 (HMSO) July

MOE, R, C (1994) 'The re-inventing government exercise. Misinterpreting the problem, misjudging the consequences', *Public Administration Review, vol 54, 2* 111–19

MOLESWORTH, W N (1886) *History of England* (London, Chapman and Hall)

MONTESQUIEU, [1748] (u/d) CL. de .S, Baron, *De L'Esprit des Lois, (1748),* (Flammarion)

MOODIE, C (1964) *The Government of Great Britain,* (London, Methuen)

MORGAN, K O (1984) *Labour in Power,* (Oxford, OUP)

—— (1997) *Callaghan,* (Oxford, OUP)

MORLEY, J (1905–6) *Life of William Ewart Gladstone,* 2 vols (London, Macmillan)

MORRISON, H (1959) *Government and Parliament,* (Oxford, OUP)

MOUNT, F (1992) *The British Constitution Now,* (Mandarin)

MOWLAM, M (2002) *Momentum* (London, Hodder and Stoughton)

MUELLER, D C (1989) *Public Choice II,* (Cambridge, CUP)

MULGAN, G (1997) *Connexity,* (London, Chatto and Windus)

MUNRO, C (1952) *The Fountains in Trafalgar Square,* (London, Heinemann)

National Audit Office (2000) *The Millennium Dome,* HC 936

NAUGHTIE, J (2002) *The Rivals,* (London, Fourth Estate)

NEILD, R (2002) *Public Corruption* (Anthem Press)

NEILL, LORD, of Bladen (2000) *Reinforcing Standards: Review of the First Report of the Committee on Standards in Public Life,* Sixth Report, Cm 4557

NEWMAN, J (2001) *Modernising Governance,* (London, Sage)

NICOLSON, H (1966) *Diaries and Letters: 1930-39* (London, Collins)

NISKANEN, WA (1971) *Bureaucracy and Representative Government,* (Aldine Atherton)

NISKANEN, WA (1973) *Structural Reform of the Federal Budget Process,* American Enterprise Association

NOLAN, LORD (1995) *First Report,* Committee of Standards in Public Life, Cm 2580.

NORTON, P (2001) in RHODES, R, *Transforming British Government* (Buckingham, Open University Press)

NOTT, J (2002) *Here To-Day, Gone Tomorrow,* (London, Politico's)

OAKESHOTT, M (1962) *Rationalism in Politics* (London, Methuen)

OBORNE, P, and WALTERS, S (2004) *Alastair Campbell,* (Aurum Press)

O'BRIEN, CC (1992) *The Great Melody,* (London, Sinclair-Stevenson)

OLIVER, D (2003) *Constitutional Reform in the UK,* (Oxford, OUP)

OLSON, M (1971) *The Logic of Collective Action,* (Cambridge, Mass, Harvard University Press)

OSBORNE, D, and GAEBLER, T (1992) *Reinventing Government,* (Addison-Wellesley)

PERRI (1997) *Holistic Government,* (Demos)

—— (1999) et al. *Governing in the Round,* (Demos)

PESTON, R (2005) *Brown's Britain* (Short Books)

PETERS, BG (2000) *Governance, Politics and the State,* (Basingstoke, Macmillan)

PIMLOTT, B (1992) *Harold Wilson* (London, HarperCollins)

PLIATSKY, L (1980) *A Review of Non-Departmental Public Bodies,* Cmnd 7797

PLOWDEN, W (1994) *Ministers and Mandarins,* Institute for Public Policy Research

PLUTARCH (undated) *Lives: Roman,* Part 2 (London, Frederick Warne)

POLLARD, S (2005) *David Blunkett* (London, Hodder and Stoughton)

POLLITT, MG and SMITH, A S J (2002) 'The Restructuring and Privatisation of British Rail: Was it really that bad?', *Fiscal Studies, vol 23, no 4, 463-502*

POWER, G (1998) *Representation of the People,* (London, Fabian Society)

PRIOR, J (1986) *A Balance of Power* (London, Hamish Hamilton)

RAC Foundation (2002) *Motoring Towards 2050* (London, RAC Foundation)

RADICE, G (2000) *Friends and Rivals: Crosland, Jenkins and Healey,* (London, Little Brown)

Railways Safety and Standards Board (2003) *Annual Safety and Standards Report: 2002/3*

RAWNSLEY, A (2000) *Servants of the People,* (London, Hamish Hamilton)

REID, G (1962) *Politics of Financial Control,* (London, Hutchinson)

RHODES, R A W (1997a) *Understanding Governance,* (Buckingham, Open University Press)

—— (1997b) 'From Marketisation to Diplomacy', *Public Policy and Administration,* 12, 31–50

—— and Dunleavy, P (1995) *Prime Minister, Cabinet and Core Executive,* (Basingstoke, Macmillan)

RICHARD, LORD (2004) *Report* (Welsh Assembly)

RICHARDS, D (1997) *The Civil Service Under the Conservatives,* (Brighton, Sussex Academic Press

RIDDELL, P (1993) *Honest Opportunism,* (London, Hamish Hamilton)

RIDDELL, P (1998) *Parliament Under Pressure,* (London, Victor Gollancz)

RIDDELL, P (2000) *Parliament Under Blair* (London, Politico's)

RIDLEY, J (1970) *Palmerston,* (London, Constable)

RIDLEY, N (1991) *My Style of Government* (London, Hutchinson)

RIPA (1987) *Top Jobs in Whitehall: Appointments and Promotions in the Senior Civil Service*

ROBERTS, A (2000) *Salisbury,* (Phoenix)

ROSE, C (1999) *England in the 1690s,* (Oxford, Blackwell)

ROSE-ACKERMAN, S (1999) *Corruption and Government,* (Cambridge, CUP)

ROSENAU, JN, and CZEMPIEL, E-O (1992) (eds) *Governance Without Government,* (Cambridge, CUP)

ROY, R (2003)' Postponing the future: a critique of short-termism,' (Railway Forum)

RUSSELL, L, SCOTT, D. and WILDING, P, 'The Funding of Local Voluntary Organisations', *Policy and Politics*, 24

SAMPSON, A (2004) *Who Runs this Place?*, (London, John Murray)

SANDFORD, M, (2004) *Commentary on the Draft Regional Assemblies Bill*, (Constitution Unit)

SCHAMA, S (1989) *Citizens* (London, Viking)

SCHWARZ, B (1987) *Lions over the Throne* (New York, New York UP)

SCHMIDT, C (1976) *The Concept of the Political*, (Rutgers University Press)

SCHMIDT, M (2003) *Political Institutions in the Federal Republic of Germany*, (Oxford, OUP)

SCOTT, D (2004) *Off Whitehall*, (London, IB Tauris)

SCOTT, G, and GORRINGE, P (1989) 'Reform of the Core Public Sector', *Australian Journal of Public Administration*, 48, 1, 81–91

SCOTT, R (1996) *Report of the Inquiry into into the Export of Defence Equipment and Dual Use Goods to Iraq and related Prosecutions*, (HMSO) 15th February

SEARLE, GR (1987) *Corruption in British Politics: 1895–1930* (Oxford, OUP)

SEDGMORE, B (1980) *The Secret Constitution* (London, Hodder and Stoughton)

SELDON, A (1996) *How Tory Governments Fall* (London, Fontana)

—— (2001) *The Blair Effect*, (London, Little Brown)

—— (2004) *Blair*, (London, Free Press)

SERPELL, SIR DAVID (1983) *Committee on the Review of Railway Finances: Report*, (HMSO)

SHAFFER, B (1973) *The Administrative Factor*, (London, Frank Cass)

SHANNON, R (2000) *Gladstone: Heroic Minister*, 1865–1898 (London, Penguin)

SISSON, C H (1959) *The Spirit of British Administration*, (London, Faber and Faber)

SMITH INSTITUTE (1999) *Empowering Government*, (Industry Forum)

SMITH, A S J (2004) 'Are Britain's Railways Costing Too Much' (Institute of Transport Studies, Leeds)

SMITH J (2003) 'What we have learned: A Comparative Perspective of Water and Rail' (CRI)

SMITH, M (1999) *The Core Executive in Britain* (Basingstoke, Macmillan)

——, RICHARDS, D, and MARSH, D (2001) 'Changing Role of Central Government Departments' in R A W Rhodes (ed) *Transforming British Government*, (Buckingham, Open University Press)

STEPHENS, P (1996) *Politics and the Pound* (Basingstoke, Macmillan)

STEVENS, R (2002) *The English Judges: Their Role in the Changing Constitution*, (Oxford, Hart Publishing)

Strategic Rail Authority (2003) *Everyone's Railway*

STUART, M (1998) *Douglas Hurd*, (Mainstream)

SUTHERLAND, K (ed) (2000) *The Rape of the Constitution*, (Imprint Academic)

—— (2004) *The Party's Over*, (Imprint Academic)

TANNER, J R (1928) *English Constitutional Conflicts of the Seventeenth Century: 1603–1689*, (Cambridge, CUP)

TAYLOR, A (1998) 'Arm's Length, but Hands Off: Mapping the New Governance', *Public Administration*, vol 76, Autumn, 441–65

TEBBITT, N (1988) *Upwardly Mobile*, (London, Weidenfeld and Nicolson)

THATCHER, M (1993) *The Downing Street Years* (London, HarperCollins)

THEAKSTON, K (1995) *The Civil Service since 1945*, (Oxford, Blackwell)

THOMAS, R M (1978) *Philosophy of British Administration* (Longman)

THOMPSON, D F (1995) *Ethics in Congress*, (Washington, Brookings Institute)

TOMKINS, A (2003) *Public Law*, (Oxford, OUP)

Treasury Solicitor (1995) *Judge over your shoulder: Judicial Review: Balancing the Scales*

TRENCH, A (2001) *The State of the Nations: 2001*, (Imprint Academic)

—— (2004) *Has Devolution made a Difference?* (Imprint Academic)

Trustees' Submission to the Senior Staff Review Board for the Review of the Parliamentary Contributory Pensions Fund (1998).

VINCENT, J R (1978) *Disraeli, Derby and the Conservative Party*, (Brighton, Harvester Press)

WADE, H W R, and FORSYTH, C F (1994) *Administrative Law*, 7th edn (Oxford, Clarendon Press)

WALDRON, J (2001) *Law and Disagreement*, (Oxford, OUP)

WALKER, P G (1970) *The Cabinet* (London, Jonathan Cape)

WEIR, S, and HALL, W (1994) *Ego-trip: Extra-Governmental Organisations in the United Kingdom and their Accountability*, (Democratic Audit and Charter 88 Trust)

WHEARE, KC (1968) *Federal Government* (Oxford, Clarendon Press)

WHITELAW W (1990) *The Whitelaw Memoirs* (London, Headline)

WICKS, N (2003) *Defining the Boundaries within the Executive: Ninth Report of the Committee on Standards in Public Life*, Cm 5775

WILKINSON, D, and APPELBAUM, E (1999) *Implementing Holistic Government*, (Demos)

WILSON OF DINTON, LORD (2002) *Portrait of a Profession*, 26 March

WILSON, H (1976) *The Governance of Britain* (Book Club Associates)

WILSON, J (1973), *CB: The Life of Sir Henry Campbell-Bannerman*, (Powell)

WILSON, W (1887) 'The Study of Administration', *Political Science Quarterly* 2 (2)

WINSOR, T (2004a)'The Future of the Railway:' *Sir Robert Reid Memorial Lecture*. (Institute of Logistics and Transport) February.

—— (2004b) *The Relationship between Government and the private sector* (ICLR) 5th April,

—— (2004c) *Submission of the Rail Regulator to the Department of Transport Rail Review* (Office of the Rail Regulator) May

—— (2004d) *The Relationship between the Government and the Private Sector:* Winsor v Bloom *in Context* (London, Incorporated Council of Law Reporting, 5th April, 2004)

WOLMAR, C (2001) *Broken Rails*, (Aurum Press)

WOODHOUSE, D (1994) *Ministers and Parliament* (Oxford, Clarendon Press)

YOUNG, H (1989) *One of Us* (London, Macmillan)

Your Right to Know: Freedom of Information, Cm 3818, December, 1997

ZIEGLER, P (1995) *Wilson* (London, HarperCollins)

Index

Major, John
  Cabinet/Cabinet system under, 69, 111–118
    legislation, lull in, 116–117
    policy direction changes, 116
  civil service under, 216–218
  Commons debates, attendance at, 131
  media and, 178
  ministerial disagreement under, 63
  rail privatisation, 118–124, 234
  shortcomings of leadership, 111, 112–114,
    117–118, 124
Mandelson, Peter, 43, 160–1, 170–1
  resignation, 25, 184
Manning, Sir David, 167
Marconi affair (1913), 13
Marghan, Deryck, 216
Marples, Ernest, 29, 39
Marquand, Professor David, 57, 142
Marr, Andrew, 191
Marsh, Dick, 28
Mayhew, Christopher, 63
Mayhew, Sir Patrick, 117, 128
Maze prison break-out, 247
Meacher, Michael, 130, 134
Media
  Blair and, 178
  House of Commons and, 131–2
  news management, objectives in relation to,
    179–180
  see also News management
Median-voter hypothesis, 89
Mellor, David, 139
Members of Parliament (MPs)
  accountability of, 9
  constituency business, 136–7
  corruption
    and accountability, 9
    prevention of, 12
    experience of, 127–8
  functions of Parliament, 12
  Labour, loyalty of, 138–140
  outside activities/employment, 128, 129
  questions, 130–1
  speech-making, deterrence from, 248
  work conditions, altered, 129–131
  see also Backbenchers; Parliament
Middleton, Sir Peter, 211
Milk Marketing Board, 117
Millbank news operation, 177
Millennium Dome, 163
Mill, John Stuart, 11, 30, 263, 270
Ministerial Code, 63
Ministerial responsibility, 20, 152–4
  accountability to Parliament, 9, 12–16, 152,
    153–4, 264–5
    historical occasions, 13
  blame avoidance, 150, 151
  diffusion of power and, 150

representative democracy, 295
Ministers
  backbenchers, meetings with, 130
  belittling of, 254–5
  Blair, Tony and, 194–1
  Brown, Gordon and, 194–5
  cascade principle, 197–9, 203, 206
  celebrity status, 179
  civil service, relationship with
    adaptability, 29–30
    Carltona principle *see* Carltona principle
    changes, 243
    experience, 24–7
    growth, 21–4
    strengths, 30–1
  decision-making by *see* Decision-making
  diminished standing of, 191–206
  discussion, ministerial, 195–7
  functions, 199–200
  junior, Scott Report on, 193, 211, 246,
    247
  lawmaking, 200
  law, power to change, 46–7
  as managers, 204–5
  Parliament as nursery of, 12, 18–19, 137
  policy delivery, 200–4
  policymaking, role in, 203
  private secretaries, 26
  resignation of, 25, 62–3, 99, 184, 247
  responsibility of *see* Ministerial
    responsibility
  Thatcher, Margaret and, 191–4
  work conditions, altered, 129–131
  see also Cabinet
Mittal, Lakshmi, 182
MMC (Monopolies and Mergers
  Commission), 34, 227
Monarchy
  veto on legislation, 7
Monck, Sir Nicholas, 26, 74, 75
Monetarist policies, 75, 78, 82, 84
Monopolies and Mergers Commission
  (MMC), 34, 227
Montesquieu, Charles-Louis de Secondat,
  Baron, 8, 61
Moore, Jo, 178
Moore, Sir John, 24
Morgan, Sally, 167
Morley, John, 63
Morris, Estelle, 138, 199, 206
Morris, John, 25, 50, 51, 83, 159, 218
Morrison, Herbert, 48, 63–4
Morton, Sir Alastair, 226
Mosley, Oswald, 63
Motorway Box, London (1969), 28, 34
Mowlam, Mo, 138, 164, 185
MPs *see* Members of Parliament (MPs)
Mundella, Anthony, 42